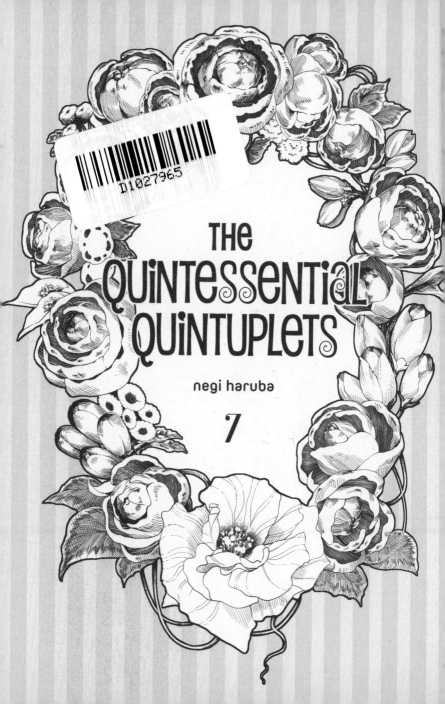

THE QUINTESSENTIAL QUINTUPLETS

negi haruba

7

Character intros

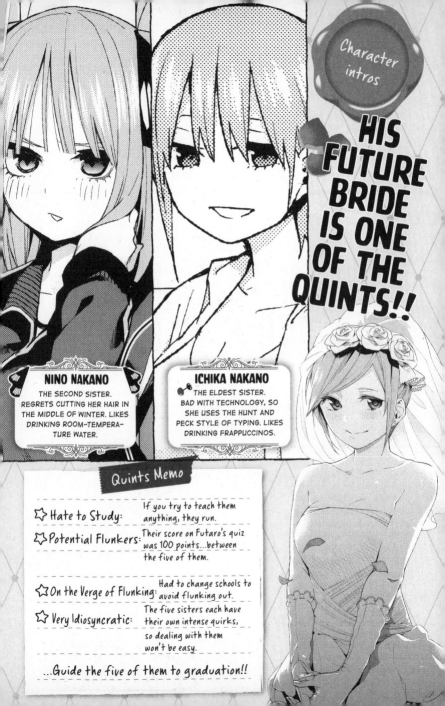

HIS FUTURE BRIDE IS ONE OF THE QUINTS!!

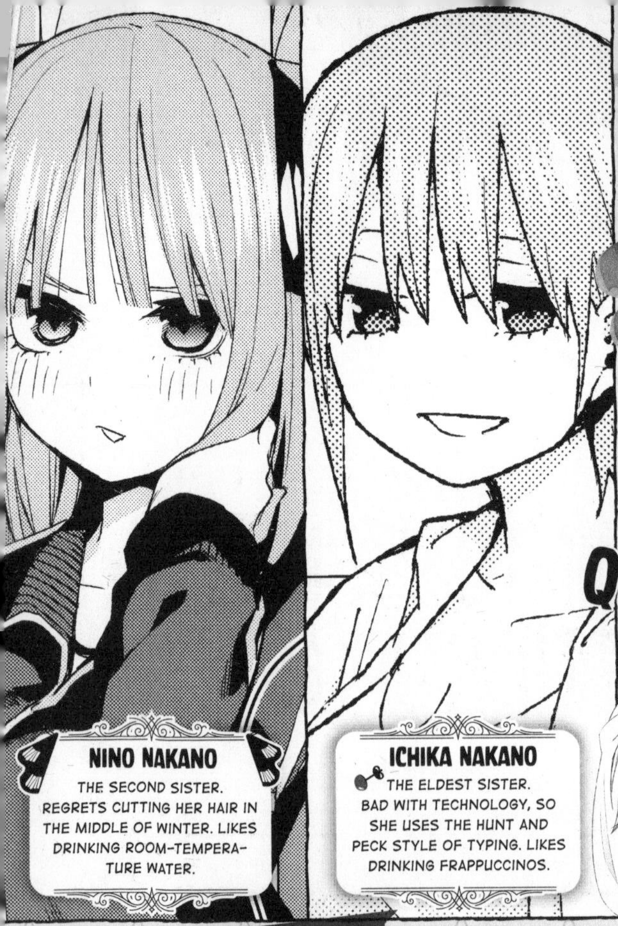
ICHIKA NAKANO
THE ELDEST SISTER. BAD WITH TECHNOLOGY, SO SHE USES THE HUNT AND PECK STYLE OF TYPING. LIKES DRINKING FRAPPUCCINOS.
NINO NAKANO
THE SECOND SISTER. REGRETS CUTTING HER HAIR IN THE MIDDLE OF WINTER. LIKES DRINKING ROOM-TEMPERATURE WATER.

Quints Memo

- ☆ **Hate to Study:** If you try to teach them anything, they run.
- ☆ **Potential Flunkers:** Their score on Futaro's quiz was 100 points...between the five of them.
- ☆ **On the Verge of Flunking:** Had to change schools to avoid flunking out.
- ☆ **Very Idiosyncratic:** The five sisters each have their own intense quirks, so dealing with them won't be easy.

...Guide the five of them to graduation!!

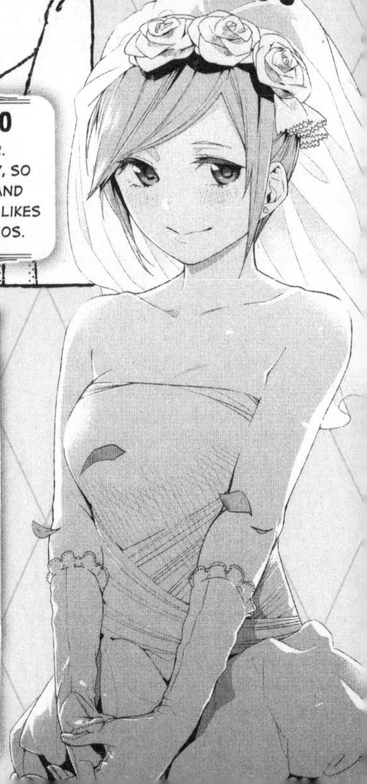

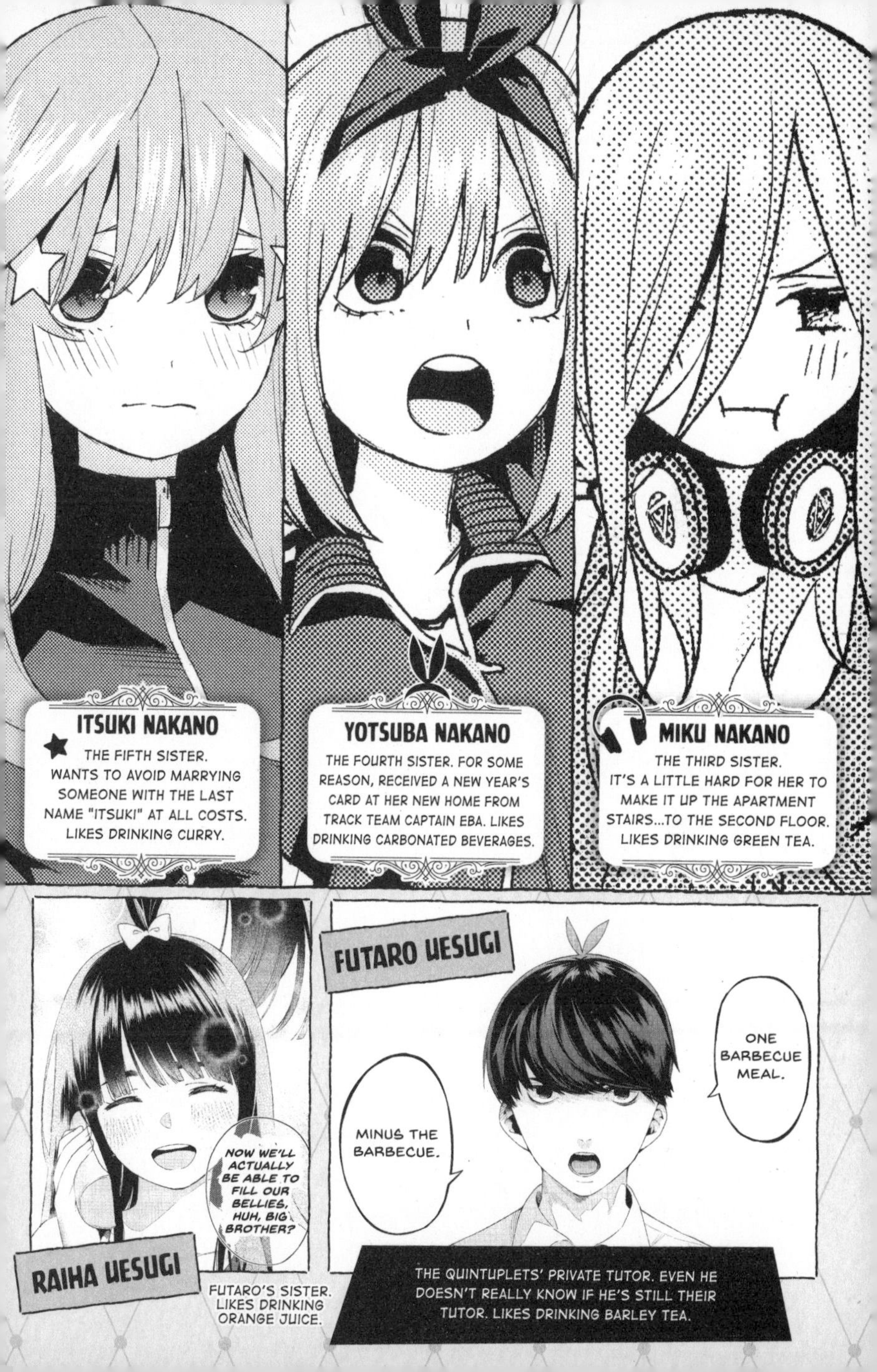
MIKU NAKANO
THE THIRD SISTER. IT'S A LITTLE HARD FOR HER TO MAKE IT UP THE APARTMENT STAIRS...TO THE SECOND FLOOR. LIKES DRINKING GREEN TEA.
YOTSUBA NAKANO
THE FOURTH SISTER. FOR SOME REASON, RECEIVED A NEW YEAR'S CARD AT HER NEW HOME FROM TRACK TEAM CAPTAIN EBA. LIKES DRINKING CARBONATED BEVERAGES.
ITSUKI NAKANO
THE FIFTH SISTER. WANTS TO AVOID MARRYING SOMEONE WITH THE LAST NAME "ITSUKI" AT ALL COSTS. LIKES DRINKING CURRY.
FUTARO UESUGI
ONE BARBECUE MEAL.
MINUS THE BARBECUE.
THE QUINTUPLETS' PRIVATE TUTOR. EVEN HE DOESN'T REALLY KNOW IF HE'S STILL THEIR TUTOR. LIKES DRINKING BARLEY TEA.
NOW WE'LL ACTUALLY BE ABLE TO FILL OUR BELLIES, HUH, BIG BROTHER?
RAIHA UESUGI
FUTARO'S SISTER. LIKES DRINKING ORANGE JUICE.

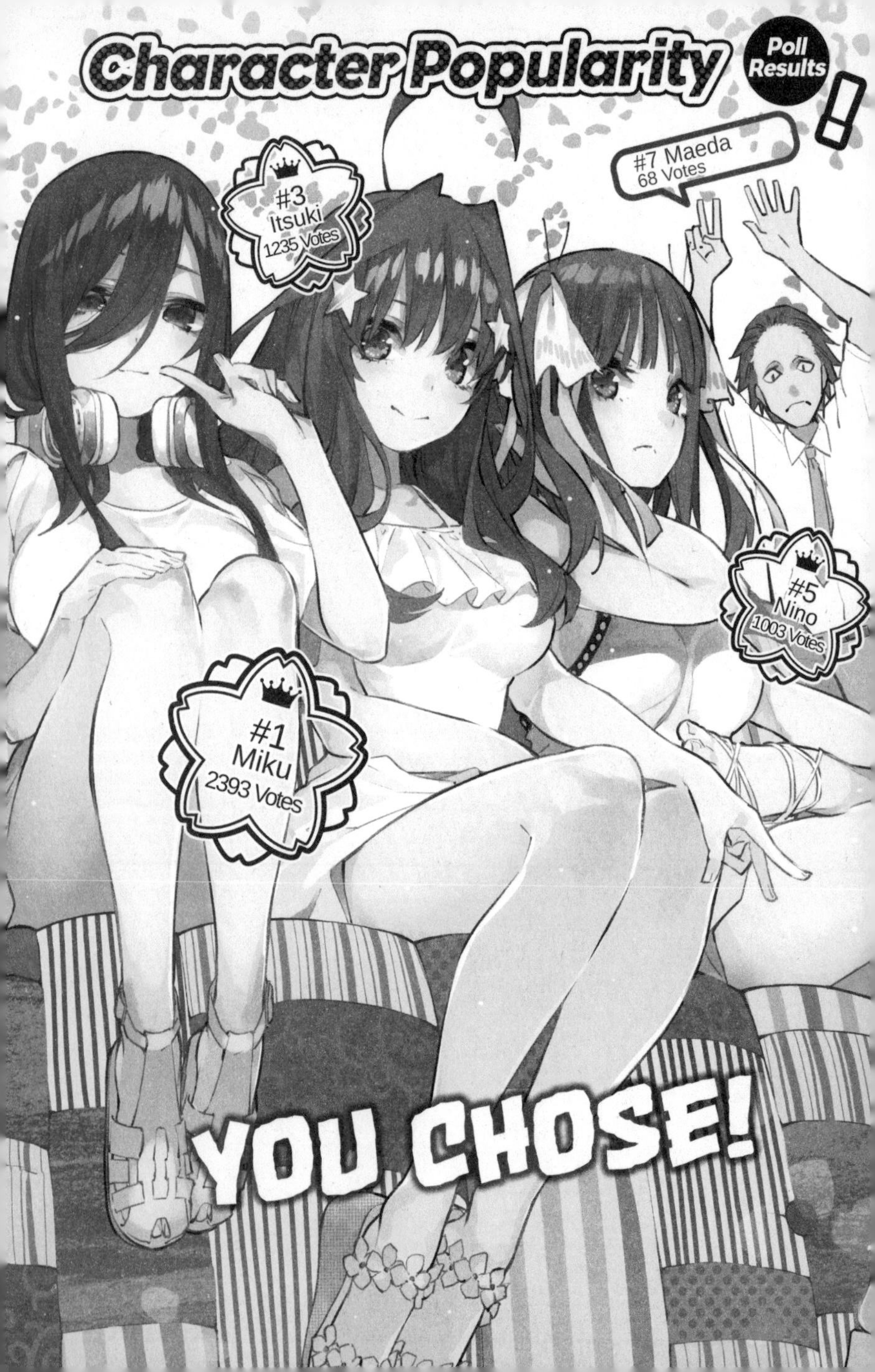
Character Popularity
Poll Results
!
#7 Maeda
68 Votes
#3
Itsuki
1235 Votes
#5
Nino
1003 Votes
#1
Miku
2393 Votes
YOU CHOSE!

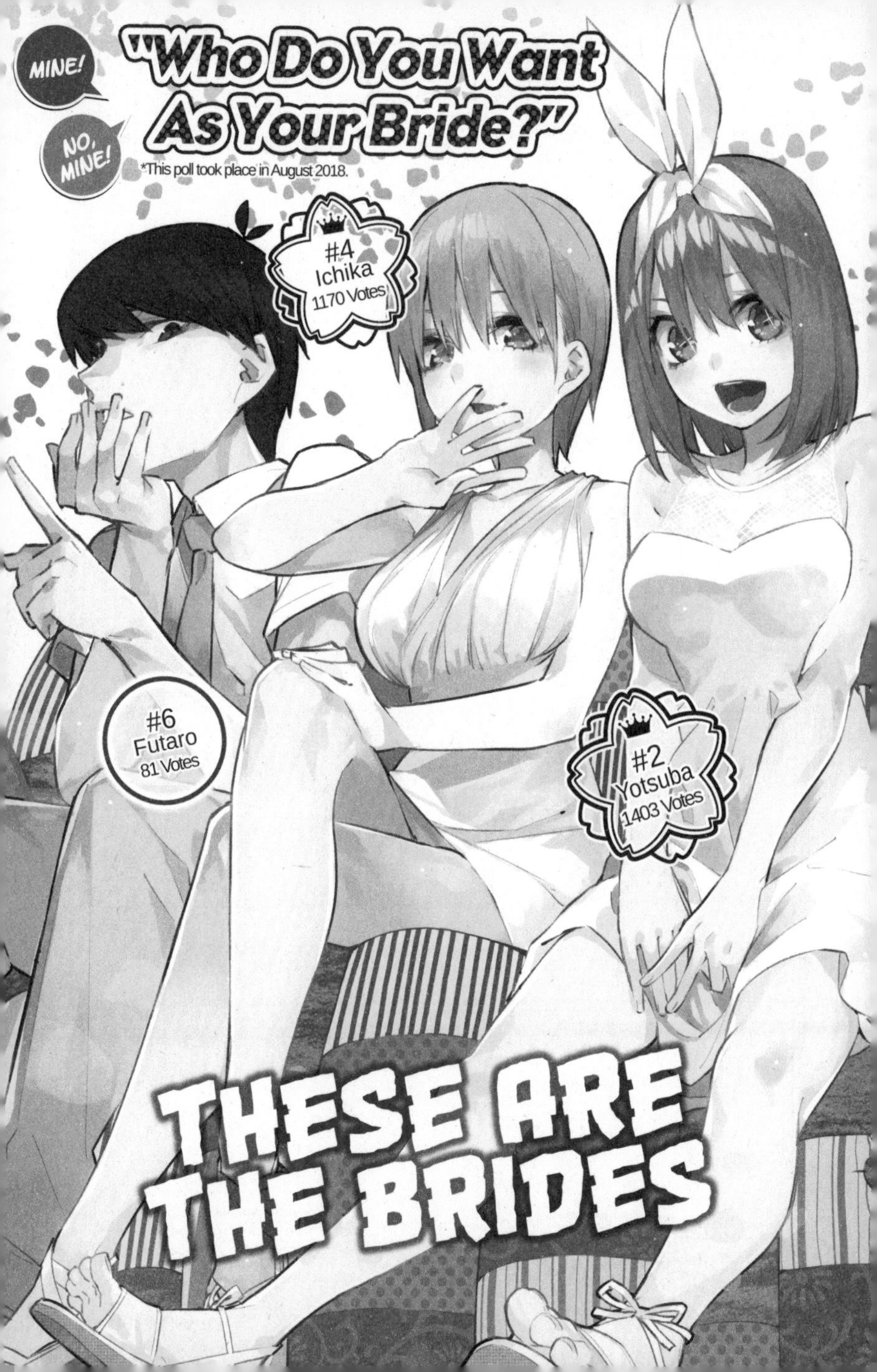
"Who Do You Want As Your Bride?"
MINE!
NO, MINE!
*This poll took place in August 2018.
#4 Ichika 1170 Votes
#6 Futaro 81 Votes
#2 Yotsuba 1403 Votes
THESE ARE THE BRIDES

CONTENTS

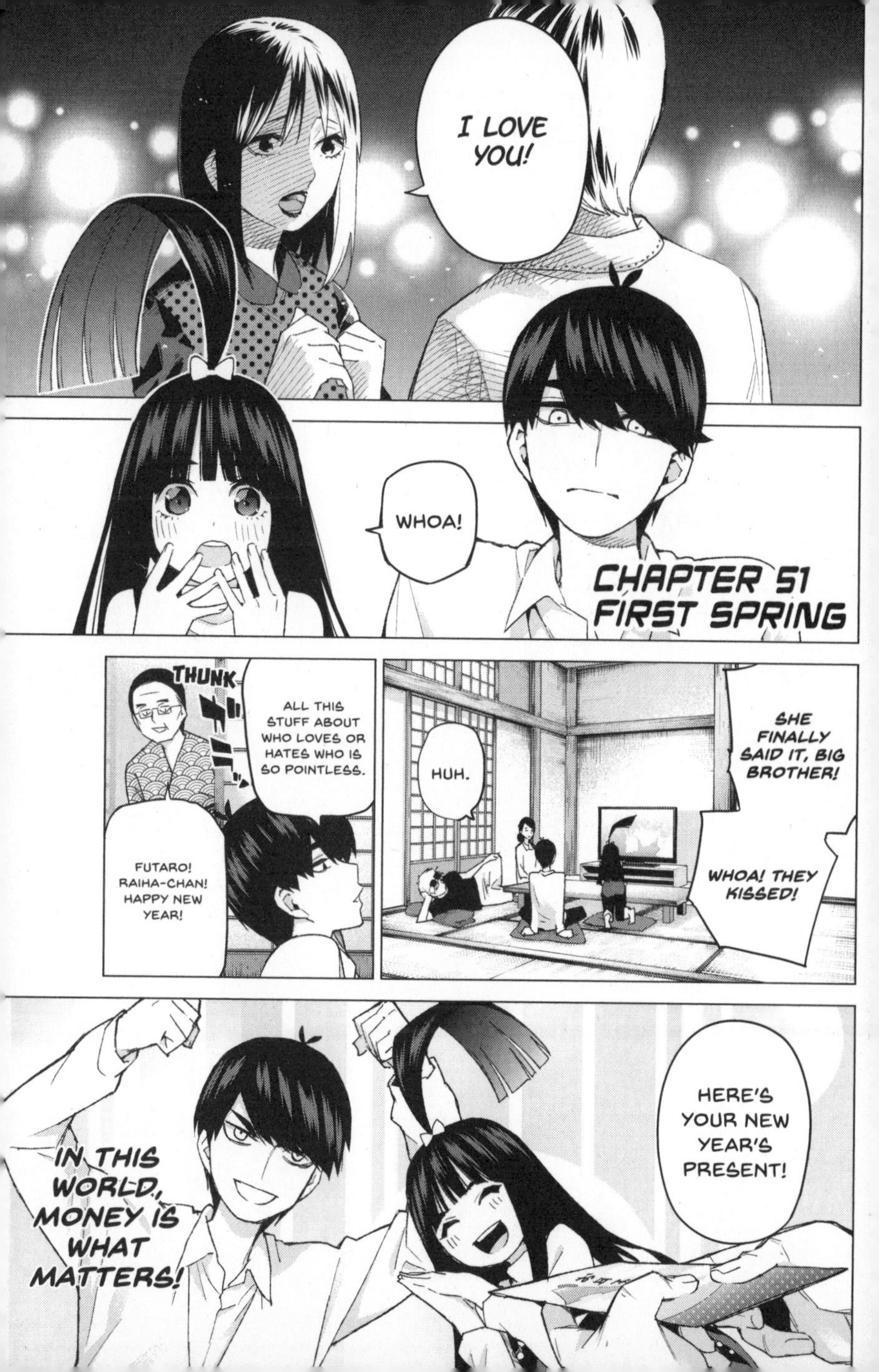
I LOVE YOU!
WHOA!
CHAPTER 51
FIRST SPRING
SHE FINALLY SAID IT, BIG BROTHER!
HUH.
WHOA! THEY KISSED!
THUNK
ALL THIS STUFF ABOUT WHO LOVES OR HATES WHO IS SO POINTLESS.
FUTARO! RAIHA-CHAN! HAPPY NEW YEAR!
HERE'S YOUR NEW YEAR'S PRESENT!
IN THIS WORLD, MONEY IS WHAT MATTERS!

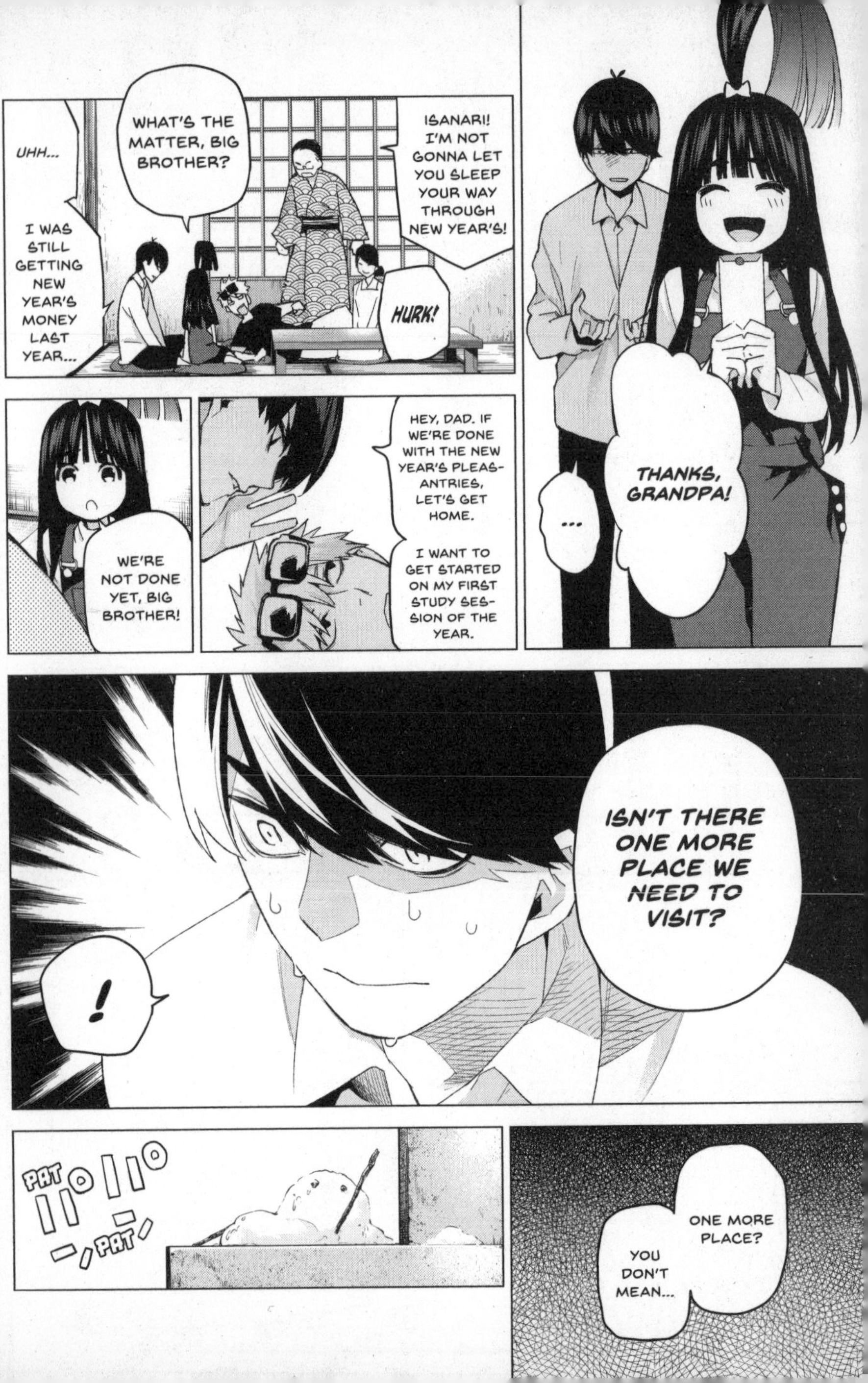

THANKS, GRANDPA!
...
ISANARI! I'M NOT GONNA LET YOU SLEEP YOUR WAY THROUGH NEW YEAR'S!
HURK!
WHAT'S THE MATTER, BIG BROTHER?
UHH...
I WAS STILL GETTING NEW YEAR'S MONEY LAST YEAR...
HEY, DAD. IF WE'RE DONE WITH THE NEW YEAR'S PLEAS-ANTRIES, LET'S GET HOME.
I WANT TO GET STARTED ON MY FIRST STUDY SES-SION OF THE YEAR.
WE'RE NOT DONE YET, BIG BROTHER!
ISN'T THERE ONE MORE PLACE WE NEED TO VISIT?
!
ONE MORE PLACE?
YOU DON'T MEAN...
PAT
PAT

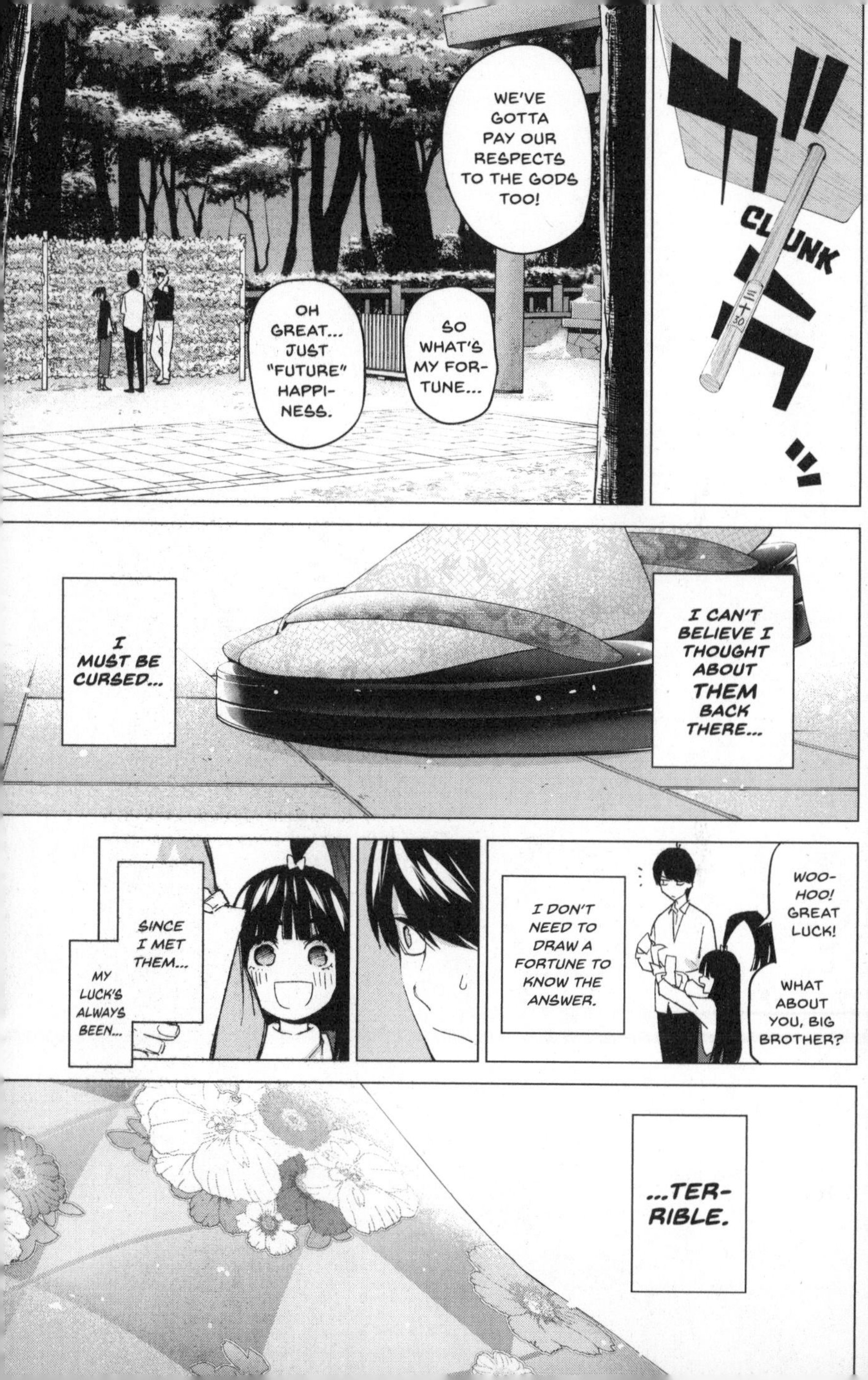
CLUNK
WE'VE GOTTA PAY OUR RESPECTS TO THE GODS TOO!
SO WHAT'S MY FOR-TUNE...
OH GREAT... JUST "FUTURE" HAPPI-NESS.
I CAN'T BELIEVE I THOUGHT ABOUT THEM BACK THERE...
I MUST BE CURSED...
WOO-HOO! GREAT LUCK!
WHAT ABOUT YOU, BIG BROTHER?
I DON'T NEED TO DRAW A FORTUNE TO KNOW THE ANSWER.
SINCE I MET THEM...
MY LUCK'S ALWAYS BEEN...
...TER-RIBLE.

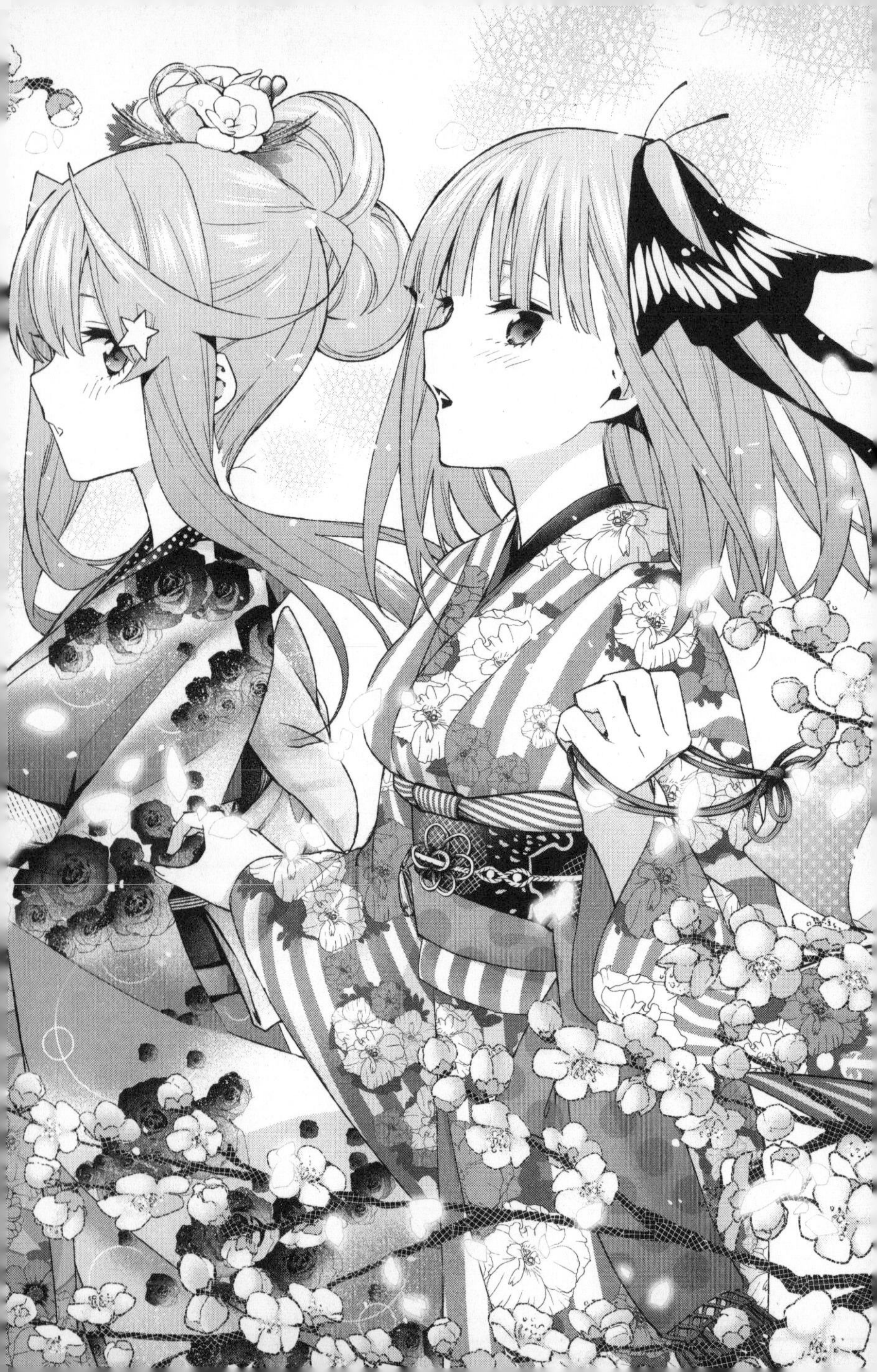

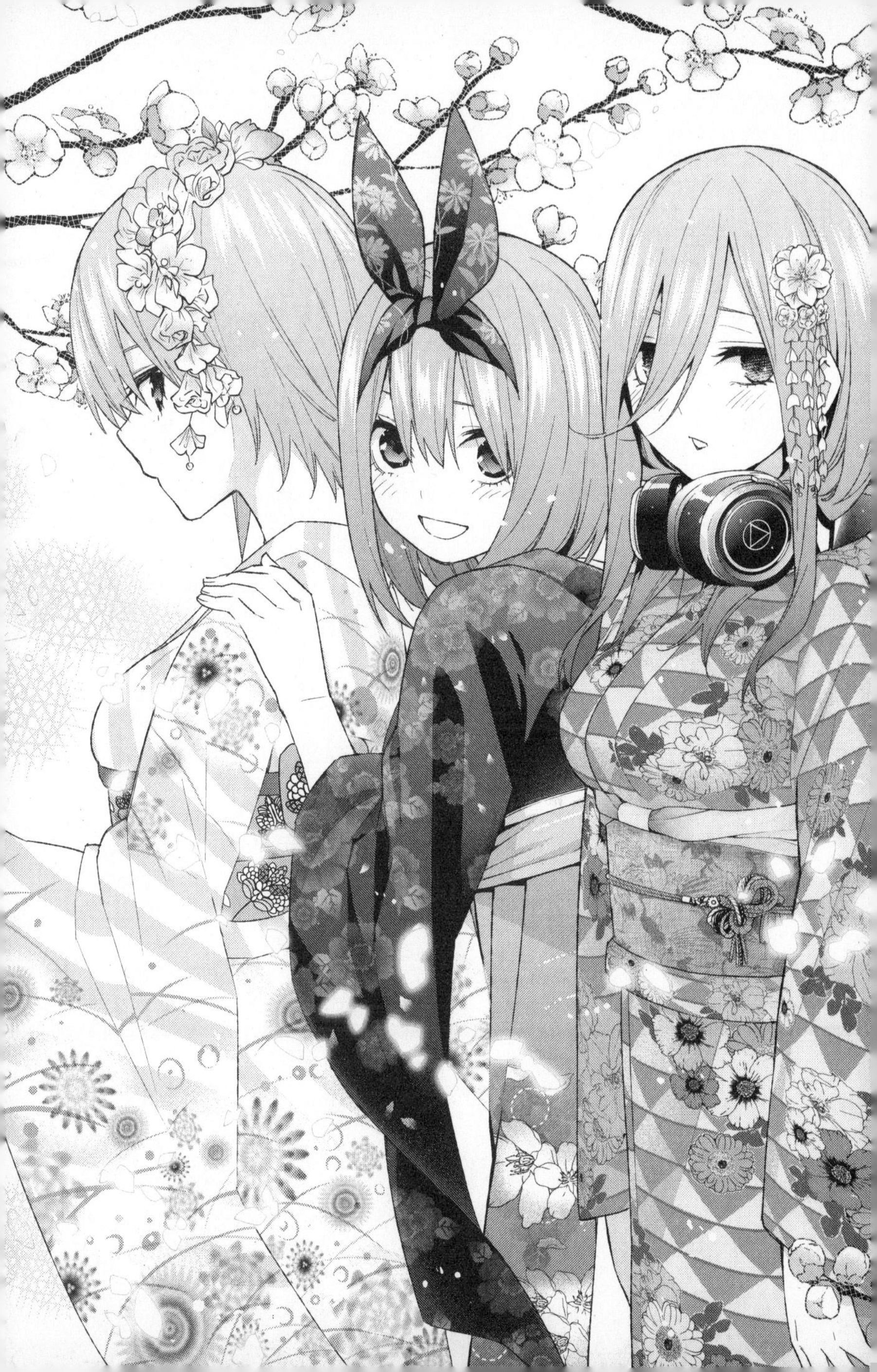

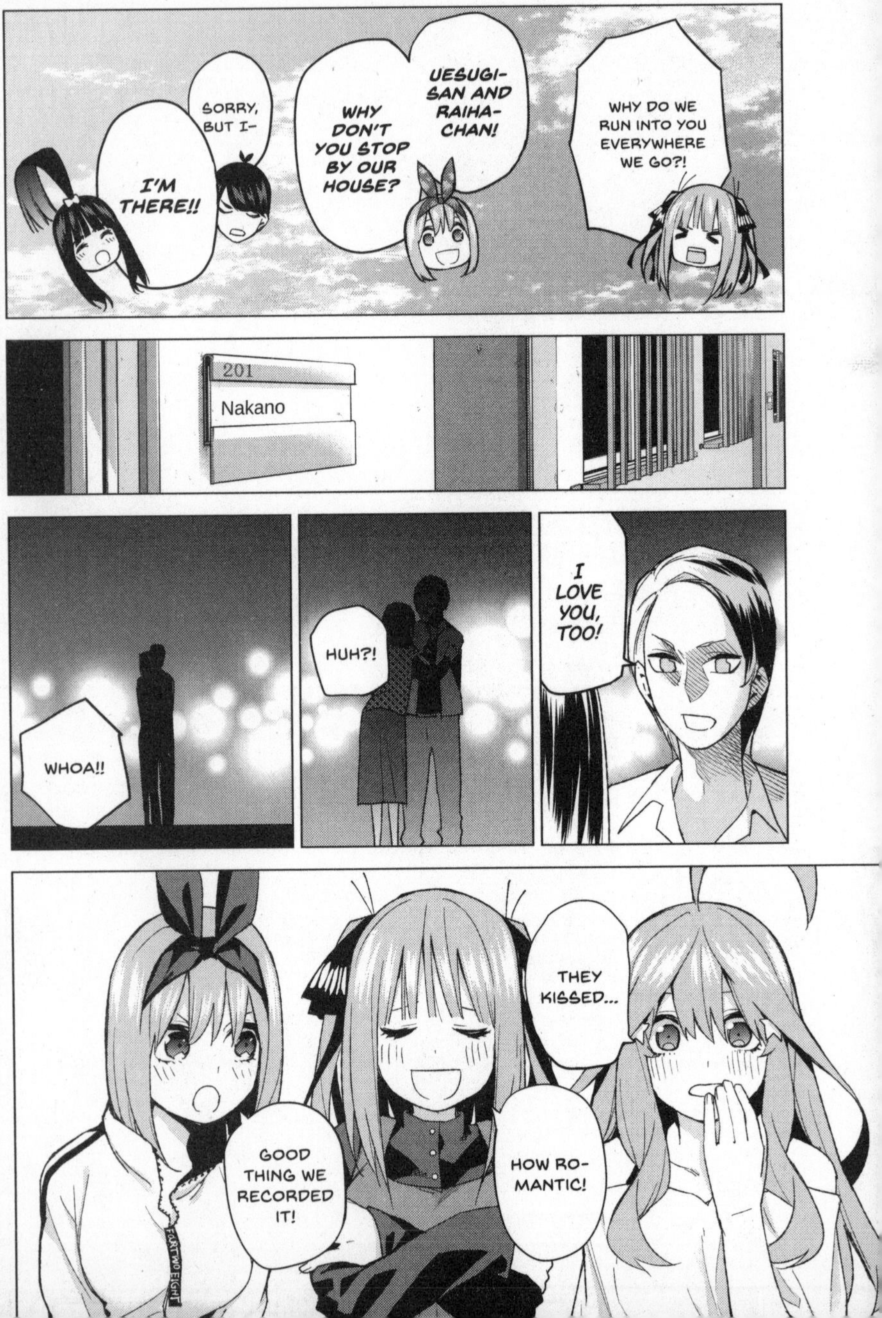
WHY DO WE RUN INTO YOU EVERYWHERE WE GO?!
UESUGI-SAN AND RAIHA-CHAN!
WHY DON'T YOU STOP BY OUR HOUSE?
SORRY, BUT I-
I'M THERE!!
201
Nakano
I LOVE YOU, TOO!
HUH?!
WHOA!!
THEY KISSED...
HOW RO-MANTIC!
GOOD THING WE RECORDED IT!

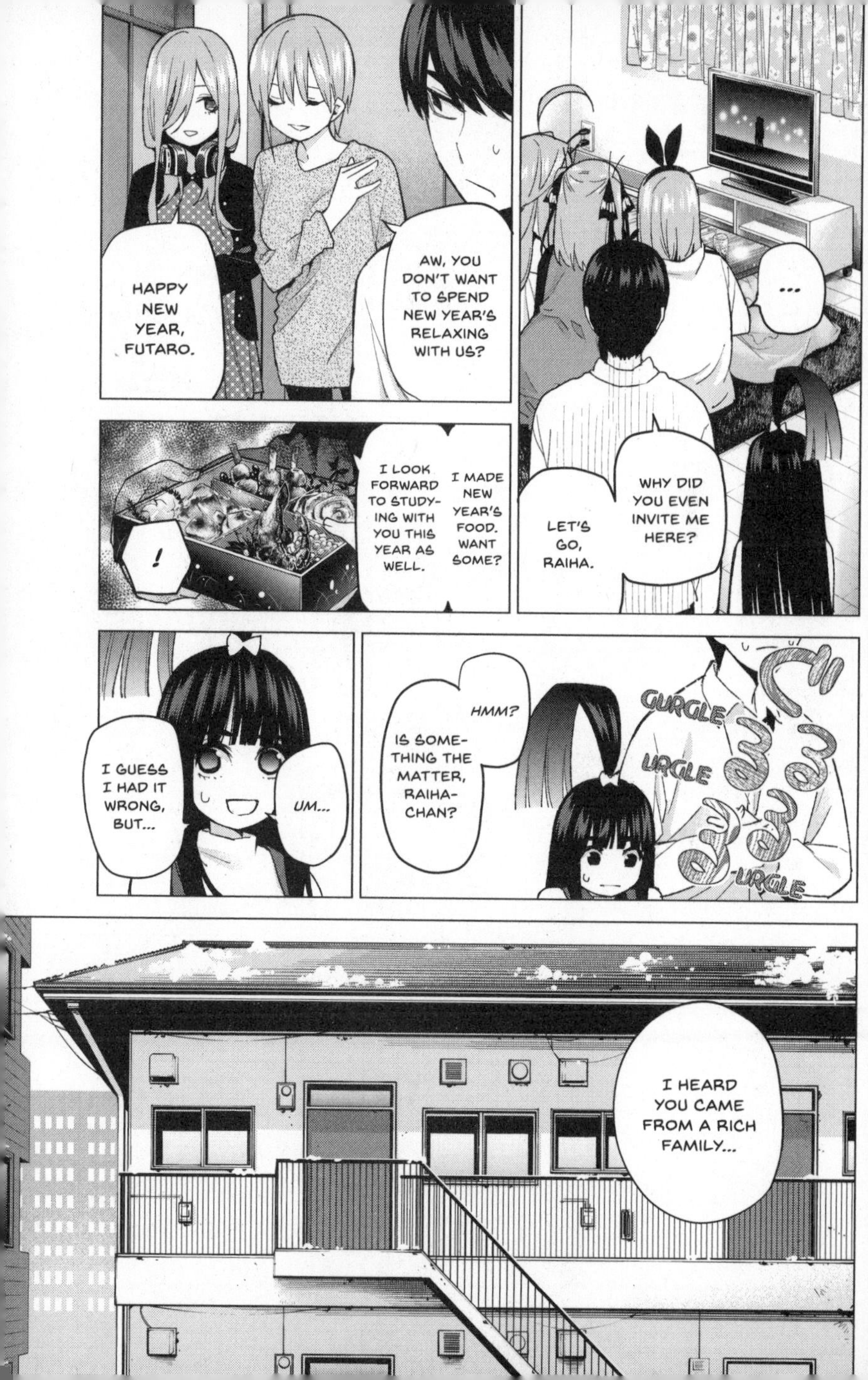
...
WHY DID YOU EVEN INVITE ME HERE?
LET'S GO, RAIHA.
AW, YOU DON'T WANT TO SPEND NEW YEAR'S RELAXING WITH US?
HAPPY NEW YEAR, FUTARO.
I MADE NEW YEAR'S FOOD. WANT SOME?
I LOOK FORWARD TO STUDYING WITH YOU THIS YEAR AS WELL.
!
HMM?
IS SOMETHING THE MATTER, RAIHA-CHAN?
GURGLE
URGLE
URGLE
UM...
I GUESS I HAD IT WRONG, BUT...
I HEARD YOU CAME FROM A RICH FAMILY...

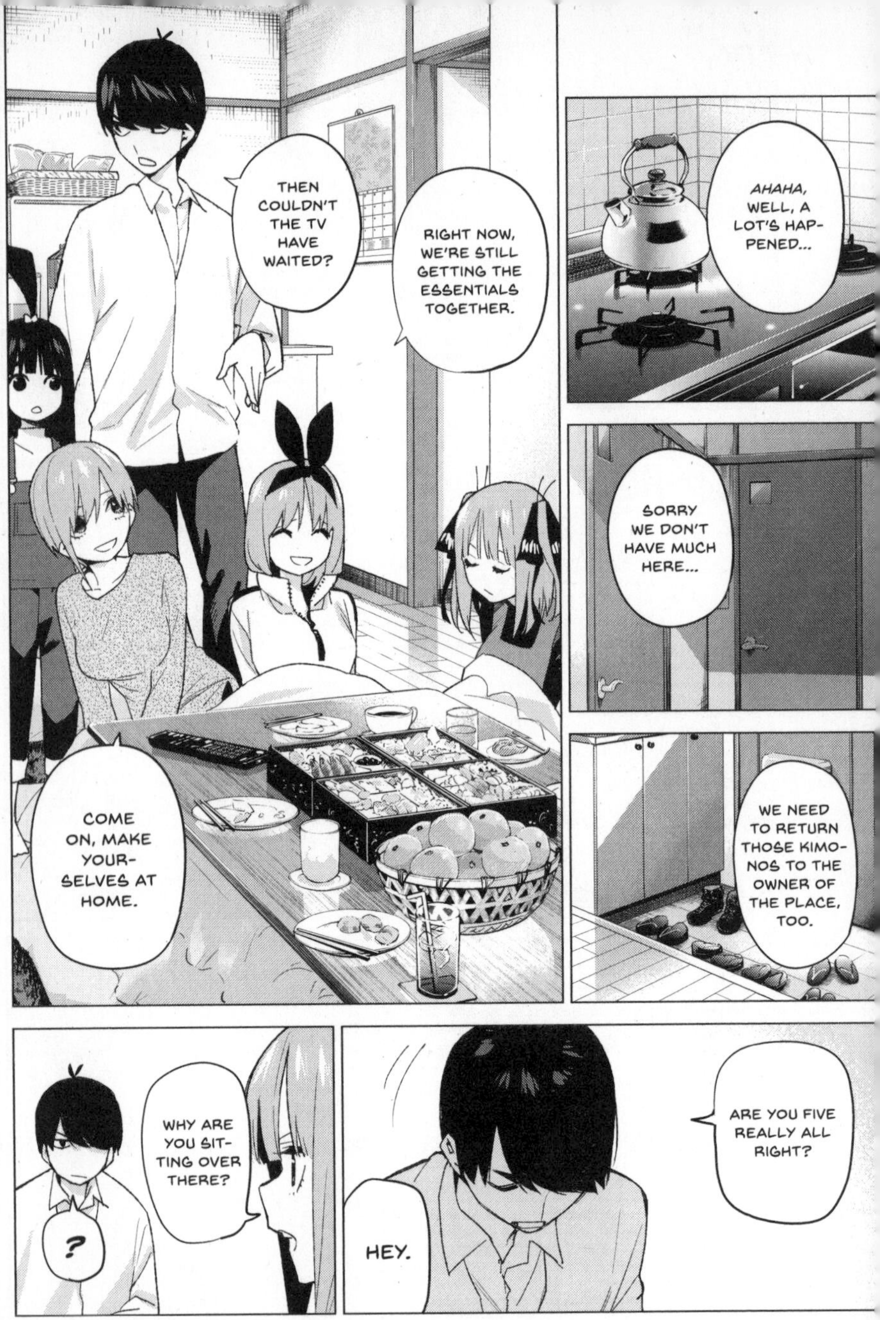
AHAHA, WELL, A LOT'S HAP-PENED...
SORRY WE DON'T HAVE MUCH HERE...
WE NEED TO RETURN THOSE KIMO-NOS TO THE OWNER OF THE PLACE, TOO.
RIGHT NOW, WE'RE STILL GETTING THE ESSENTIALS TOGETHER.
THEN COULDN'T THE TV HAVE WAITED?
COME ON, MAKE YOUR-SELVES AT HOME.
ARE YOU FIVE REALLY ALL RIGHT?
HEY.
WHY ARE YOU SIT-TING OVER THERE?
?

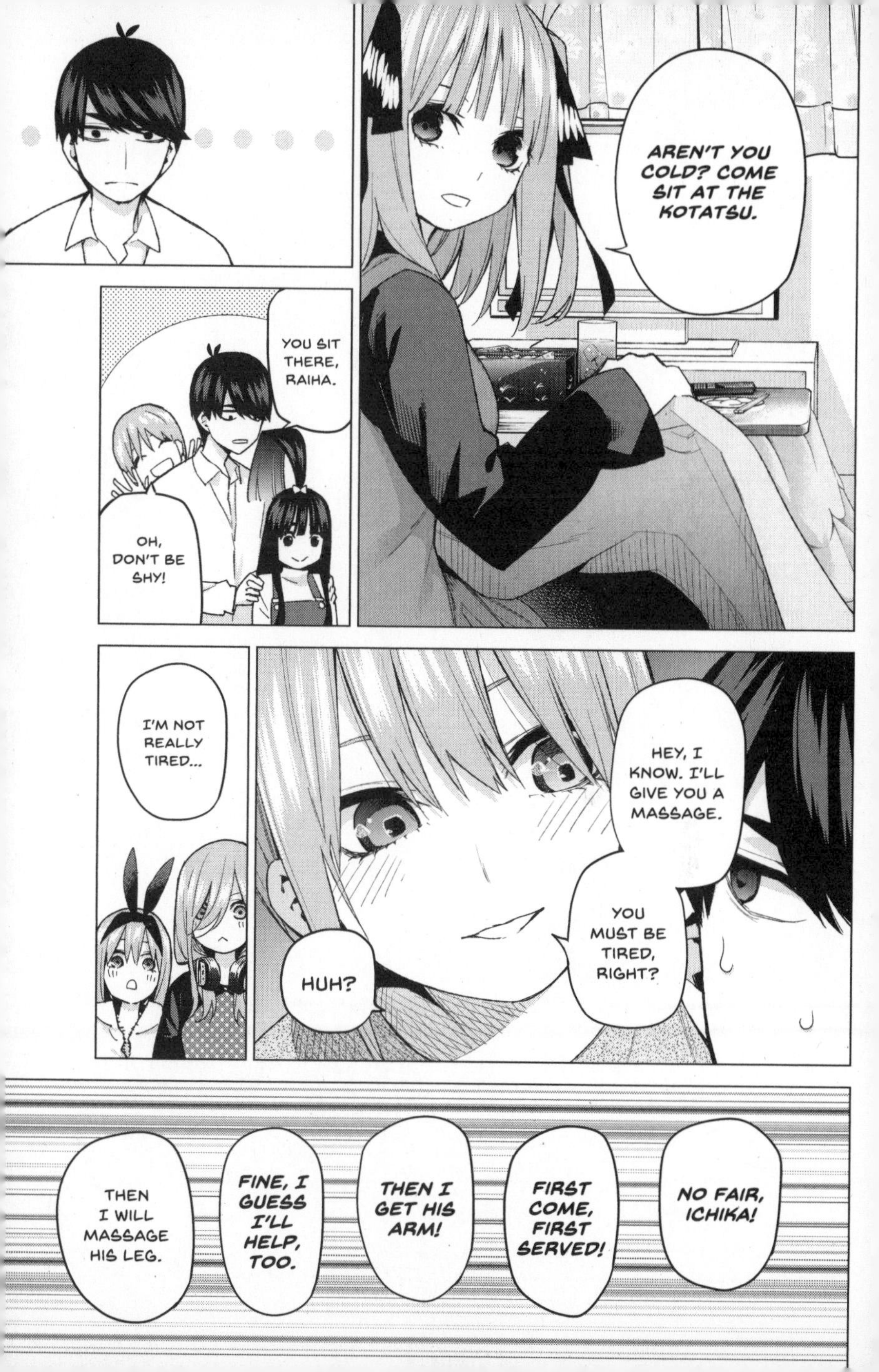
AREN'T YOU COLD? COME SIT AT THE KOTATSU.
YOU SIT THERE, RAIHA.
OH, DON'T BE SHY!
HEY, I KNOW. I'LL GIVE YOU A MASSAGE.
YOU MUST BE TIRED, RIGHT?
HUH?
I'M NOT REALLY TIRED...
NO FAIR, ICHIKA!
FIRST COME, FIRST SERVED!
THEN I GET HIS ARM!
FINE, I GUESS I'LL HELP, TOO.
THEN I WILL MASSAGE HIS LEG.

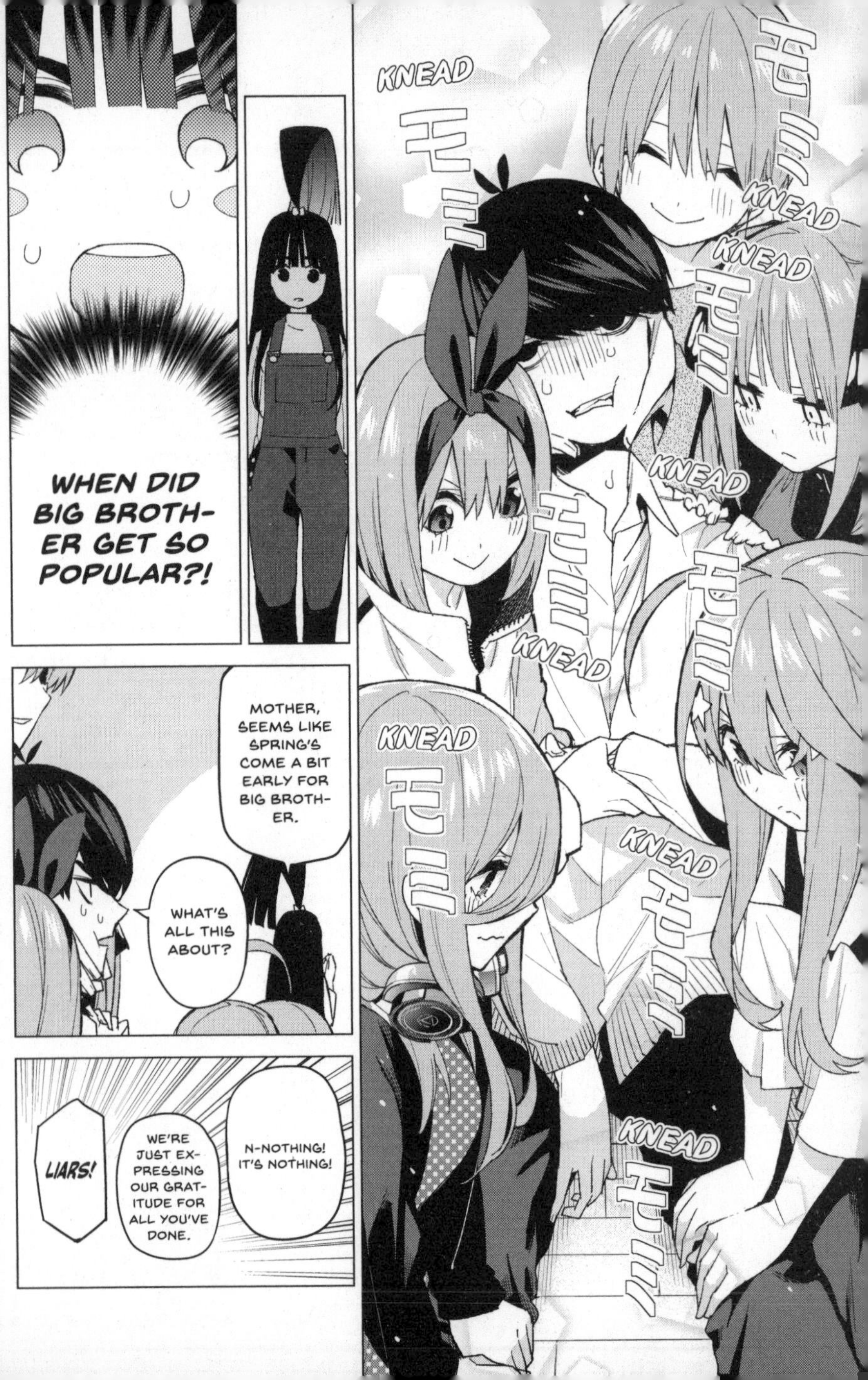
KNEAD
モミ
KNEAD
モミ
KNEAD
モミ
KNEAD
モミ
KNEAD
モミ
KNEAD
モミ
KNEAD
モミ
KNEAD
モミ
WHEN DID BIG BROTHER GET SO POPULAR?!
MOTHER, SEEMS LIKE SPRING'S COME A BIT EARLY FOR BIG BROTHER.
WHAT'S ALL THIS ABOUT?
N-NOTHING! IT'S NOTHING!
WE'RE JUST EXPRESSING OUR GRATITUDE FOR ALL YOU'VE DONE.
LIARS!

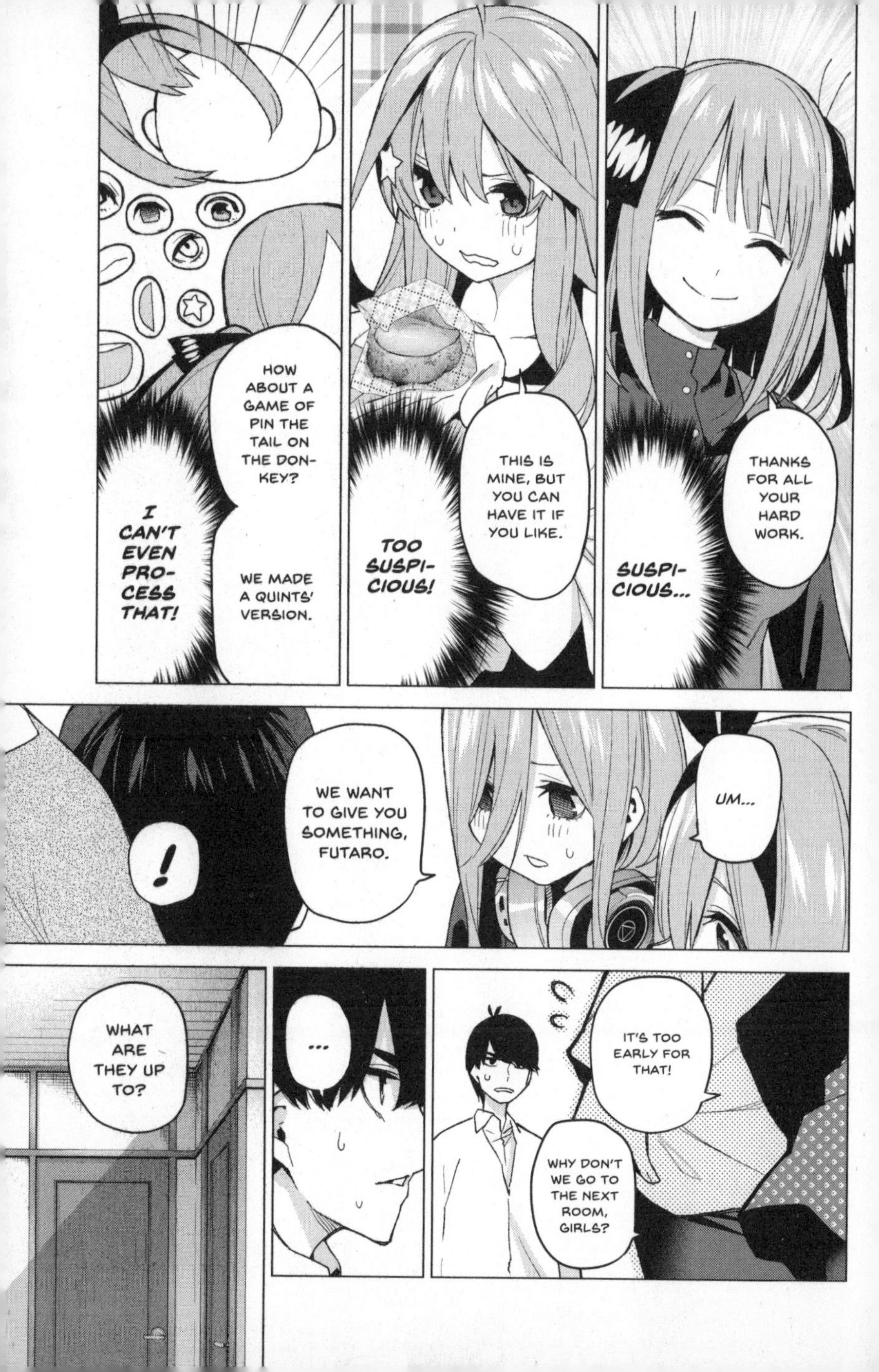
THANKS FOR ALL YOUR HARD WORK.
SUSPICIOUS...
THIS IS MINE, BUT YOU CAN HAVE IT IF YOU LIKE.
TOO SUSPICIOUS!
HOW ABOUT A GAME OF PIN THE TAIL ON THE DONKEY?
WE MADE A QUINTS' VERSION.
I CAN'T EVEN PROCESS THAT!
UM...
WE WANT TO GIVE YOU SOMETHING, FUTARO.
!
IT'S TOO EARLY FOR THAT!
WHY DON'T WE GO TO THE NEXT ROOM, GIRLS?
...
WHAT ARE THEY UP TO?

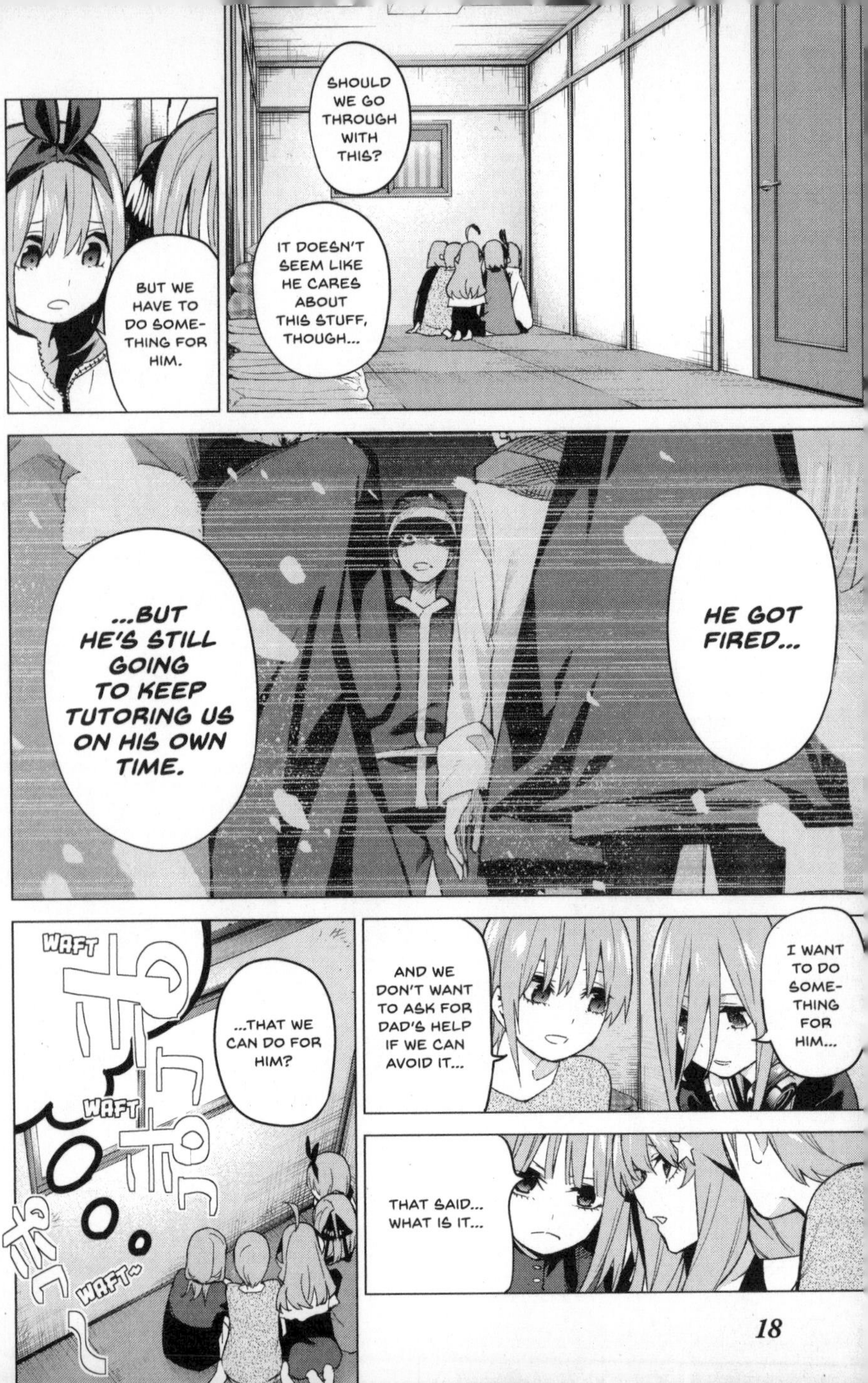
SHOULD WE GO THROUGH WITH THIS?
IT DOESN'T SEEM LIKE HE CARES ABOUT THIS STUFF, THOUGH...
BUT WE HAVE TO DO SOME-THING FOR HIM.
HE GOT FIRED...
...BUT HE'S STILL GOING TO KEEP TUTORING US ON HIS OWN TIME.
I WANT TO DO SOME-THING FOR HIM...
AND WE DON'T WANT TO ASK FOR DAD'S HELP IF WE CAN AVOID IT...
THAT SAID... WHAT IS IT...
...THAT WE CAN DO FOR HIM?
WAFT
WAFT
WAFT~

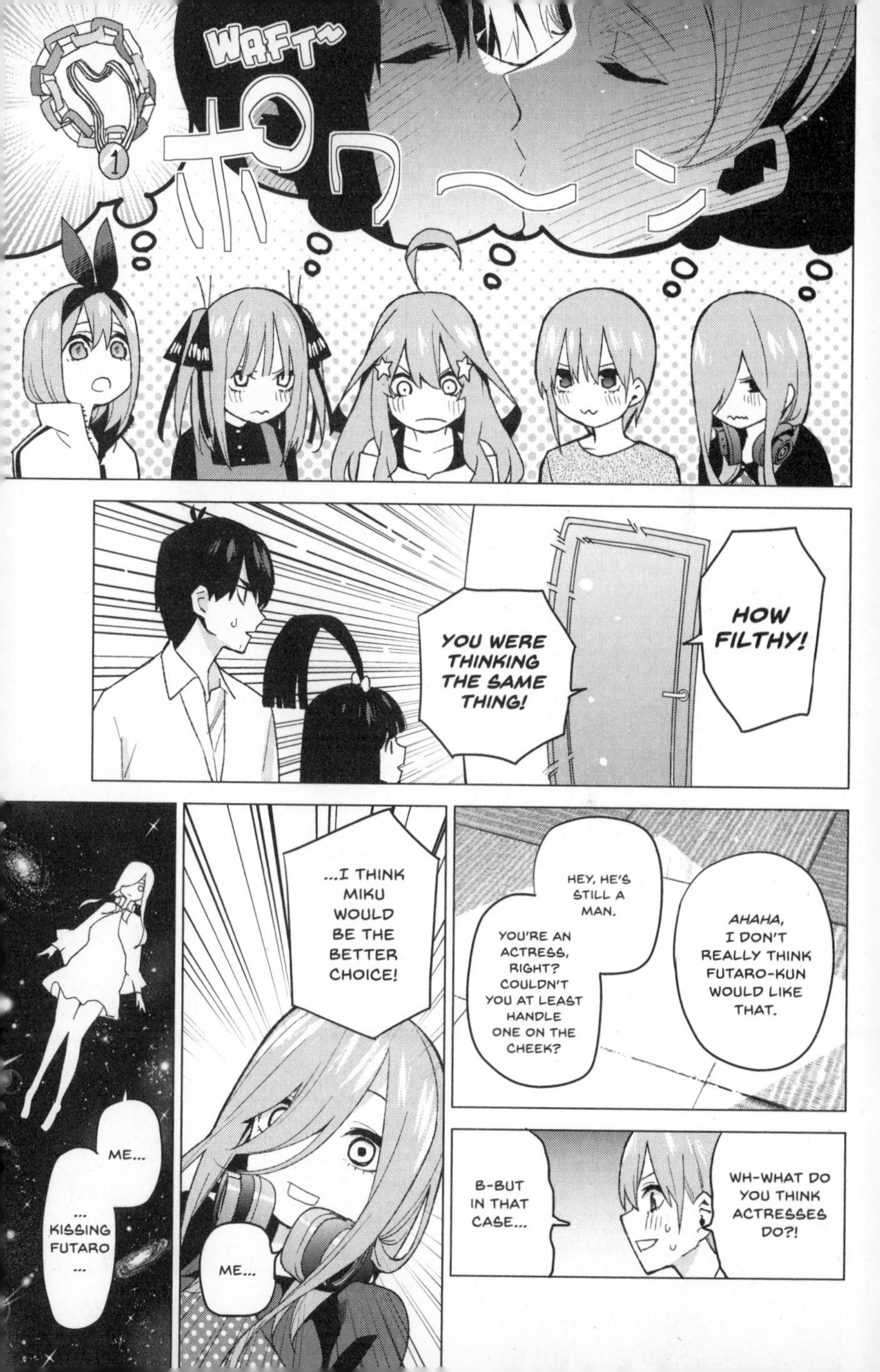
WAFT~
HOW FILTHY!
YOU WERE THINKING THE SAME THING!
AHAHA, I DON'T REALLY THINK FUTARO-KUN WOULD LIKE THAT.
HEY, HE'S STILL A MAN.
YOU'RE AN ACTRESS, RIGHT? COULDN'T YOU AT LEAST HANDLE ONE ON THE CHEEK?
WH-WHAT DO YOU THINK ACTRESSES DO?!
B-BUT IN THAT CASE...
...I THINK MIKU WOULD BE THE BETTER CHOICE!
ME...
ME...
... KISSING FUTARO ...

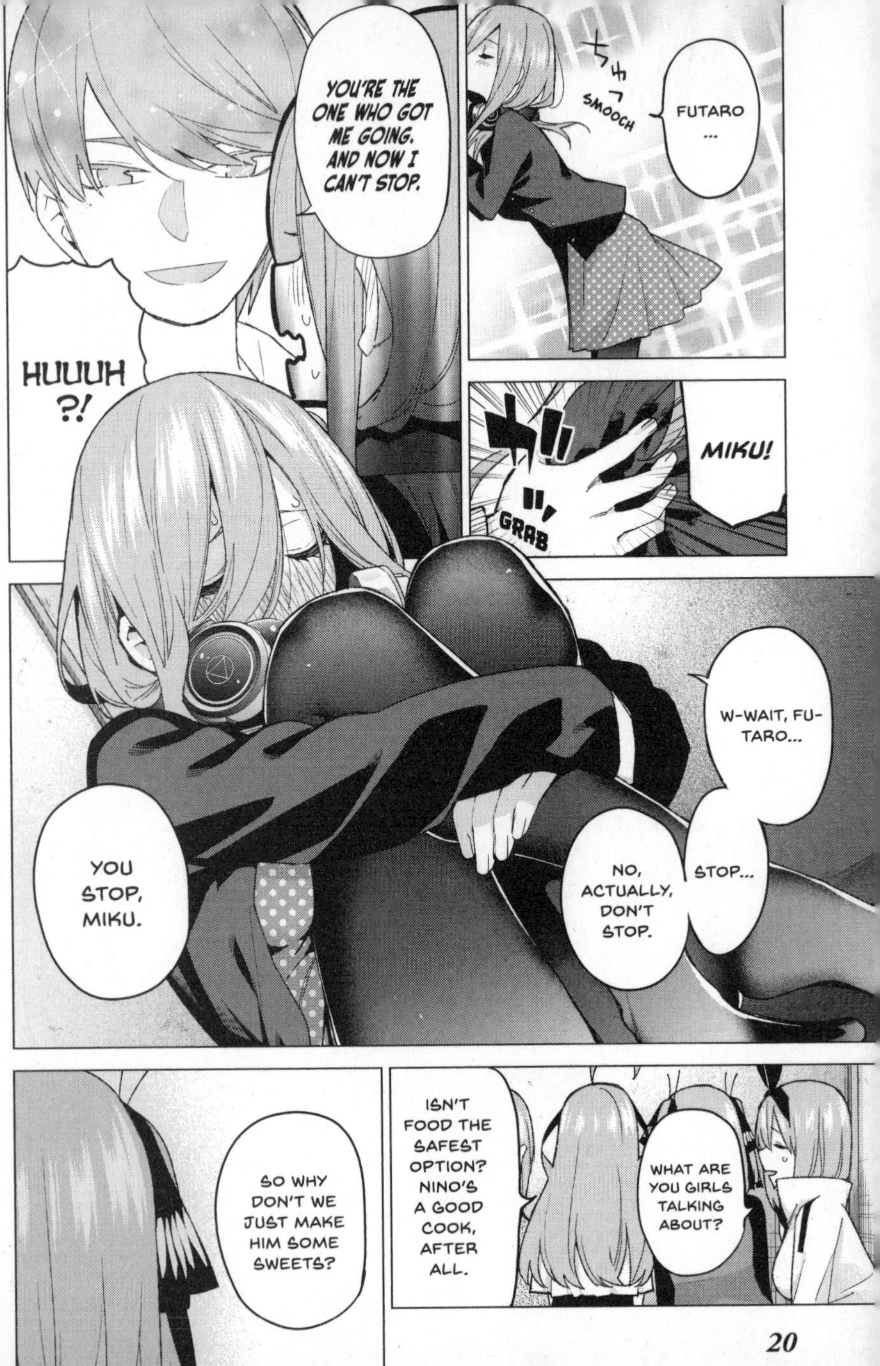
SMOOCH
FUTARO ...
GRAB
MIKU!
YOU'RE THE ONE WHO GOT ME GOING. AND NOW I CAN'T STOP.
HUUUH ?!
W-WAIT, FU-TARO...
STOP...
NO, ACTUALLY, DON'T STOP.
YOU STOP, MIKU.
WHAT ARE YOU GIRLS TALKING ABOUT?
ISN'T FOOD THE SAFEST OPTION? NINO'S A GOOD COOK, AFTER ALL.
SO WHY DON'T WE JUST MAKE HIM SOME SWEETS?

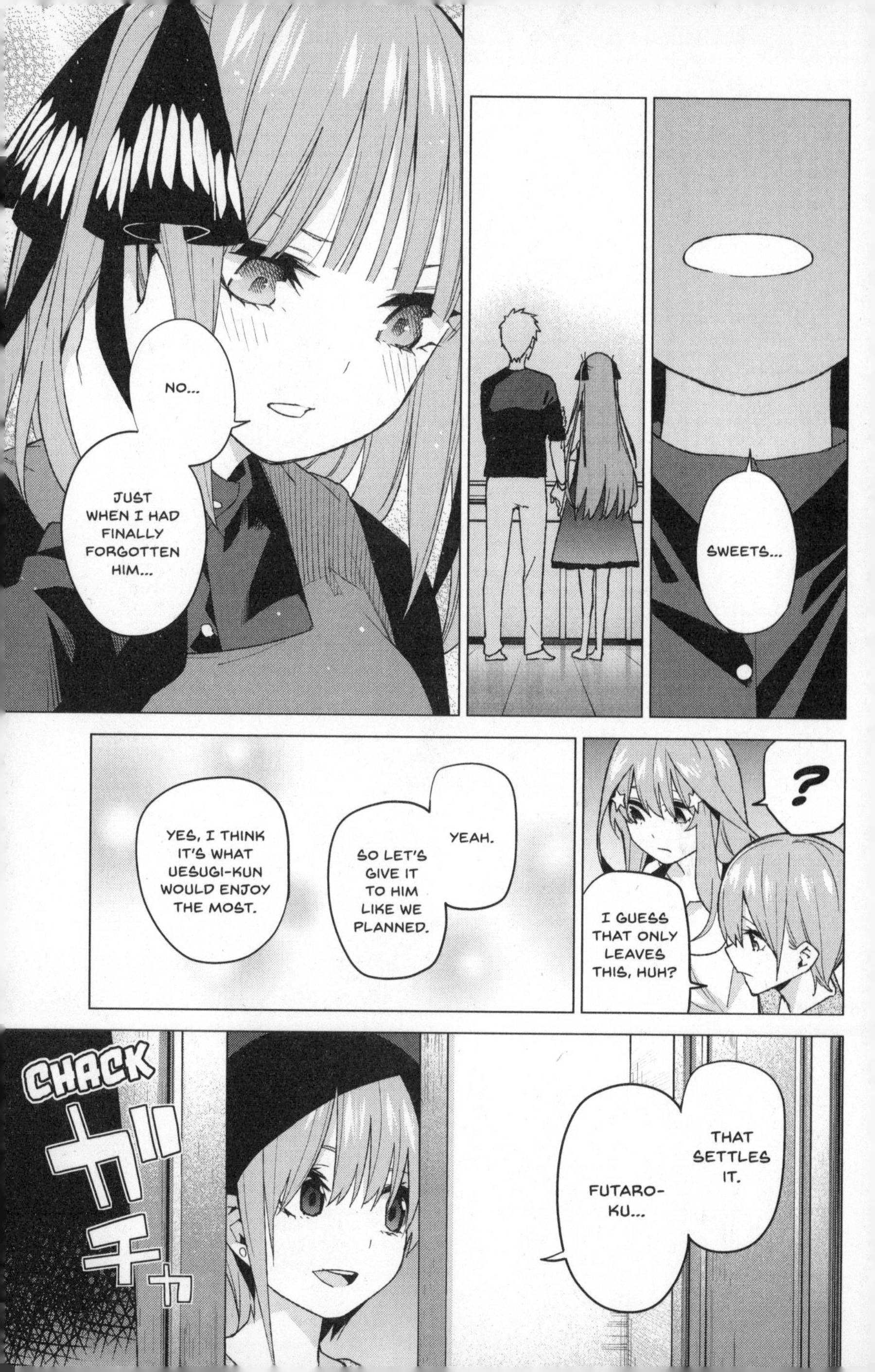
SWEETS...
NO...
JUST WHEN I HAD FINALLY FORGOTTEN HIM...
?
I GUESS THAT ONLY LEAVES THIS, HUH?
YEAH.
SO LET'S GIVE IT TO HIM LIKE WE PLANNED.
YES, I THINK IT'S WHAT UESUGI-KUN WOULD ENJOY THE MOST.
THAT SETTLES IT.
FUTARO-KU...
CHACK
ガチャ

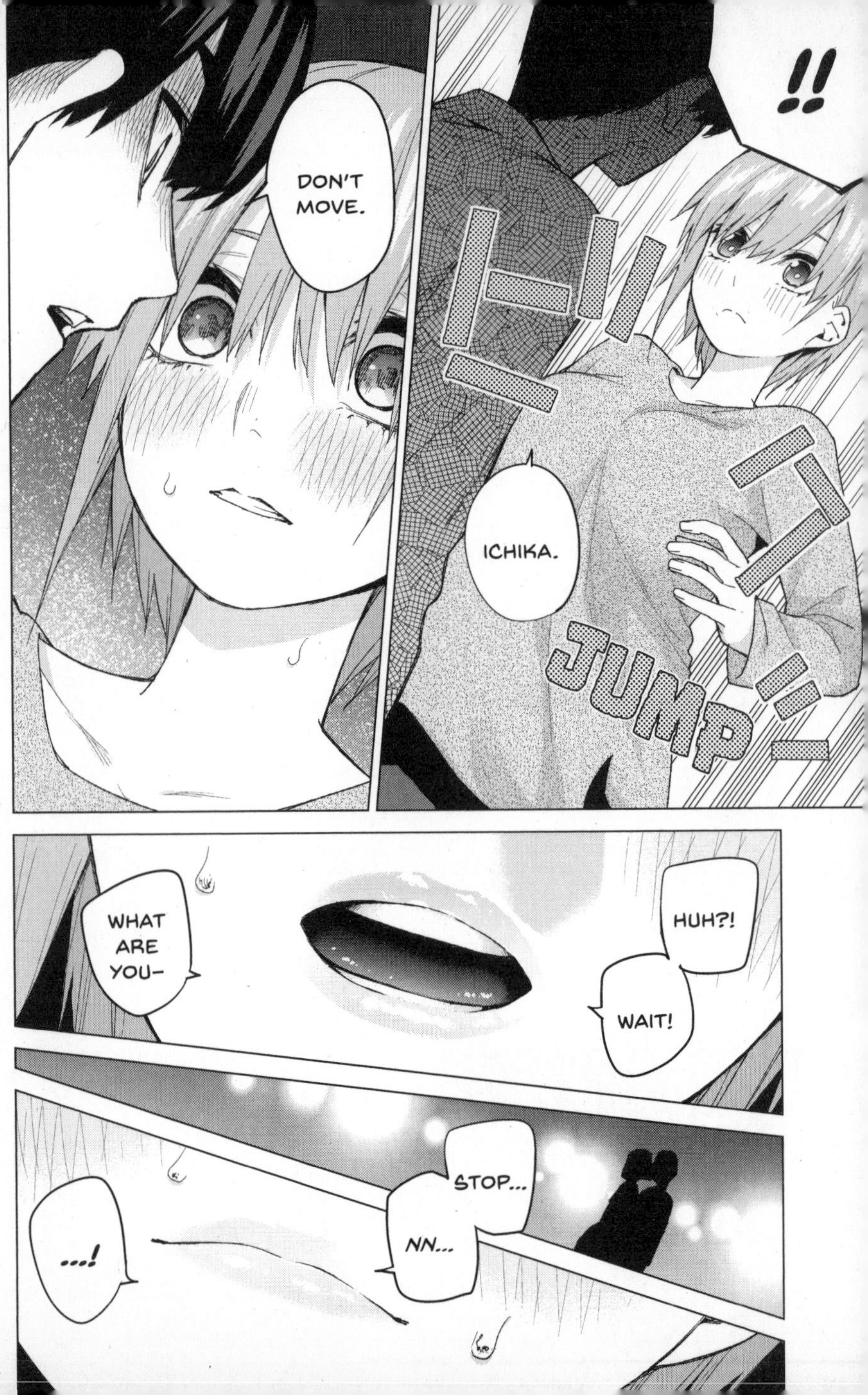
!!
ICHIKA.
JUMP!!
DON'T MOVE.
HUH?!
WAIT!
WHAT ARE YOU–
STOP...
NN...
...!

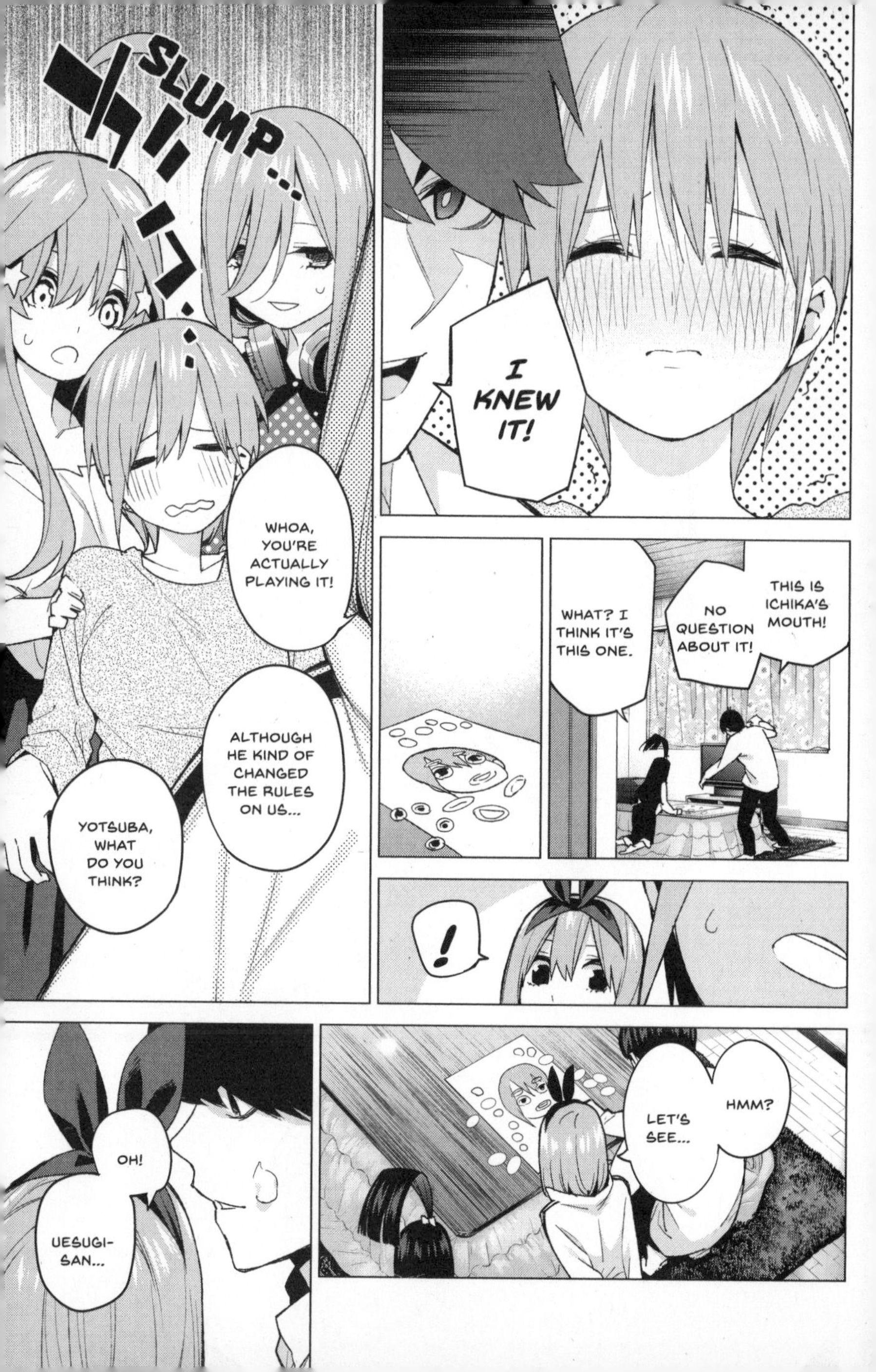
I KNEW IT!
THIS IS ICHIKA'S MOUTH!
NO QUESTION ABOUT IT!
WHAT? I THINK IT'S THIS ONE.
!
SLUMP...
WHOA, YOU'RE ACTUALLY PLAYING IT!
ALTHOUGH HE KIND OF CHANGED THE RULES ON US...
YOTSUBA, WHAT DO YOU THINK?
HMM?
LET'S SEE...
OH!
UESUGI-SAN...

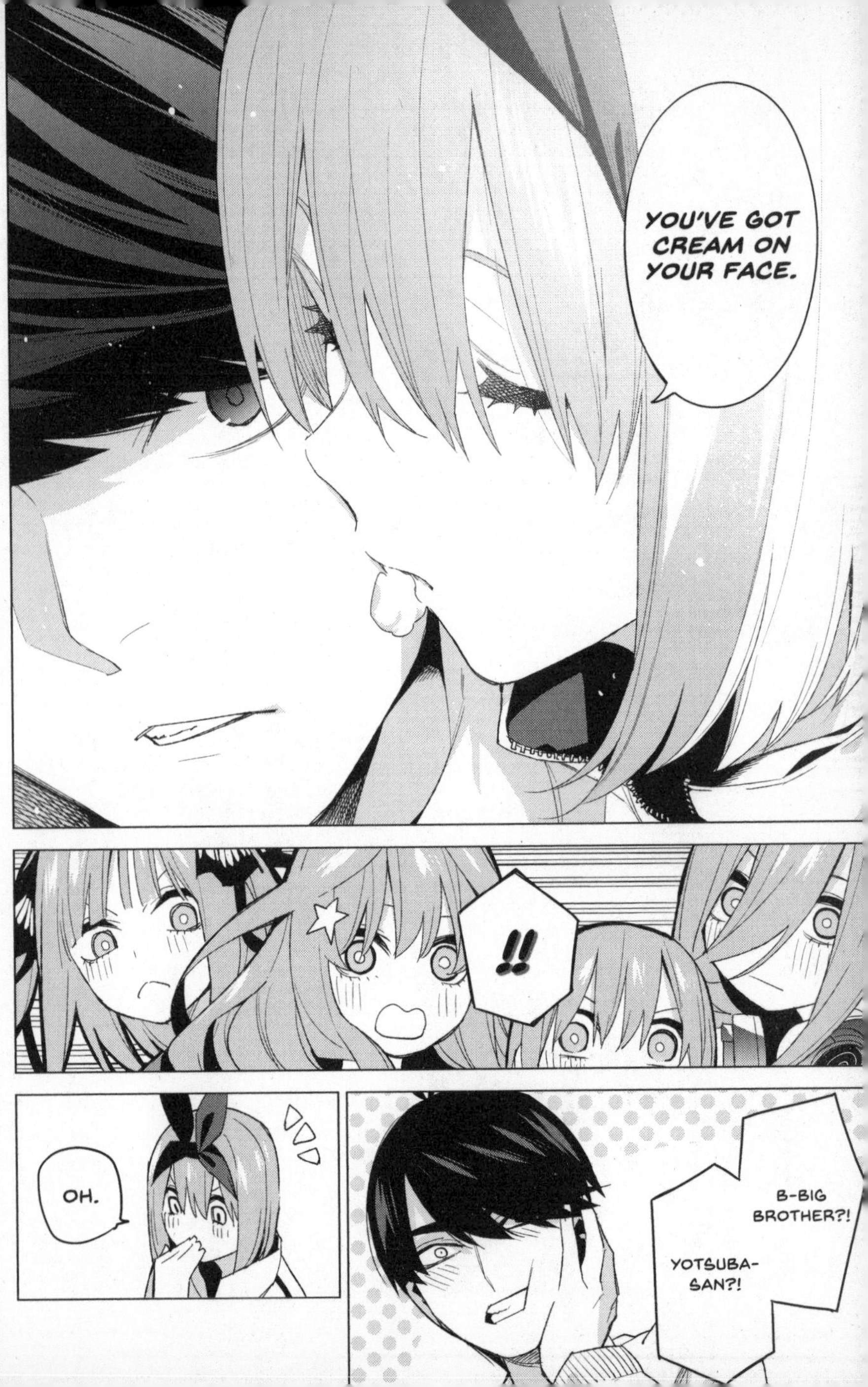
YOU'VE GOT CREAM ON YOUR FACE.
!!
B-BIG BROTHER?!
YOTSUBA-SAN?!
OH.

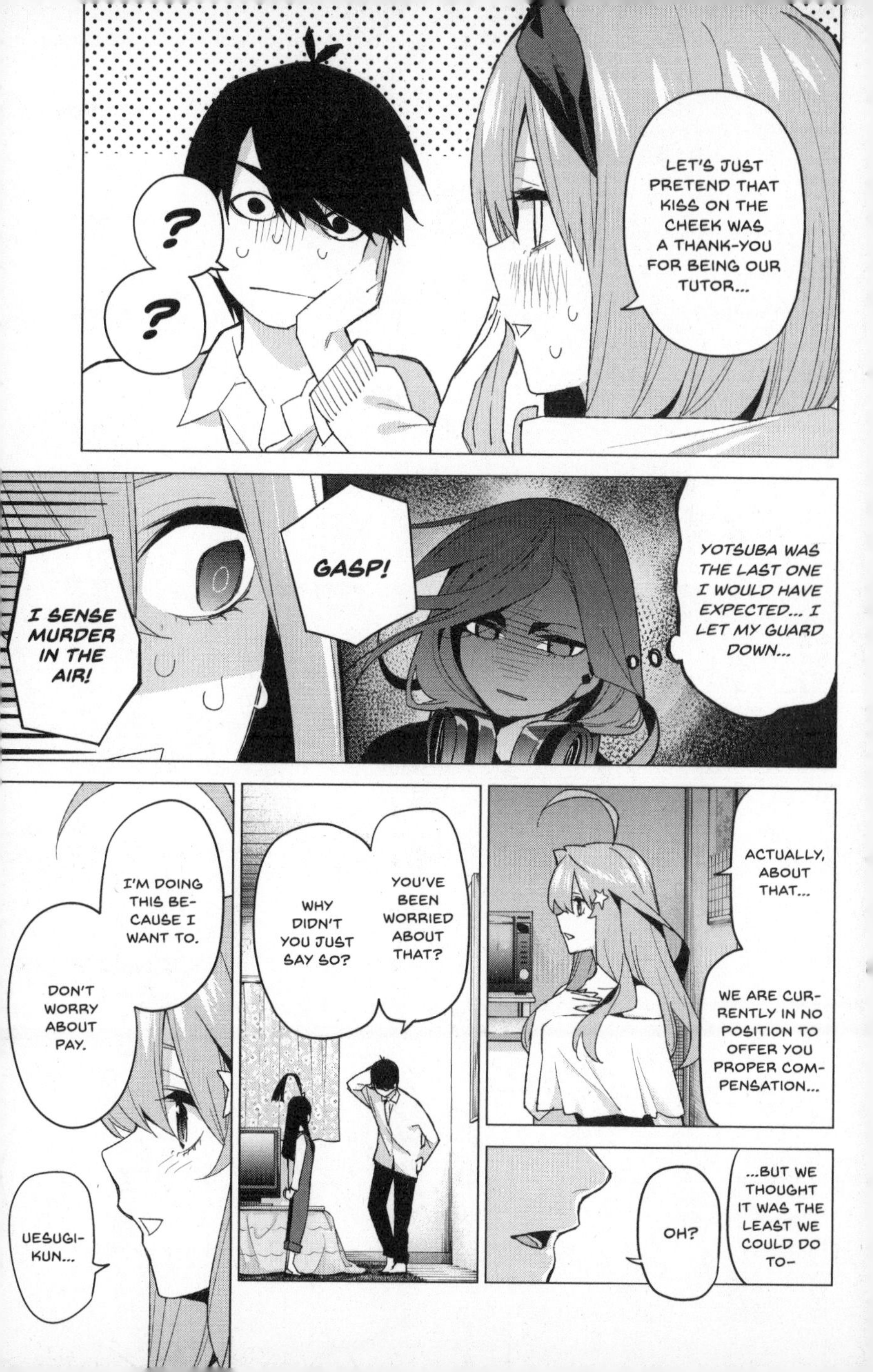
LET'S JUST PRETEND THAT KISS ON THE CHEEK WAS A THANK-YOU FOR BEING OUR TUTOR...
?
?
YOTSUBA WAS THE LAST ONE I WOULD HAVE EXPECTED... I LET MY GUARD DOWN...
GASP!
I SENSE MURDER IN THE AIR!
ACTUALLY, ABOUT THAT...
WE ARE CUR-RENTLY IN NO POSITION TO OFFER YOU PROPER COMPEN-SATION...
...BUT WE THOUGHT IT WAS THE LEAST WE COULD DO TO-
OH?
YOU'VE BEEN WORRIED ABOUT THAT?
WHY DIDN'T YOU JUST SAY SO?
I'M DOING THIS BE-CAUSE I WANT TO.
DON'T WORRY ABOUT PAY.
UESUGI-KUN...

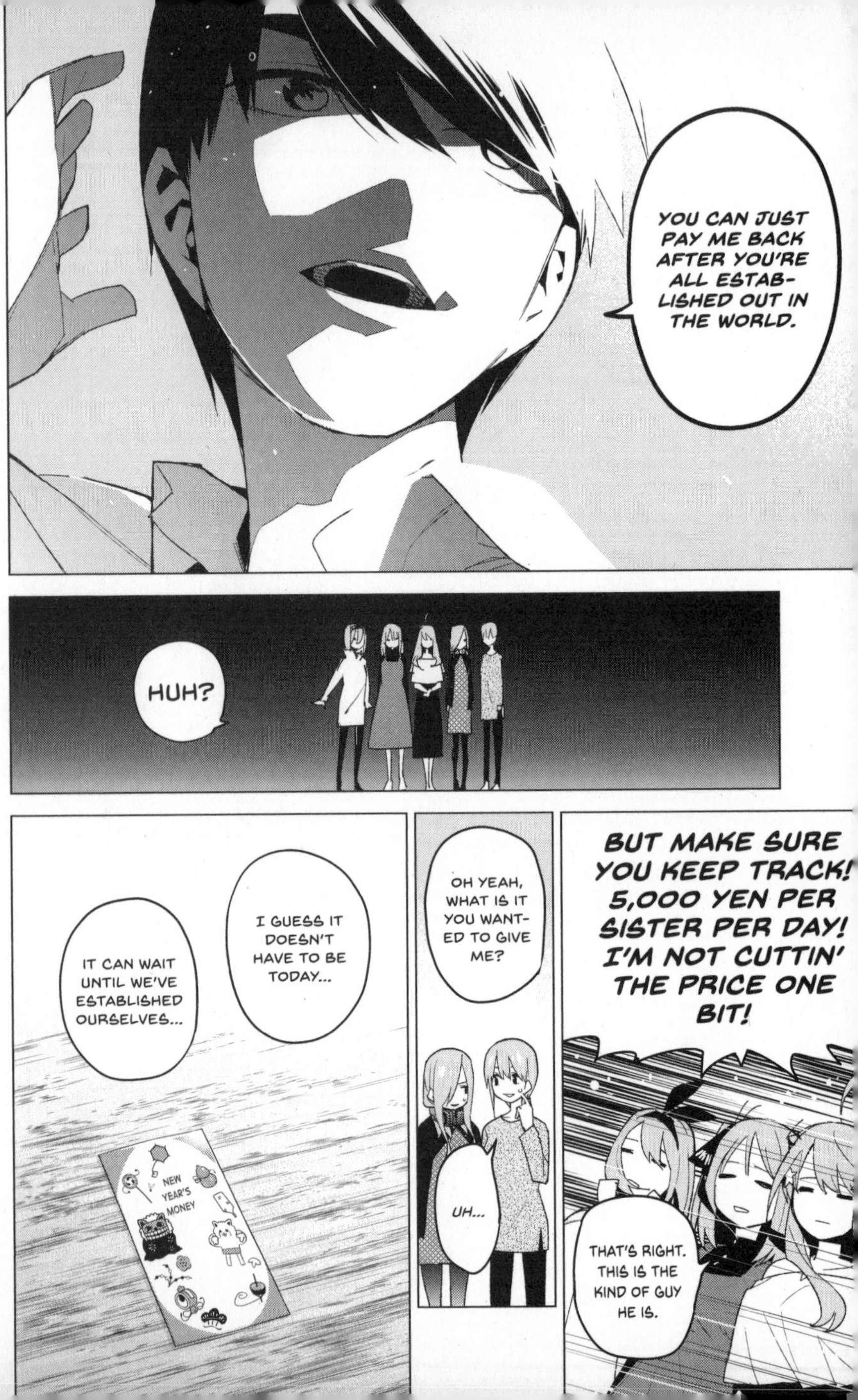
YOU CAN JUST PAY ME BACK AFTER YOU'RE ALL ESTAB-LISHED OUT IN THE WORLD.
HUH?
BUT MAKE SURE YOU KEEP TRACK! 5,000 YEN PER SISTER PER DAY! I'M NOT CUTTIN' THE PRICE ONE BIT!
THAT'S RIGHT. THIS IS THE KIND OF GUY HE IS.
OH YEAH, WHAT IS IT YOU WANT-ED TO GIVE ME?
UH...
I GUESS IT DOESN'T HAVE TO BE TODAY...
IT CAN WAIT UNTIL WE'VE ESTABLISHED OURSELVES...
NEW YEAR'S MONEY

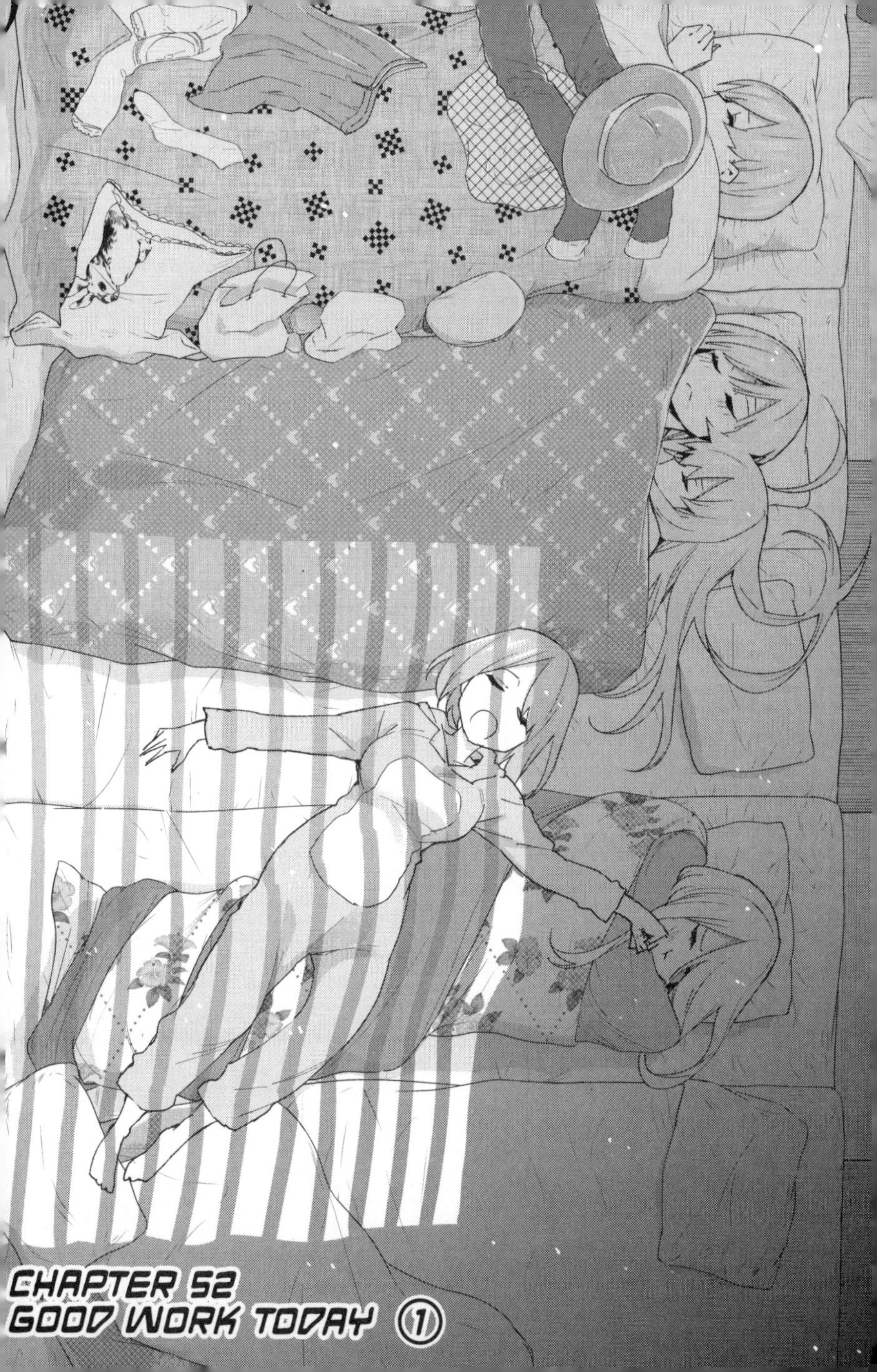

CHAPTER 52
GOOD WORK TODAY ①

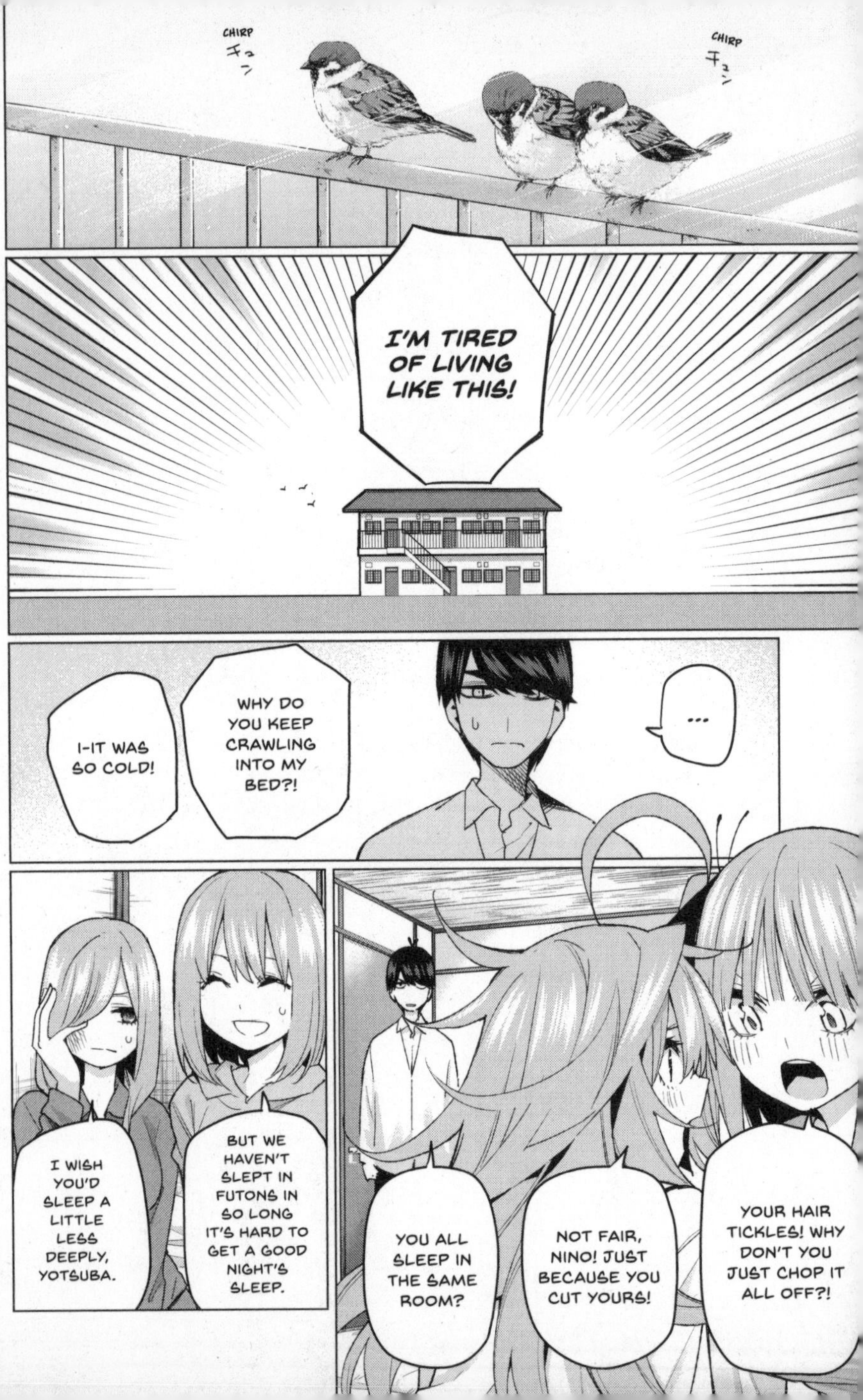

CHIRP チュン
CHIRP チュン
I'M TIRED OF LIVING LIKE THIS!
...
WHY DO YOU KEEP CRAWLING INTO MY BED?!
I-IT WAS SO COLD!
YOUR HAIR TICKLES! WHY DON'T YOU JUST CHOP IT ALL OFF?!
NOT FAIR, NINO! JUST BECAUSE YOU CUT YOURS!
YOU ALL SLEEP IN THE SAME ROOM?
BUT WE HAVEN'T SLEPT IN FUTONS IN SO LONG IT'S HARD TO GET A GOOD NIGHT'S SLEEP.
I WISH YOU'D SLEEP A LITTLE LESS DEEPLY, YOTSUBA.

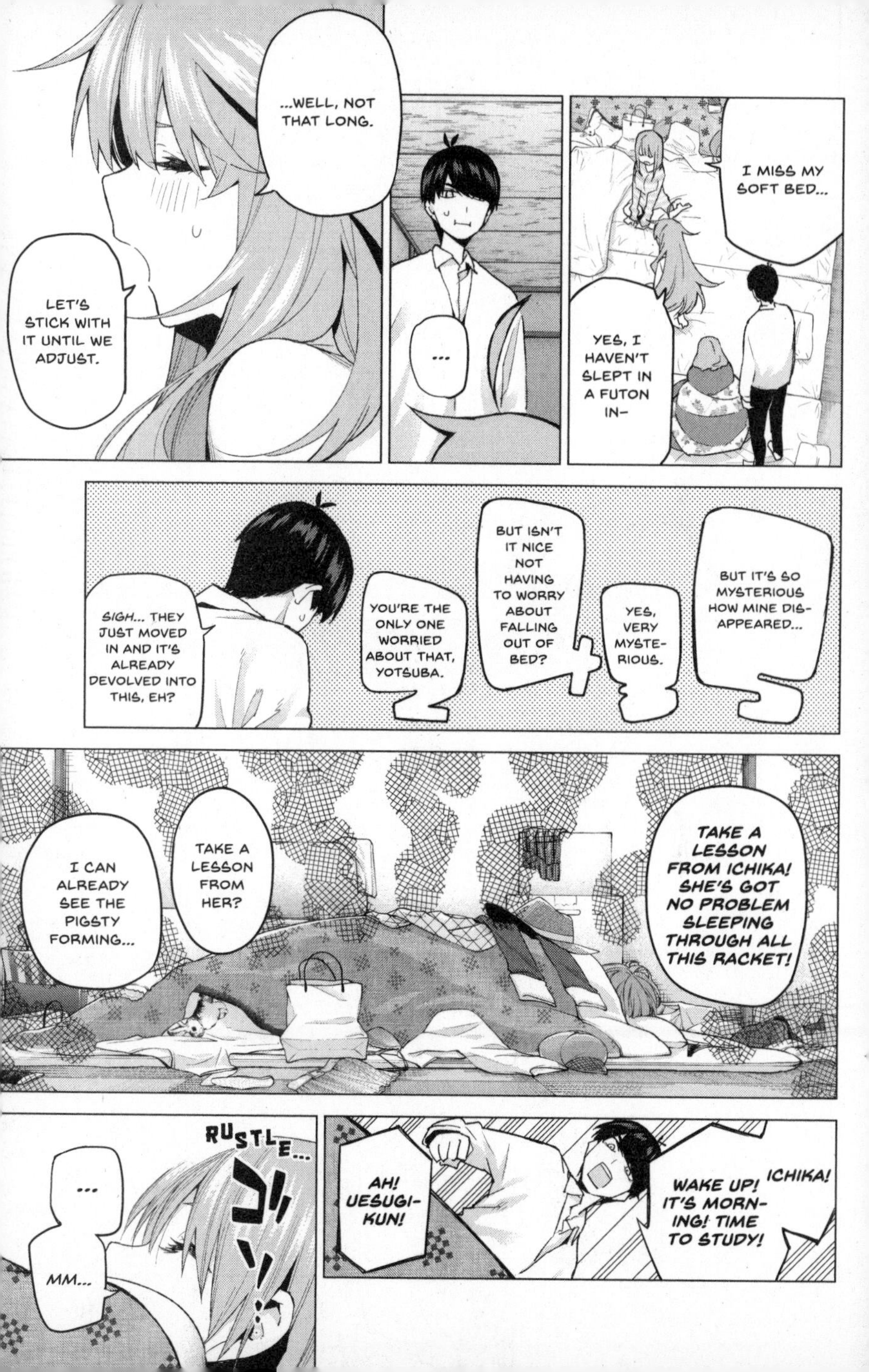
I MISS MY SOFT BED...
YES, I HAVEN'T SLEPT IN A FUTON IN–
...WELL, NOT THAT LONG.
...
LET'S STICK WITH IT UNTIL WE ADJUST.
BUT IT'S SO MYSTERIOUS HOW MINE DIS-APPEARED...
YES, VERY MYSTE-RIOUS.
BUT ISN'T IT NICE NOT HAVING TO WORRY ABOUT FALLING OUT OF BED?
YOU'RE THE ONLY ONE WORRIED ABOUT THAT, YOTSUBA.
SIGH... THEY JUST MOVED IN AND IT'S ALREADY DEVOLVED INTO THIS, EH?
TAKE A LESSON FROM ICHIKA! SHE'S GOT NO PROBLEM SLEEPING THROUGH ALL THIS RACKET!
TAKE A LESSON FROM HER?
I CAN ALREADY SEE THE PIGSTY FORMING...
ICHIKA!
WAKE UP! IT'S MORN-ING! TIME TO STUDY!
AH! UESUGI-KUN!
RUSTLE...
...
MM...

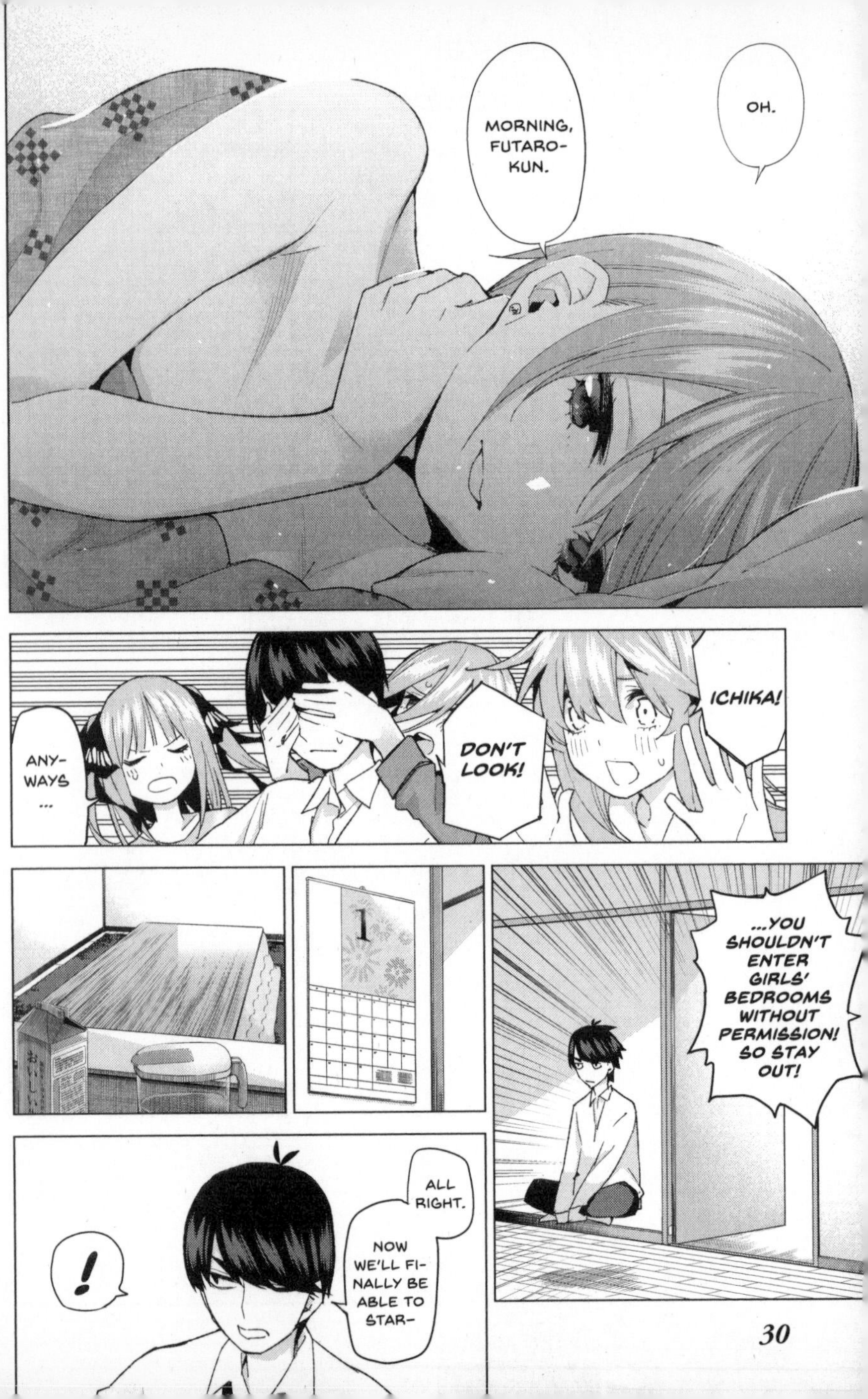
OH.
MORNING, FUTARO-KUN.
ICHIKA!
DON'T LOOK!
ANY-WAYS...
...YOU SHOULDN'T ENTER GIRLS' BEDROOMS WITHOUT PERMISSION! SO STAY OUT!
ALL RIGHT.
NOW WE'LL FI-NALLY BE ABLE TO STAR-
!

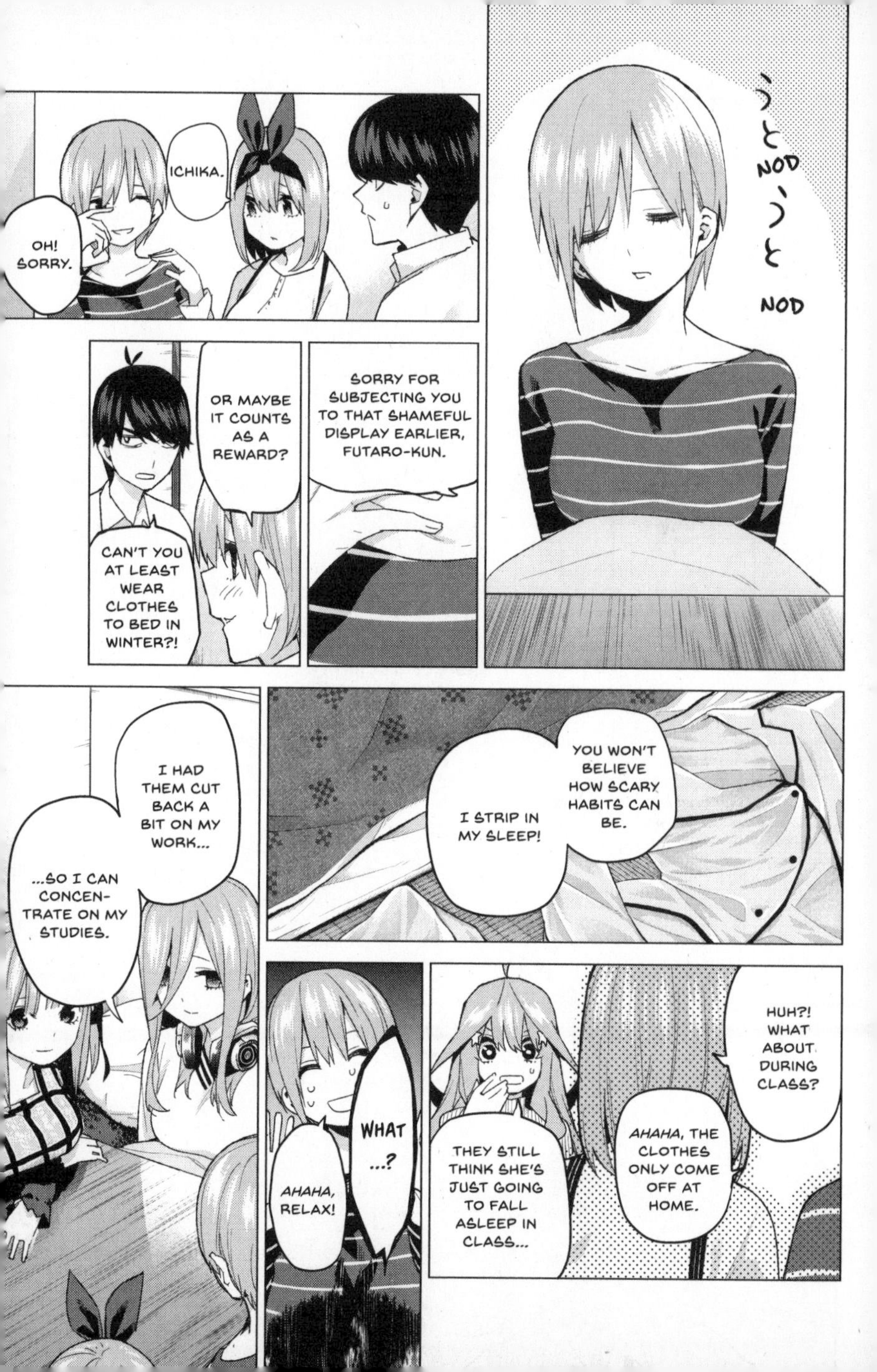
うと
NOD
うと
NOD
ICHIKA.
OH! SORRY.
SORRY FOR SUBJECTING YOU TO THAT SHAMEFUL DISPLAY EARLIER, FUTARO-KUN.
OR MAYBE IT COUNTS AS A REWARD?
CAN'T YOU AT LEAST WEAR CLOTHES TO BED IN WINTER?!
YOU WON'T BELIEVE HOW SCARY HABITS CAN BE.
I STRIP IN MY SLEEP!
HUH?! WHAT ABOUT DURING CLASS?
AHAHA, THE CLOTHES ONLY COME OFF AT HOME.
THEY STILL THINK SHE'S JUST GOING TO FALL ASLEEP IN CLASS...
WHAT ...?
AHAHA, RELAX!
I HAD THEM CUT BACK A BIT ON MY WORK...
...SO I CAN CONCENTRATE ON MY STUDIES.

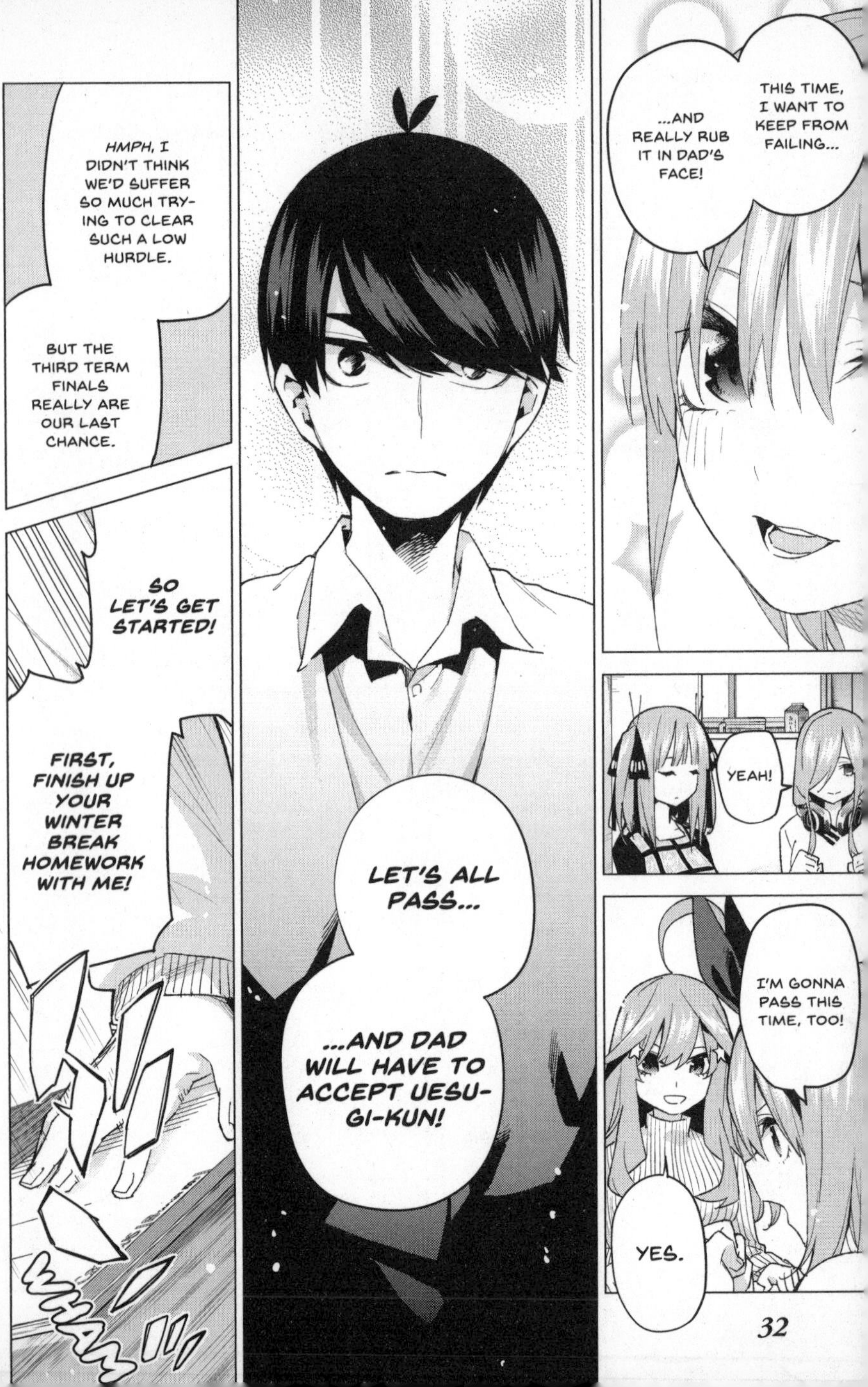

THIS TIME, I WANT TO KEEP FROM FAILING...
...AND REALLY RUB IT IN DAD'S FACE!
YEAH!
I'M GONNA PASS THIS TIME, TOO!
YES.
LET'S ALL PASS...
...AND DAD WILL HAVE TO ACCEPT UESU-GI-KUN!
HMPH, I DIDN'T THINK WE'D SUFFER SO MUCH TRY-ING TO CLEAR SUCH A LOW HURDLE.
BUT THE THIRD TERM FINALS REALLY ARE OUR LAST CHANCE.
SO LET'S GET STARTED!
FIRST, FINISH UP YOUR WINTER BREAK HOMEWORK WITH ME!
WHAM!!!

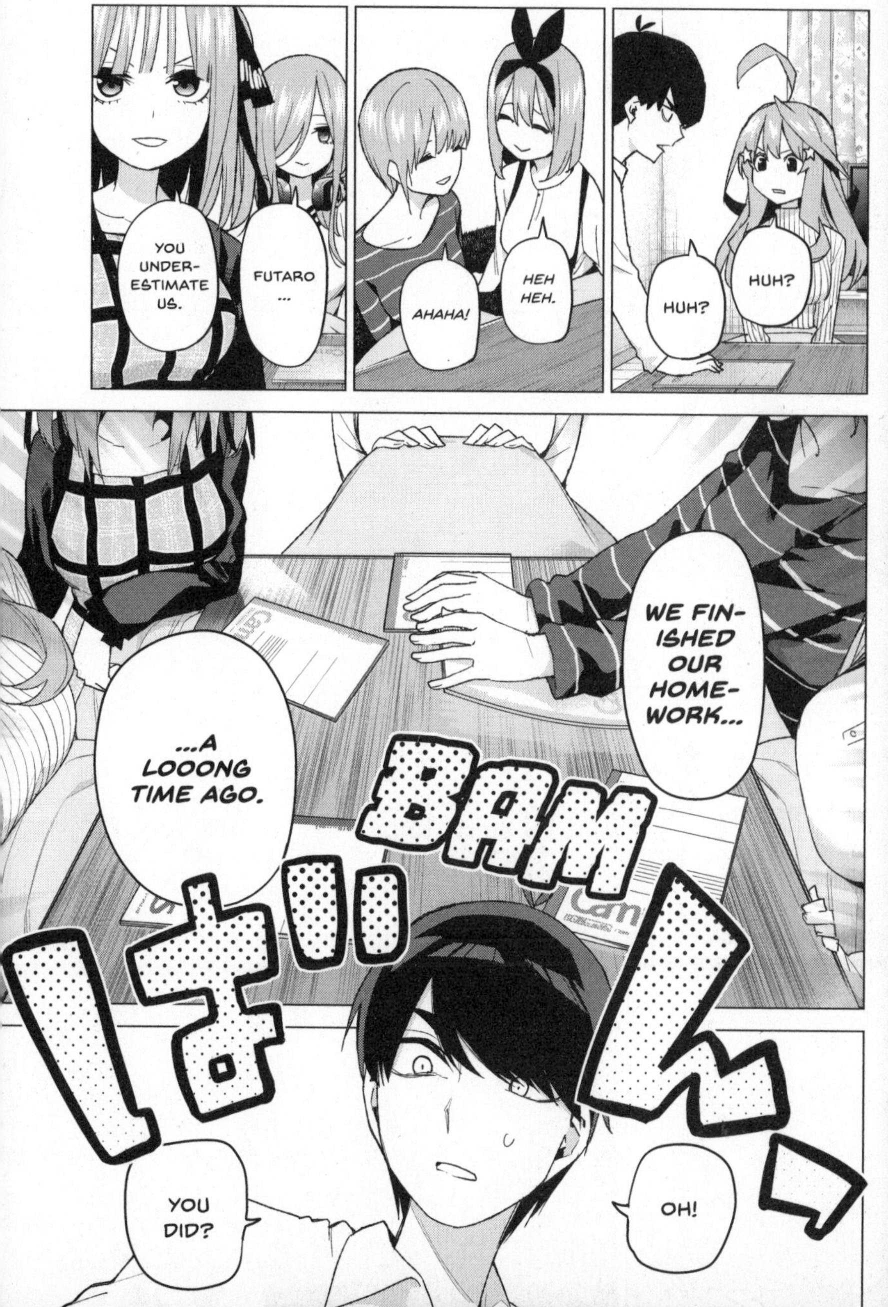
HUH?
HUH?
HEH HEH.
AHAHA!
FUTARO ...
YOU UNDER-ESTIMATE US.
WE FIN-ISHED OUR HOME-WORK...
...A LOOONG TIME AGO.
BAM
OH!
YOU DID?

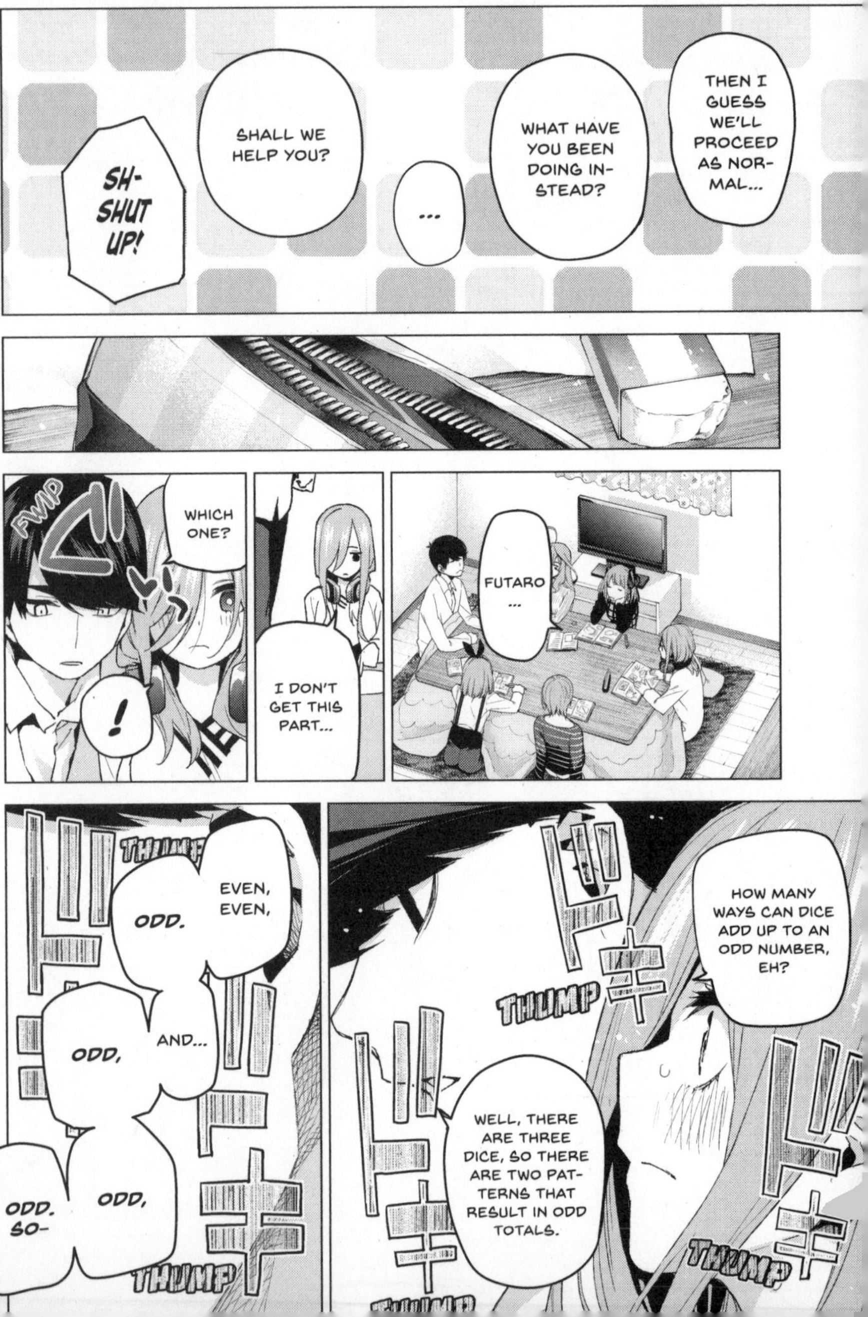
THEN I GUESS WE'LL PROCEED AS NOR-MAL...
WHAT HAVE YOU BEEN DOING IN-STEAD?
...
SHALL WE HELP YOU?
SH-SHUT UP!
FUTARO ...
I DON'T GET THIS PART...
WHICH ONE?
FWIP
!
HOW MANY WAYS CAN DICE ADD UP TO AN ODD NUMBER, EH?
THUMP
WELL, THERE ARE THREE DICE, SO THERE ARE TWO PAT-TERNS THAT RESULT IN ODD TOTALS.
THUMP
THUMP
EVEN, EVEN,
ODD.
AND...
ODD,
ODD,
ODD. SO-
THUMP

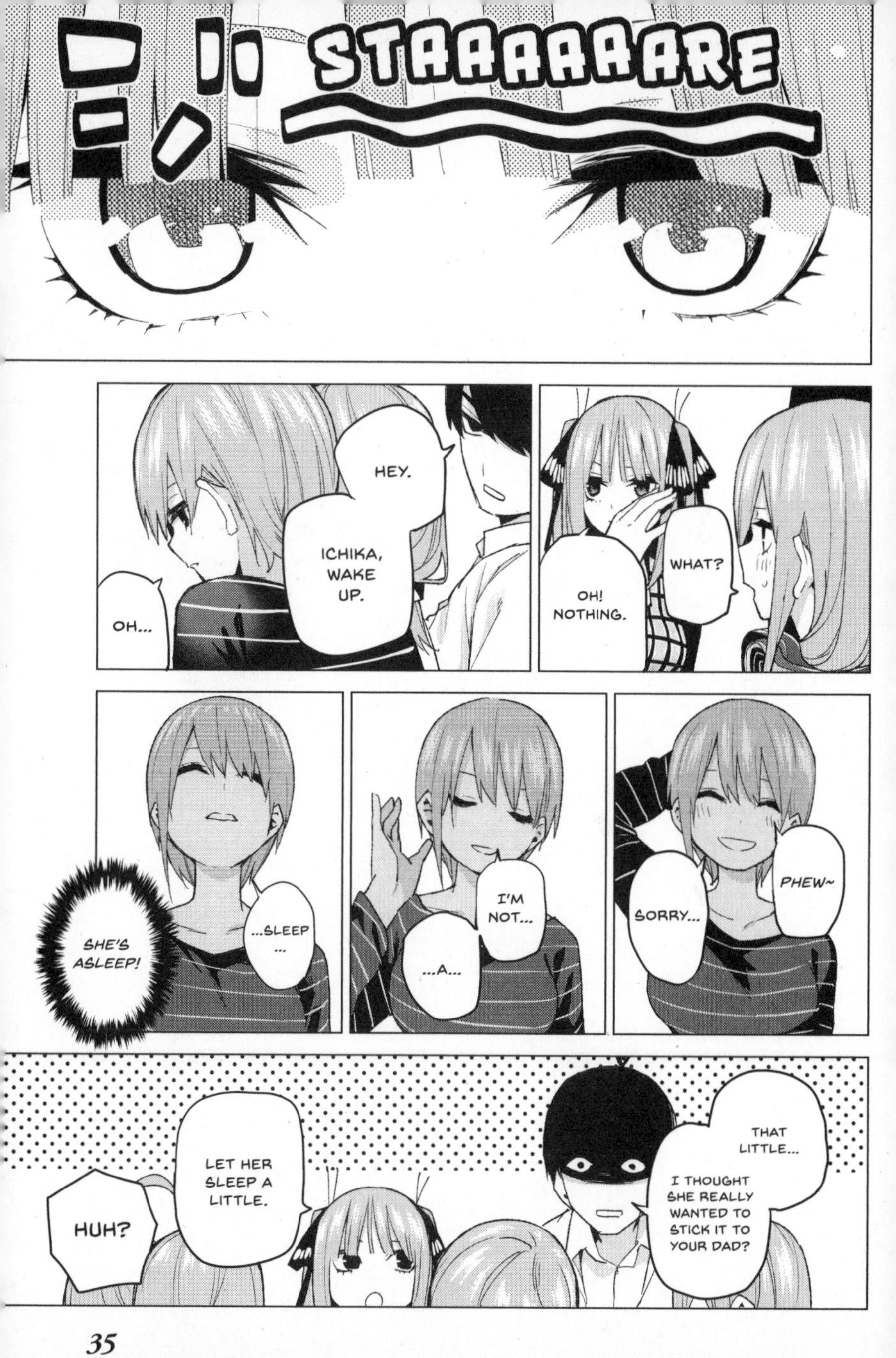
!!
STAAAAAAARE
WHAT?
OH! NOTHING.
HEY.
ICHIKA, WAKE UP.
OH...
PHEW~
SORRY...
I'M NOT...
...A...
...SLEEP ...
SHE'S ASLEEP!
THAT LITTLE...
I THOUGHT SHE REALLY WANTED TO STICK IT TO YOUR DAD?
LET HER SLEEP A LITTLE.
HUH?

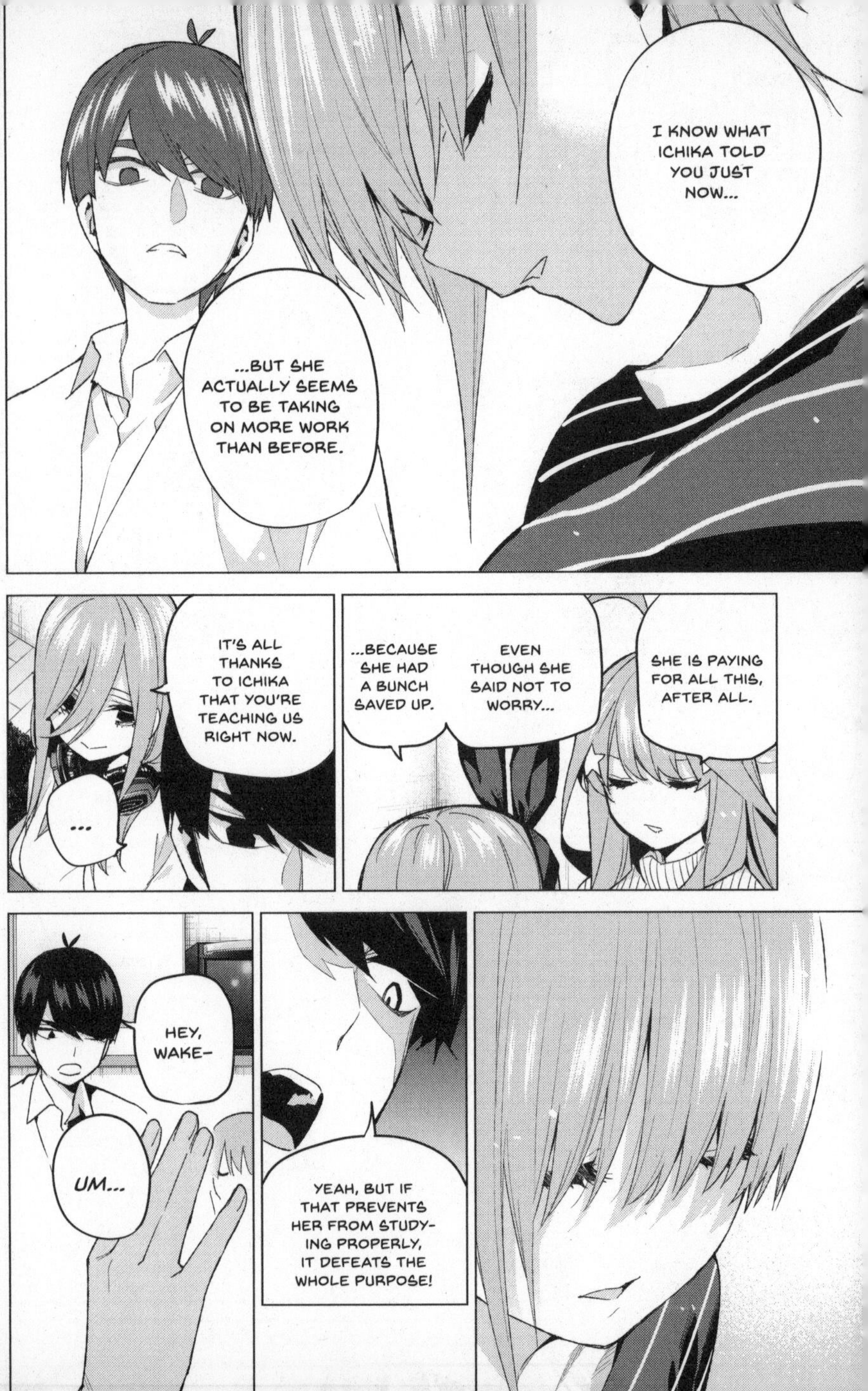
I KNOW WHAT ICHIKA TOLD YOU JUST NOW...
...BUT SHE ACTUALLY SEEMS TO BE TAKING ON MORE WORK THAN BEFORE.
SHE IS PAYING FOR ALL THIS, AFTER ALL.
EVEN THOUGH SHE SAID NOT TO WORRY...
...BECAUSE SHE HAD A BUNCH SAVED UP.
IT'S ALL THANKS TO ICHIKA THAT YOU'RE TEACHING US RIGHT NOW.
...
YEAH, BUT IF THAT PREVENTS HER FROM STUDY-ING PROPERLY, IT DEFEATS THE WHOLE PURPOSE!
HEY, WAKE-
UM...

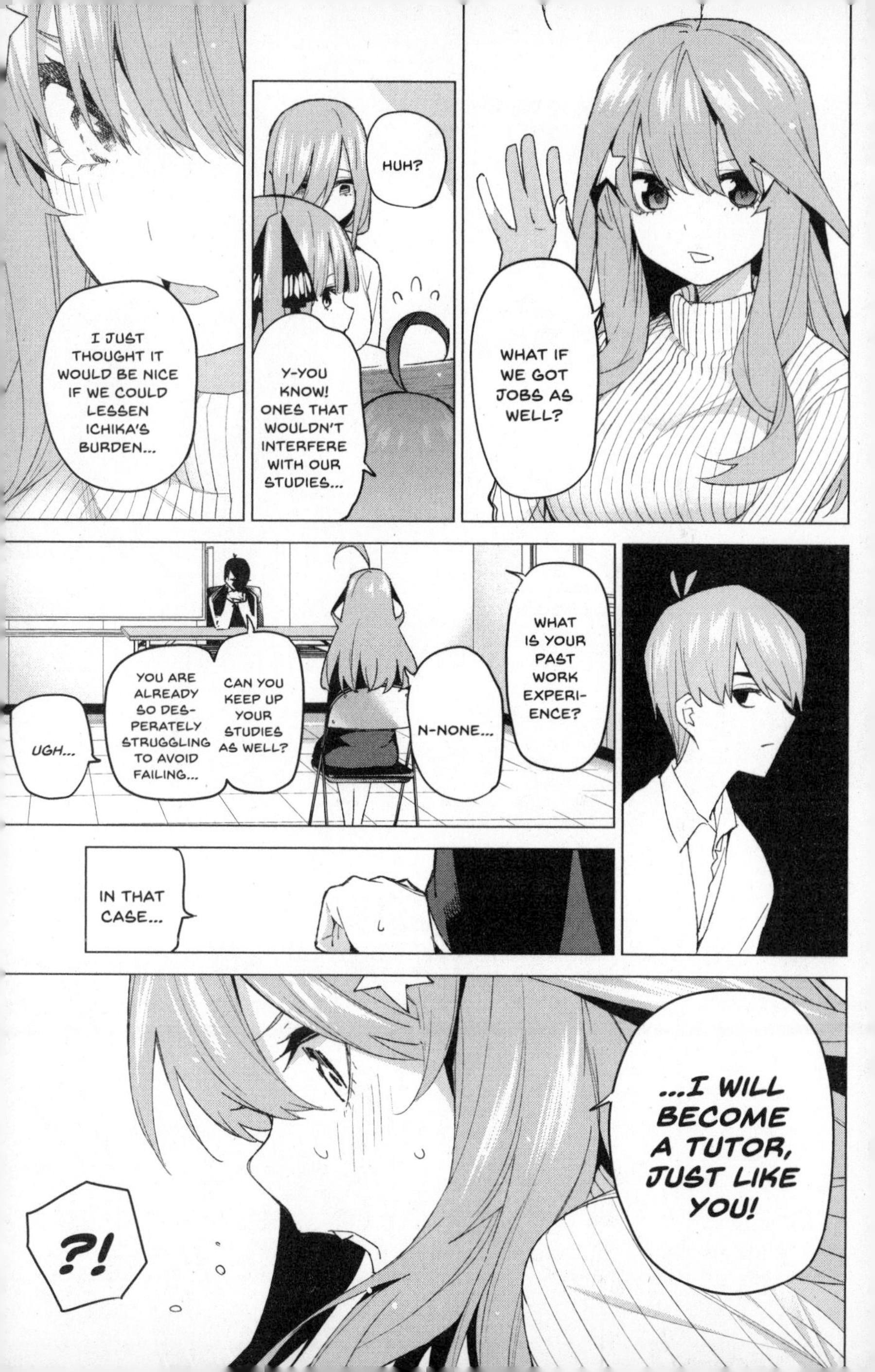

WHAT IF WE GOT JOBS AS WELL?
HUH?
Y-YOU KNOW! ONES THAT WOULDN'T INTERFERE WITH OUR STUDIES...
I JUST THOUGHT IT WOULD BE NICE IF WE COULD LESSEN ICHIKA'S BURDEN...
WHAT IS YOUR PAST WORK EXPERIENCE?
N-NONE...
CAN YOU KEEP UP YOUR STUDIES AS WELL?
YOU ARE ALREADY SO DESPERATELY STRUGGLING TO AVOID FAILING...
UGH...
IN THAT CASE...
...I WILL BECOME A TUTOR, JUST LIKE YOU!
?!

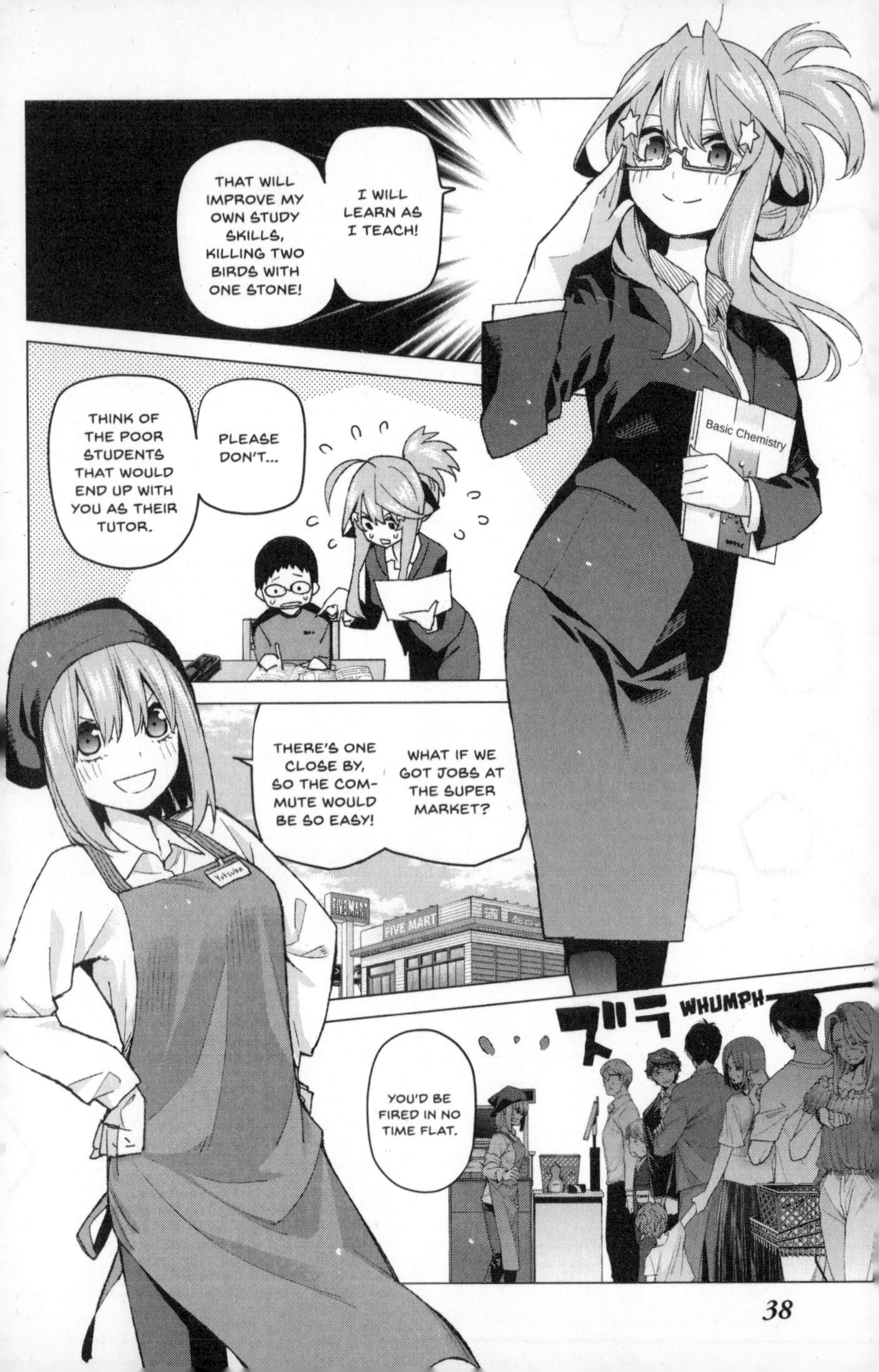
I WILL LEARN AS I TEACH!
THAT WILL IMPROVE MY OWN STUDY SKILLS, KILLING TWO BIRDS WITH ONE STONE!
Basic Chemistry
PLEASE DON'T...
THINK OF THE POOR STUDENTS THAT WOULD END UP WITH YOU AS THEIR TUTOR.
WHAT IF WE GOT JOBS AT THE SUPER MARKET?
THERE'S ONE CLOSE BY, SO THE COMMUTE WOULD BE SO EASY!
FIVE MART
WHUMPH
YOU'D BE FIRED IN NO TIME FLAT.

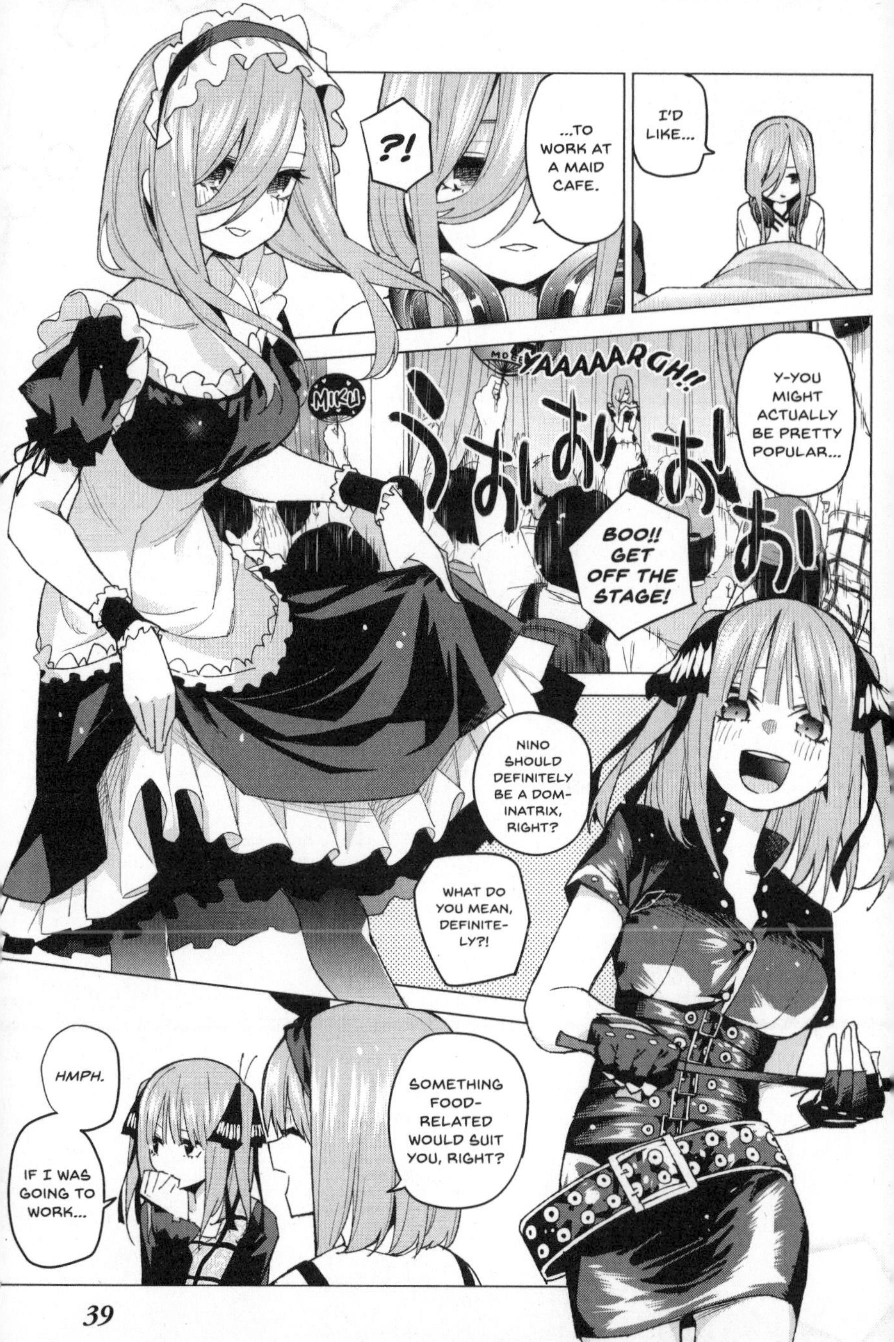

I'D LIKE...
...TO WORK AT A MAID CAFE.
?!
Y-YOU MIGHT ACTUALLY BE PRETTY POPULAR...
YAAAAARGH!!
MOE
MIKU
うおおおお
BOO!! GET OFF THE STAGE!
NINO SHOULD DEFINITELY BE A DOM-INATRIX, RIGHT?
WHAT DO YOU MEAN, DEFINITE-LY?!
SOMETHING FOOD-RELATED WOULD SUIT YOU, RIGHT?
HMPH.
IF I WAS GOING TO WORK...

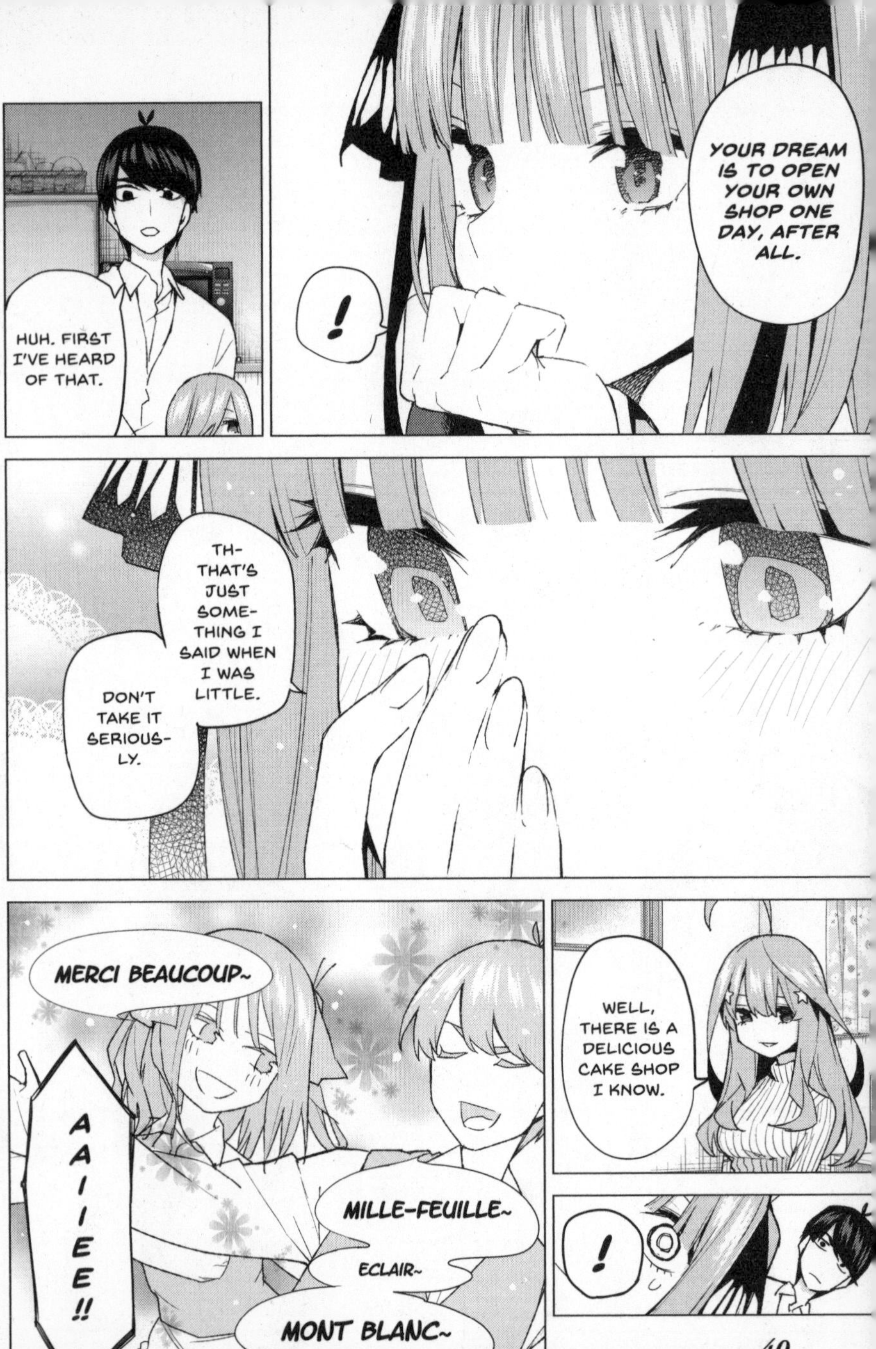
YOUR DREAM IS TO OPEN YOUR OWN SHOP ONE DAY, AFTER ALL.
!
HUH. FIRST I'VE HEARD OF THAT.
TH- THAT'S JUST SOME-THING I SAID WHEN I WAS LITTLE.
DON'T TAKE IT SERIOUS-LY.
WELL, THERE IS A DELICIOUS CAKE SHOP I KNOW.
!
MERCI BEAUCOUP~
AAIIEE!!
MILLE-FEUILLE~
ECLAIR~
MONT BLANC~

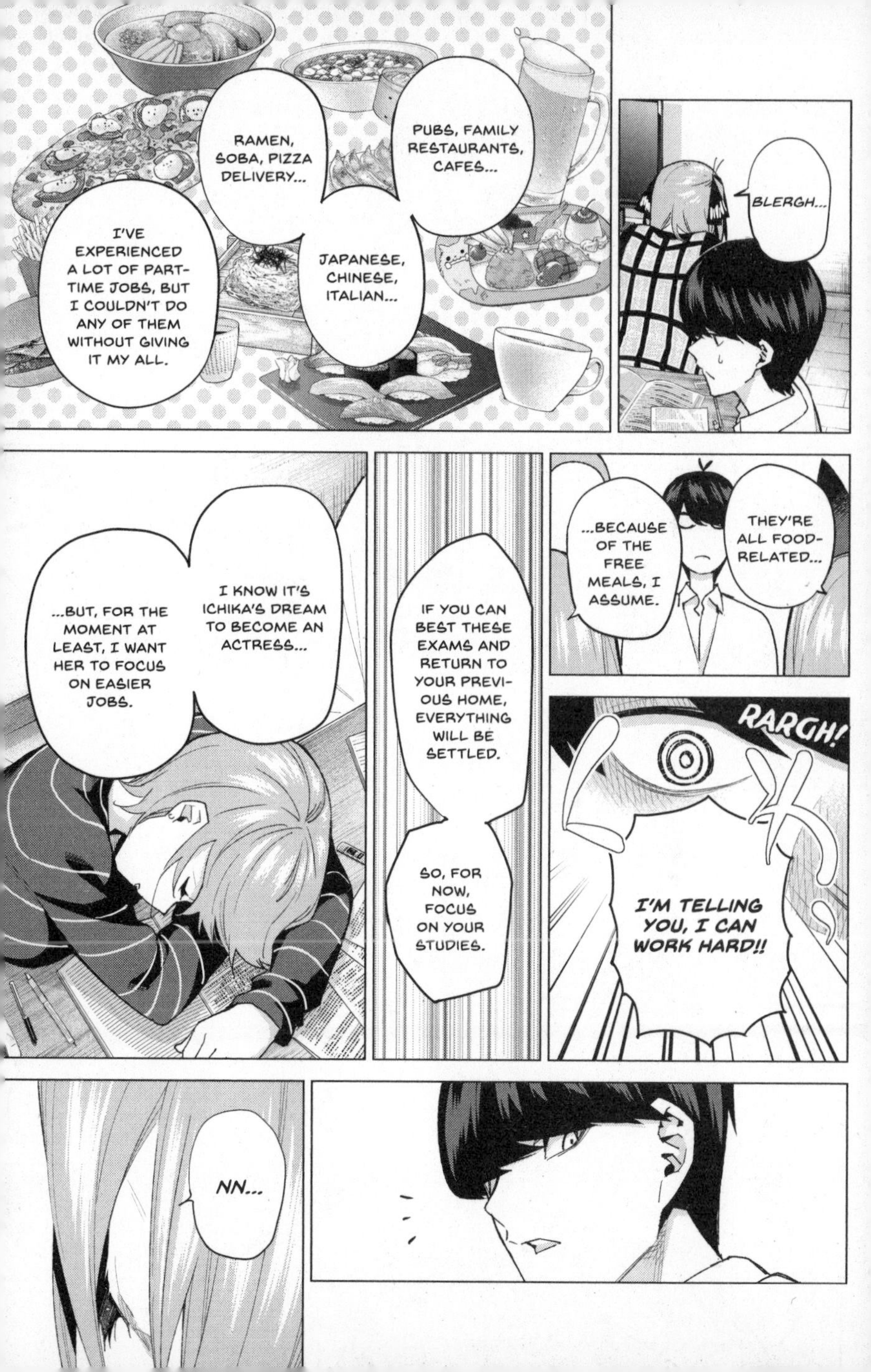
BLERGH...
PUBS, FAMILY RESTAURANTS, CAFES...
RAMEN, SOBA, PIZZA DELIVERY...
JAPANESE, CHINESE, ITALIAN...
I'VE EXPERIENCED A LOT OF PART-TIME JOBS, BUT I COULDN'T DO ANY OF THEM WITHOUT GIVING IT MY ALL.
THEY'RE ALL FOOD-RELATED...
...BECAUSE OF THE FREE MEALS, I ASSUME.
RARGH!
I'M TELLING YOU, I CAN WORK HARD!!
IF YOU CAN BEST THESE EXAMS AND RETURN TO YOUR PREVIOUS HOME, EVERYTHING WILL BE SETTLED.
SO, FOR NOW, FOCUS ON YOUR STUDIES.
I KNOW IT'S ICHIKA'S DREAM TO BECOME AN ACTRESS...
...BUT, FOR THE MOMENT AT LEAST, I WANT HER TO FOCUS ON EASIER JOBS.
NN...

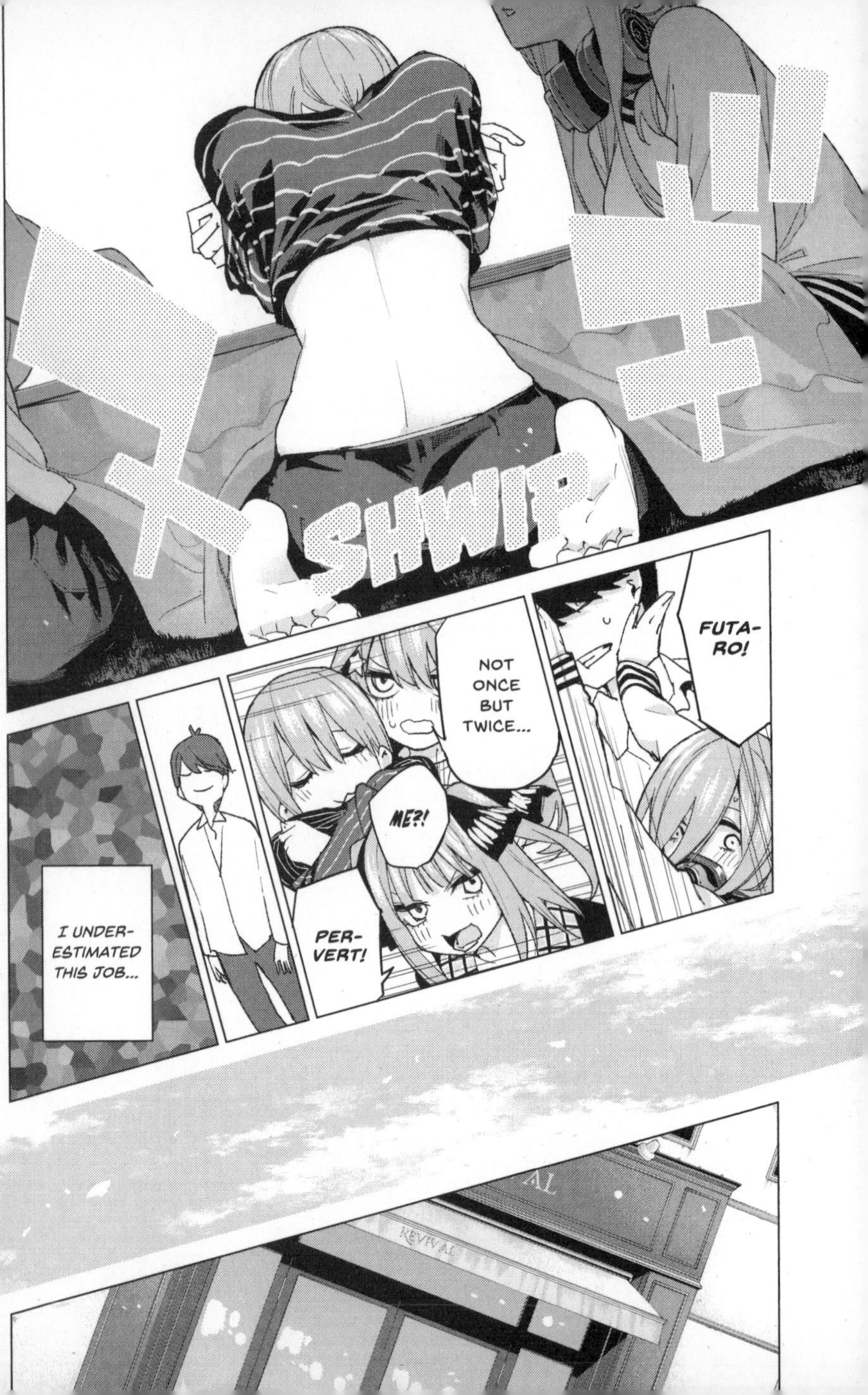
SHWIP
FUTA-RO!
NOT ONCE BUT TWICE...
ME?!
PER-VERT!
I UNDER-ESTIMATED THIS JOB...
REVIVAL
REVIVAL

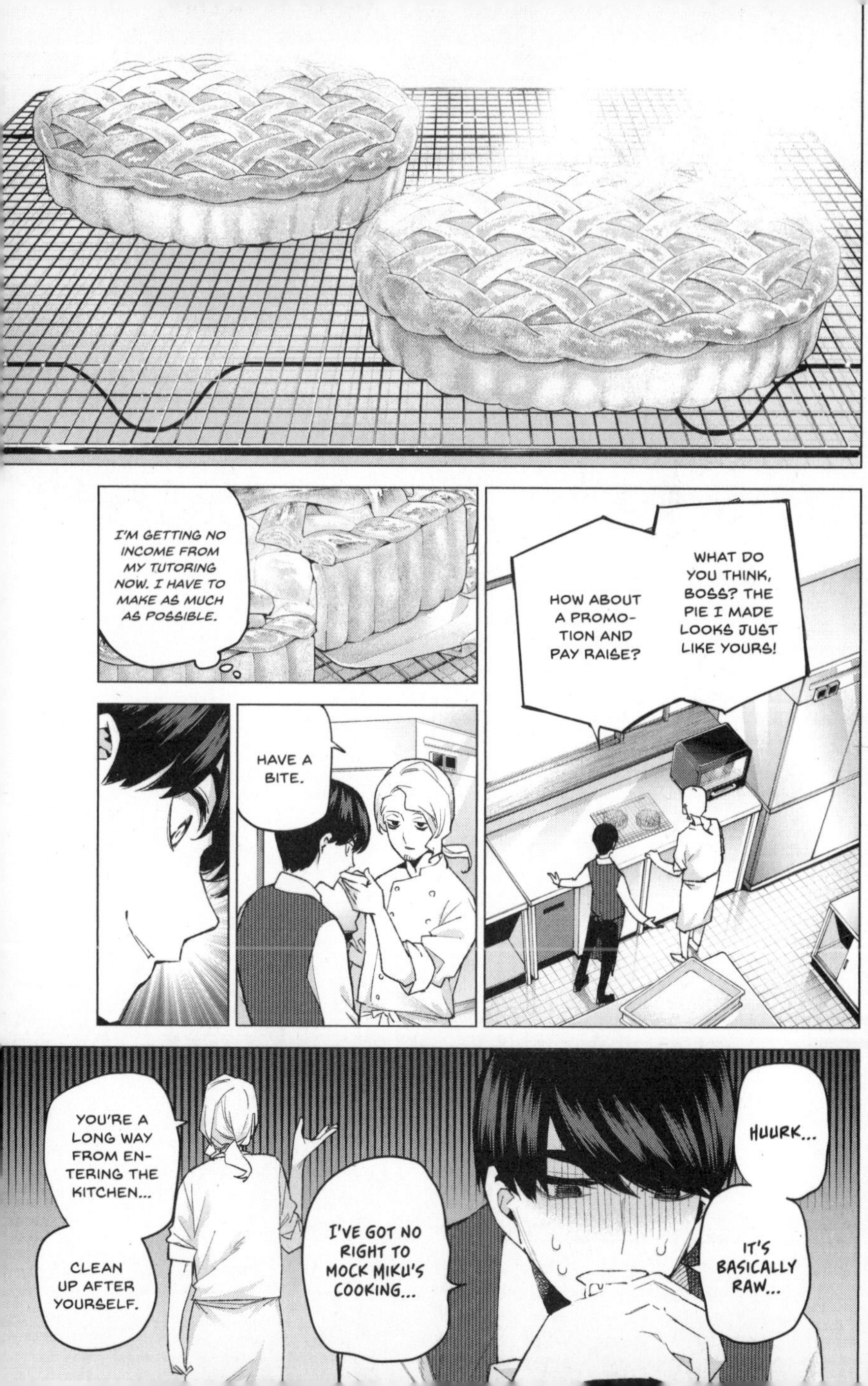
WHAT DO YOU THINK, BOSS? THE PIE I MADE LOOKS JUST LIKE YOURS!
HOW ABOUT A PROMO-TION AND PAY RAISE?
I'M GETTING NO INCOME FROM MY TUTORING NOW. I HAVE TO MAKE AS MUCH AS POSSIBLE.
HAVE A BITE.
HUURK...
IT'S BASICALLY RAW...
I'VE GOT NO RIGHT TO MOCK MIKU'S COOKING...
YOU'RE A LONG WAY FROM EN-TERING THE KITCHEN...
CLEAN UP AFTER YOURSELF.

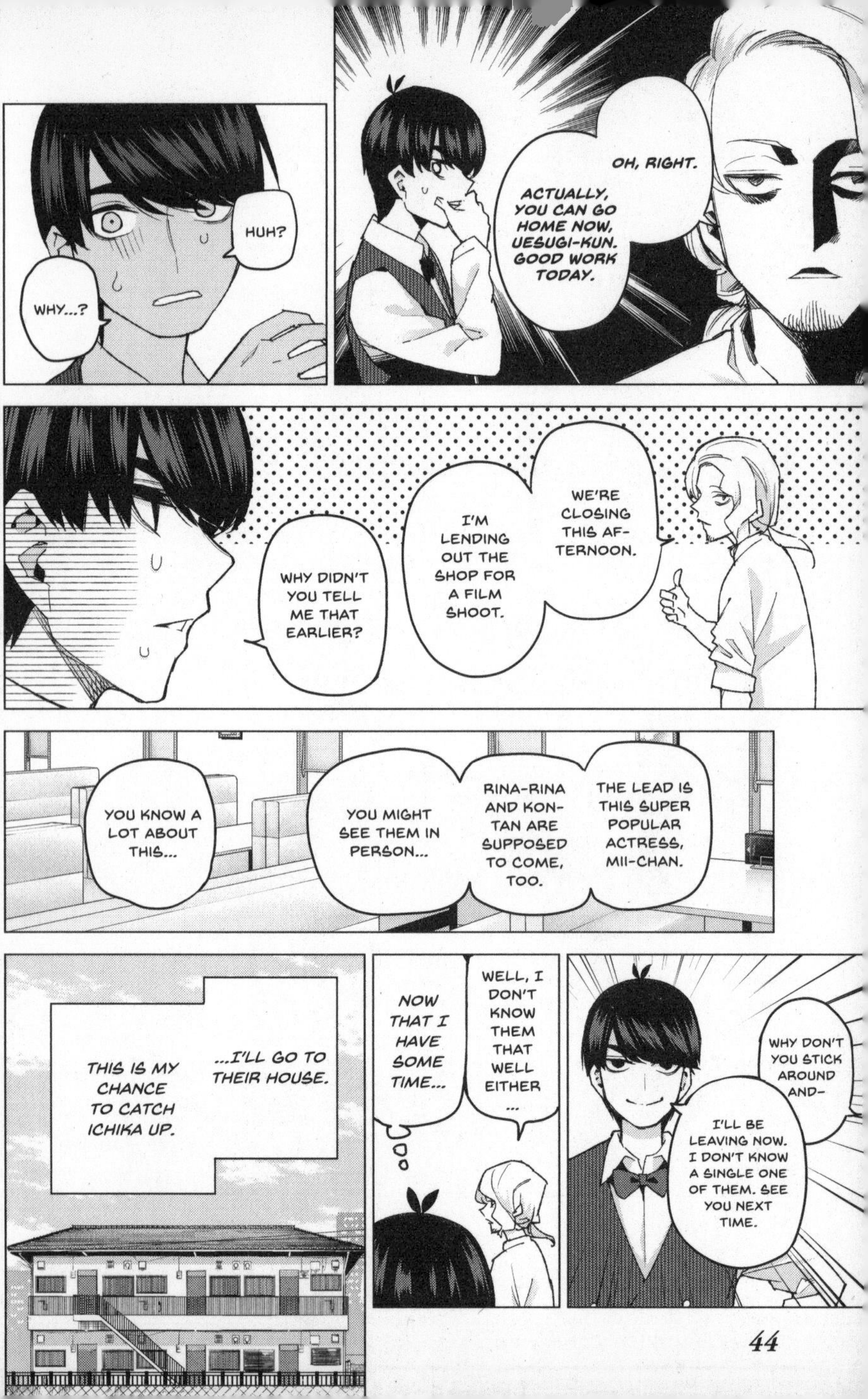
OH, RIGHT.
ACTUALLY, YOU CAN GO HOME NOW, UESUGI-KUN. GOOD WORK TODAY.
HUH?
WHY...?
WE'RE CLOSING THIS AF-TERNOON.
I'M LENDING OUT THE SHOP FOR A FILM SHOOT.
WHY DIDN'T YOU TELL ME THAT EARLIER?
THE LEAD IS THIS SUPER POPULAR ACTRESS, MII-CHAN.
RINA-RINA AND KON-TAN ARE SUPPOSED TO COME, TOO.
YOU MIGHT SEE THEM IN PERSON...
YOU KNOW A LOT ABOUT THIS...
WHY DON'T YOU STICK AROUND AND-
I'LL BE LEAVING NOW. I DON'T KNOW A SINGLE ONE OF THEM. SEE YOU NEXT TIME.
WELL, I DON'T KNOW THEM THAT WELL EITHER...
NOW THAT I HAVE SOME TIME...
...I'LL GO TO THEIR HOUSE.
THIS IS MY CHANCE TO CATCH ICHIKA UP.

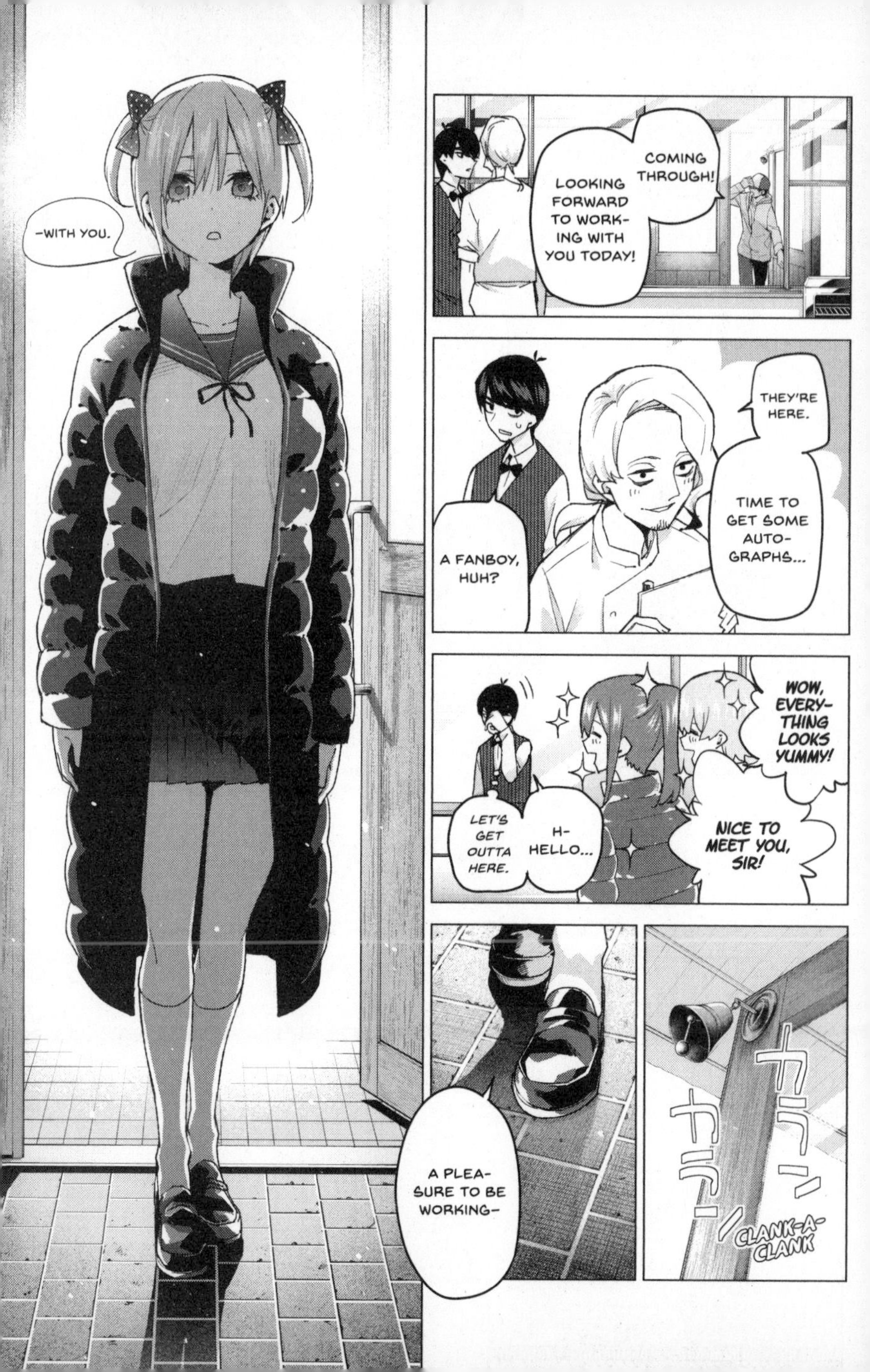
COMING THROUGH!
LOOKING FORWARD TO WORKING WITH YOU TODAY!
THEY'RE HERE.
TIME TO GET SOME AUTOGRAPHS...
A FANBOY, HUH?
WOW, EVERYTHING LOOKS YUMMY!
NICE TO MEET YOU, SIR!
H-HELLO...
LET'S GET OUTTA HERE.
CLANK-A-CLANK
A PLEASURE TO BE WORKING-
-WITH YOU.

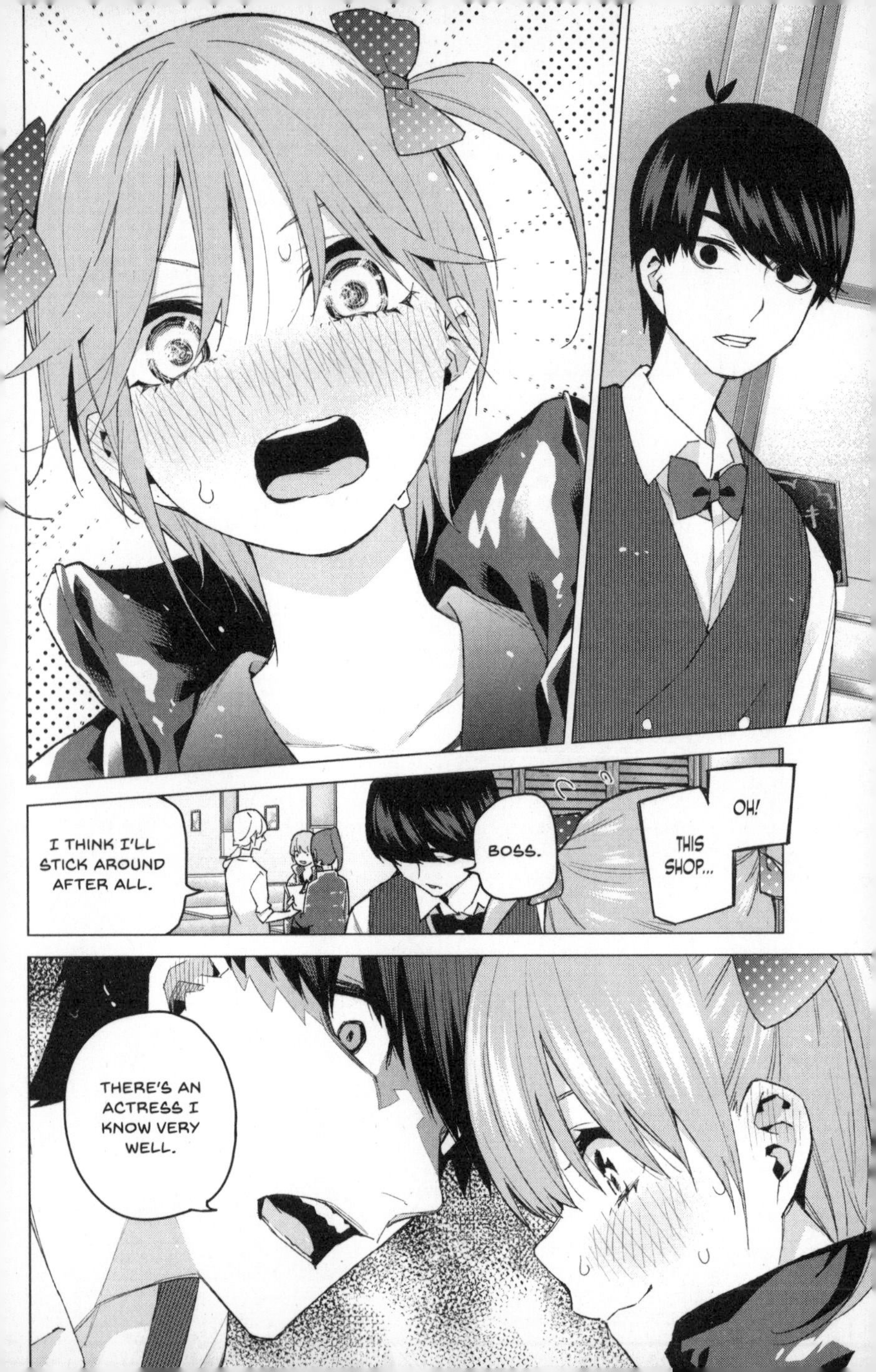
OH! THIS SHOP...
BOSS.
I THINK I'LL STICK AROUND AFTER ALL.
THERE'S AN ACTRESS I KNOW VERY WELL.

CHAPTER 53 GOOD WORK TODAY ②

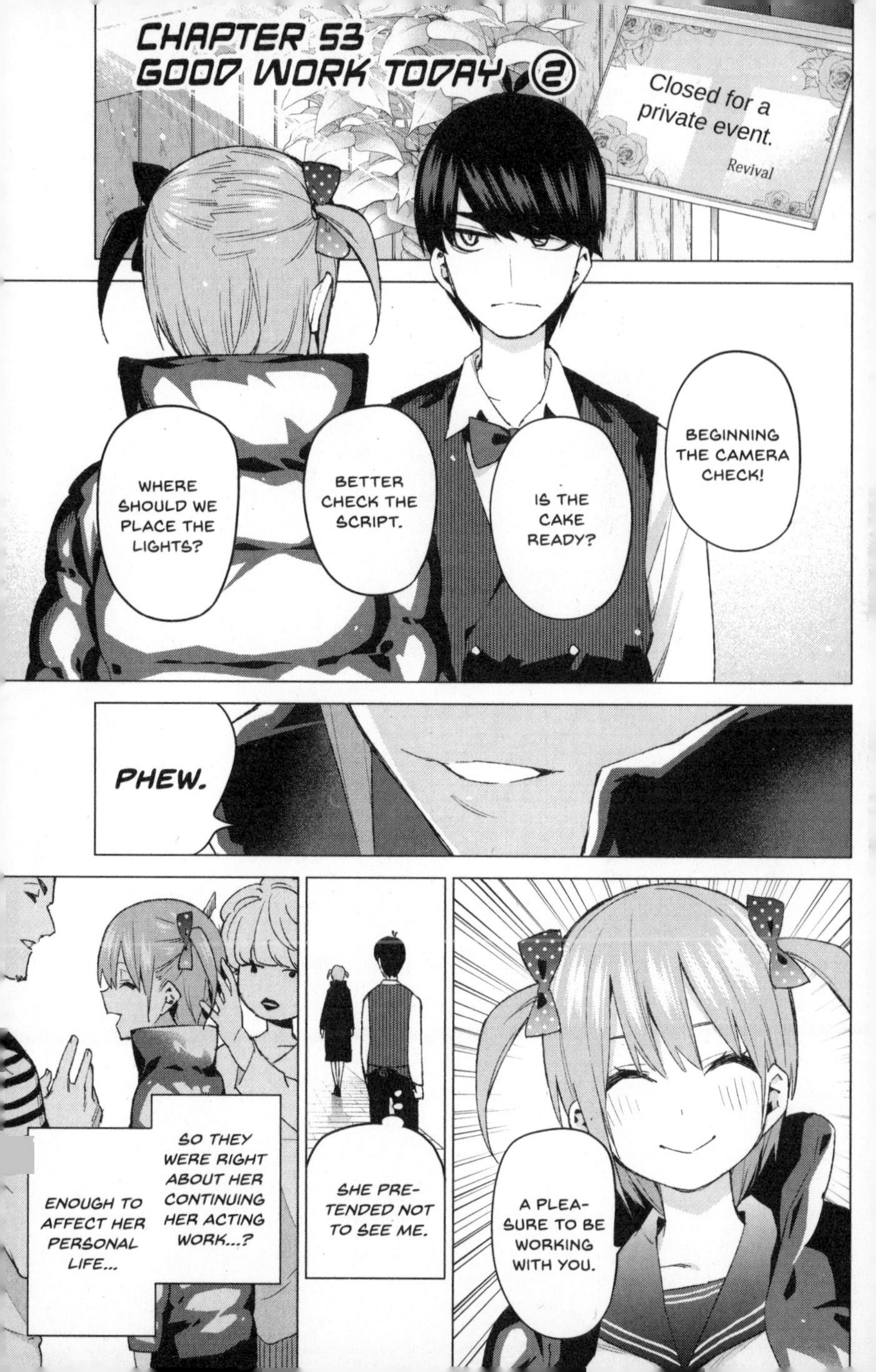
Closed for a private event.
Revival
BEGINNING THE CAMERA CHECK!
IS THE CAKE READY?
BETTER CHECK THE SCRIPT.
WHERE SHOULD WE PLACE THE LIGHTS?
PHEW.
A PLEA-SURE TO BE WORKING WITH YOU.
SHE PRE-TENDED NOT TO SEE ME.
SO THEY WERE RIGHT ABOUT HER CONTINUING HER ACTING WORK...?
ENOUGH TO AFFECT HER PERSONAL LIFE...

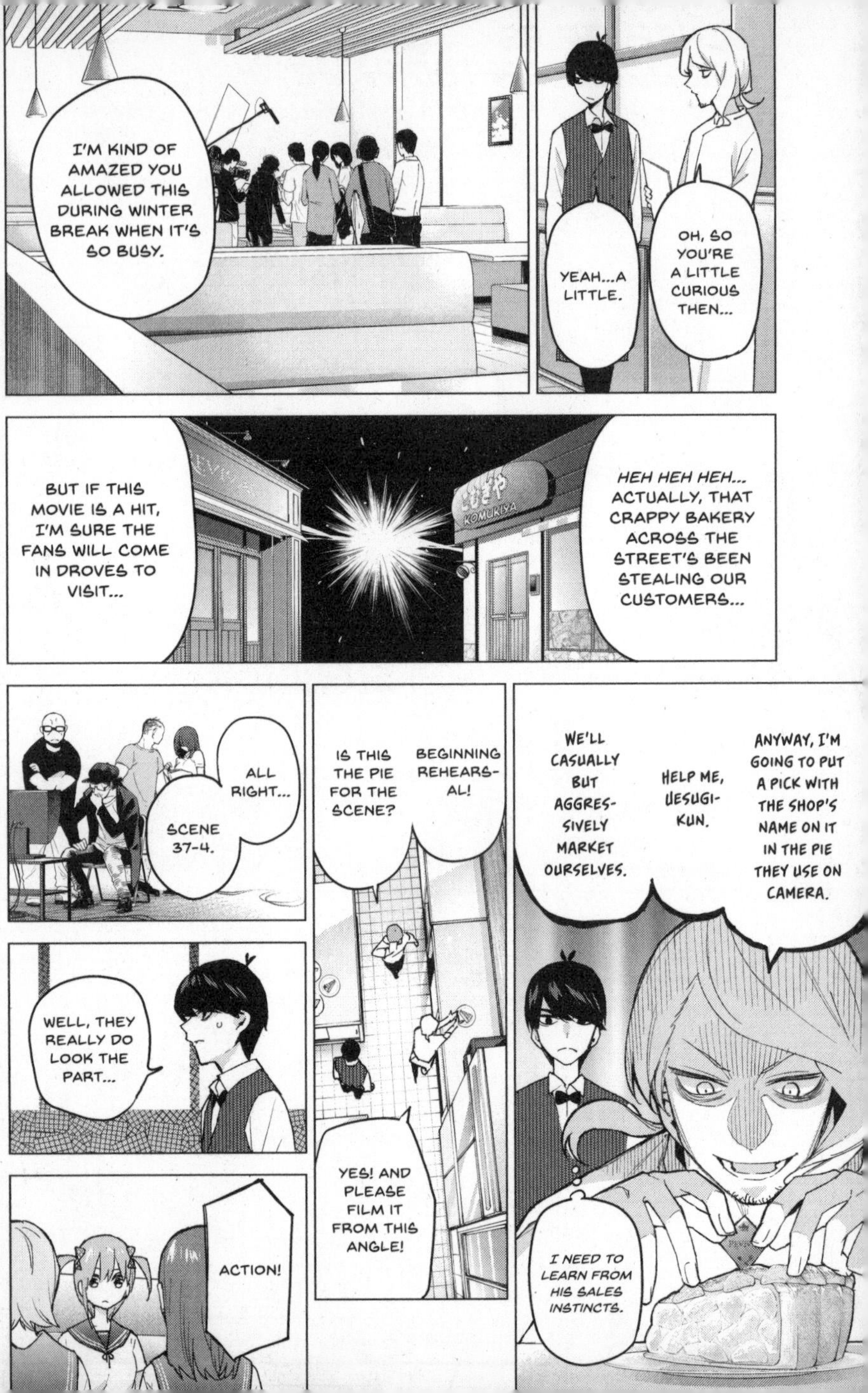
OH, SO YOU'RE A LITTLE CURIOUS THEN...
YEAH...A LITTLE.
I'M KIND OF AMAZED YOU ALLOWED THIS DURING WINTER BREAK WHEN IT'S SO BUSY.
HEH HEH HEH... ACTUALLY, THAT CRAPPY BAKERY ACROSS THE STREET'S BEEN STEALING OUR CUSTOMERS...
こむぎや
KOMUKIYA
BUT IF THIS MOVIE IS A HIT, I'M SURE THE FANS WILL COME IN DROVES TO VISIT...
ANYWAY, I'M GOING TO PUT A PICK WITH THE SHOP'S NAME ON IT IN THE PIE THEY USE ON CAMERA.
HELP ME, UESUGI-KUN.
WE'LL CASUALLY BUT AGGRESSIVELY MARKET OURSELVES.
I NEED TO LEARN FROM HIS SALES INSTINCTS.
BEGINNING REHEARSAL!
IS THIS THE PIE FOR THE SCENE?
YES! AND PLEASE FILM IT FROM THIS ANGLE!
ALL RIGHT...
SCENE 37-4.
WELL, THEY REALLY DO LOOK THE PART...
ACTION!

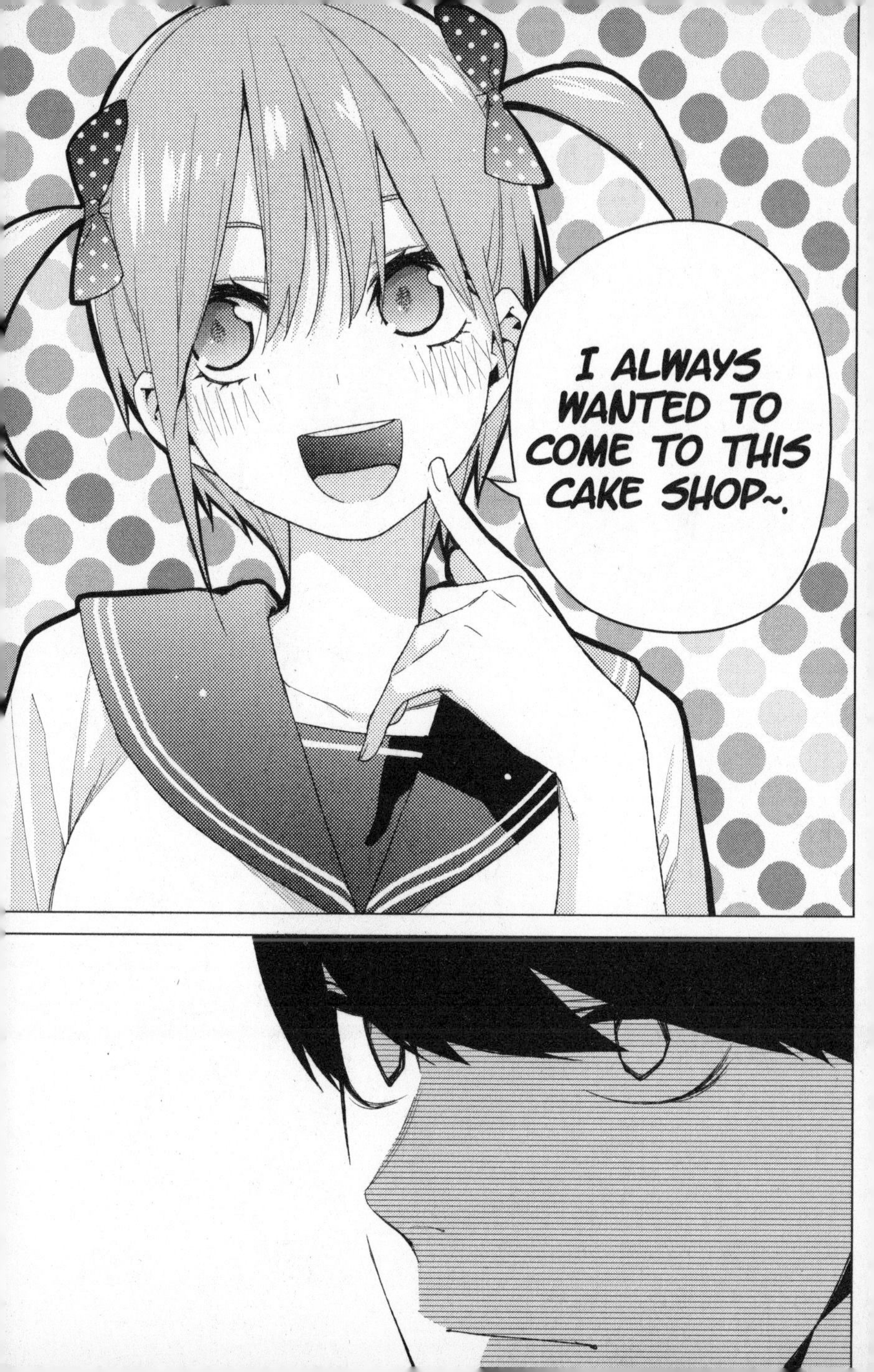
I ALWAYS WANTED TO COME TO THIS CAKE SHOP~.

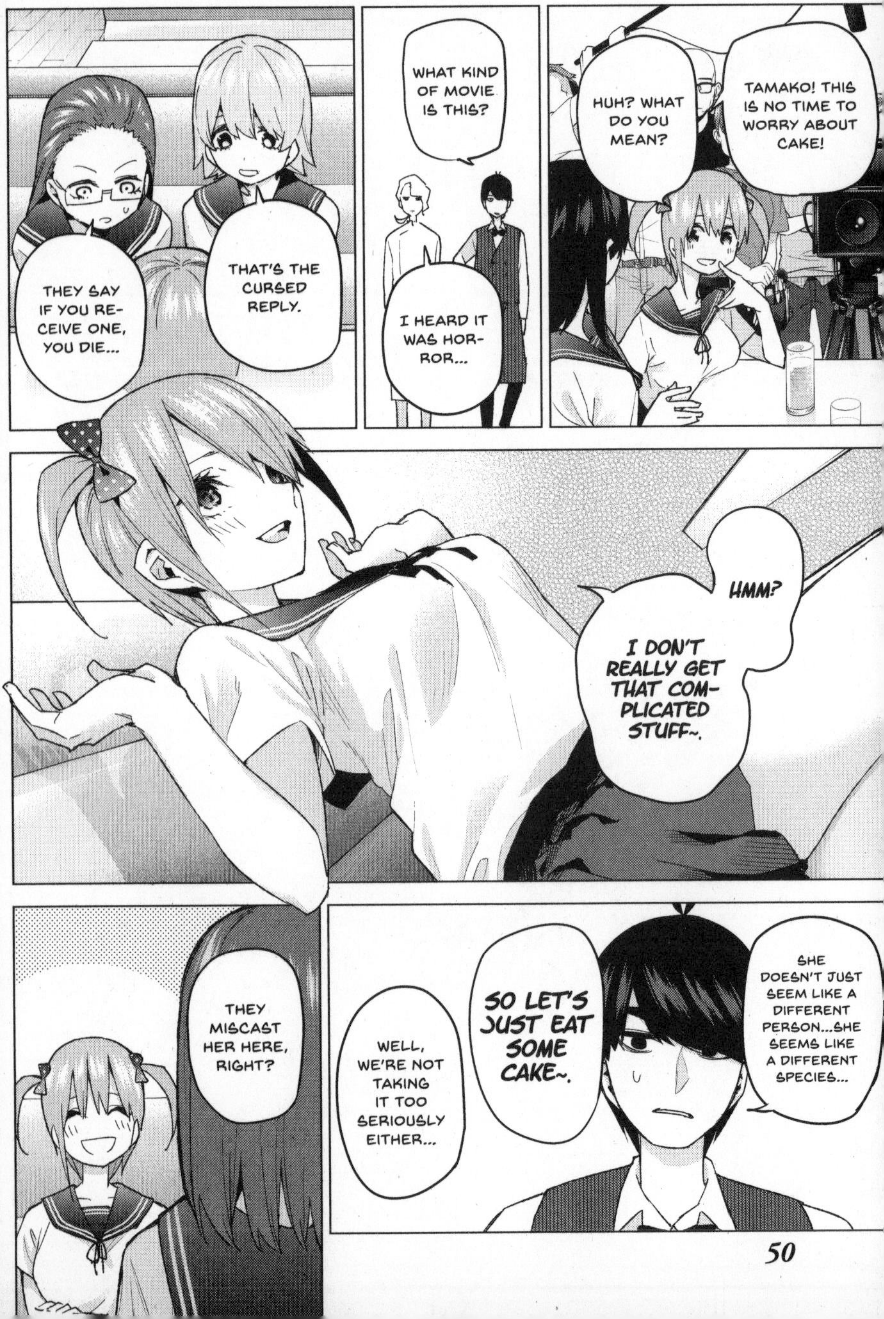
TAMAKO! THIS IS NO TIME TO WORRY ABOUT CAKE!
HUH? WHAT DO YOU MEAN?
WHAT KIND OF MOVIE IS THIS?
I HEARD IT WAS HOR-ROR...
THAT'S THE CURSED REPLY.
THEY SAY IF YOU RE-CEIVE ONE, YOU DIE...
HMM?
I DON'T REALLY GET THAT COM-PLICATED STUFF~.
SHE DOESN'T JUST SEEM LIKE A DIFFERENT PERSON...SHE SEEMS LIKE A DIFFERENT SPECIES...
SO LET'S JUST EAT SOME CAKE~.
WELL, WE'RE NOT TAKING IT TOO SERIOUSLY EITHER...
THEY MISCAST HER HERE, RIGHT?

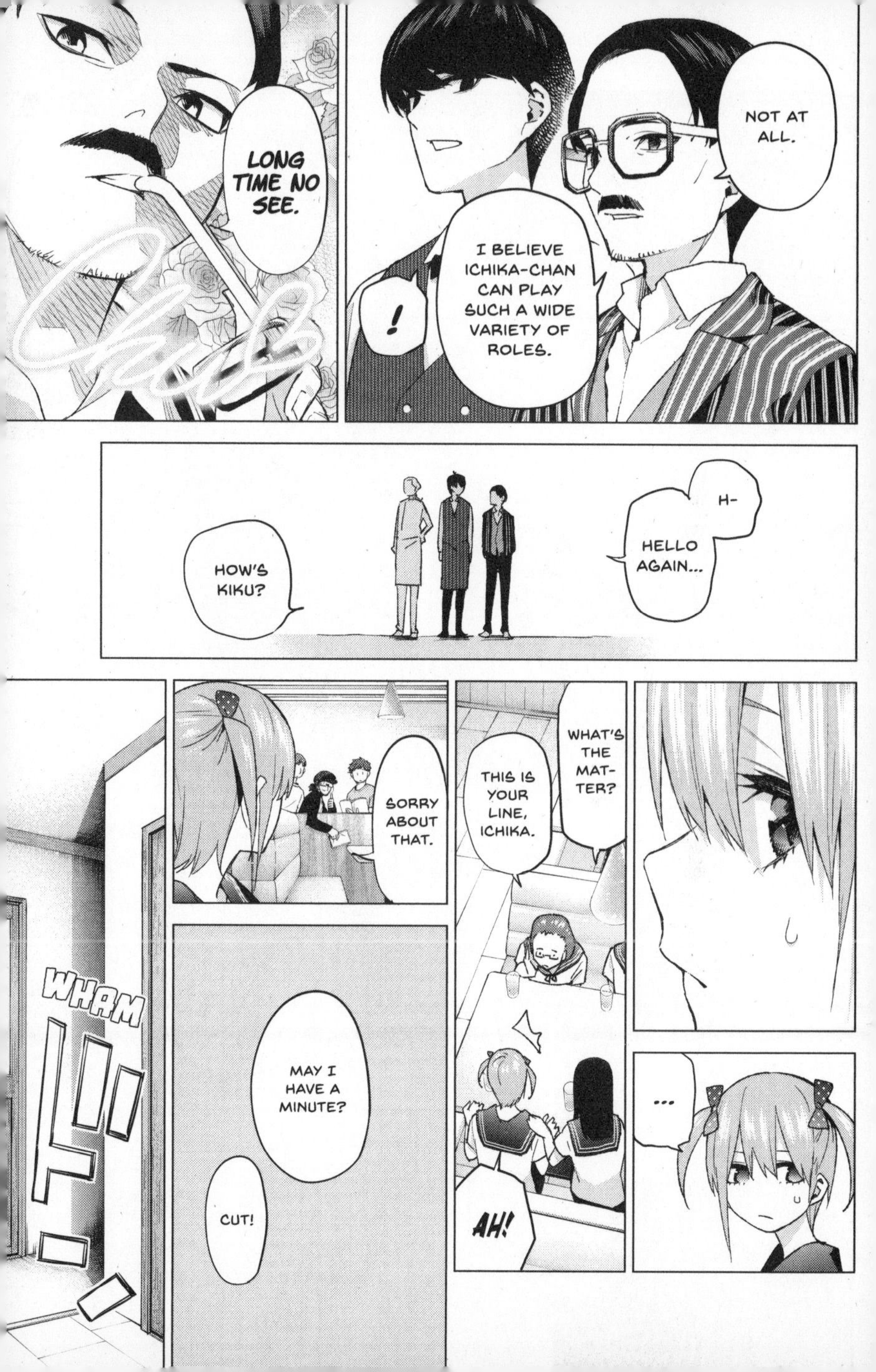
NOT AT ALL.
I BELIEVE ICHIKA-CHAN CAN PLAY SUCH A WIDE VARIETY OF ROLES.
!
LONG TIME NO SEE.
H-
HELLO AGAIN...
HOW'S KIKU?
...
WHAT'S THE MAT-TER?
THIS IS YOUR LINE, ICHIKA.
AH!
SORRY ABOUT THAT.
MAY I HAVE A MINUTE?
CUT!
WHAM

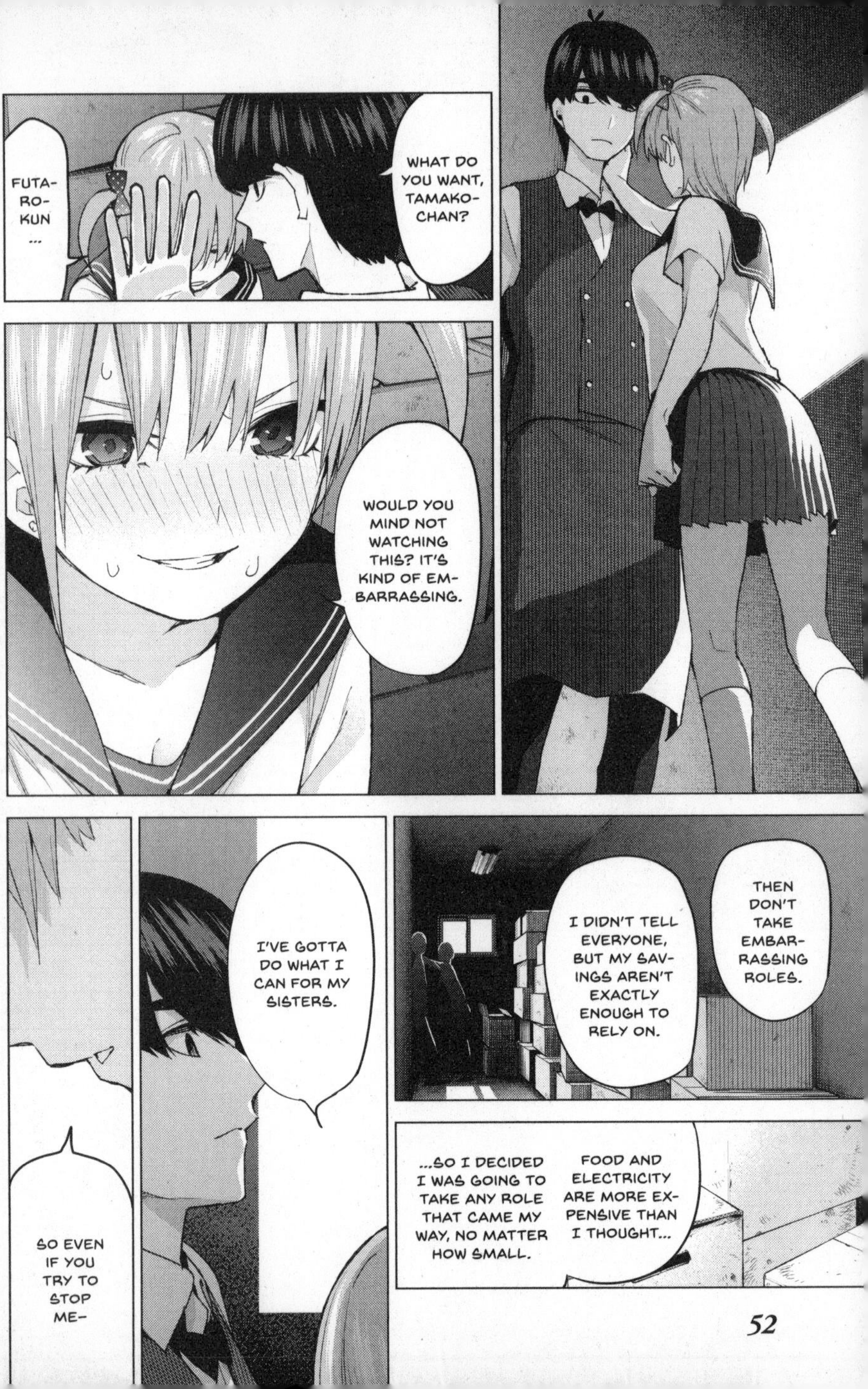
WHAT DO YOU WANT, TAMAKO-CHAN?
FUTA-RO-KUN ...
WOULD YOU MIND NOT WATCHING THIS? IT'S KIND OF EM-BARRASSING.
THEN DON'T TAKE EMBAR-RASSING ROLES.
I DIDN'T TELL EVERYONE, BUT MY SAV-INGS AREN'T EXACTLY ENOUGH TO RELY ON.
FOOD AND ELECTRICITY ARE MORE EX-PENSIVE THAN I THOUGHT...
...SO I DECIDED I WAS GOING TO TAKE ANY ROLE THAT CAME MY WAY, NO MATTER HOW SMALL.
I'VE GOTTA DO WHAT I CAN FOR MY SISTERS.
SO EVEN IF YOU TRY TO STOP ME-

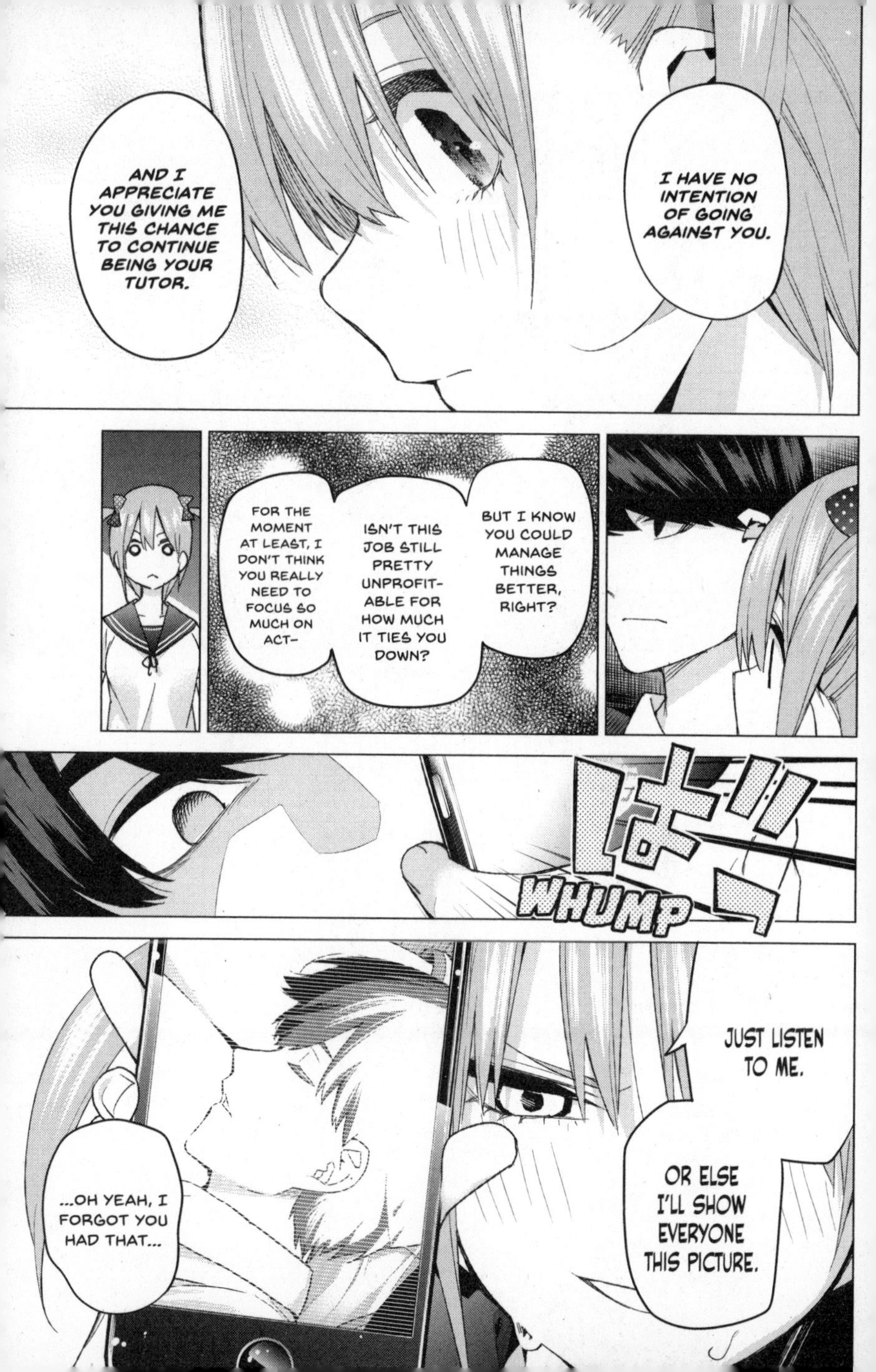
I HAVE NO INTENTION OF GOING AGAINST YOU.
AND I APPRECIATE YOU GIVING ME THIS CHANCE TO CONTINUE BEING YOUR TUTOR.
BUT I KNOW YOU COULD MANAGE THINGS BETTER, RIGHT?
ISN'T THIS JOB STILL PRETTY UNPROFIT-ABLE FOR HOW MUCH IT TIES YOU DOWN?
FOR THE MOMENT AT LEAST, I DON'T THINK YOU REALLY NEED TO FOCUS SO MUCH ON ACT–
は!!
WHUMP
JUST LISTEN TO ME.
OR ELSE I'LL SHOW EVERYONE THIS PICTURE.
...OH YEAH, I FORGOT YOU HAD THAT...

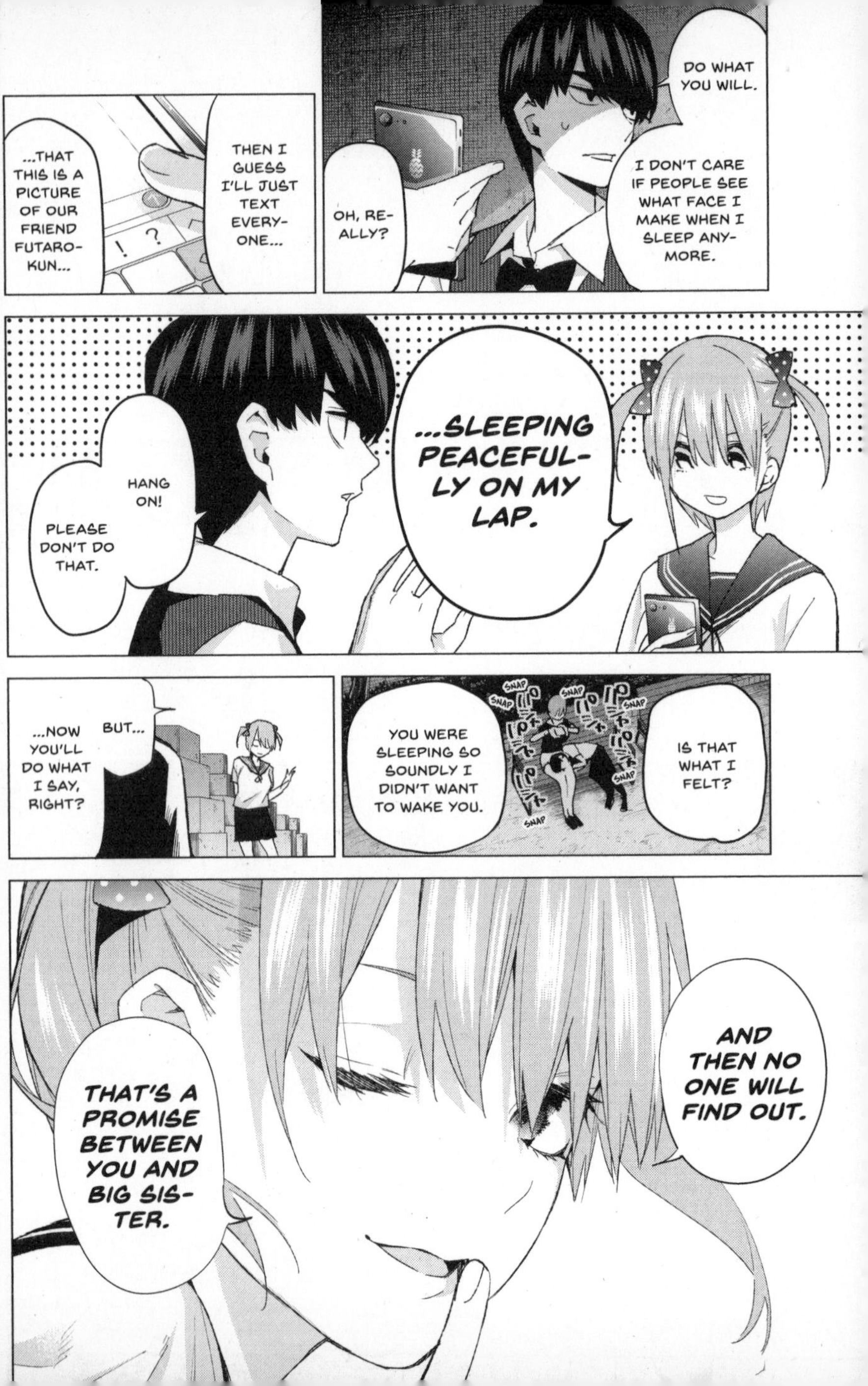
DO WHAT YOU WILL.
I DON'T CARE IF PEOPLE SEE WHAT FACE I MAKE WHEN I SLEEP ANYMORE.
OH, REALLY?
THEN I GUESS I'LL JUST TEXT EVERYONE...
...THAT THIS IS A PICTURE OF OUR FRIEND FUTARO-KUN...
...SLEEPING PEACEFULLY ON MY LAP.
HANG ON!
PLEASE DON'T DO THAT.
IS THAT WHAT I FELT?
SNAP SNAP SNAP SNAP SNAP SNAP
YOU WERE SLEEPING SO SOUNDLY I DIDN'T WANT TO WAKE YOU.
BUT...
...NOW YOU'LL DO WHAT I SAY, RIGHT?
AND THEN NO ONE WILL FIND OUT.
THAT'S A PROMISE BETWEEN YOU AND BIG SISTER.

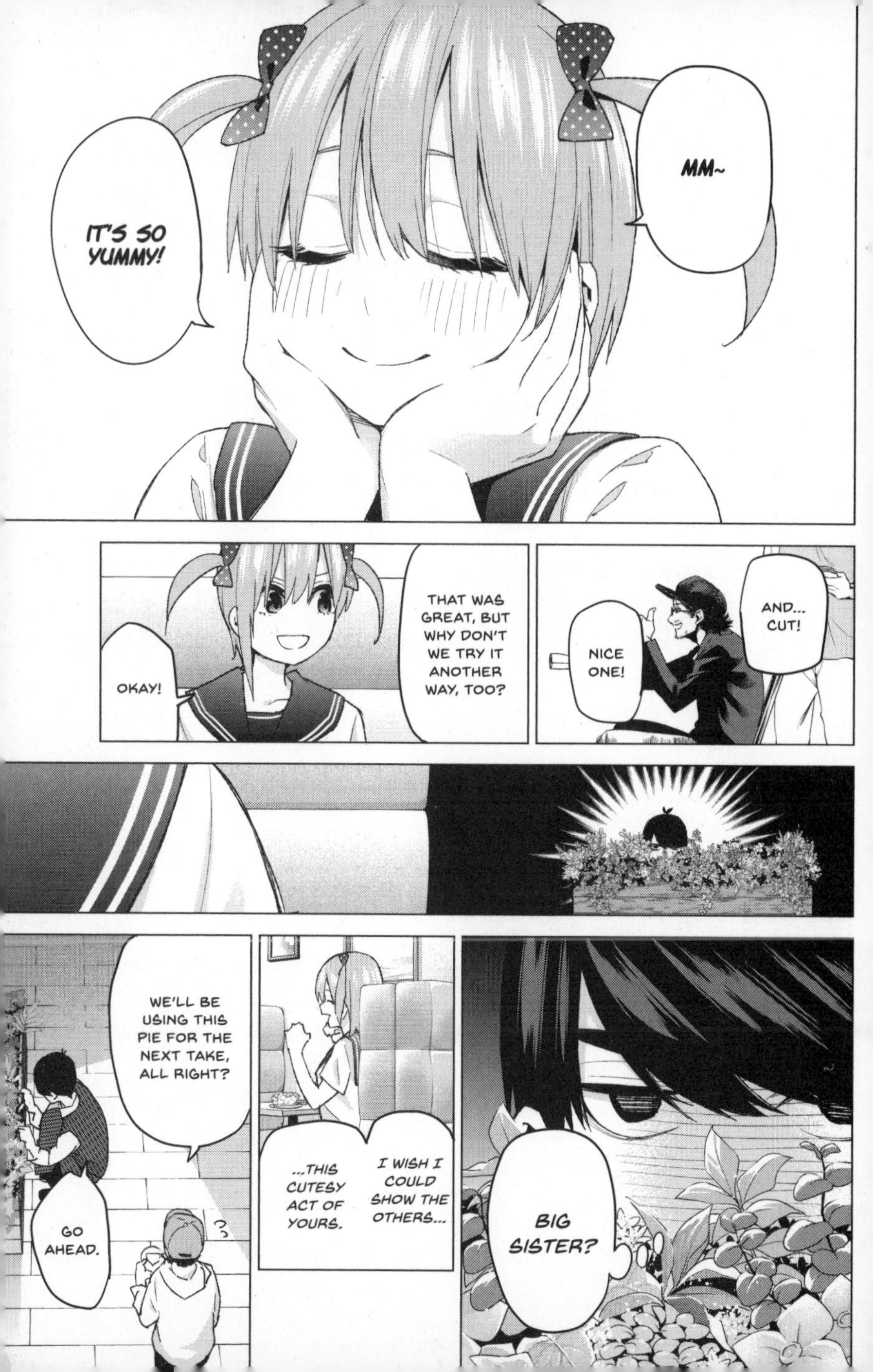
MM~
IT'S SO YUMMY!
AND... CUT!
NICE ONE!
THAT WAS GREAT, BUT WHY DON'T WE TRY IT ANOTHER WAY, TOO?
OKAY!
BIG SISTER?
I WISH I COULD SHOW THE OTHERS...
...THIS CUTESY ACT OF YOURS.
WE'LL BE USING THIS PIE FOR THE NEXT TAKE, ALL RIGHT?
GO AHEAD.
?

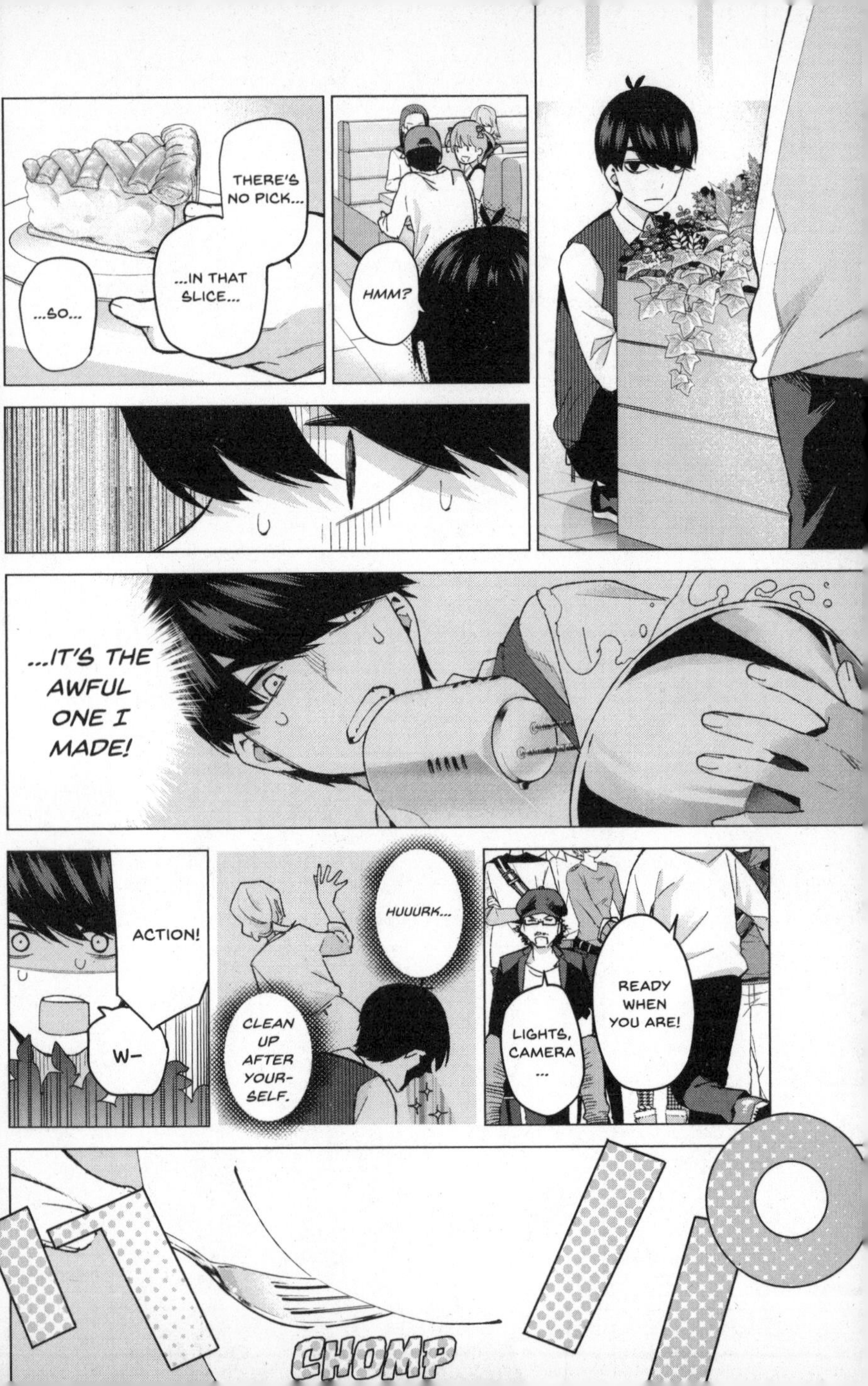
HMM?
THERE'S NO PICK...
...IN THAT SLICE...
...SO...
...IT'S THE AWFUL ONE I MADE!
READY WHEN YOU ARE!
LIGHTS, CAMERA ...
HUUURK...
CLEAN UP AFTER YOUR-SELF.
ACTION!
W-
CHOMP

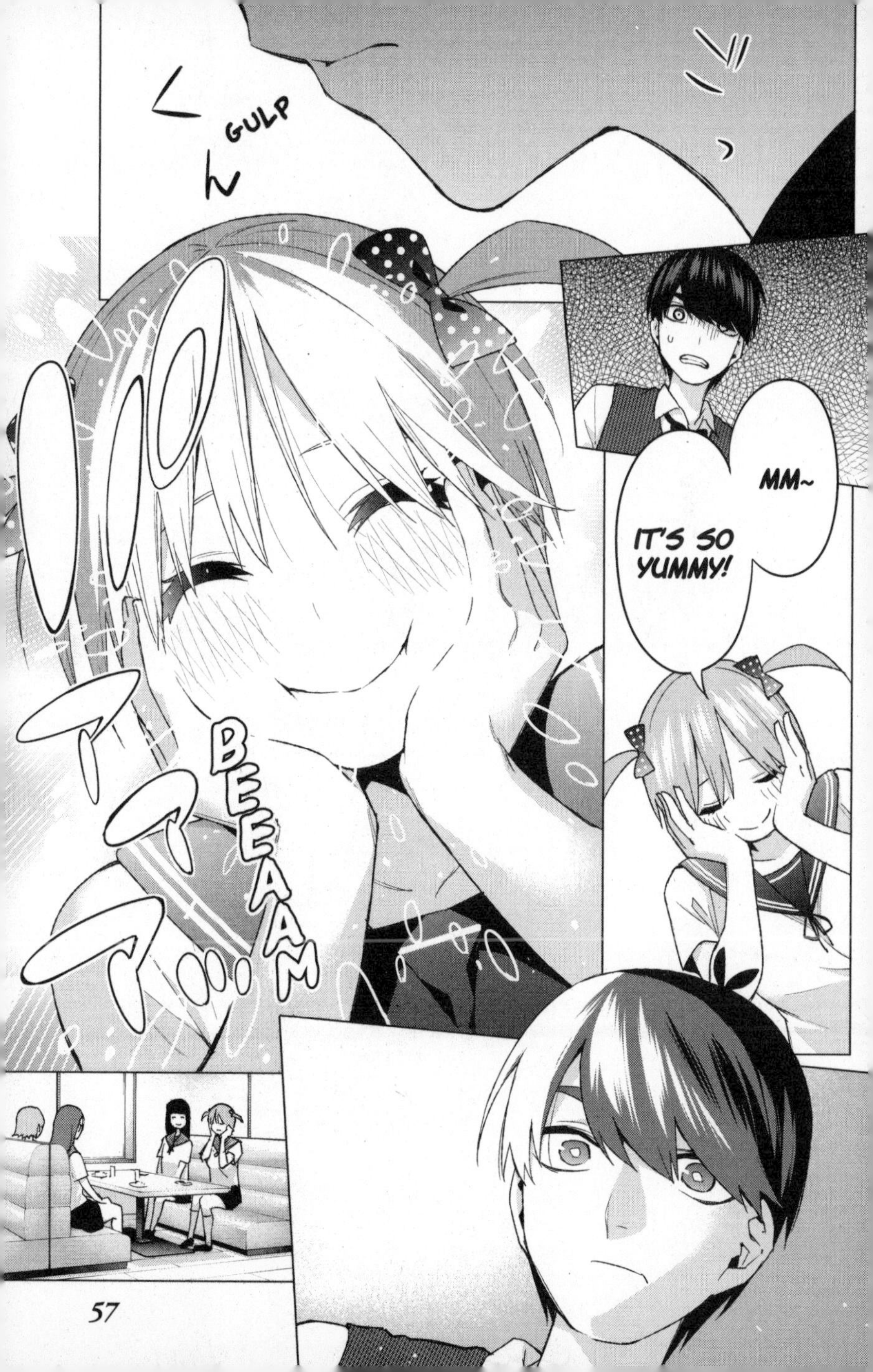
GULP
MM~
IT'S SO YUMMY!
BEEAAM

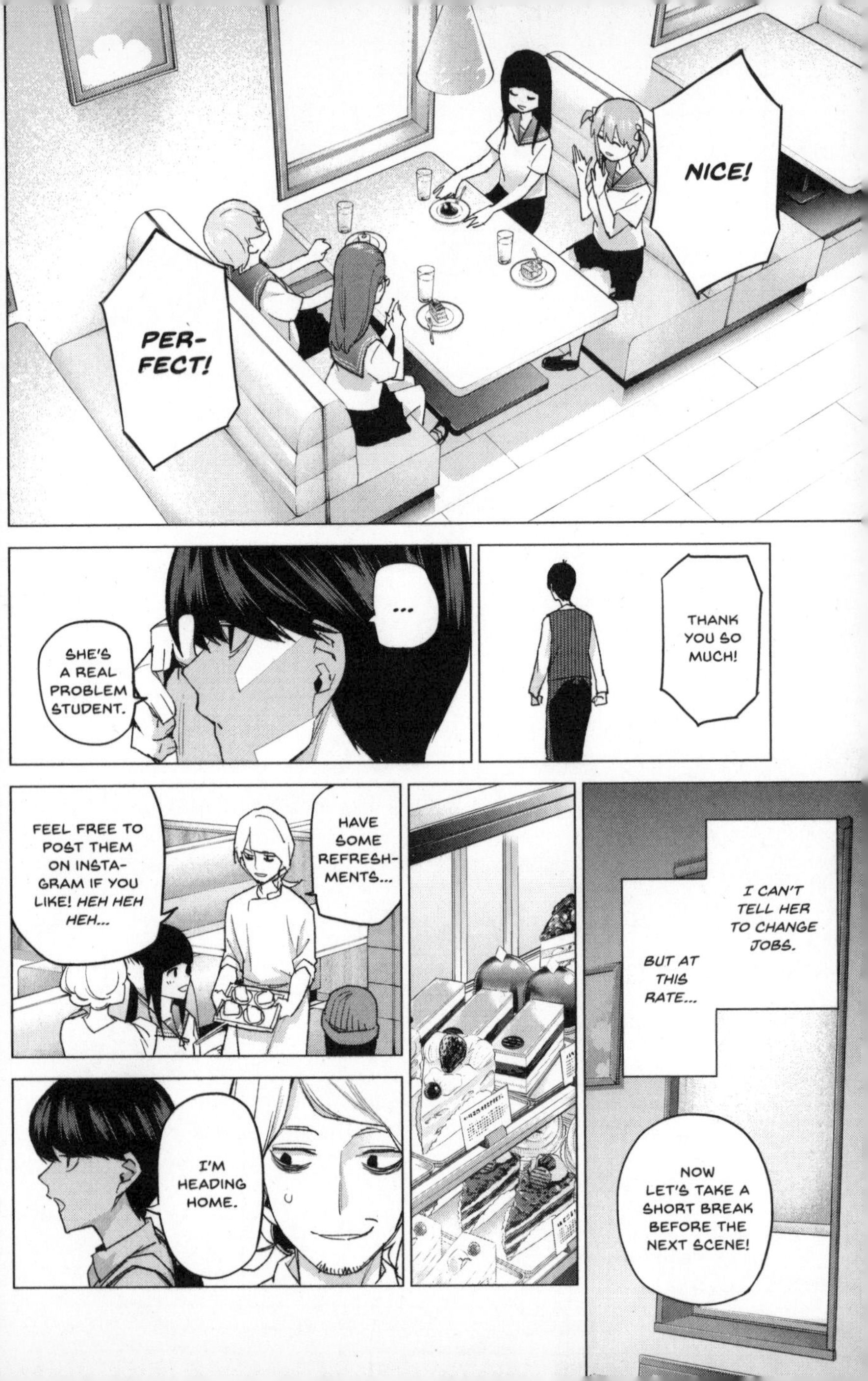
NICE!
PER-FECT!
THANK YOU SO MUCH!
...
SHE'S A REAL PROBLEM STUDENT.
I CAN'T TELL HER TO CHANGE JOBS.
BUT AT THIS RATE...
NOW LET'S TAKE A SHORT BREAK BEFORE THE NEXT SCENE!
HAVE SOME REFRESH-MENTS...
FEEL FREE TO POST THEM ON INSTA-GRAM IF YOU LIKE! *HEH HEH HEH...*
I'M HEADING HOME.

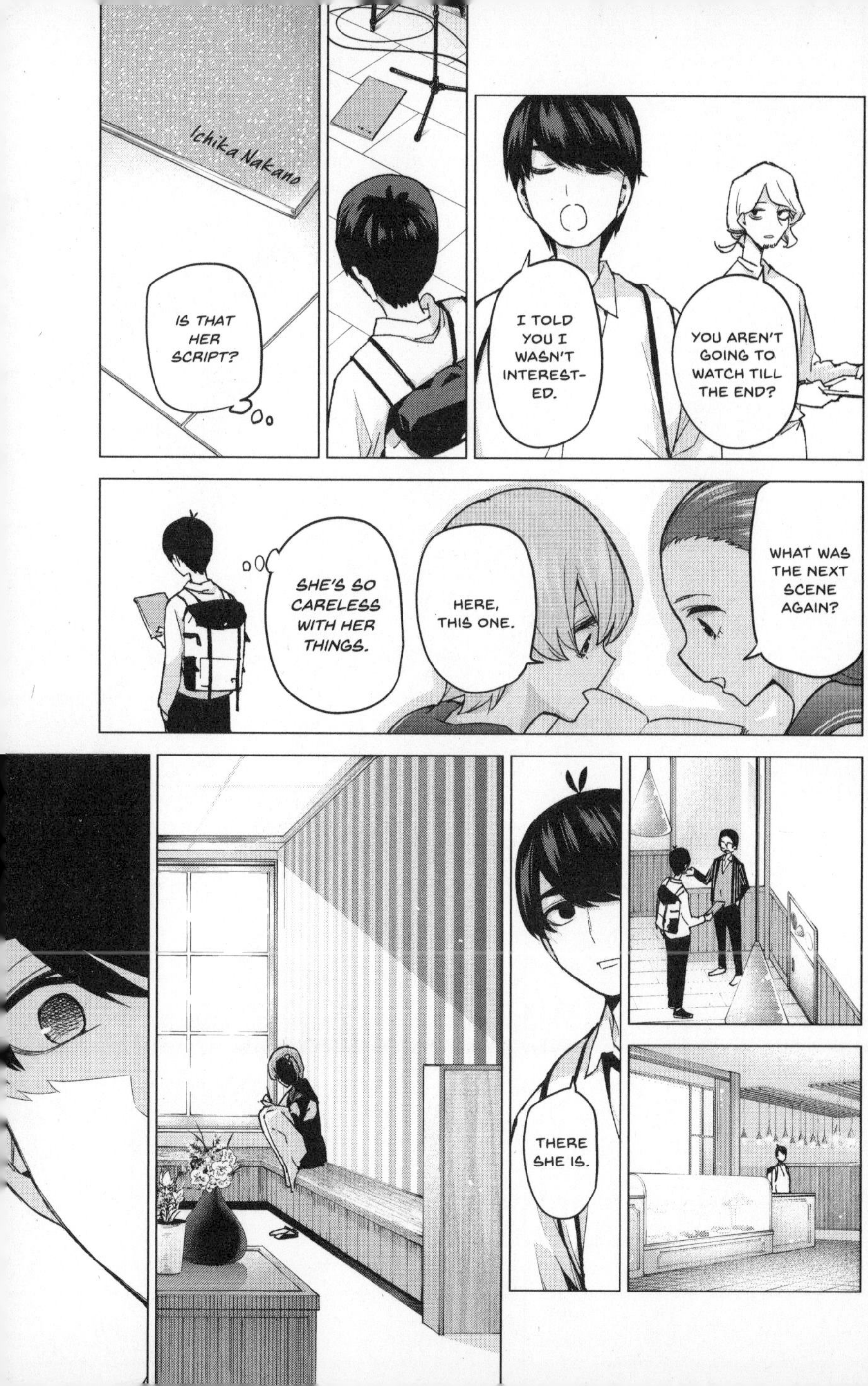
YOU AREN'T GOING TO WATCH TILL THE END?
I TOLD YOU I WASN'T INTEREST-ED.
Ichika Nakano
IS THAT HER SCRIPT?
WHAT WAS THE NEXT SCENE AGAIN?
HERE, THIS ONE.
SHE'S SO CARELESS WITH HER THINGS.
THERE SHE IS.

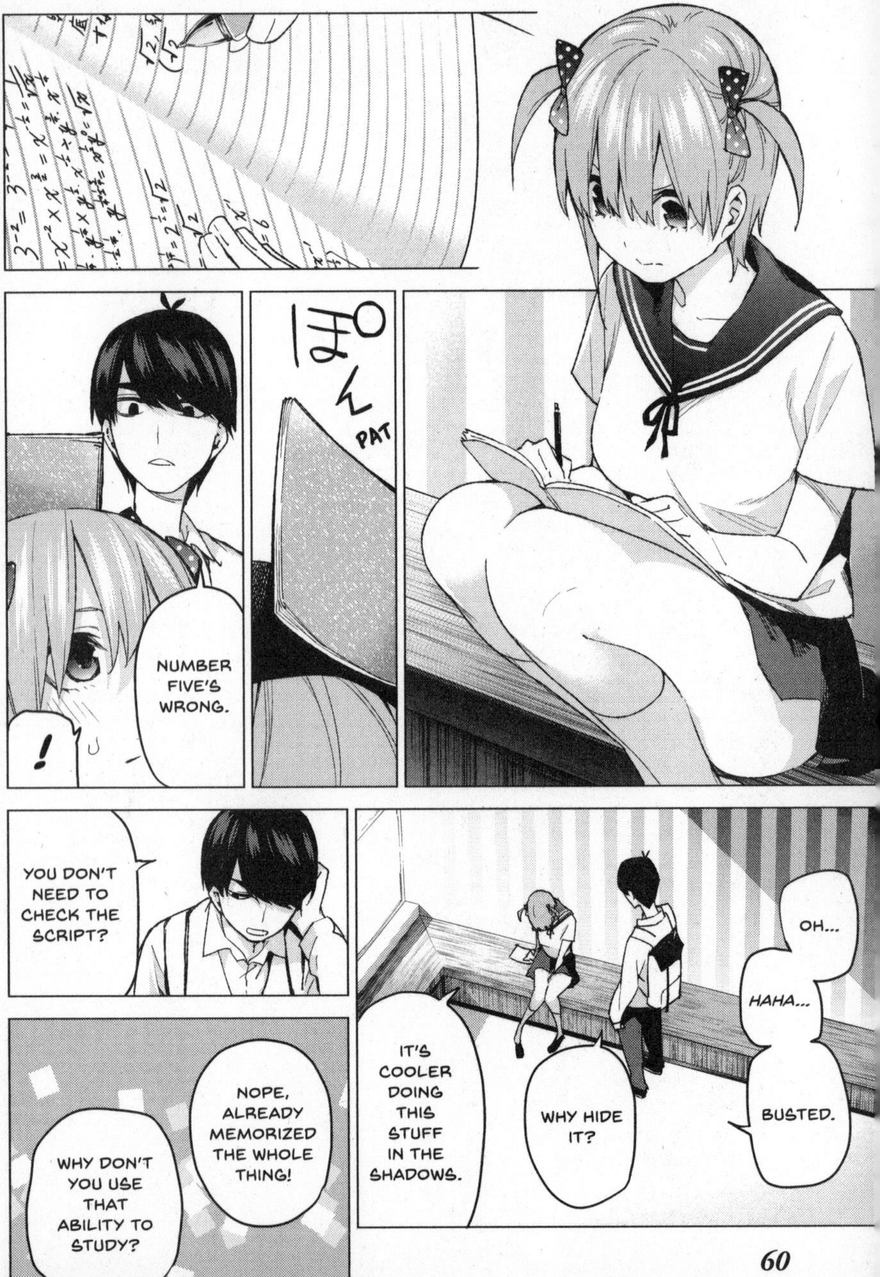
ぽん
PAT
NUMBER FIVE'S WRONG.
!
OH...
HAHA...
BUSTED.
WHY HIDE IT?
IT'S COOLER DOING THIS STUFF IN THE SHADOWS.
YOU DON'T NEED TO CHECK THE SCRIPT?
NOPE, ALREADY MEMORIZED THE WHOLE THING!
WHY DON'T YOU USE THAT ABILITY TO STUDY?

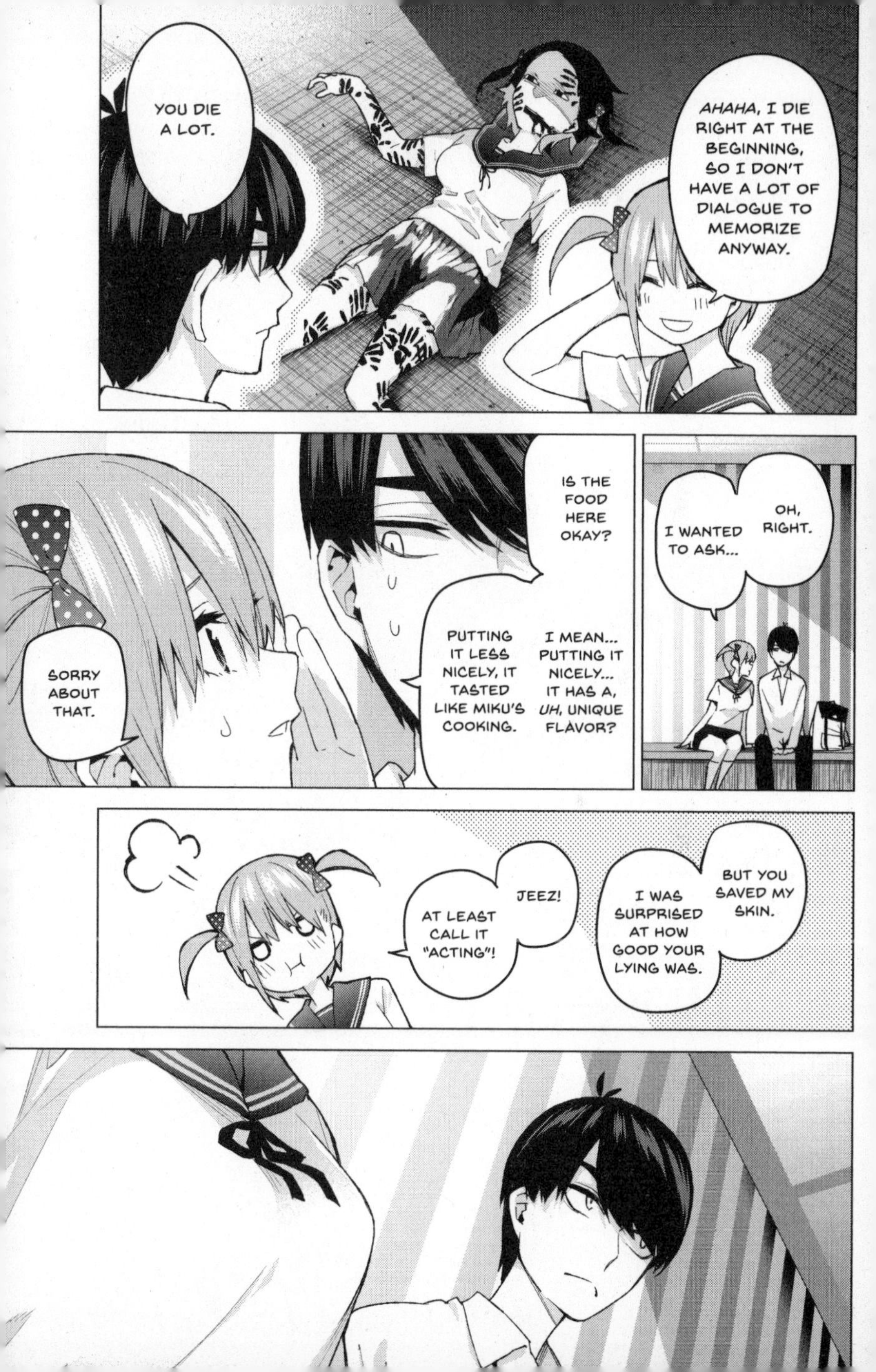
YOU DIE A LOT.
AHAHA, I DIE RIGHT AT THE BEGINNING, SO I DON'T HAVE A LOT OF DIALOGUE TO MEMORIZE ANYWAY.
OH, RIGHT.
I WANTED TO ASK...
IS THE FOOD HERE OKAY?
I MEAN... PUTTING IT NICELY... IT HAS A, *UH*, UNIQUE FLAVOR?
PUTTING IT LESS NICELY, IT TASTED LIKE MIKU'S COOKING.
SORRY ABOUT THAT.
BUT YOU SAVED MY SKIN.
I WAS SURPRISED AT HOW GOOD YOUR LYING WAS.
JEEZ!
AT LEAST CALL IT "ACTING"!

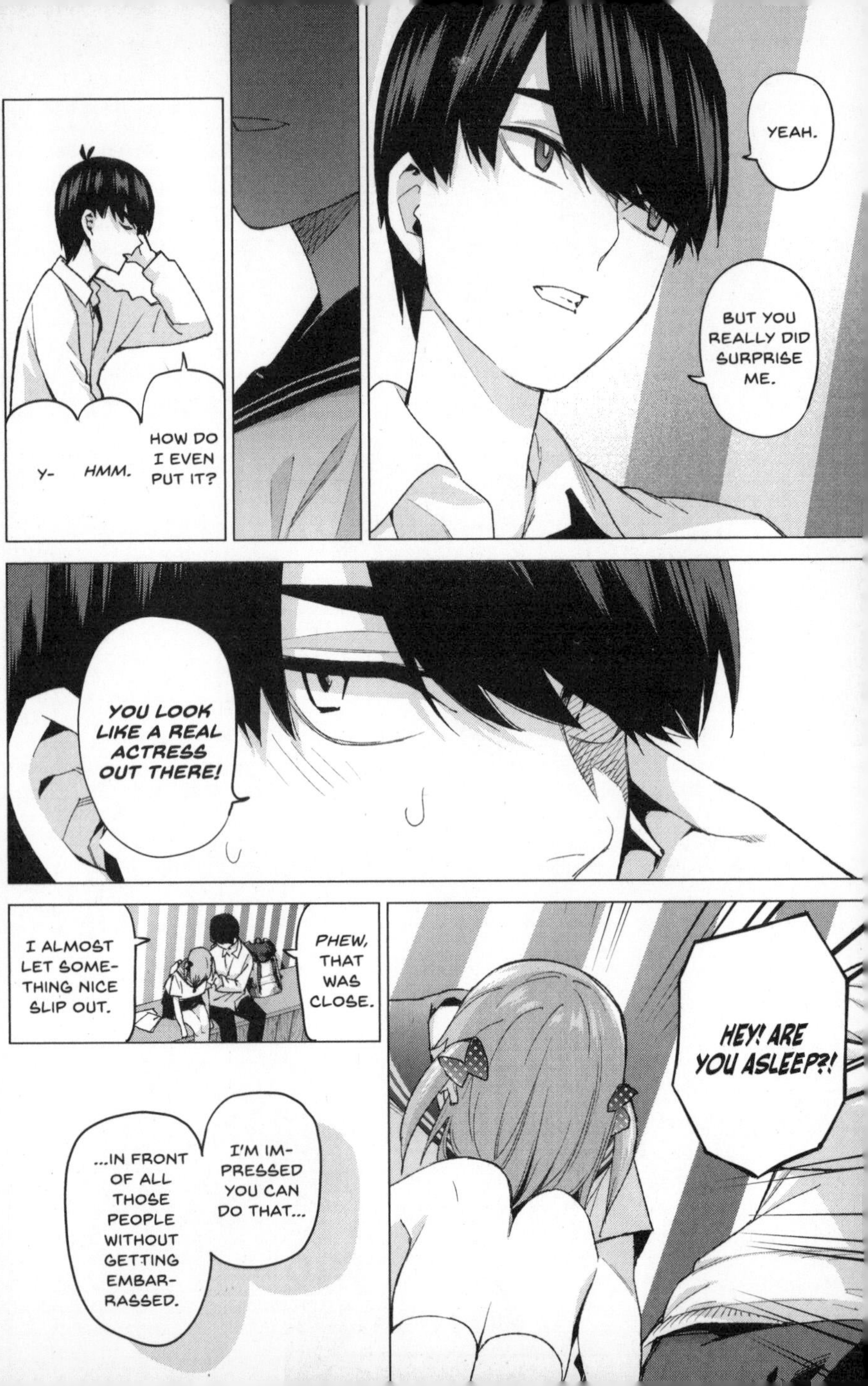
YEAH.
BUT YOU REALLY DID SURPRISE ME.
Y- HMM. HOW DO I EVEN PUT IT?
YOU LOOK LIKE A REAL ACTRESS OUT THERE!
HEY! ARE YOU ASLEEP?!
PHEW, THAT WAS CLOSE.
I ALMOST LET SOME-THING NICE SLIP OUT.
I'M IM-PRESSED YOU CAN DO THAT...
...IN FRONT OF ALL THOSE PEOPLE WITHOUT GETTING EMBAR-RASSED.

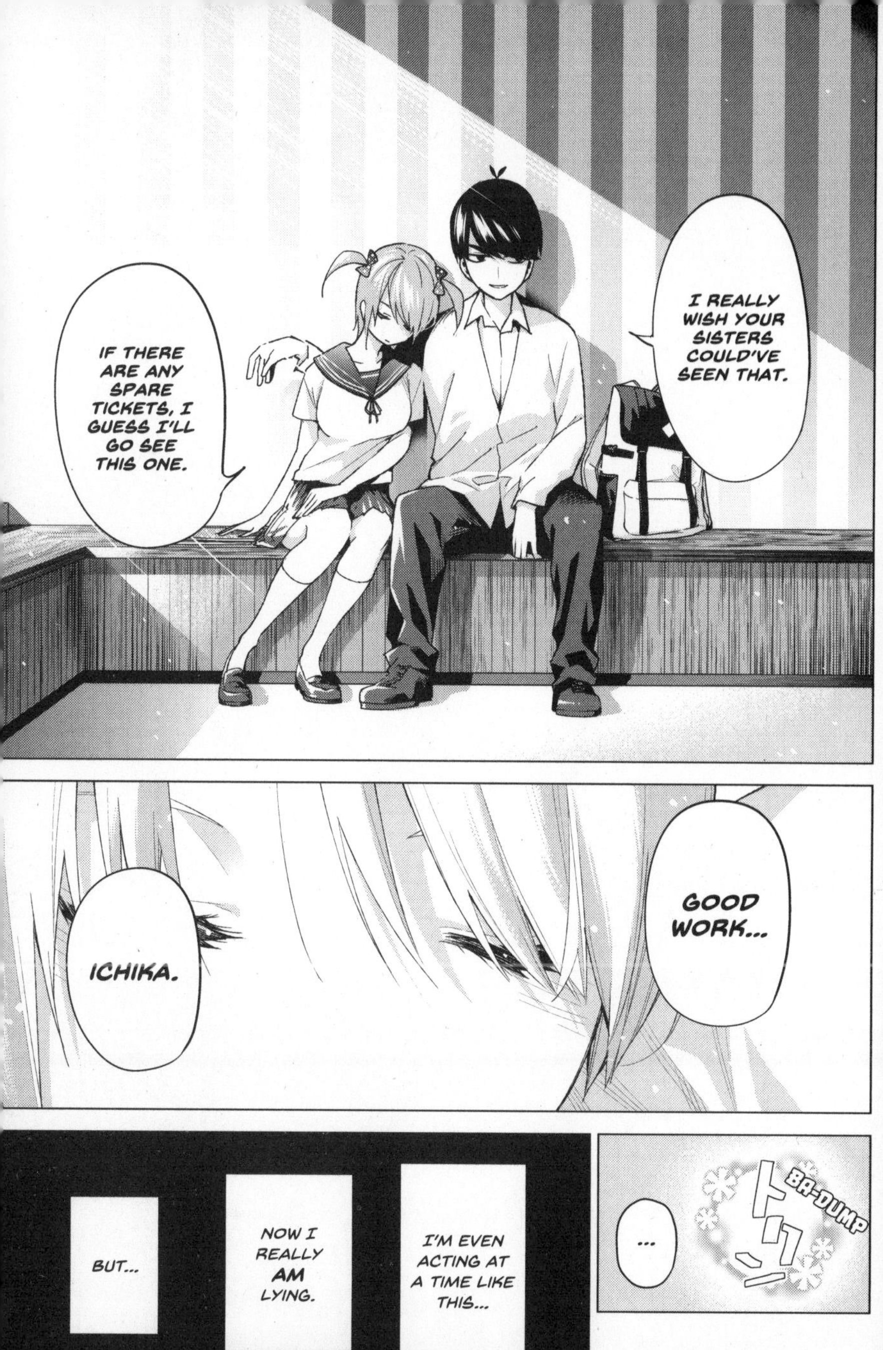
I REALLY WISH YOUR SISTERS COULD'VE SEEN THAT.
IF THERE ARE ANY SPARE TICKETS, I GUESS I'LL GO SEE THIS ONE.
GOOD WORK...
ICHIKA.
BA-DUMP
...
I'M EVEN ACTING AT A TIME LIKE THIS...
NOW I REALLY AM LYING.
BUT...

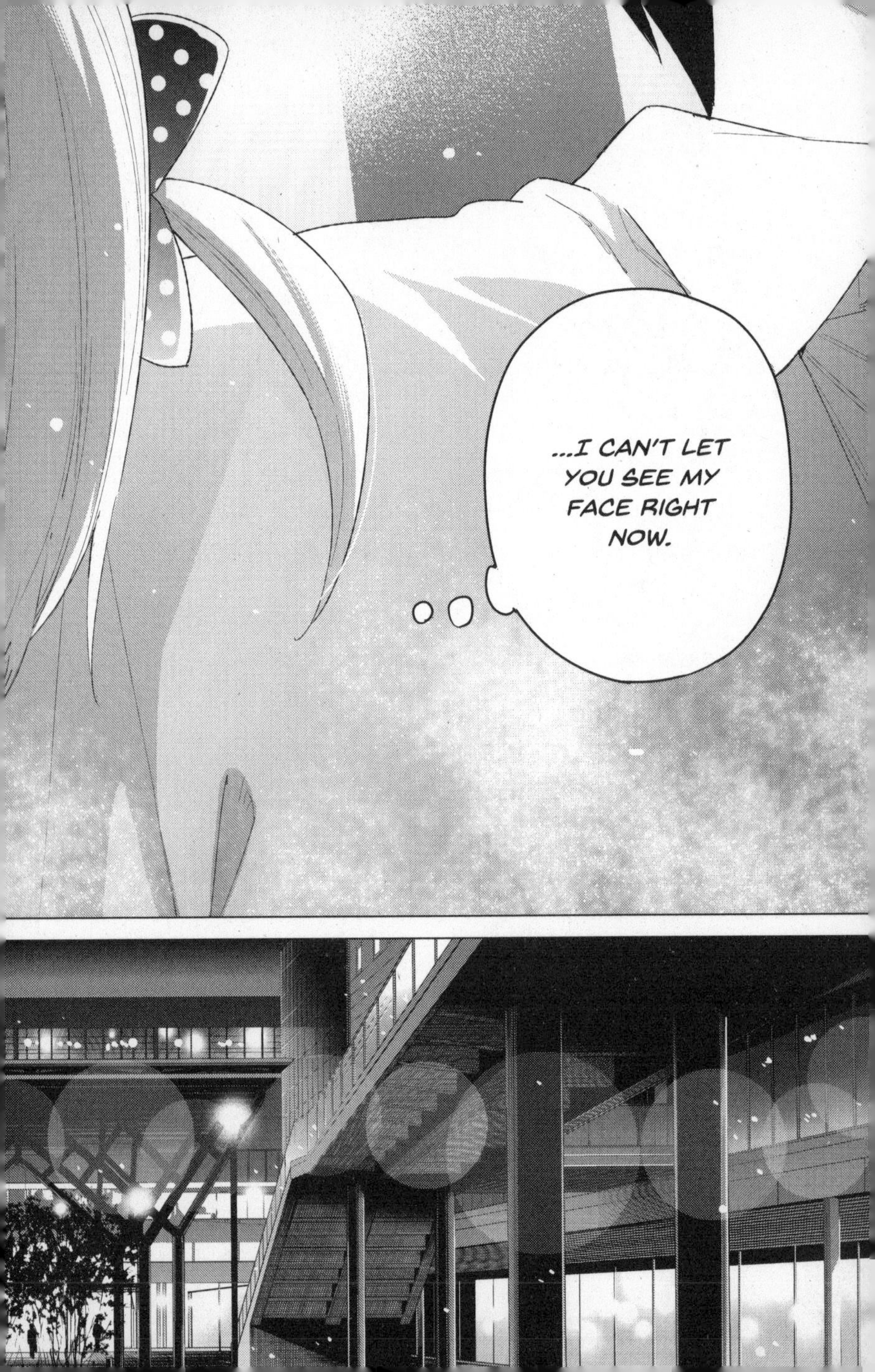
...I CAN'T LET YOU SEE MY FACE RIGHT NOW.

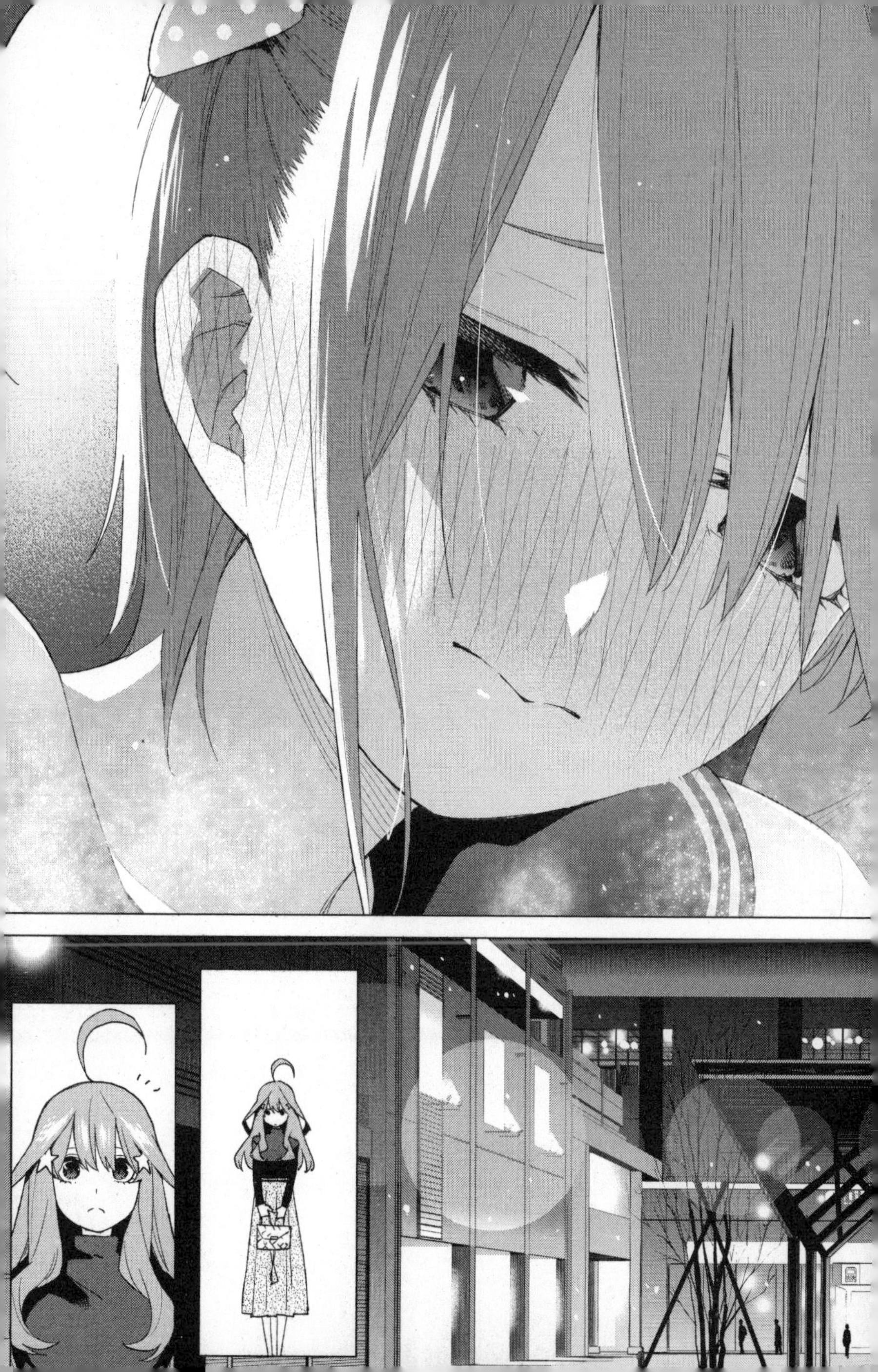

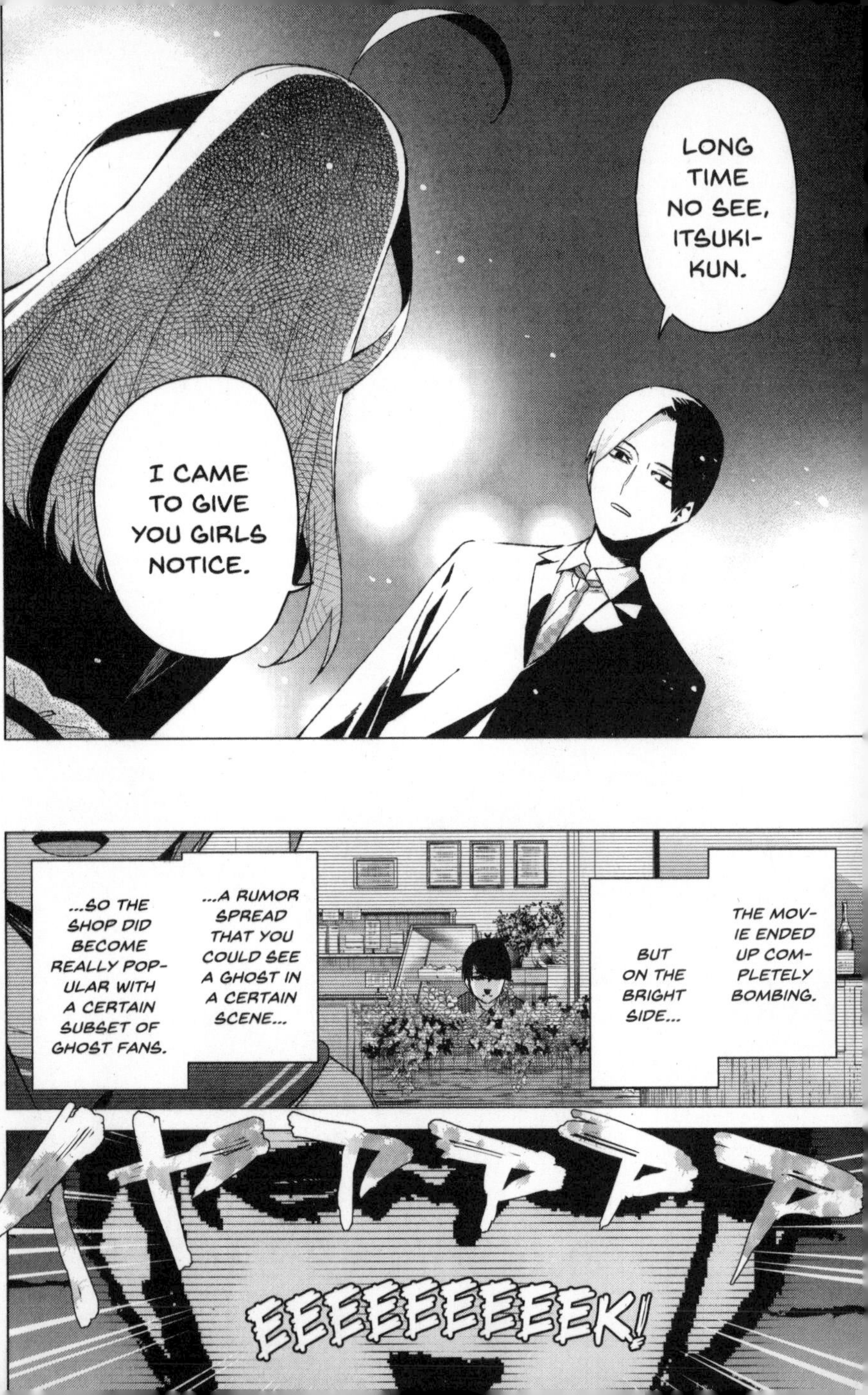
LONG TIME NO SEE, ITSUKI-KUN.
I CAME TO GIVE YOU GIRLS NOTICE.
THE MOVIE ENDED UP COMPLETELY BOMBING.
BUT ON THE BRIGHT SIDE...
...A RUMOR SPREAD THAT YOU COULD SEE A GHOST IN A CERTAIN SCENE...
...SO THE SHOP DID BECOME REALLY POPULAR WITH A CERTAIN SUBSET OF GHOST FANS.
EEEEEEEEEEK!!

CHAPTER 54
THE FOOL'S BATTLE

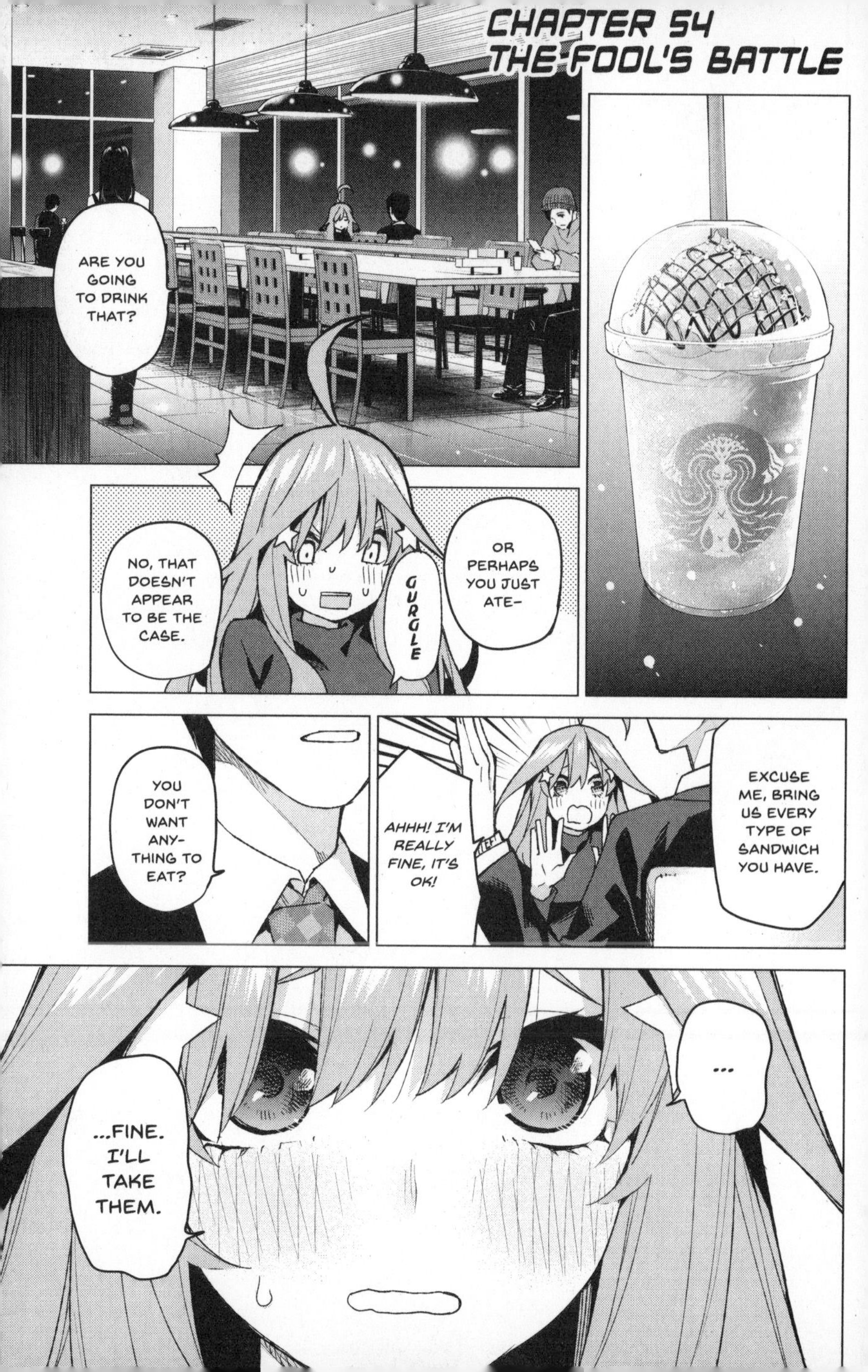
ARE YOU GOING TO DRINK THAT?
OR PERHAPS YOU JUST ATE-
GURGLE
NO, THAT DOESN'T APPEAR TO BE THE CASE.
EXCUSE ME, BRING US EVERY TYPE OF SANDWICH YOU HAVE.
AHHH! I'M REALLY FINE, IT'S OK!
YOU DON'T WANT ANY-THING TO EAT?
...
...FINE. I'LL TAKE THEM.

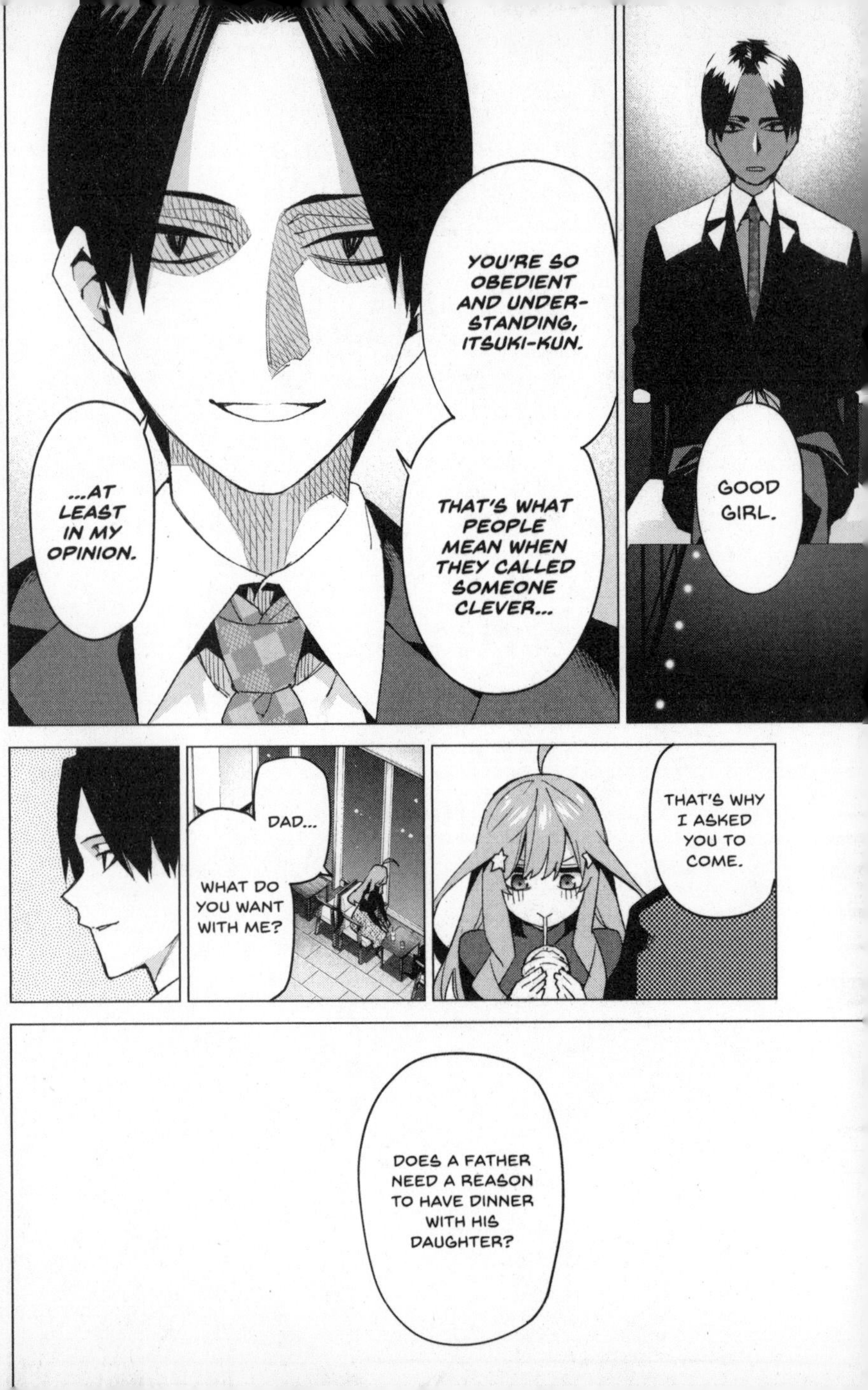
GOOD GIRL.
YOU'RE SO OBEDIENT AND UNDER-STANDING, ITSUKI-KUN.
THAT'S WHAT PEOPLE MEAN WHEN THEY CALLED SOMEONE CLEVER...
...AT LEAST IN MY OPINION.
THAT'S WHY I ASKED YOU TO COME.
DAD...
WHAT DO YOU WANT WITH ME?
DOES A FATHER NEED A REASON TO HAVE DINNER WITH HIS DAUGHTER?

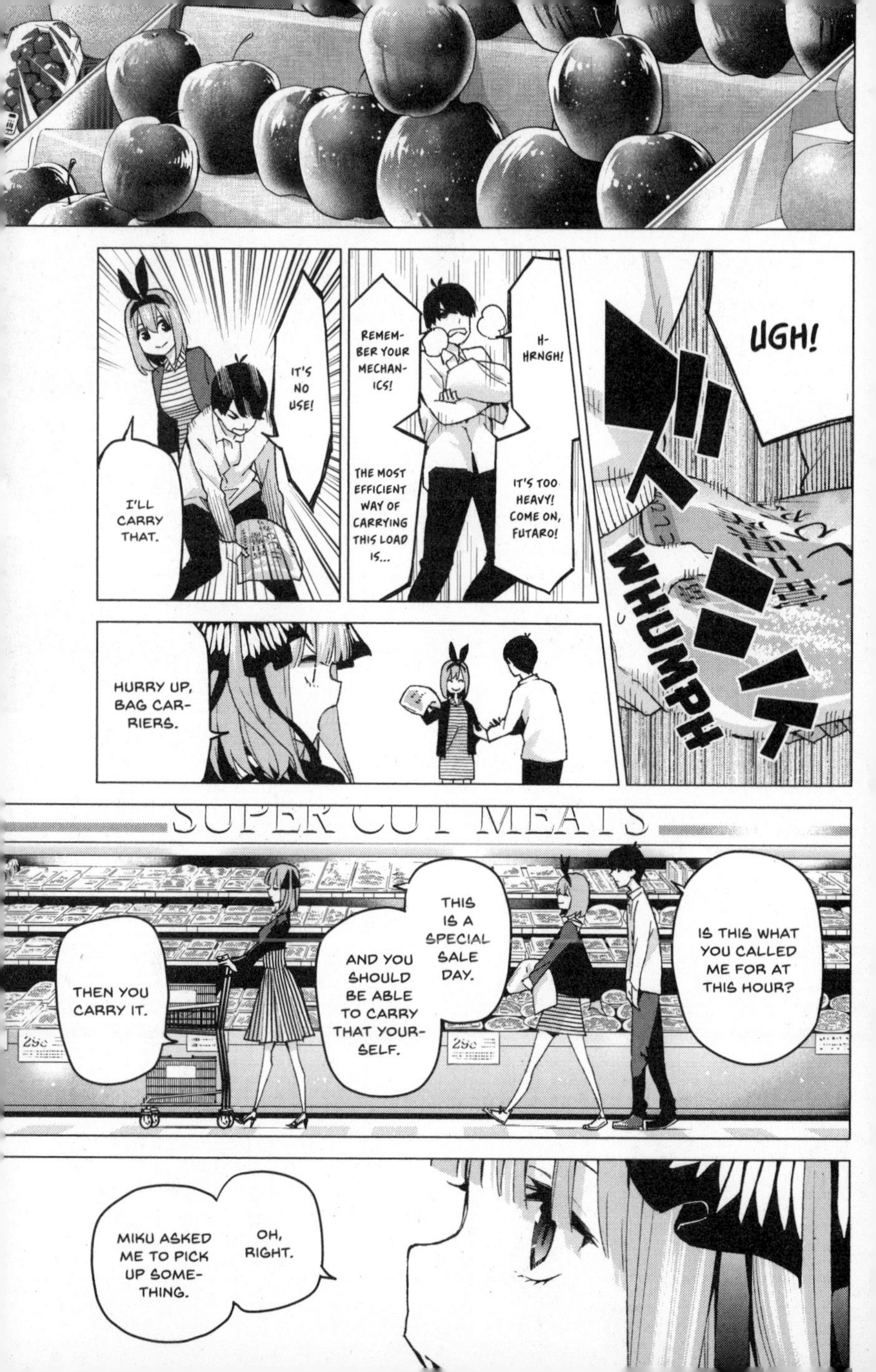
UGH!
WHUMPH
H-HRNGH!
REMEMBER YOUR MECHANICS!
IT'S TOO HEAVY! COME ON, FUTARO!
THE MOST EFFICIENT WAY OF CARRYING THIS LOAD IS...
IT'S NO USE!
I'LL CARRY THAT.
HURRY UP, BAG CARRIERS.
SUPER CUT MEATS
IS THIS WHAT YOU CALLED ME FOR AT THIS HOUR?
THIS IS A SPECIAL SALE DAY.
AND YOU SHOULD BE ABLE TO CARRY THAT YOURSELF.
THEN YOU CARRY IT.
OH, RIGHT.
MIKU ASKED ME TO PICK UP SOMETHING.

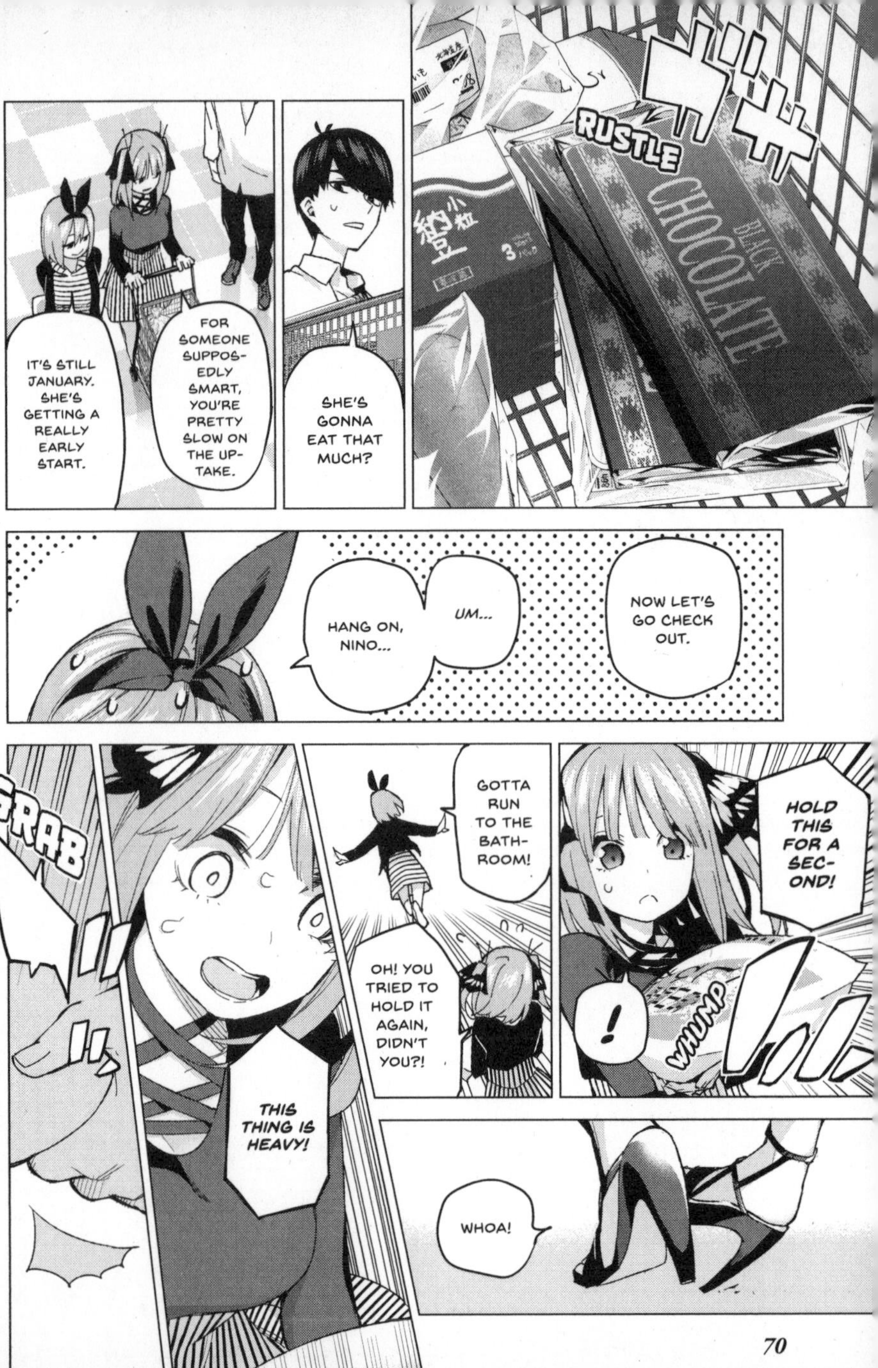
RUSTLE
BLACK CHOCOLATE
SHE'S GONNA EAT THAT MUCH?
FOR SOMEONE SUPPOS-EDLY SMART, YOU'RE PRETTY SLOW ON THE UP-TAKE.
IT'S STILL JANUARY. SHE'S GETTING A REALLY EARLY START.
NOW LET'S GO CHECK OUT.
UM...
HANG ON, NINO...
HOLD THIS FOR A SEC-OND!
!
WHUMP
GOTTA RUN TO THE BATH-ROOM!
OH! YOU TRIED TO HOLD IT AGAIN, DIDN'T YOU?!
WHOA!
GRAB
THIS THING IS HEAVY!

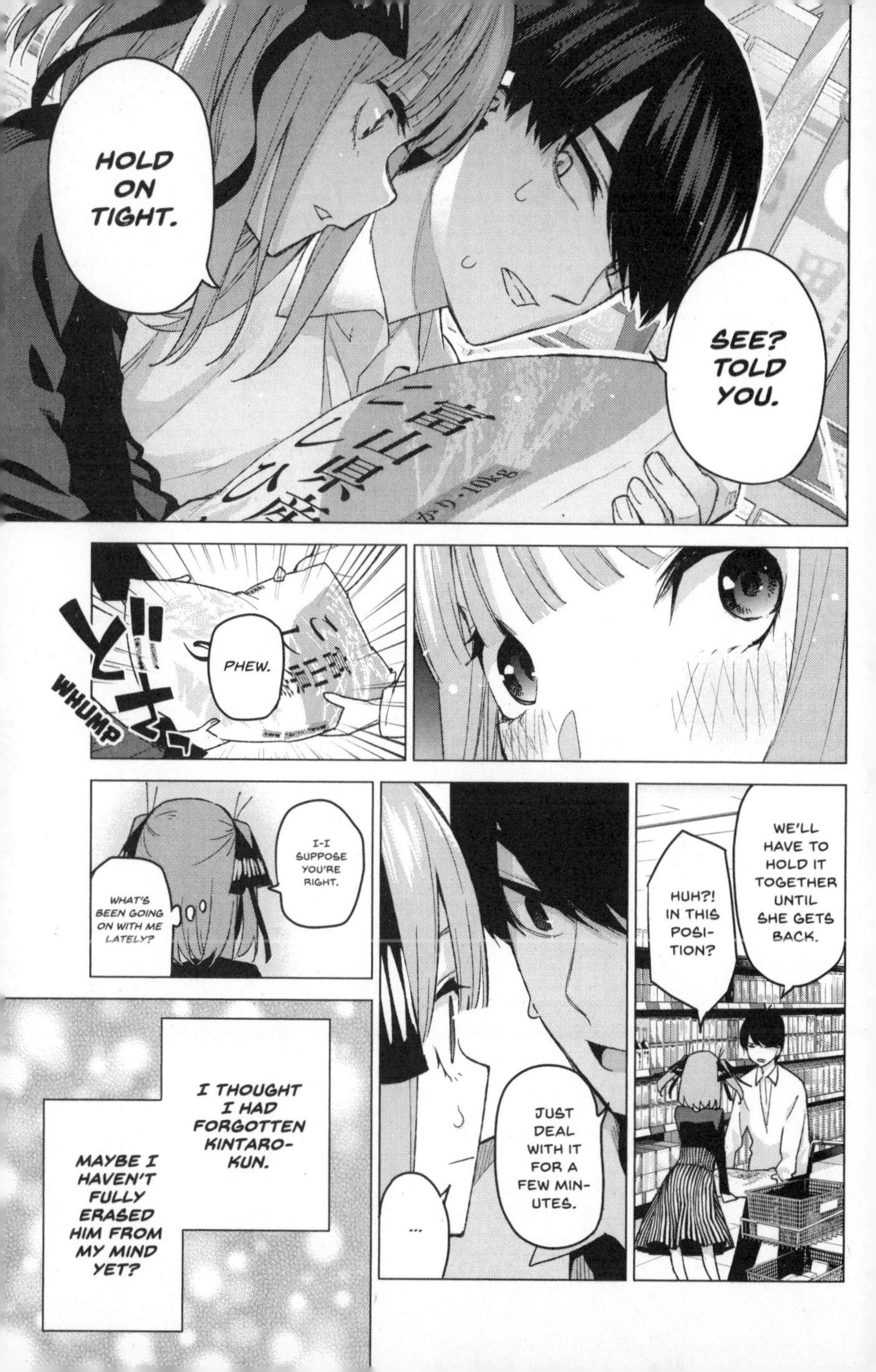
HOLD ON TIGHT.
SEE? TOLD YOU.
PHEW.
WHUMP
WE'LL HAVE TO HOLD IT TOGETHER UNTIL SHE GETS BACK.
HUH?! IN THIS POSITION?
JUST DEAL WITH IT FOR A FEW MINUTES.
...
I-I SUPPOSE YOU'RE RIGHT.
WHAT'S BEEN GOING ON WITH ME LATELY?
I THOUGHT I HAD FORGOTTEN KINTARO-KUN.
MAYBE I HAVEN'T FULLY ERASED HIM FROM MY MIND YET?

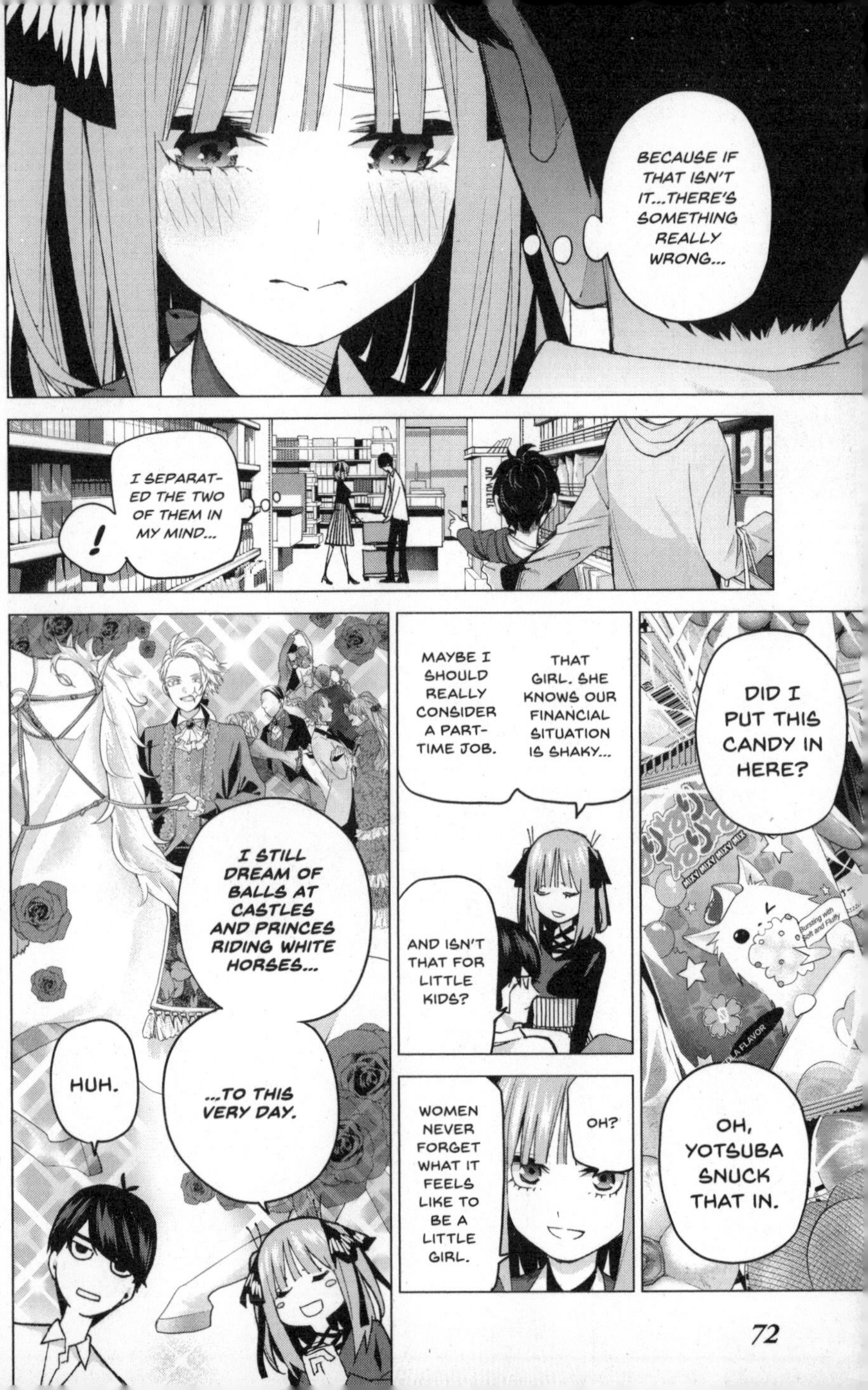
BECAUSE IF THAT ISN'T IT...THERE'S SOMETHING REALLY WRONG...
I SEPARATED THE TWO OF THEM IN MY MIND...
!
DID I PUT THIS CANDY IN HERE?
Bursting with Soft and Fluffy
OH, YOTSUBA SNUCK THAT IN.
THAT GIRL. SHE KNOWS OUR FINANCIAL SITUATION IS SHAKY...
MAYBE I SHOULD REALLY CONSIDER A PART-TIME JOB.
AND ISN'T THAT FOR LITTLE KIDS?
OH?
WOMEN NEVER FORGET WHAT IT FEELS LIKE TO BE A LITTLE GIRL.
I STILL DREAM OF BALLS AT CASTLES AND PRINCES RIDING WHITE HORSES...
...TO THIS VERY DAY.
HUH.

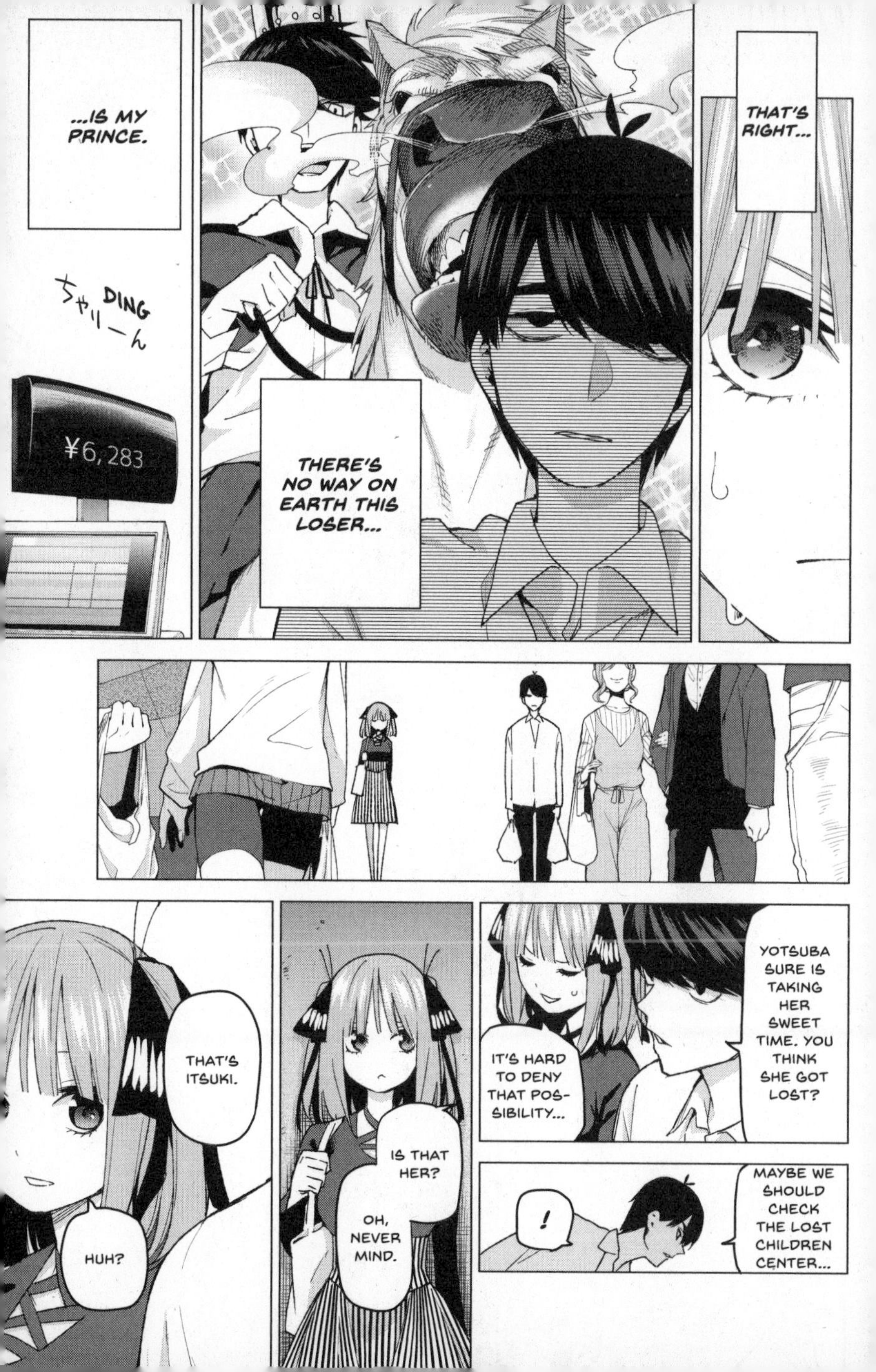
THAT'S RIGHT...
THERE'S NO WAY ON EARTH THIS LOSER...
...IS MY PRINCE.
ちゃりーん DING
¥6,283
YOTSUBA SURE IS TAKING HER SWEET TIME. YOU THINK SHE GOT LOST?
IT'S HARD TO DENY THAT POSSIBILITY...
MAYBE WE SHOULD CHECK THE LOST CHILDREN CENTER...
!
IS THAT HER?
OH, NEVER MIND.
THAT'S ITSUKI.
HUH?

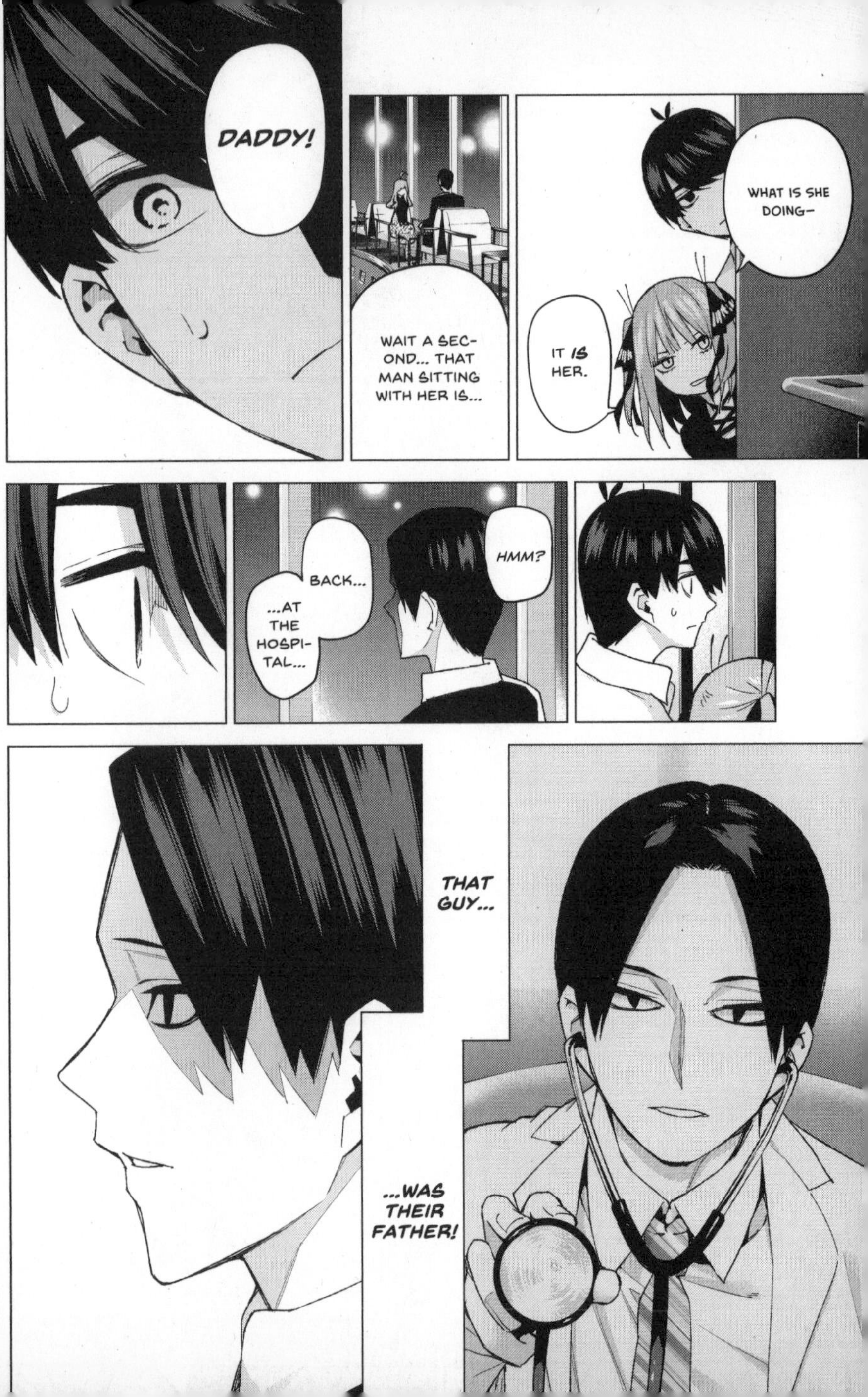
WHAT IS SHE DOING—
IT IS HER.
WAIT A SEC-OND... THAT MAN SITTING WITH HER IS...
DADDY!
HMM?
BACK...
...AT THE HOSPI-TAL...
THAT GUY...
...WAS THEIR FATHER!

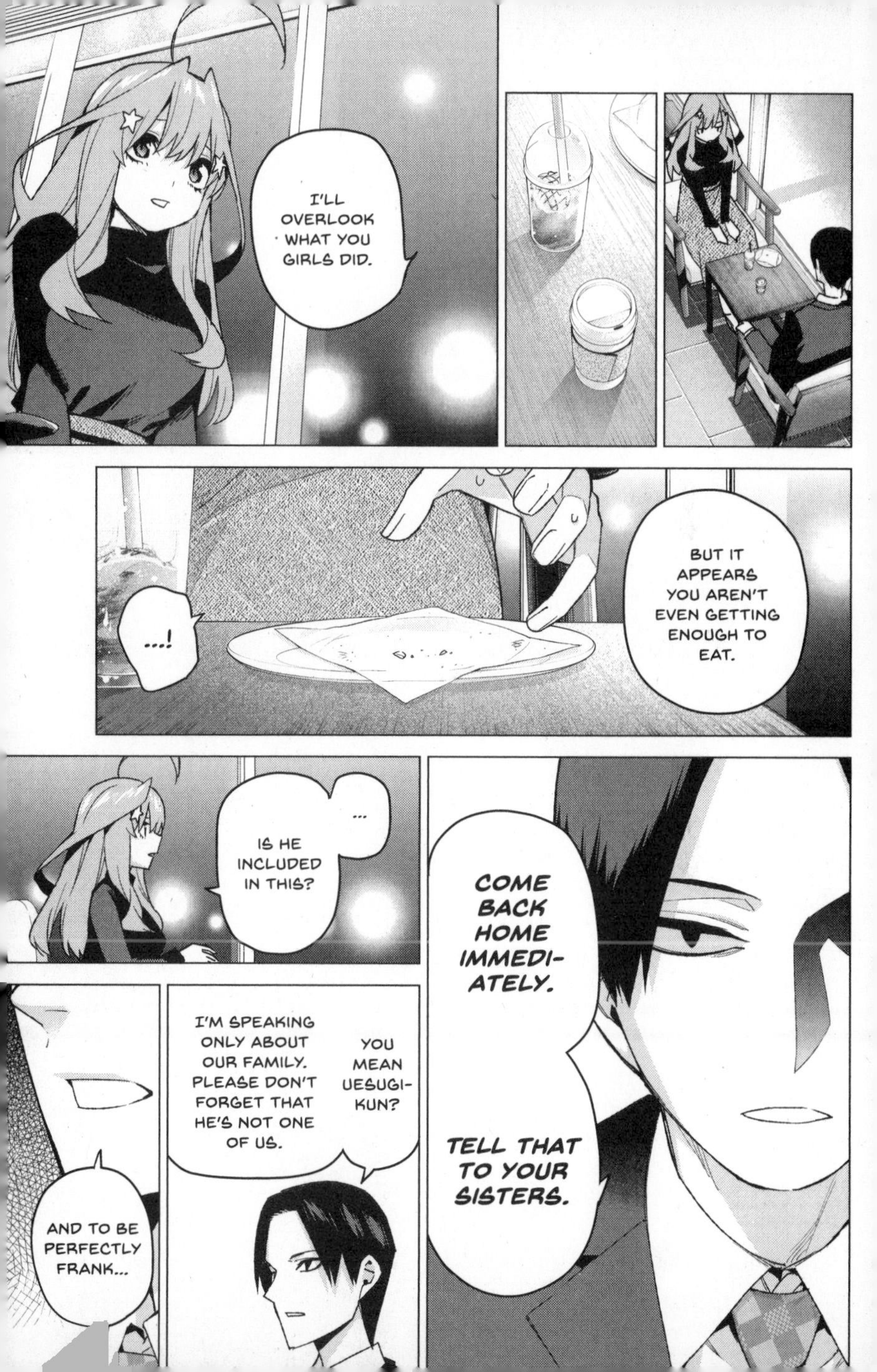
I'LL OVERLOOK WHAT YOU GIRLS DID.
BUT IT APPEARS YOU AREN'T EVEN GETTING ENOUGH TO EAT.
...!
COME BACK HOME IMMEDI-ATELY.
TELL THAT TO YOUR SISTERS.
... IS HE INCLUDED IN THIS?
YOU MEAN UESUGI-KUN?
I'M SPEAKING ONLY ABOUT OUR FAMILY. PLEASE DON'T FORGET THAT HE'S NOT ONE OF US.
AND TO BE PERFECTLY FRANK...

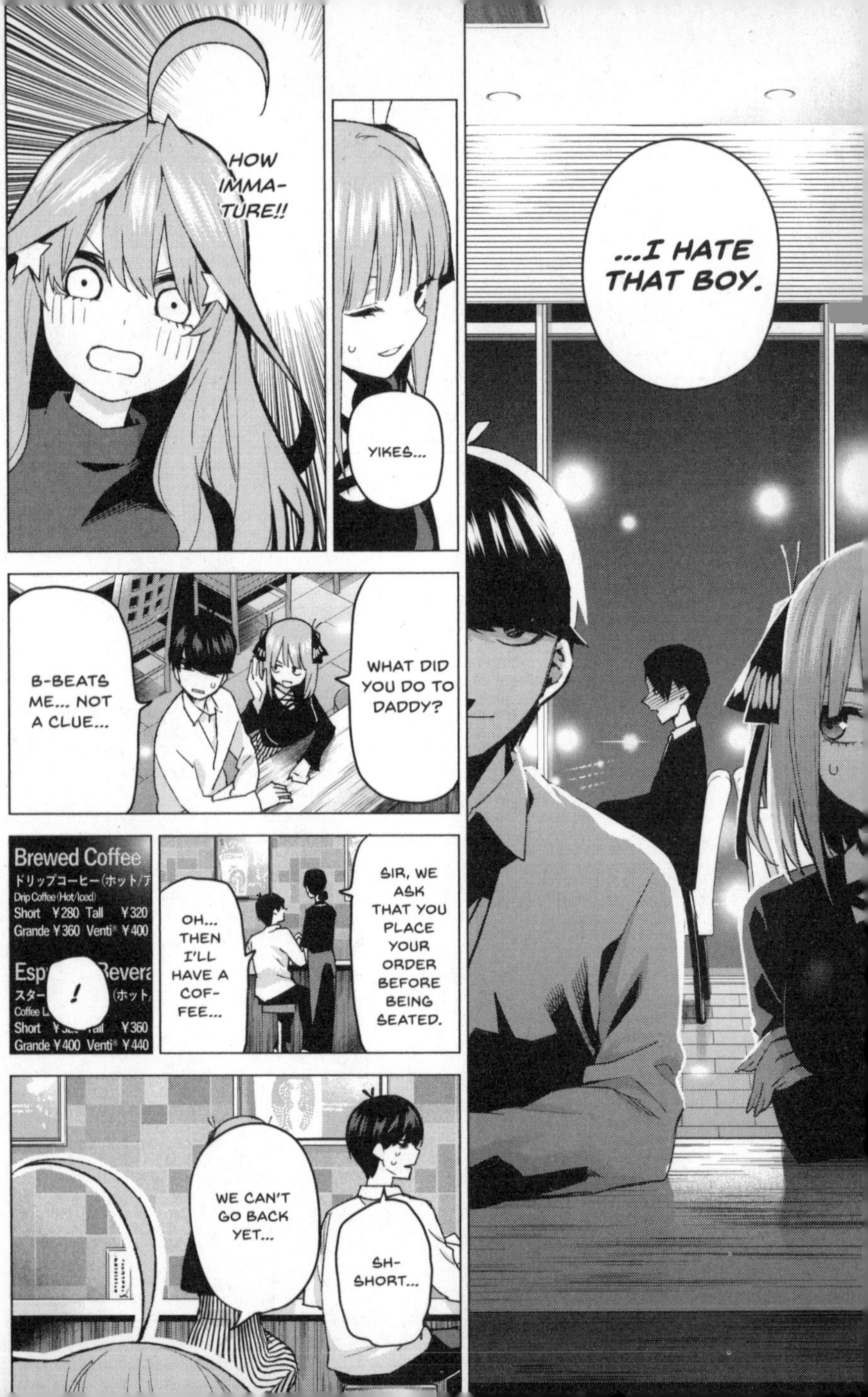
...I HATE THAT BOY.
YIKES...
HOW IMMA-TURE!!
WHAT DID YOU DO TO DADDY?
B-BEATS ME... NOT A CLUE...
SIR, WE ASK THAT YOU PLACE YOUR ORDER BEFORE BEING SEATED.
OH... THEN I'LL HAVE A COF-FEE...
Brewed Coffee
Drip Coffee (Hot/Iced)
Short ¥280 Tall ¥320
Grande ¥360 Venti ¥400
!
Short ¥360
Grande ¥400 Venti ¥440
WE CAN'T GO BACK YET...
SH-SHORT...

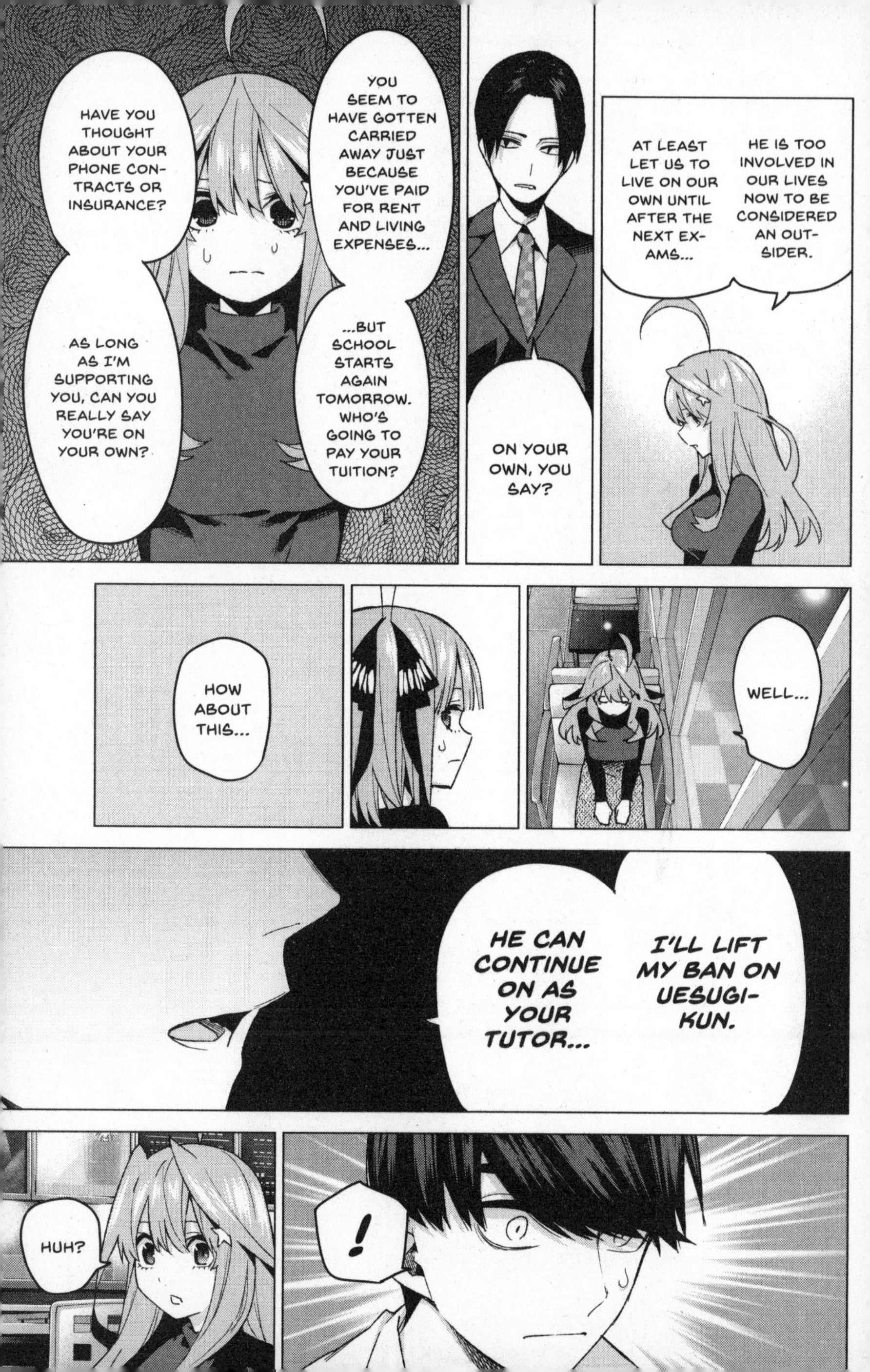
HE IS TOO INVOLVED IN OUR LIVES NOW TO BE CONSIDERED AN OUT-SIDER.
AT LEAST LET US TO LIVE ON OUR OWN UNTIL AFTER THE NEXT EX-AMS...
ON YOUR OWN, YOU SAY?
YOU SEEM TO HAVE GOTTEN CARRIED AWAY JUST BECAUSE YOU'VE PAID FOR RENT AND LIVING EXPENSES...
...BUT SCHOOL STARTS AGAIN TOMORROW. WHO'S GOING TO PAY YOUR TUITION?
HAVE YOU THOUGHT ABOUT YOUR PHONE CON-TRACTS OR INSURANCE?
AS LONG AS I'M SUPPORTING YOU, CAN YOU REALLY SAY YOU'RE ON YOUR OWN?
WELL...
HOW ABOUT THIS...
I'LL LIFT MY BAN ON UESUGI-KUN.
HE CAN CONTINUE ON AS YOUR TUTOR...
!
HUH?

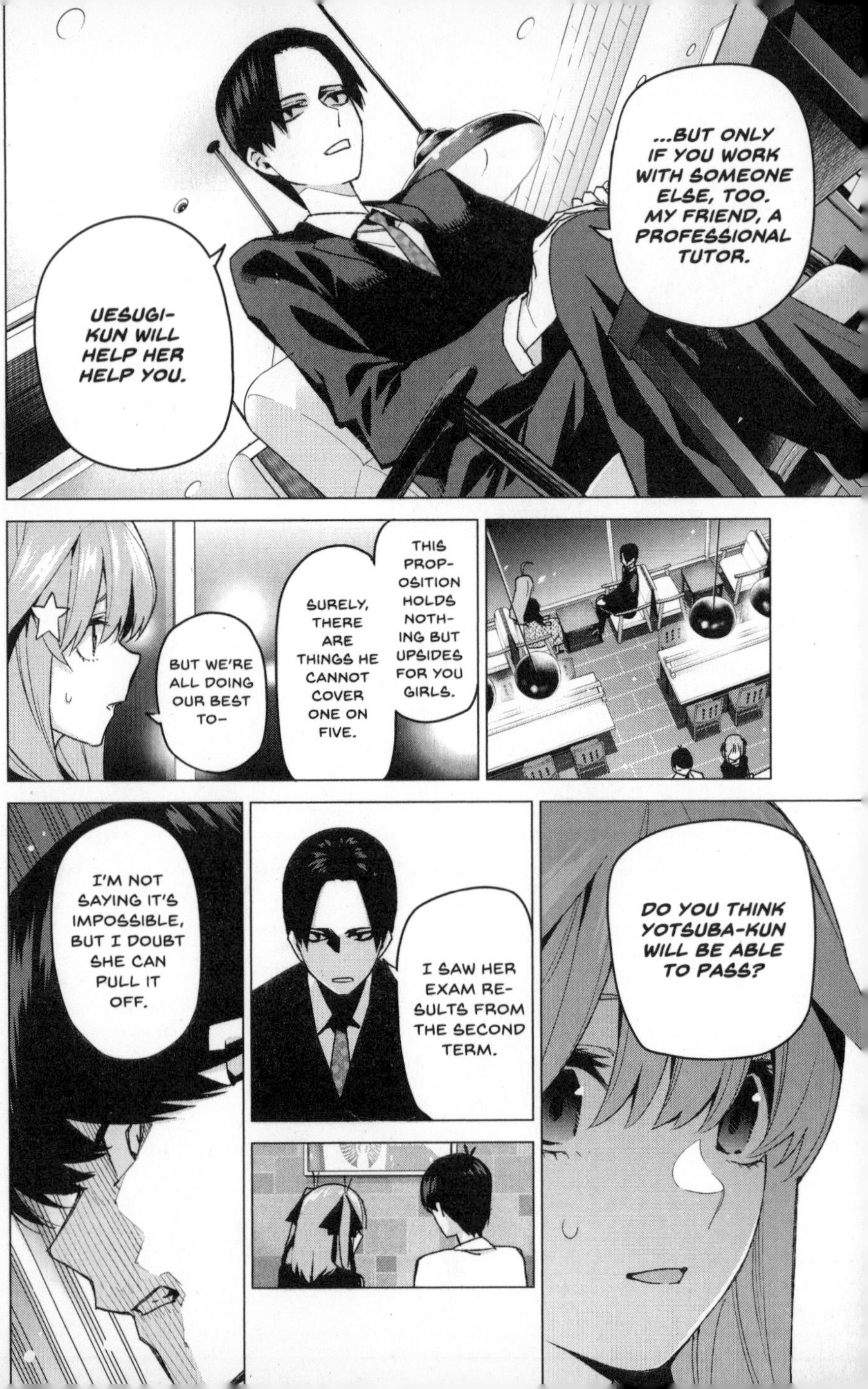
...BUT ONLY IF YOU WORK WITH SOMEONE ELSE, TOO. MY FRIEND, A PROFESSIONAL TUTOR.
UESUGI-KUN WILL HELP HER HELP YOU.
THIS PROPOSITION HOLDS NOTHING BUT UPSIDES FOR YOU GIRLS.
SURELY, THERE ARE THINGS HE CANNOT COVER ONE ON FIVE.
BUT WE'RE ALL DOING OUR BEST TO-
DO YOU THINK YOTSUBA-KUN WILL BE ABLE TO PASS?
I SAW HER EXAM RESULTS FROM THE SECOND TERM.
I'M NOT SAYING IT'S IMPOSSIBLE, BUT I DOUBT SHE CAN PULL IT OFF.

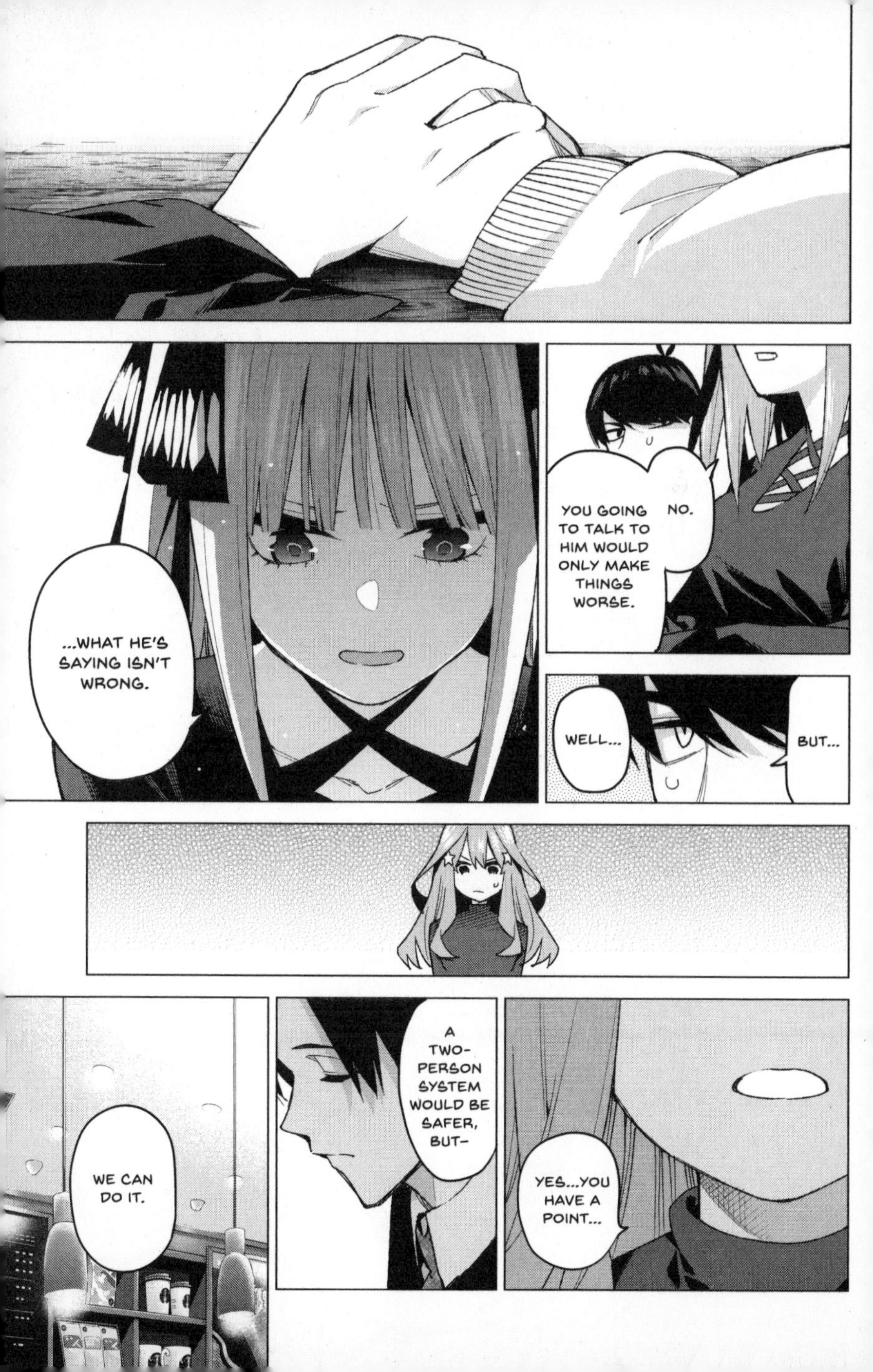
NO.
YOU GOING TO TALK TO HIM WOULD ONLY MAKE THINGS WORSE.
BUT...
WELL...
...WHAT HE'S SAYING ISN'T WRONG.
YES...YOU HAVE A POINT...
A TWO-PERSON SYSTEM WOULD BE SAFER, BUT-
WE CAN DO IT.

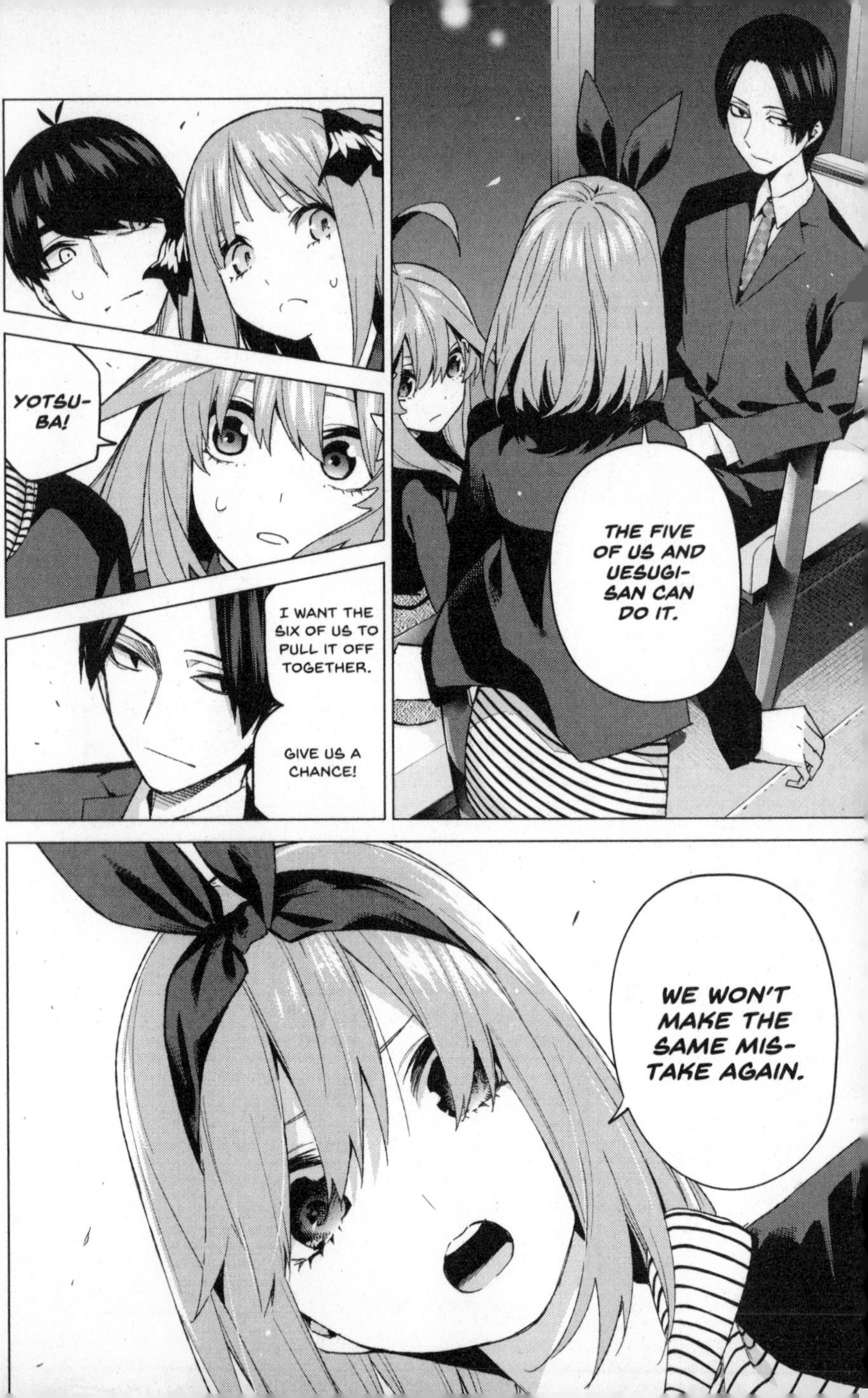
THE FIVE OF US AND UESUGI-SAN CAN DO IT.
YOTSU-BA!
I WANT THE SIX OF US TO PULL IT OFF TOGETHER.
GIVE US A CHANCE!
WE WON'T MAKE THE SAME MIS-TAKE AGAIN.

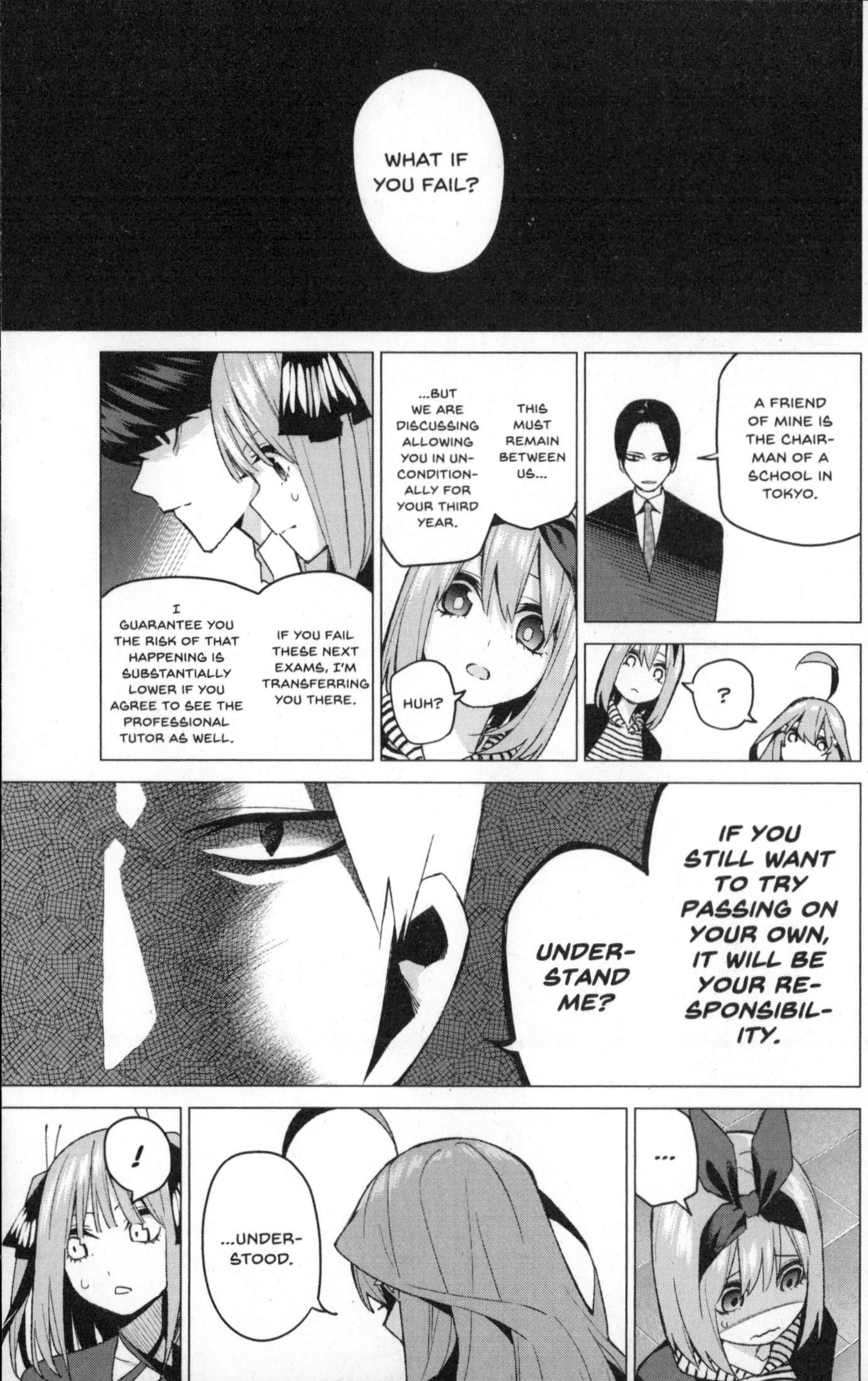
WHAT IF YOU FAIL?
A FRIEND OF MINE IS THE CHAIR-MAN OF A SCHOOL IN TOKYO.
?
THIS MUST REMAIN BETWEEN US...
...BUT WE ARE DISCUSSING ALLOWING YOU IN UN-CONDITION-ALLY FOR YOUR THIRD YEAR.
HUH?
IF YOU FAIL THESE NEXT EXAMS, I'M TRANSFERRING YOU THERE.
I GUARANTEE YOU THE RISK OF THAT HAPPENING IS SUBSTANTIALLY LOWER IF YOU AGREE TO SEE THE PROFESSIONAL TUTOR AS WELL.
IF YOU STILL WANT TO TRY PASSING ON YOUR OWN, IT WILL BE YOUR RE-SPONSIBIL-ITY.
UNDER-STAND ME?
...
...UNDER-STOOD.
!

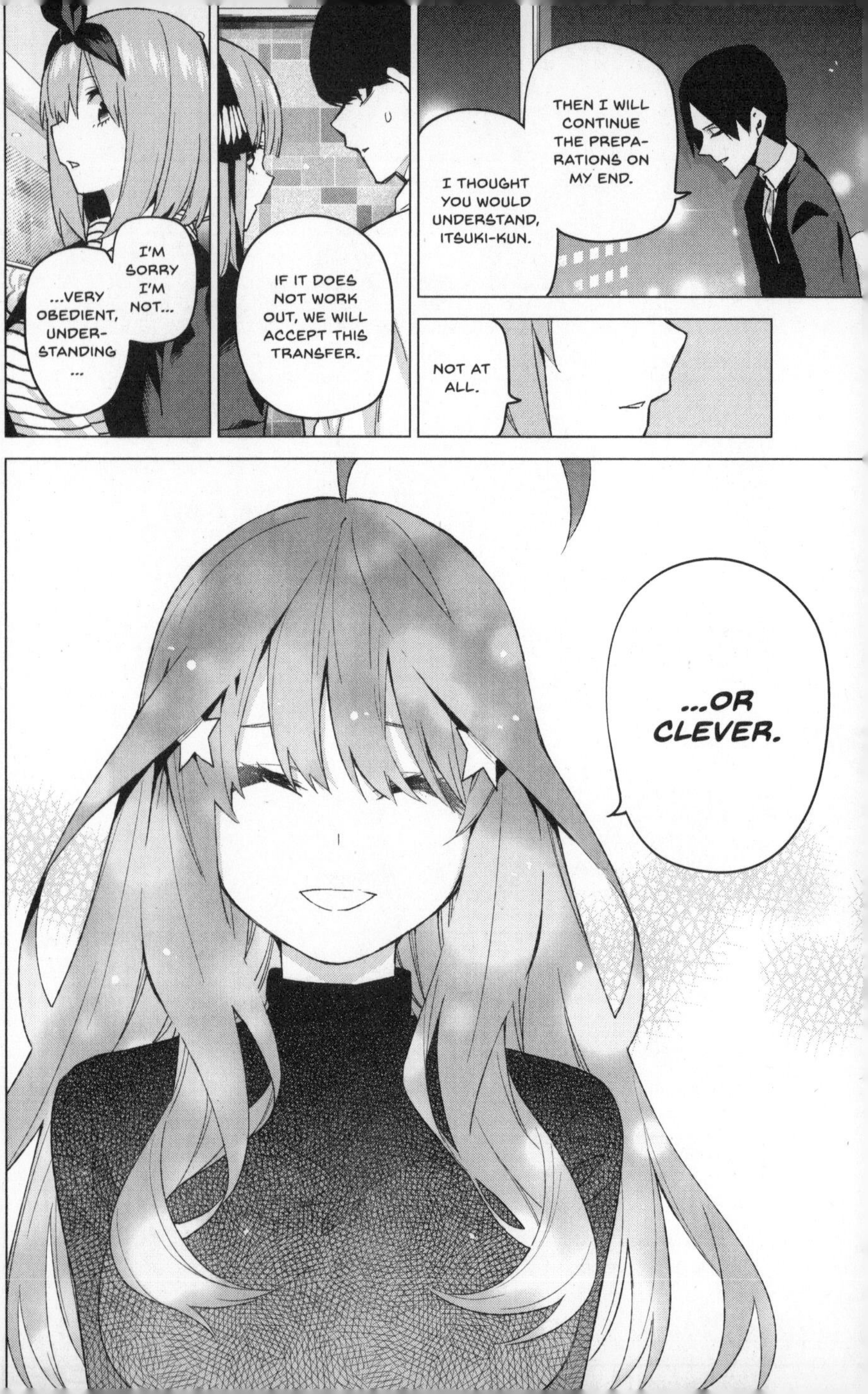
THEN I WILL CONTINUE THE PREPARATIONS ON MY END.
I THOUGHT YOU WOULD UNDERSTAND, ITSUKI-KUN.
NOT AT ALL.
IF IT DOES NOT WORK OUT, WE WILL ACCEPT THIS TRANSFER.
I'M SORRY I'M NOT...
...VERY OBEDIENT, UNDERSTANDING ...
...OR CLEVER.

I SUPPOSE IT IS MY JOB AS A PARENT TO LISTEN TO MY CHILDREN'S SELFISH DEMANDS.

AND THEN TEACH THEM A LESSON.

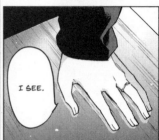

I SEE.

THIS IS YOUR ONLY CHANCE.

WE'LL SEE.

THIS WON'T BE LIKE AT OUR LAST SCHOOL.

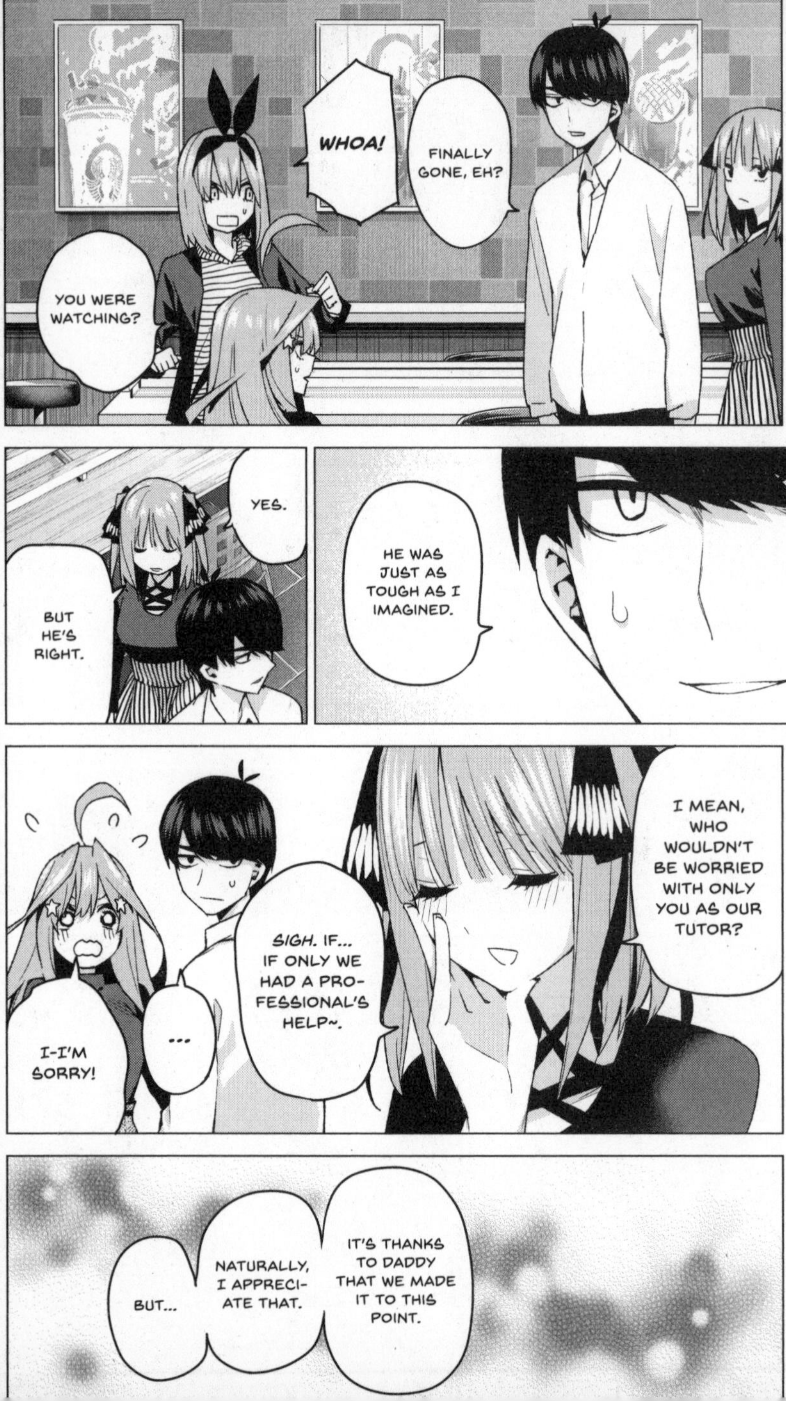
FINALLY GONE, EH?
WHOA!
YOU WERE WATCHING?
HE WAS JUST AS TOUGH AS I IMAGINED.
YES.
BUT HE'S RIGHT.
I MEAN, WHO WOULDN'T BE WORRIED WITH ONLY YOU AS OUR TUTOR?
SIGH. IF... IF ONLY WE HAD A PRO-FESSIONAL'S HELP~.
...
I-I'M SORRY!
IT'S THANKS TO DADDY THAT WE MADE IT TO THIS POINT.
NATURALLY, I APPRECIATE THAT.
BUT...

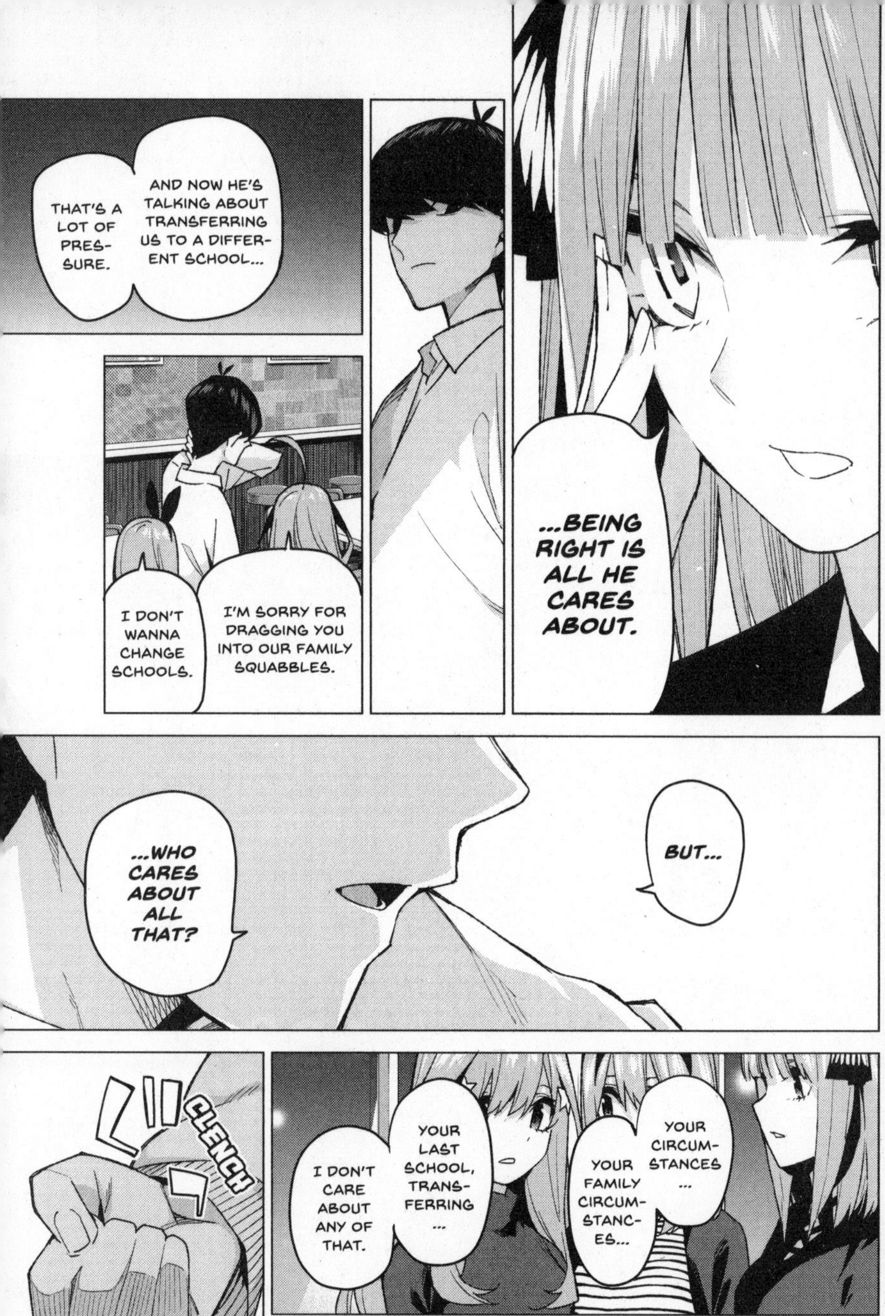
...BEING RIGHT IS ALL HE CARES ABOUT.
AND NOW HE'S TALKING ABOUT TRANSFERRING US TO A DIFFERENT SCHOOL...
THAT'S A LOT OF PRESSURE.
I'M SORRY FOR DRAGGING YOU INTO OUR FAMILY SQUABBLES.
I DON'T WANNA CHANGE SCHOOLS.
BUT...
...WHO CARES ABOUT ALL THAT?
YOUR CIRCUMSTANCES...
YOUR FAMILY CIRCUMSTANCES...
YOUR LAST SCHOOL, TRANSFERRING...
I DON'T CARE ABOUT ANY OF THAT.
CLENCH

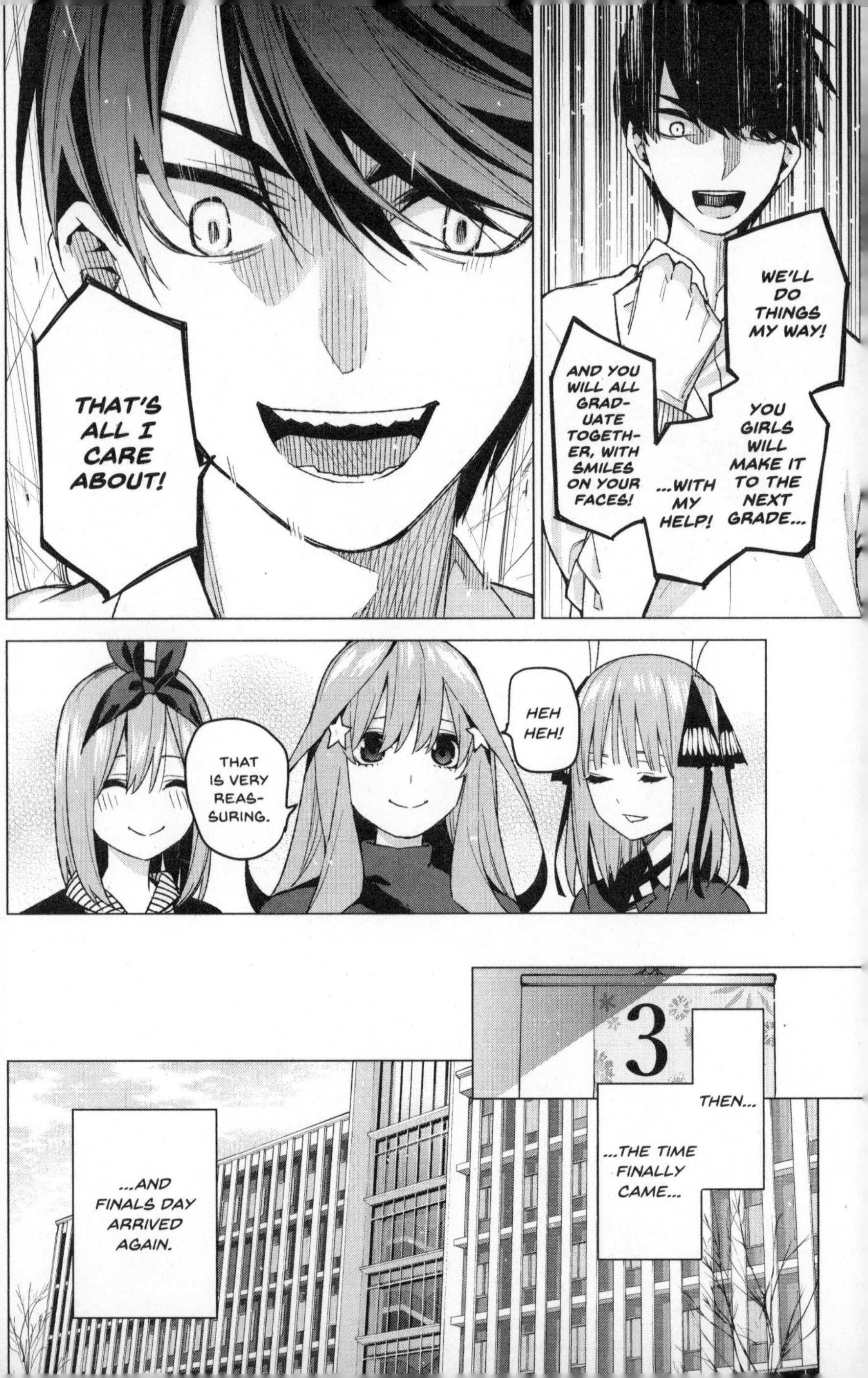
WE'LL DO THINGS MY WAY!
YOU GIRLS WILL MAKE IT TO THE NEXT GRADE...
...WITH MY HELP!
AND YOU WILL ALL GRAD-UATE TOGETH-ER, WITH SMILES ON YOUR FACES!
THAT'S ALL I CARE ABOUT!
HEH HEH!
THAT IS VERY REAS-SURING.
3
THEN...
...THE TIME FINALLY CAME...
...AND FINALS DAY ARRIVED AGAIN.

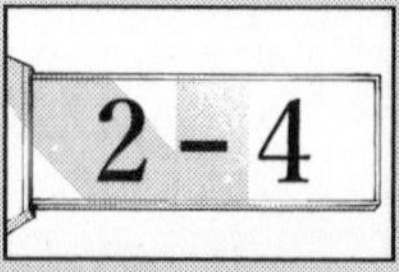
2 - 4

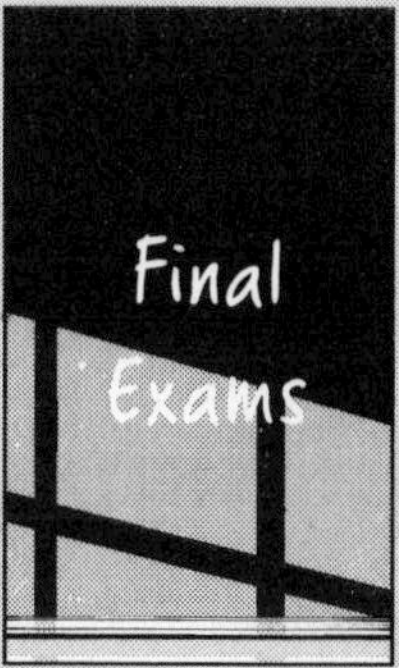
Final Exams

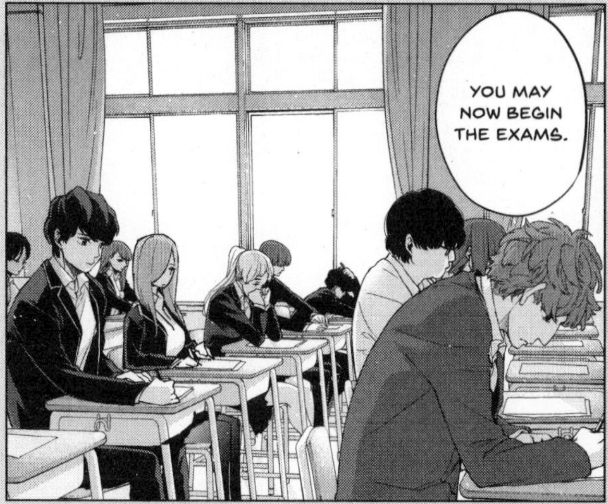
YOU MAY NOW BEGIN THE EXAMS.

CHAPTER 55
IF THE LAST EXAM WAS MIKU'S

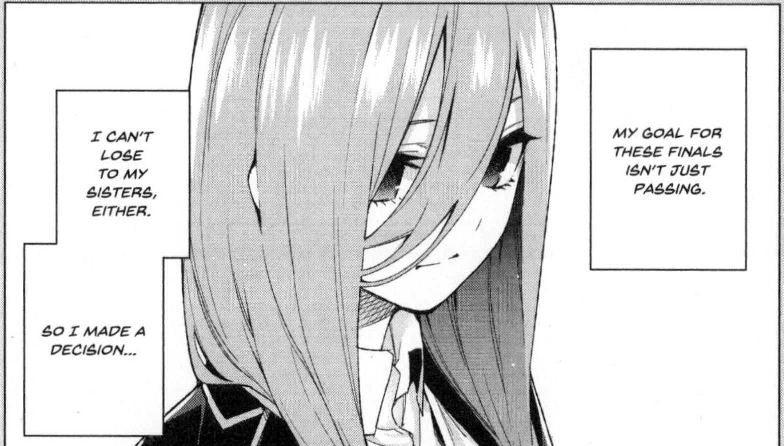
MY GOAL FOR THESE FINALS ISN'T JUST PASSING.
I CAN'T LOSE TO MY SISTERS, EITHER.
SO I MADE A DECISION...

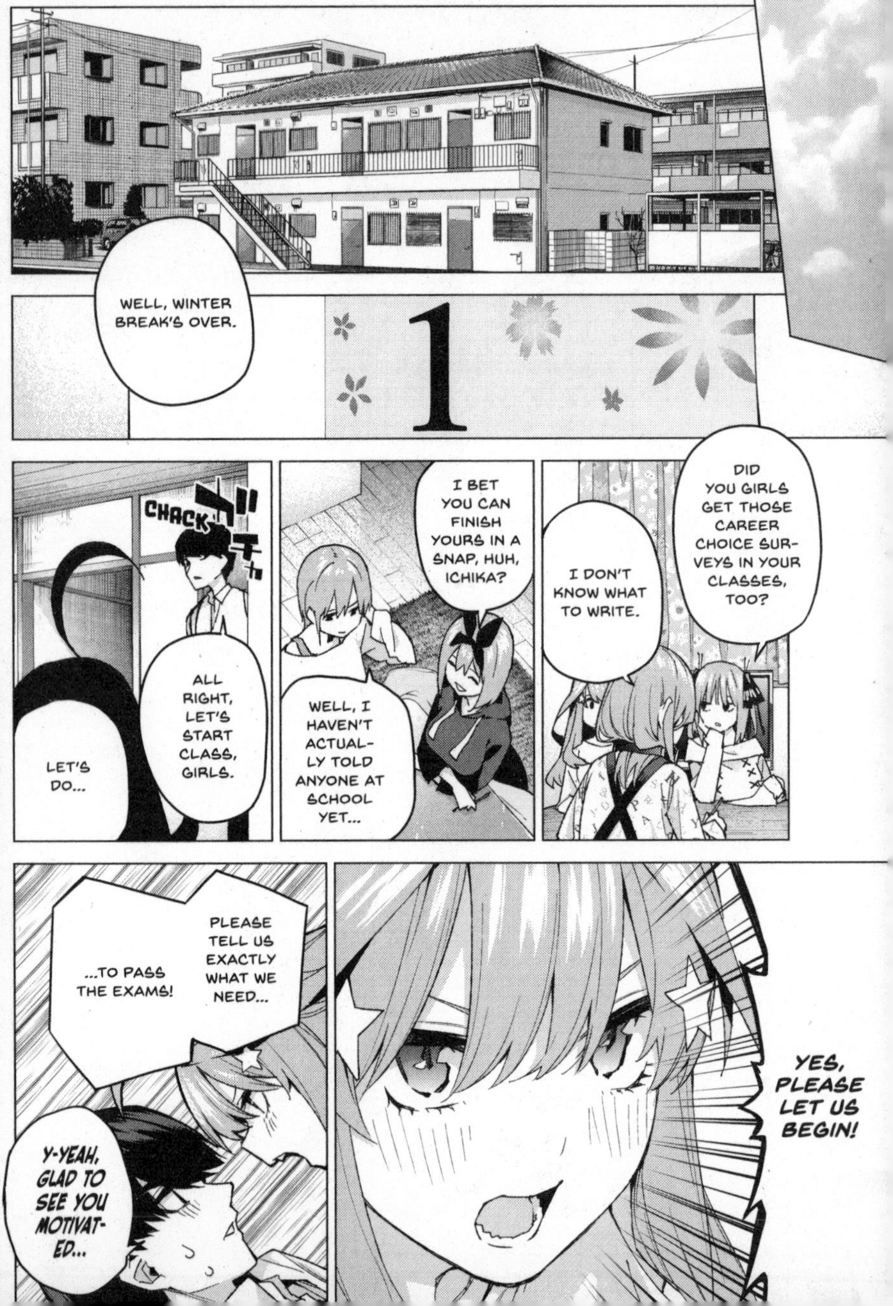
WELL, WINTER BREAK'S OVER.
1
DID YOU GIRLS GET THOSE CAREER CHOICE SURVEYS IN YOUR CLASSES, TOO?
I DON'T KNOW WHAT TO WRITE.
I BET YOU CAN FINISH YOURS IN A SNAP, HUH, ICHIKA?
WELL, I HAVEN'T ACTUALLY TOLD ANYONE AT SCHOOL YET...
CHACK
ALL RIGHT, LET'S START CLASS, GIRLS.
LET'S DO...
YES, PLEASE LET US BEGIN!
PLEASE TELL US EXACTLY WHAT WE NEED...
...TO PASS THE EXAMS!
Y-YEAH, GLAD TO SEE YOU MOTIVATED...

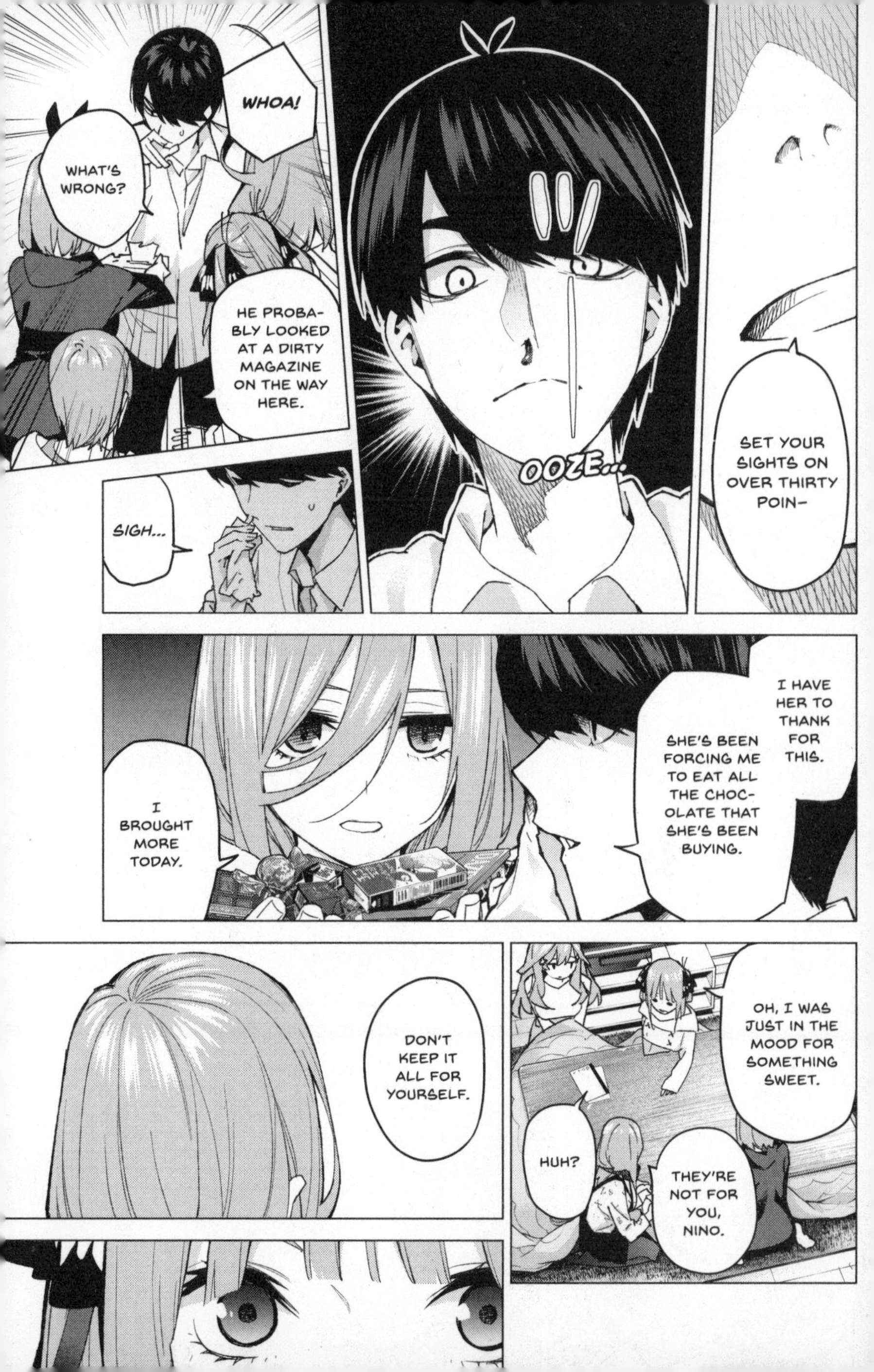
SET YOUR SIGHTS ON OVER THIRTY POIN-
OOZE...
WHOA!
WHAT'S WRONG?
HE PROBABLY LOOKED AT A DIRTY MAGAZINE ON THE WAY HERE.
SIGH...
I HAVE HER TO THANK FOR THIS.
SHE'S BEEN FORCING ME TO EAT ALL THE CHOCOLATE THAT SHE'S BEEN BUYING.
I BROUGHT MORE TODAY.
OH, I WAS JUST IN THE MOOD FOR SOMETHING SWEET.
THEY'RE NOT FOR YOU, NINO.
HUH?
DON'T KEEP IT ALL FOR YOURSELF.

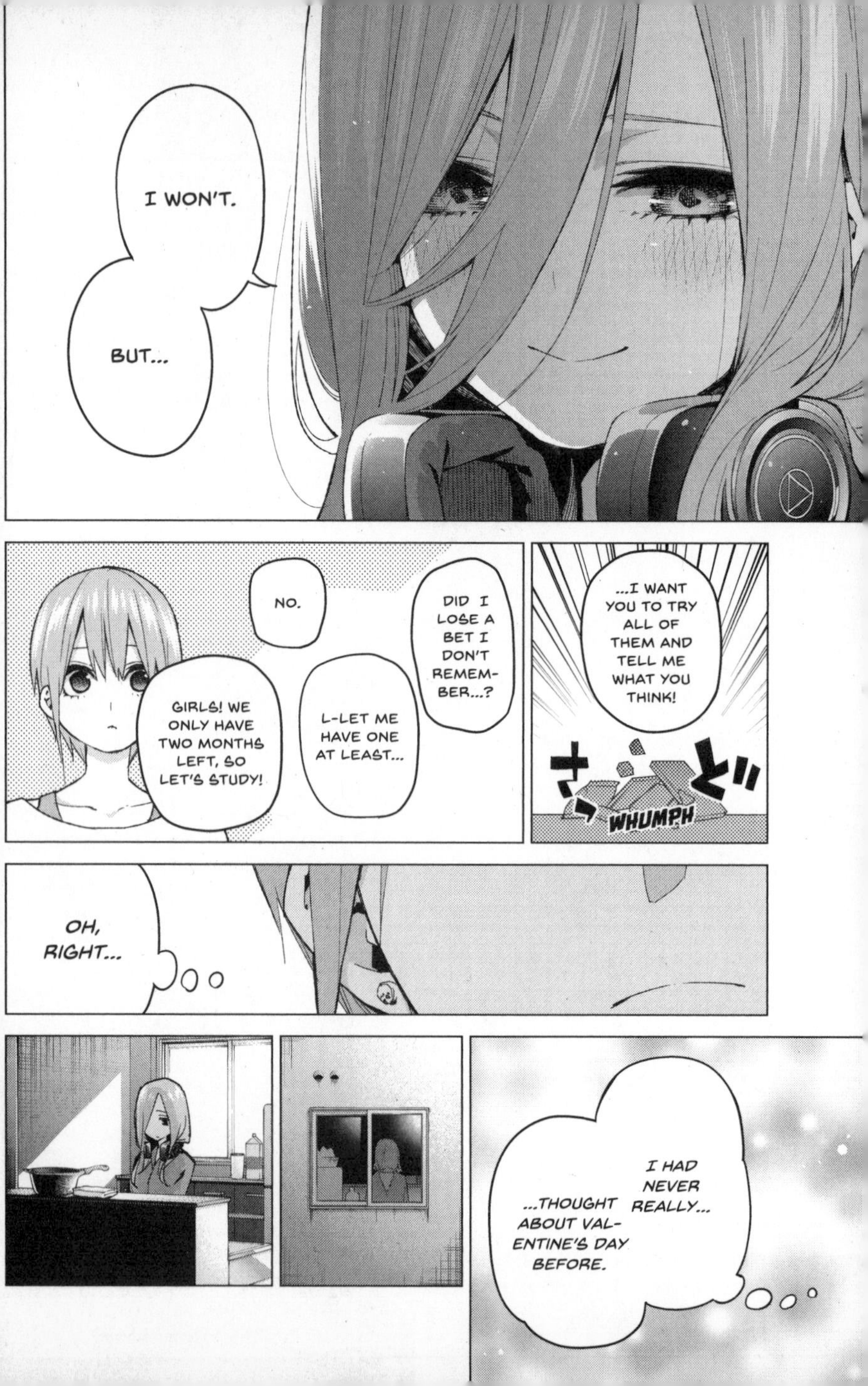
I WON'T.
BUT...
...I WANT YOU TO TRY ALL OF THEM AND TELL ME WHAT YOU THINK!
WHUMPH
DID I LOSE A BET I DON'T REMEMBER...?
NO.
L-LET ME HAVE ONE AT LEAST...
GIRLS! WE ONLY HAVE TWO MONTHS LEFT, SO LET'S STUDY!
OH, RIGHT...
I HAD NEVER REALLY... ...THOUGHT ABOUT VALENTINE'S DAY BEFORE.

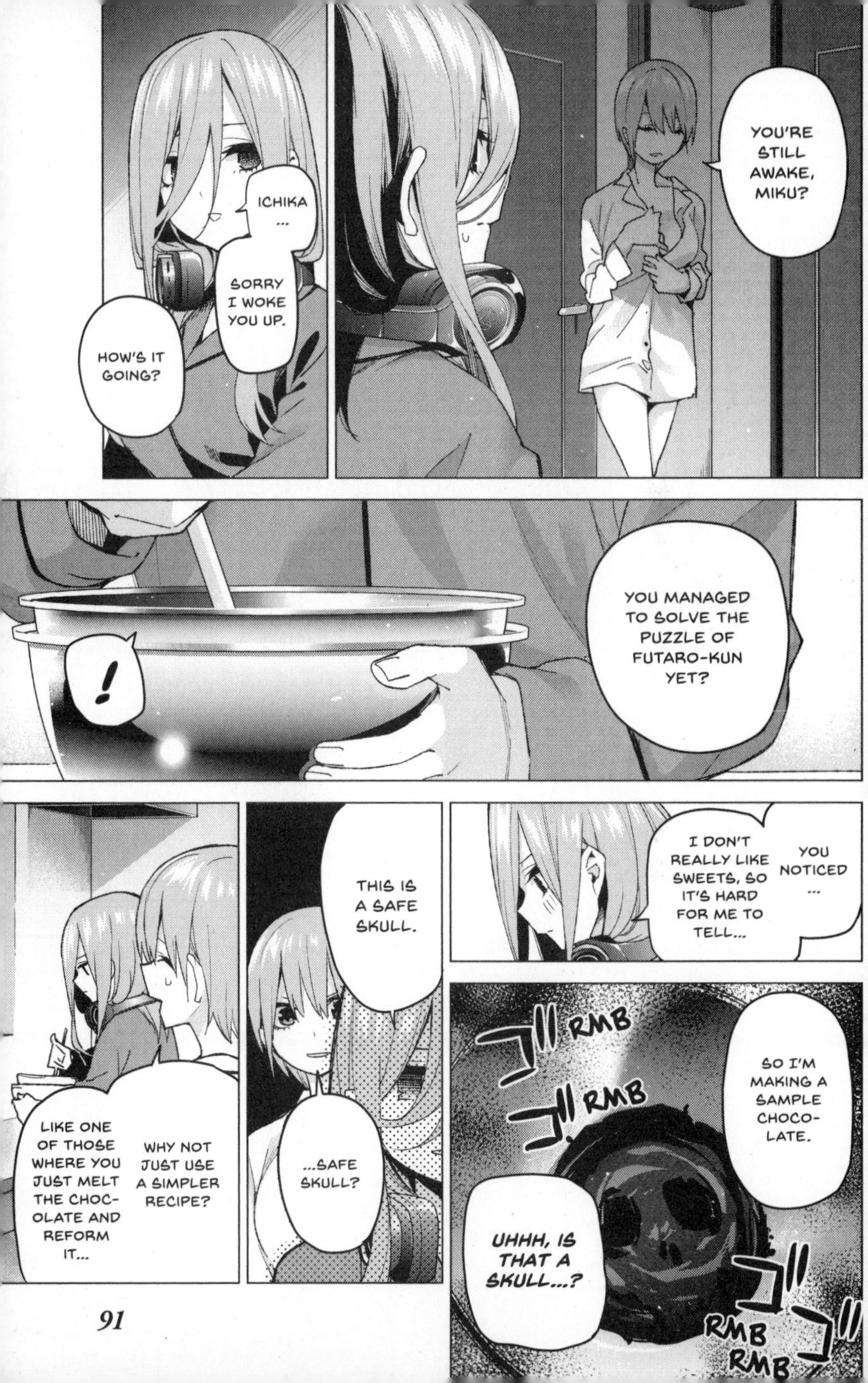
YOU'RE STILL AWAKE, MIKU?
ICHIKA ...
SORRY I WOKE YOU UP.
HOW'S IT GOING?
YOU MANAGED TO SOLVE THE PUZZLE OF FUTARO-KUN YET?
!
YOU NOTICED ...
I DON'T REALLY LIKE SWEETS, SO IT'S HARD FOR ME TO TELL...
RMB
RMB
SO I'M MAKING A SAMPLE CHOCO-LATE.
UHHH, IS THAT A SKULL...?
RMB
RMB
THIS IS A SAFE SKULL.
...SAFE SKULL?
WHY NOT JUST USE A SIMPLER RECIPE?
LIKE ONE OF THOSE WHERE YOU JUST MELT THE CHOC-OLATE AND REFORM IT...

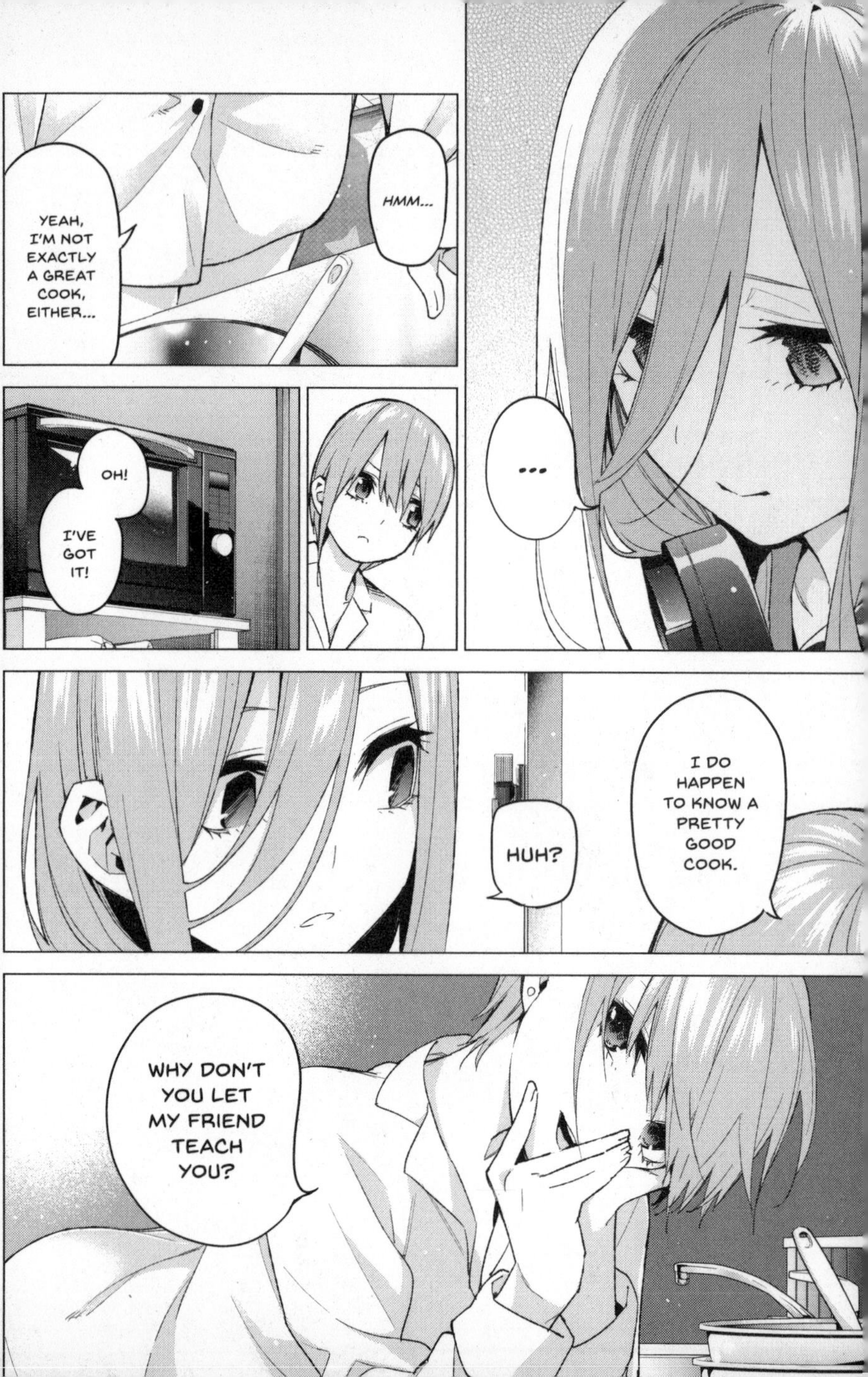
...
HMM...
YEAH, I'M NOT EXACTLY A GREAT COOK, EITHER...
OH!
I'VE GOT IT!
I DO HAPPEN TO KNOW A PRETTY GOOD COOK.
HUH?
WHY DON'T YOU LET MY FRIEND TEACH YOU?

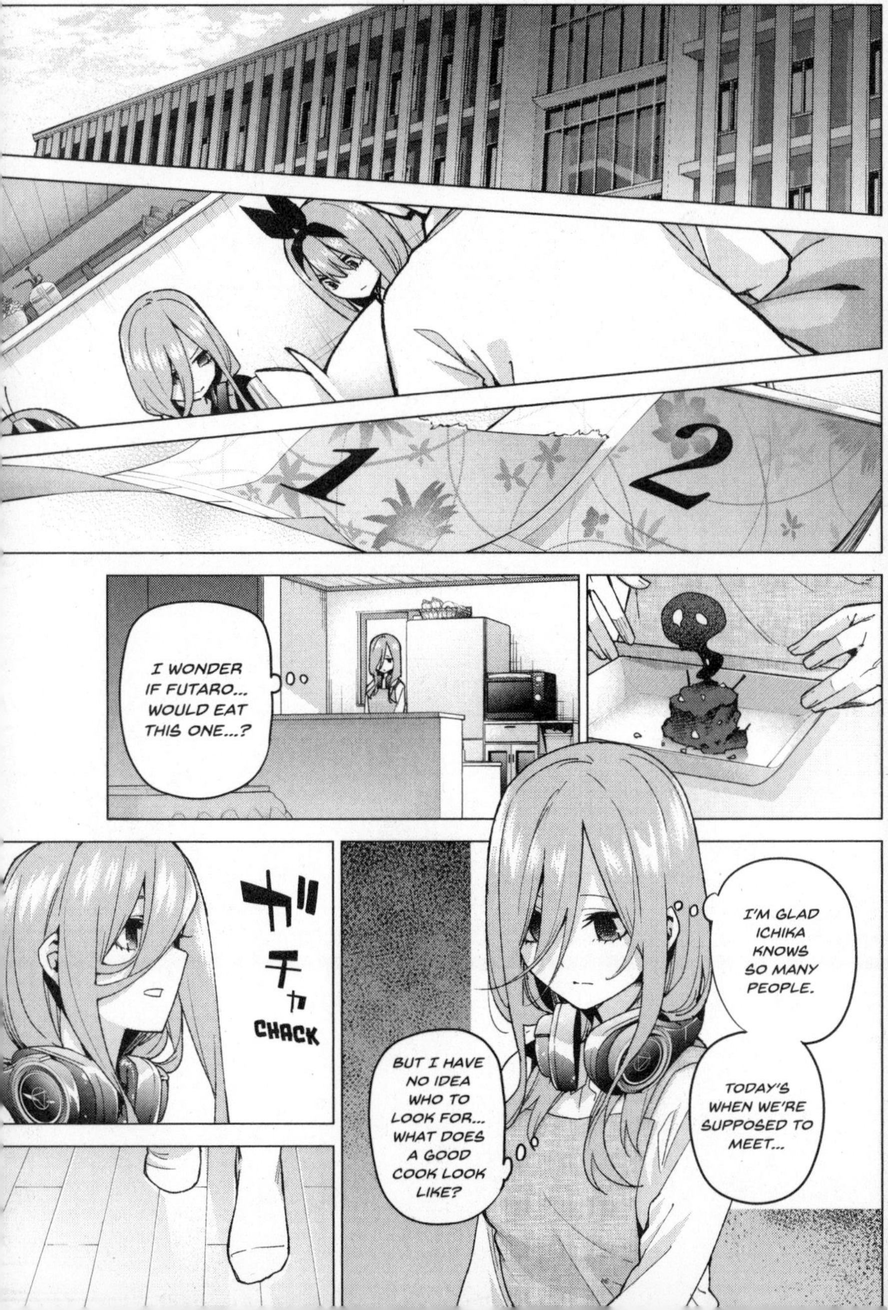
I WONDER IF FUTARO... WOULD EAT THIS ONE...?
I'M GLAD ICHIKA KNOWS SO MANY PEOPLE.
TODAY'S WHEN WE'RE SUPPOSED TO MEET...
BUT I HAVE NO IDEA WHO TO LOOK FOR... WHAT DOES A GOOD COOK LOOK LIKE?
ガチャ
CHACK

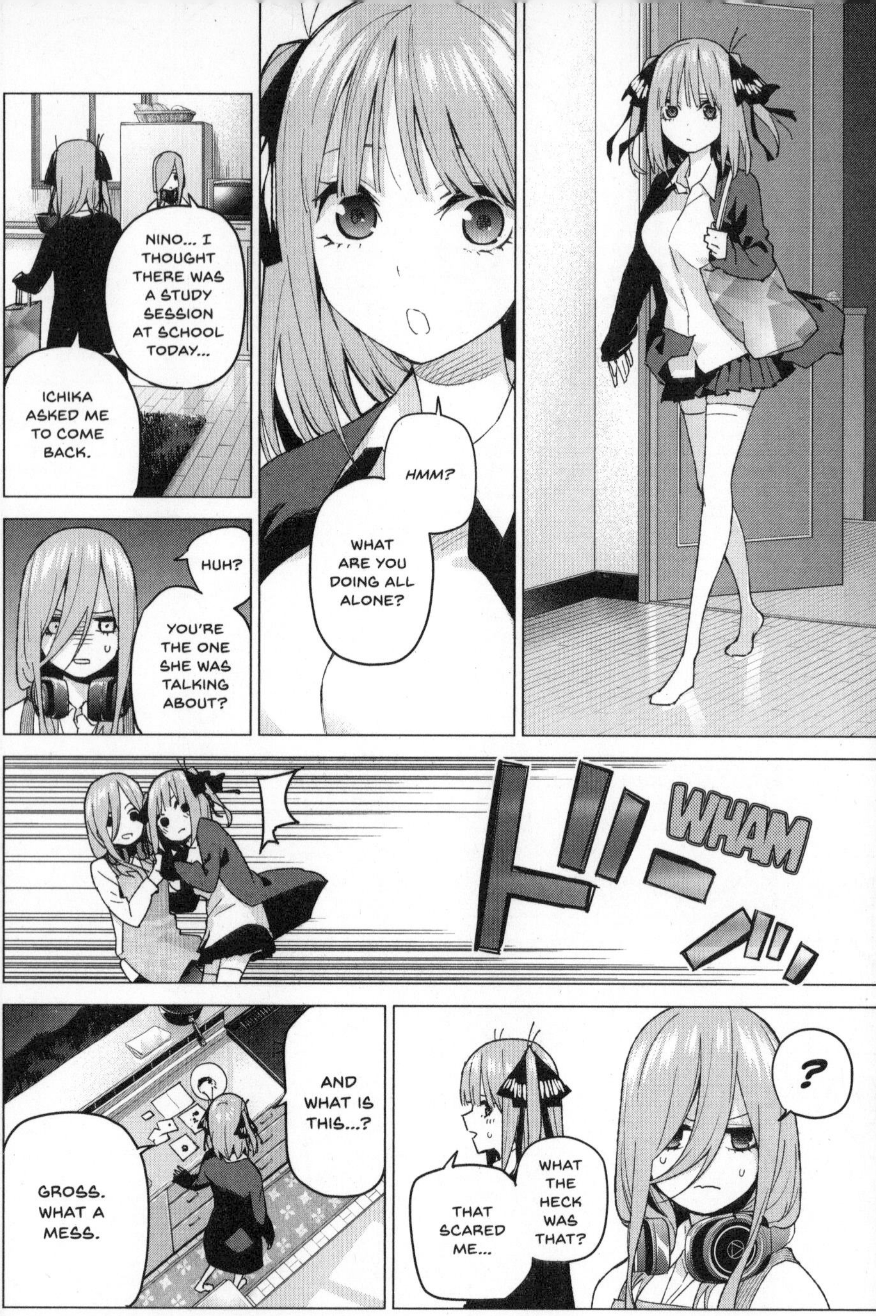
HMM?
WHAT ARE YOU DOING ALL ALONE?
NINO... I THOUGHT THERE WAS A STUDY SESSION AT SCHOOL TODAY...
ICHIKA ASKED ME TO COME BACK.
HUH?
YOU'RE THE ONE SHE WAS TALKING ABOUT?
WHAM
!
?
WHAT THE HECK WAS THAT?
THAT SCARED ME...
AND WHAT IS THIS...?
GROSS. WHAT A MESS.

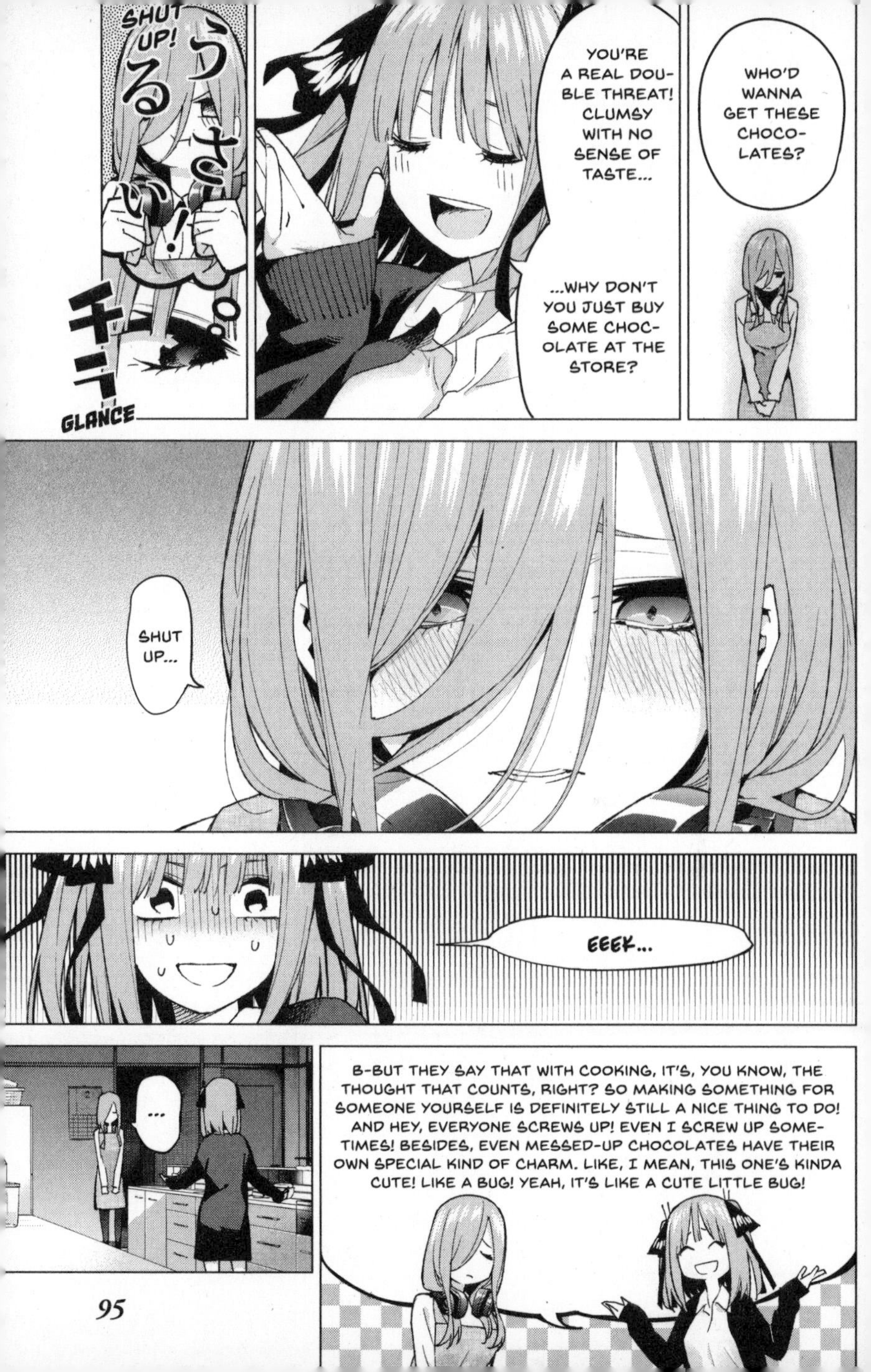
WHO'D WANNA GET THESE CHOCOLATES?
YOU'RE A REAL DOUBLE THREAT! CLUMSY WITH NO SENSE OF TASTE...
...WHY DON'T YOU JUST BUY SOME CHOCOLATE AT THE STORE?
うるさい!
SHUT UP!
チラ
GLANCE
SHUT UP...
EEEK...
B-BUT THEY SAY THAT WITH COOKING, IT'S, YOU KNOW, THE THOUGHT THAT COUNTS, RIGHT? SO MAKING SOMETHING FOR SOMEONE YOURSELF IS DEFINITELY STILL A NICE THING TO DO! AND HEY, EVERYONE SCREWS UP! EVEN I SCREW UP SOMETIMES! BESIDES, EVEN MESSED-UP CHOCOLATES HAVE THEIR OWN SPECIAL KIND OF CHARM. LIKE, I MEAN, THIS ONE'S KINDA CUTE! LIKE A BUG! YEAH, IT'S LIKE A CUTE LITTLE BUG!
...

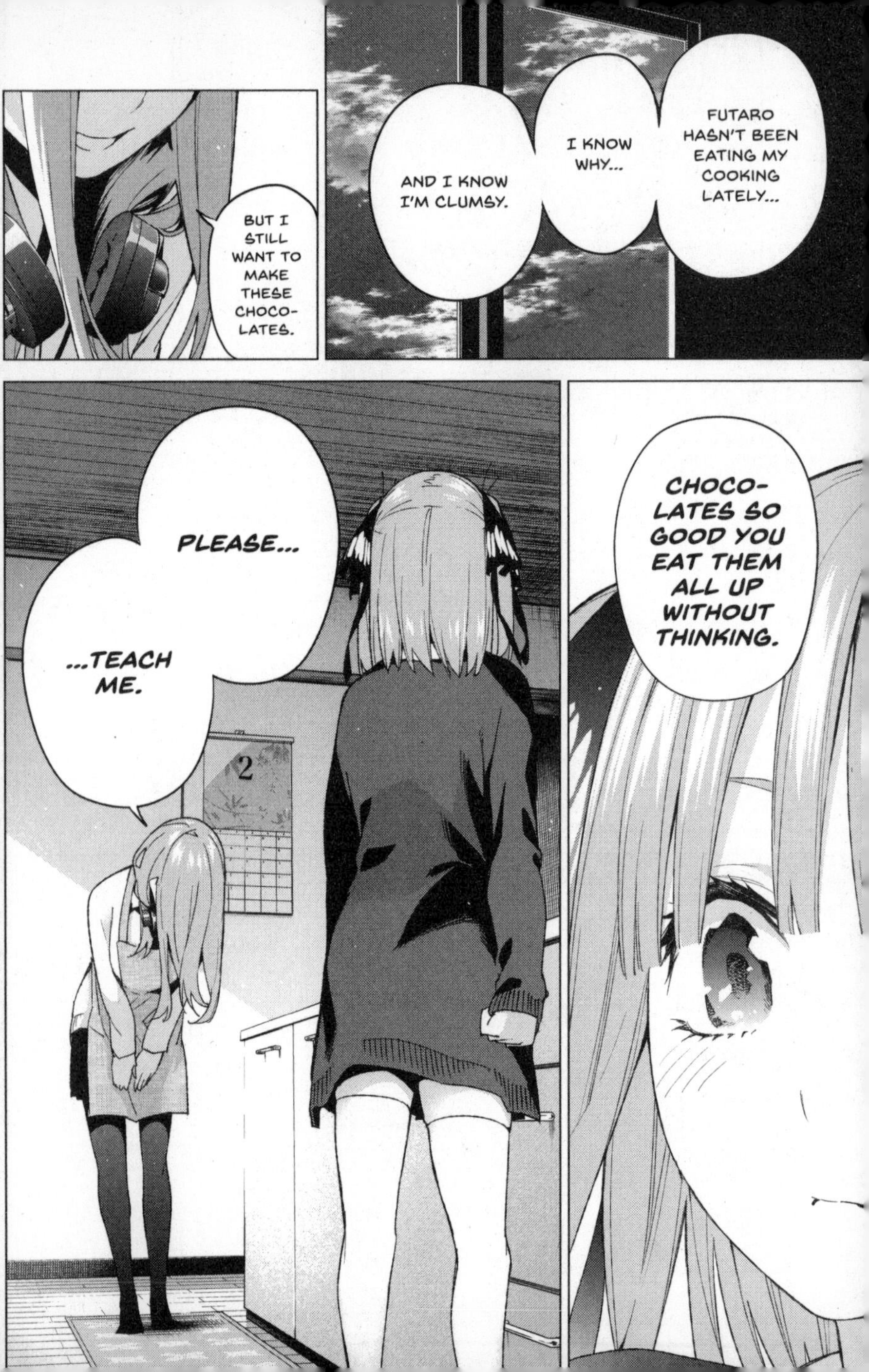
FUTARO HASN'T BEEN EATING MY COOKING LATELY...
I KNOW WHY...
AND I KNOW I'M CLUMSY.
BUT I STILL WANT TO MAKE THESE CHOCO-LATES.
CHOCO-LATES SO GOOD YOU EAT THEM ALL UP WITHOUT THINKING.
PLEASE...
...TEACH ME.
2

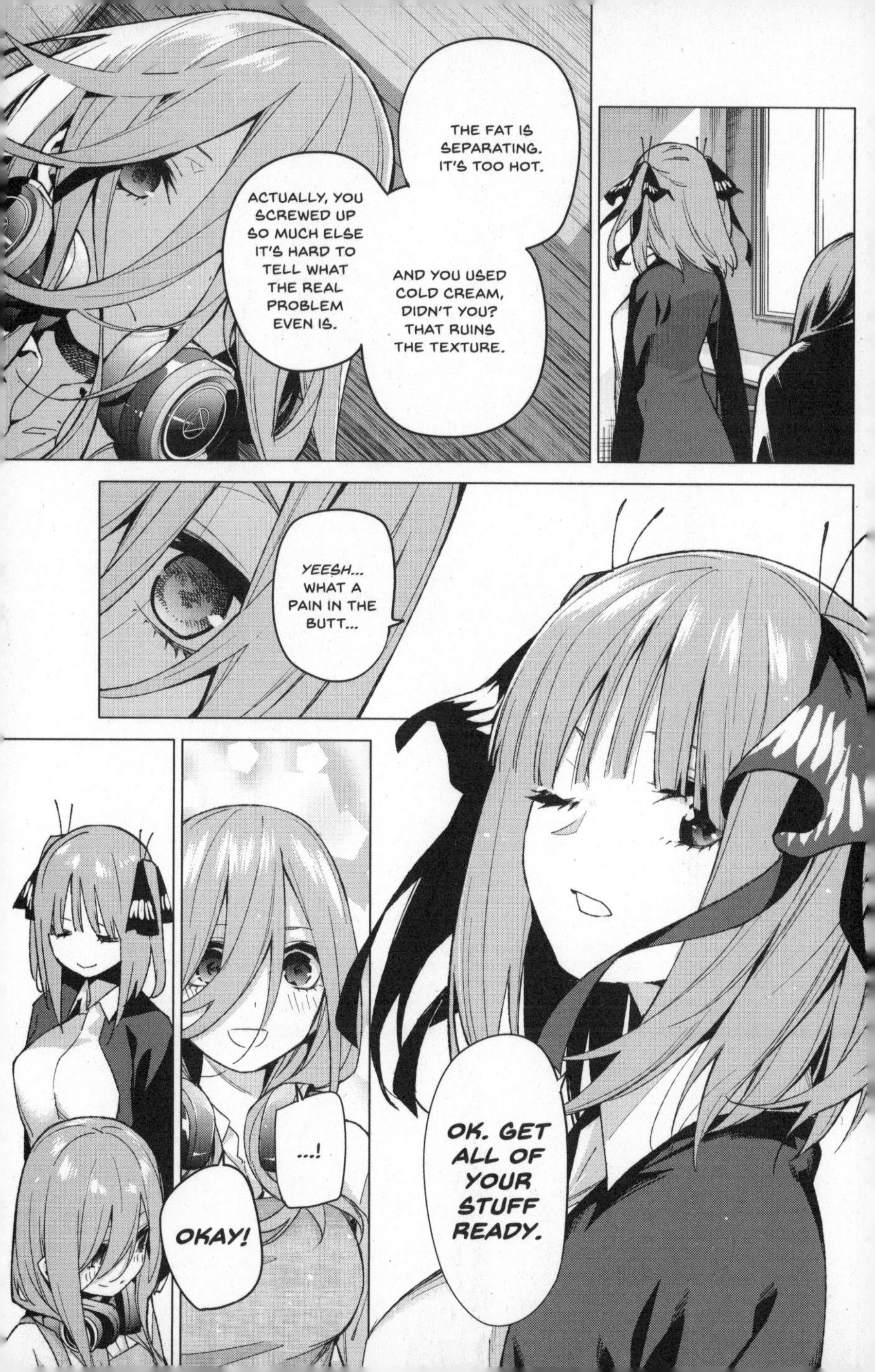
THE FAT IS SEPARATING. IT'S TOO HOT.
AND YOU USED COLD CREAM, DIDN'T YOU? THAT RUINS THE TEXTURE.
ACTUALLY, YOU SCREWED UP SO MUCH ELSE IT'S HARD TO TELL WHAT THE REAL PROBLEM EVEN IS.
OK. GET ALL OF YOUR STUFF READY.
YEESH... WHAT A PAIN IN THE BUTT...
...!
OKAY!

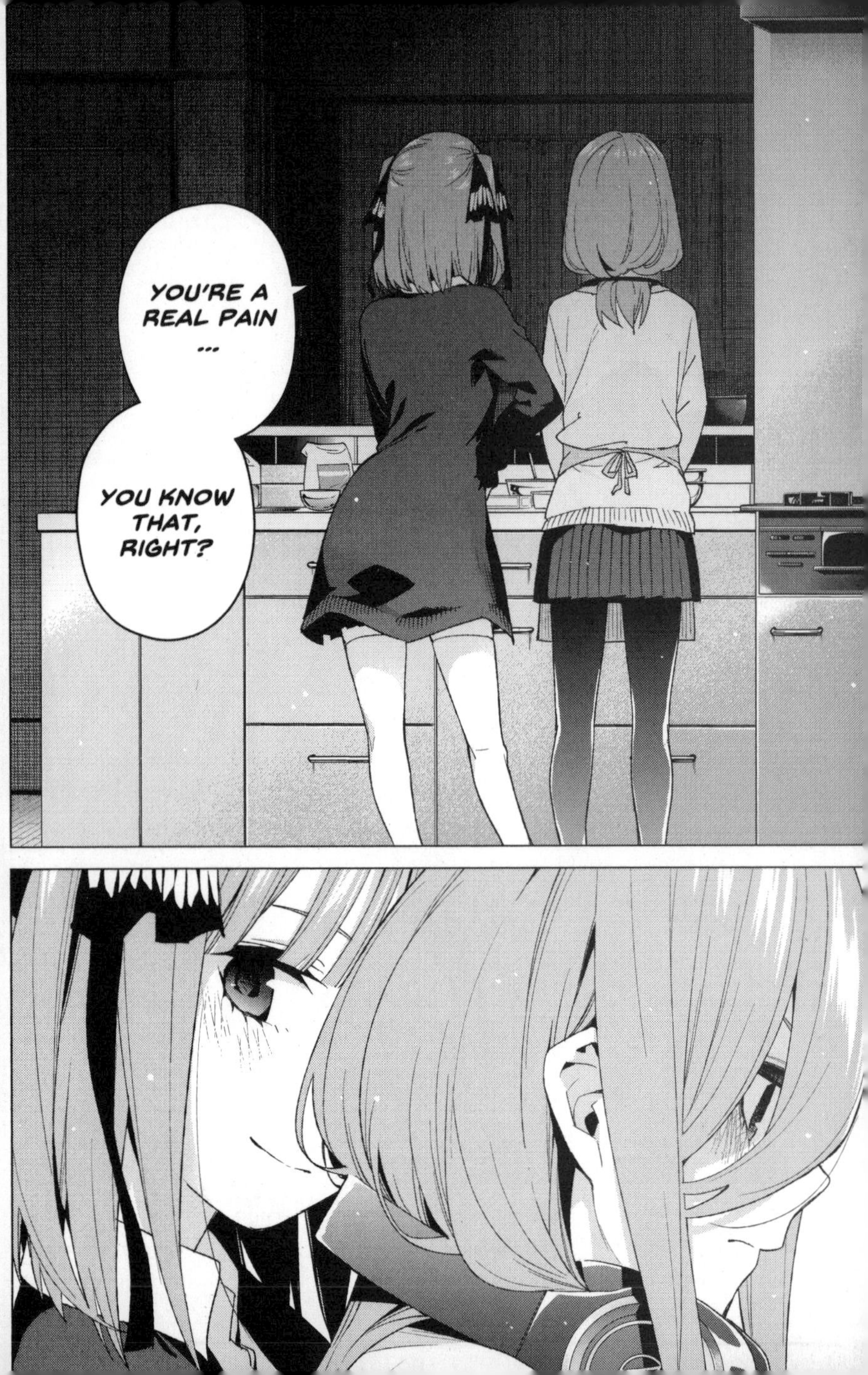
YOU'RE A REAL PAIN ...
YOU KNOW THAT, RIGHT?

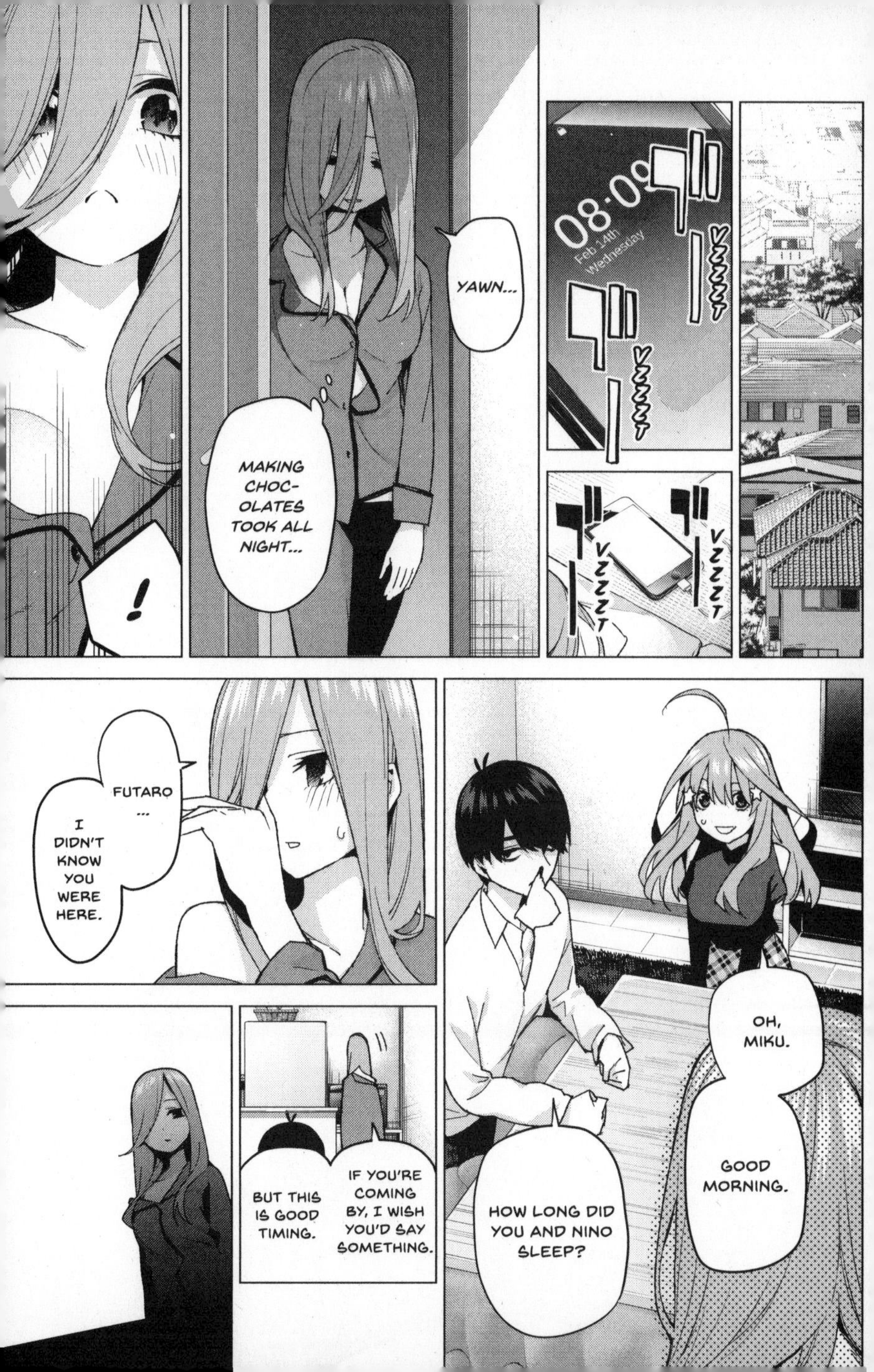
08:00
Feb 14th
Wednesday
VZZZT
VZZZT
VZZZT
VZZZT
YAWN...
MAKING CHOC-OLATES TOOK ALL NIGHT...
!
OH, MIKU.
GOOD MORNING.
HOW LONG DID YOU AND NINO SLEEP?
FUTARO ...
I DIDN'T KNOW YOU WERE HERE.
IF YOU'RE COMING BY, I WISH YOU'D SAY SOMETHING.
BUT THIS IS GOOD TIMING.

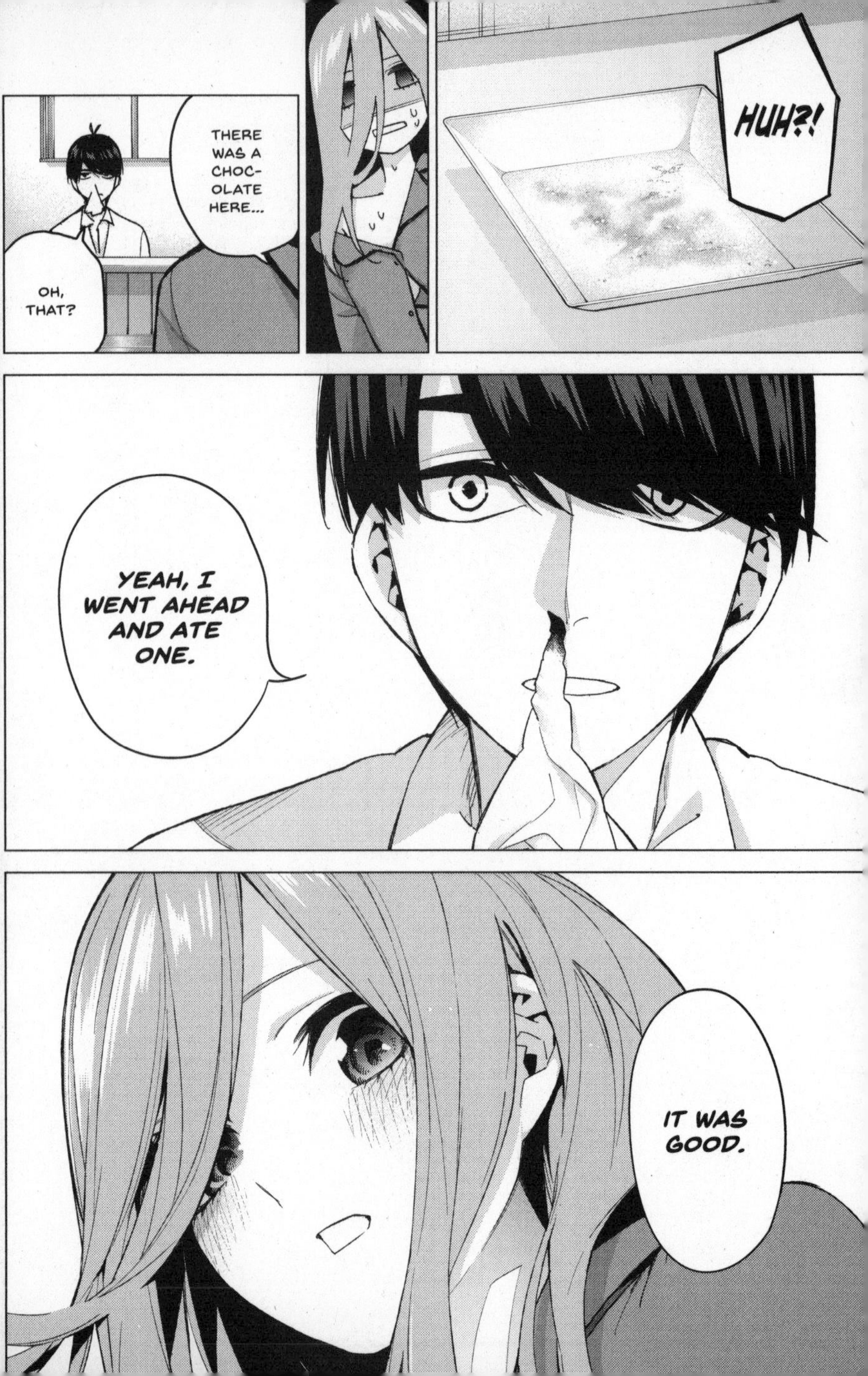
HUH?!
THERE WAS A CHOCOLATE HERE...
OH, THAT?
YEAH, I WENT AHEAD AND ATE ONE.
IT WAS GOOD.

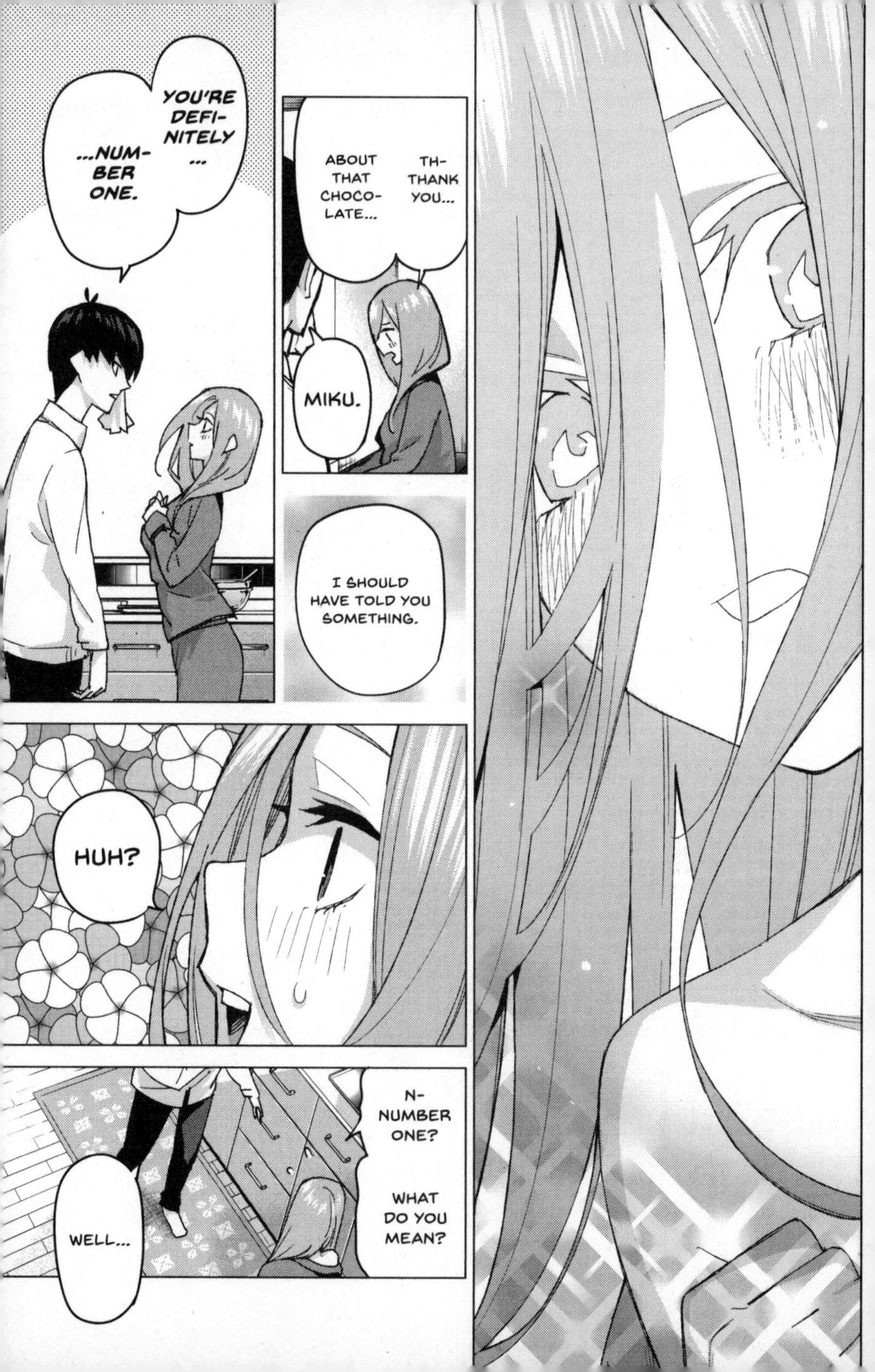
TH-THANK YOU... ABOUT THAT CHOCOLATE...
MIKU.
I SHOULD HAVE TOLD YOU SOMETHING.
YOU'RE DEFINITELY ... ...NUMBER ONE.
HUH?
N-NUMBER ONE? WHAT DO YOU MEAN?
WELL...

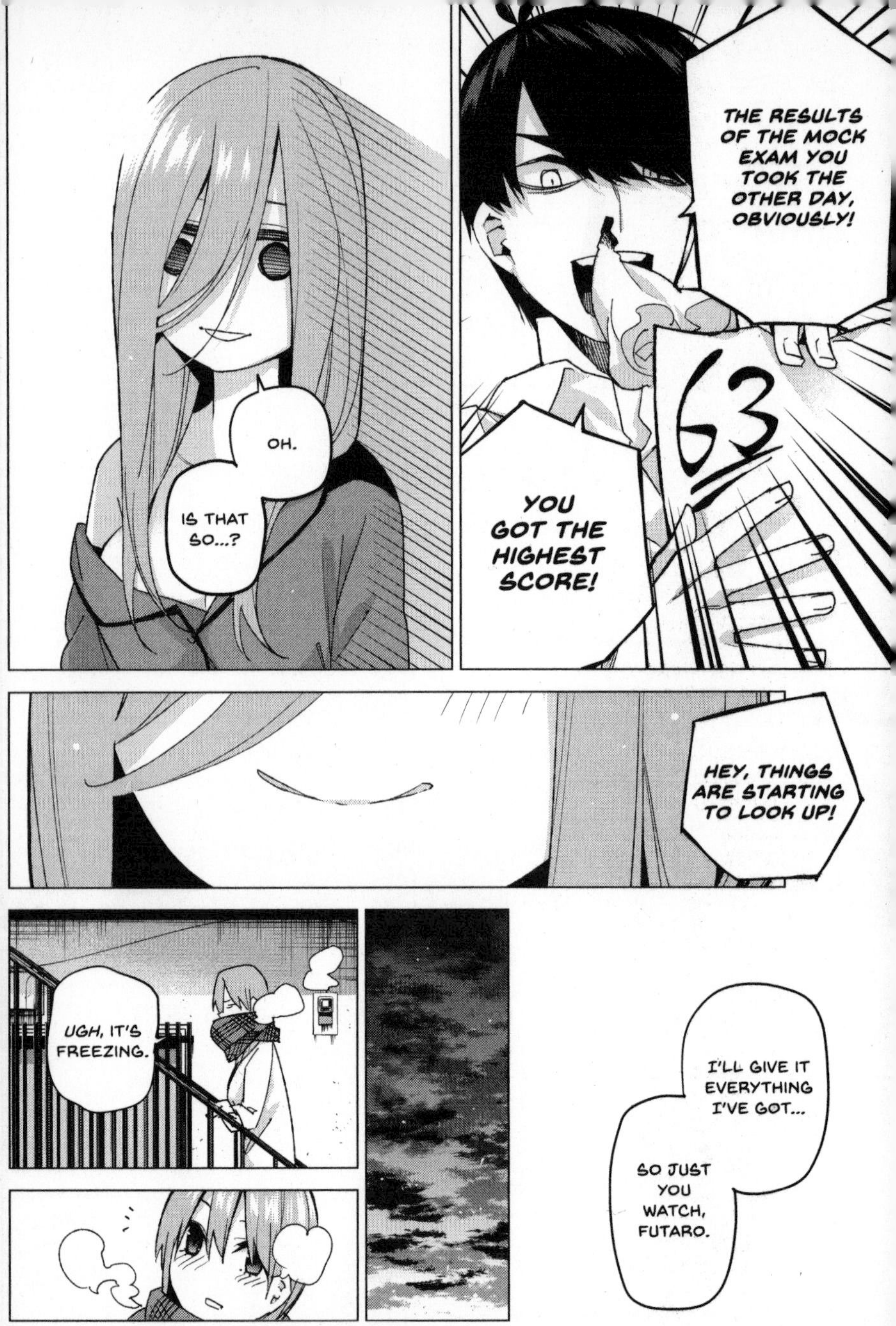
THE RESULTS OF THE MOCK EXAM YOU TOOK THE OTHER DAY, OBVIOUSLY!
63
YOU GOT THE HIGHEST SCORE!
OH.
IS THAT SO...?
HEY, THINGS ARE STARTING TO LOOK UP!
I'LL GIVE IT EVERYTHING I'VE GOT...
SO JUST YOU WATCH, FUTARO.
UGH, IT'S FREEZING.

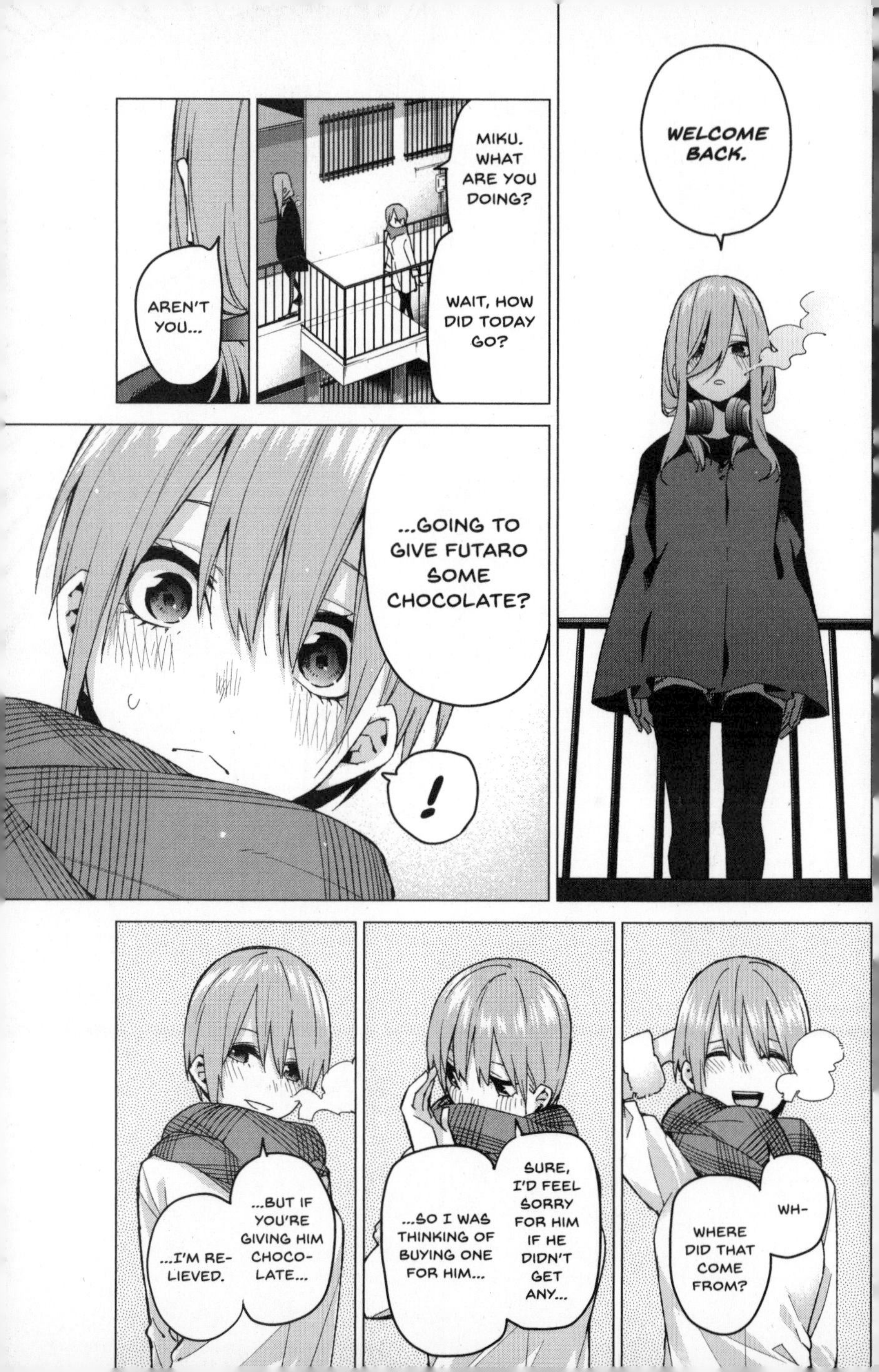
WELCOME BACK.
MIKU. WHAT ARE YOU DOING?
WAIT, HOW DID TODAY GO?
AREN'T YOU...
...GOING TO GIVE FUTARO SOME CHOCOLATE?
!
WH-
WHERE DID THAT COME FROM?
SURE, I'D FEEL SORRY FOR HIM IF HE DIDN'T GET ANY...
...SO I WAS THINKING OF BUYING ONE FOR HIM...
...BUT IF YOU'RE GIVING HIM CHOCO-LATE...
...I'M RE-LIEVED.

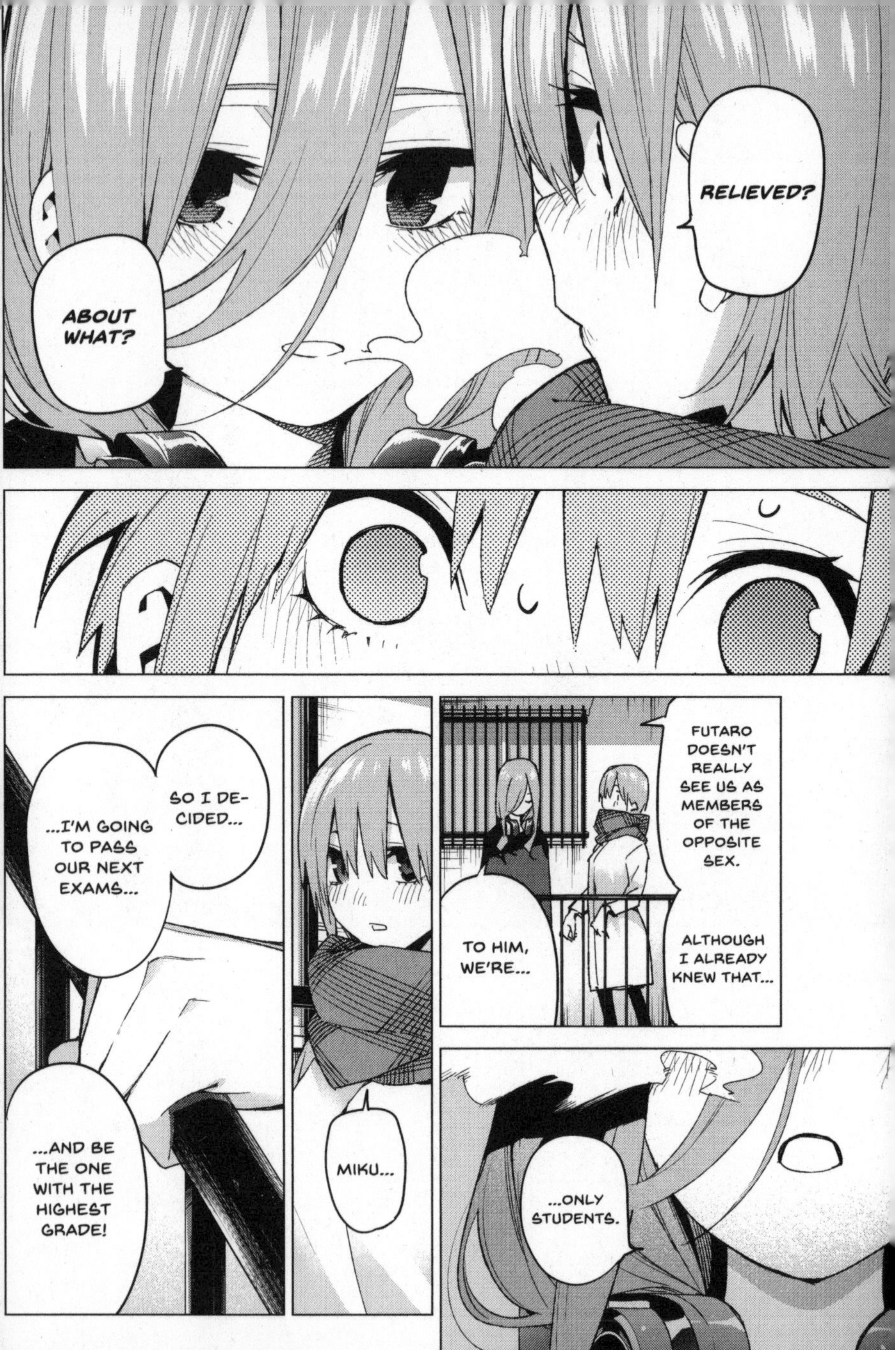
RELIEVED?
ABOUT WHAT?
FUTARO DOESN'T REALLY SEE US AS MEMBERS OF THE OPPOSITE SEX.
ALTHOUGH I ALREADY KNEW THAT...
TO HIM, WE'RE...
...ONLY STUDENTS.
MIKU...
SO I DE-CIDED...
...I'M GOING TO PASS OUR NEXT EXAMS...
...AND BE THE ONE WITH THE HIGHEST GRADE!

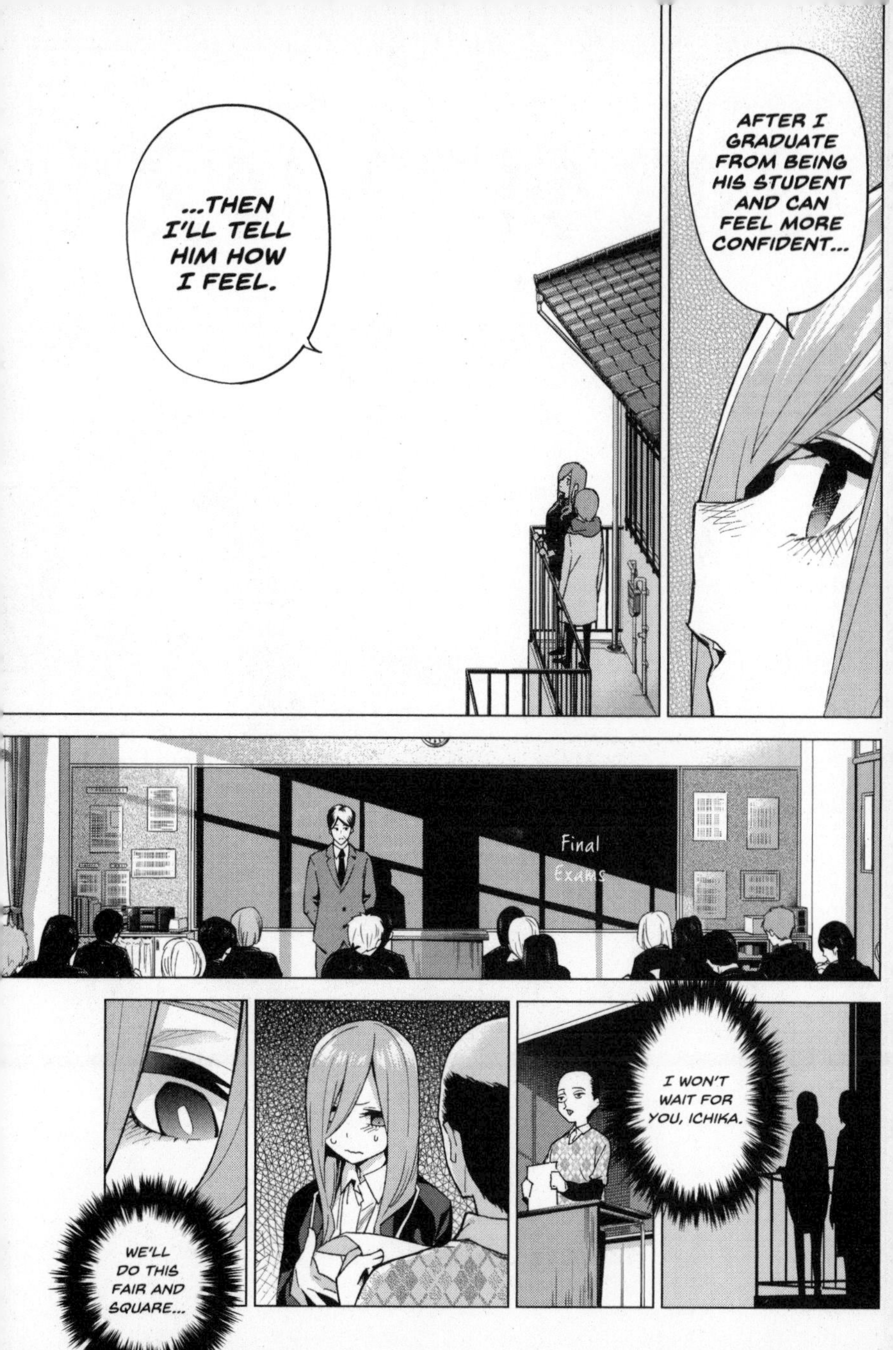
AFTER I GRADUATE FROM BEING HIS STUDENT AND CAN FEEL MORE CONFIDENT...
...THEN I'LL TELL HIM HOW I FEEL.
Final Exams
I WON'T WAIT FOR YOU, ICHIKA.
WE'LL DO THIS FAIR AND SQUARE...

Lan-guage Arts	Math	Science	Social Studies	English	Total
43	48	41	72	34	238

FIRST COME, FIRST SERVED!

VERY WELL DONE

PASSED

Miku Nakano

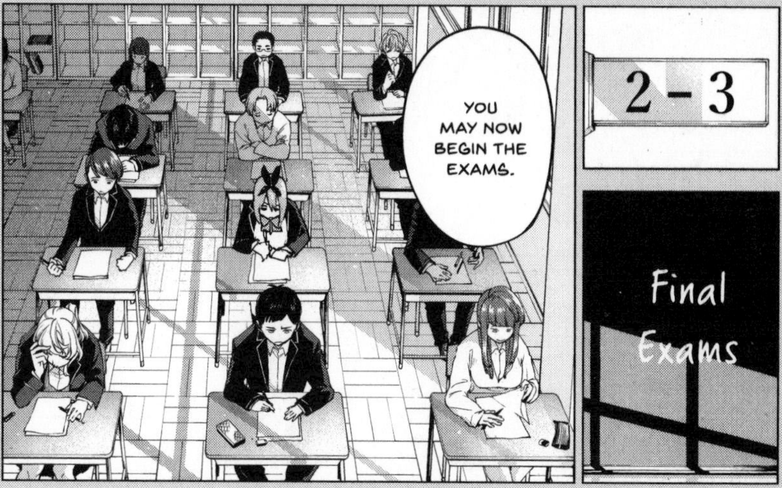
2-3
Final Exams
YOU MAY NOW BEGIN THE EXAMS.

CHAPTER 56
IF THE LAST EXAM WAS YOTSUBA'S

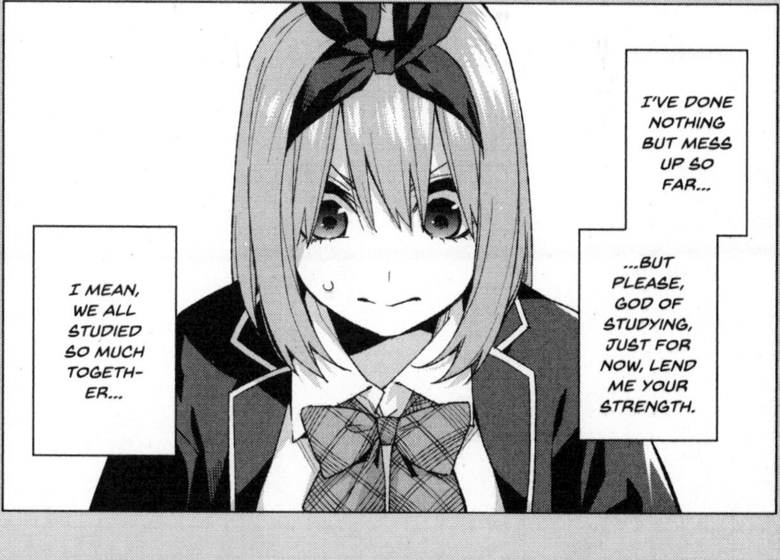
I'VE DONE NOTHING BUT MESS UP SO FAR...
...BUT PLEASE, GOD OF STUDYING, JUST FOR NOW, LEND ME YOUR STRENGTH.
I MEAN, WE ALL STUDIED SO MUCH TOGETH-ER...

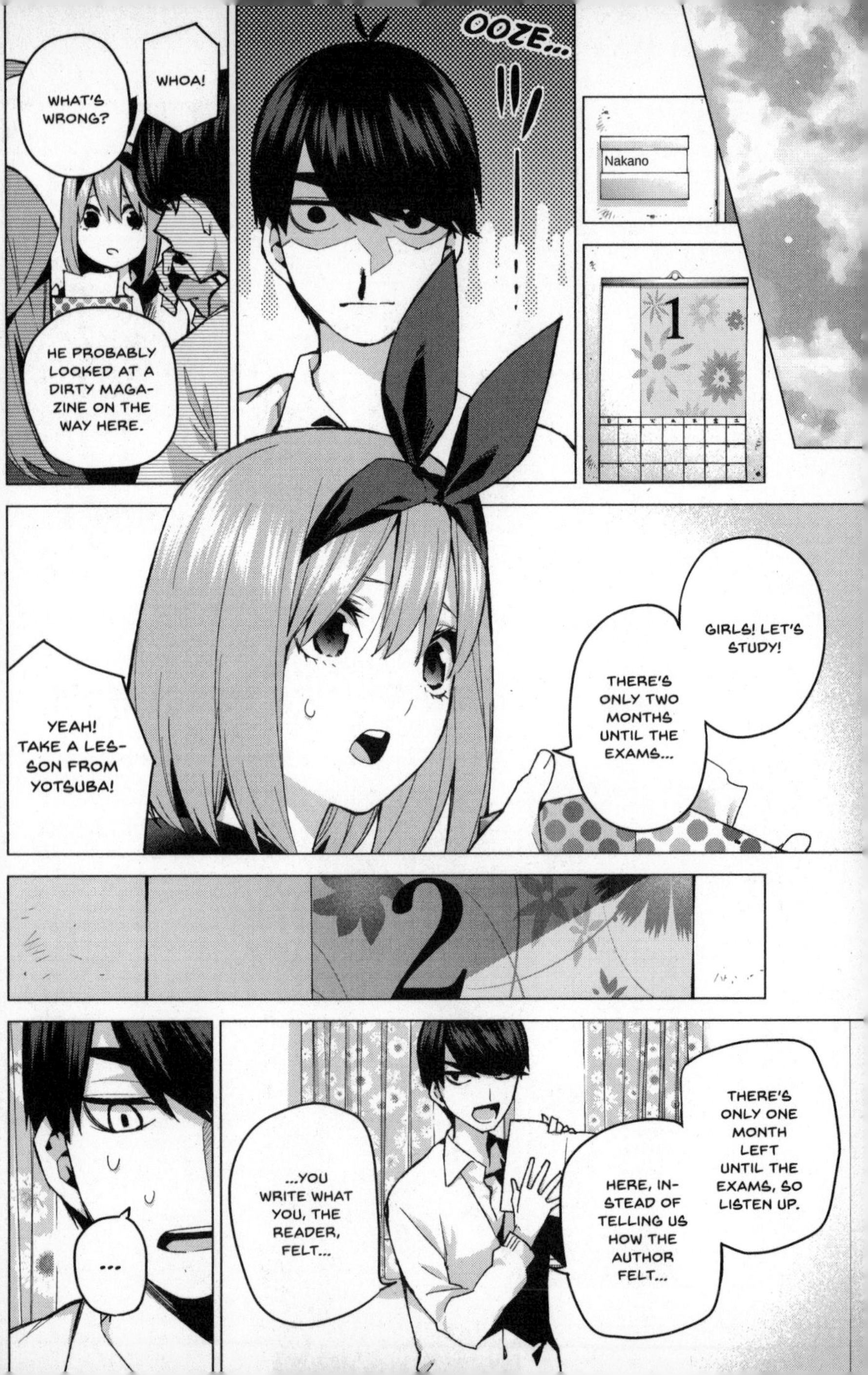
Nakano
1
OOZE...
WHOA!
WHAT'S WRONG?
HE PROBABLY LOOKED AT A DIRTY MAGA-ZINE ON THE WAY HERE.
GIRLS! LET'S STUDY!
THERE'S ONLY TWO MONTHS UNTIL THE EXAMS...
YEAH! TAKE A LES-SON FROM YOTSUBA!
2
THERE'S ONLY ONE MONTH LEFT UNTIL THE EXAMS, SO LISTEN UP.
HERE, IN-STEAD OF TELLING US HOW THE AUTHOR FELT...
...YOU WRITE WHAT YOU, THE READER, FELT...
...

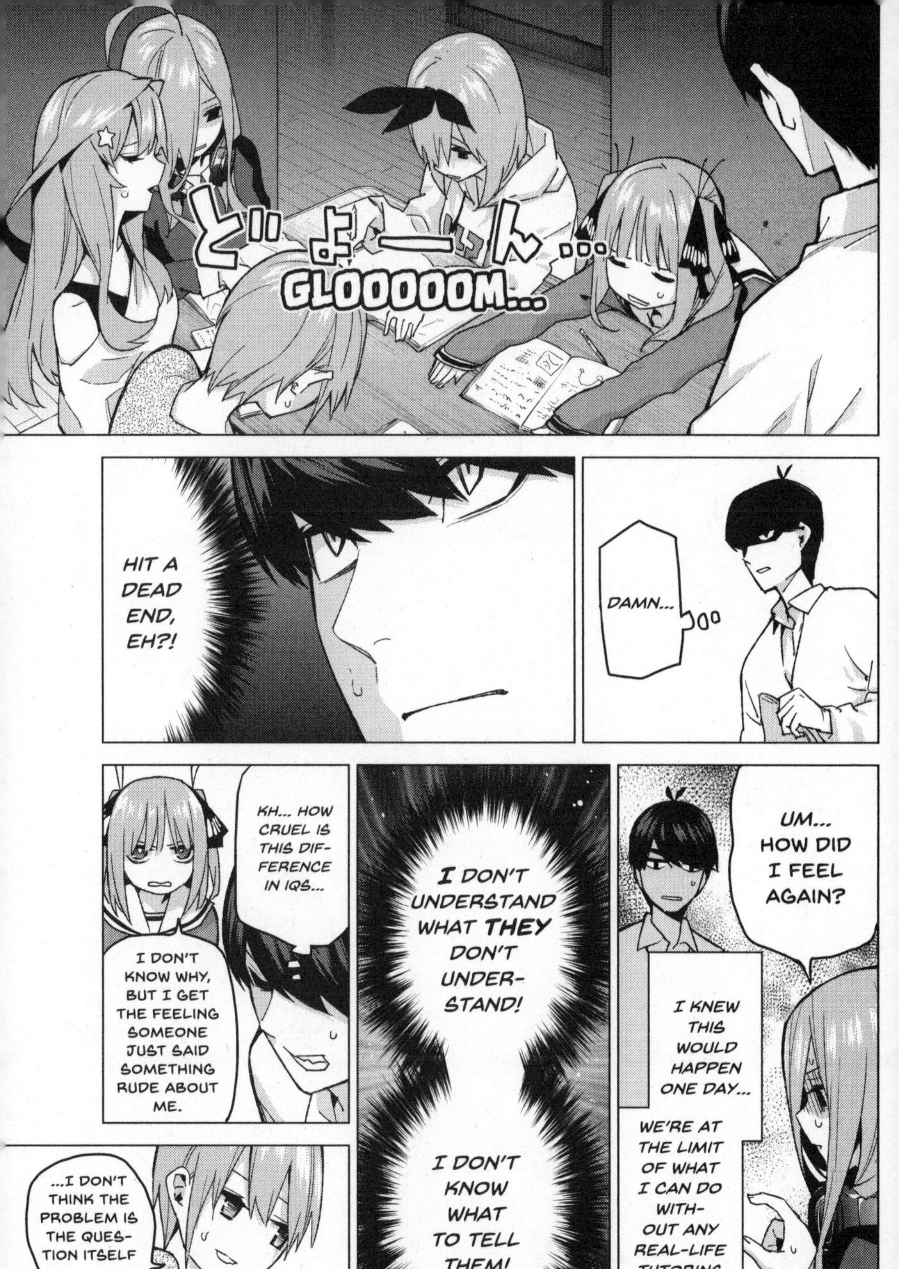
どよーーん...
GLOOOOOM...
DAMN...
HIT A DEAD END, EH?!
UM... HOW DID I FEEL AGAIN?
I KNEW THIS WOULD HAPPEN ONE DAY...
WE'RE AT THE LIMIT OF WHAT I CAN DO WITHOUT ANY REAL-LIFE TUTORING SKILLS...
I DON'T UNDERSTAND WHAT THEY DON'T UNDERSTAND!
I DON'T KNOW WHAT TO TELL THEM!
KH... HOW CRUEL IS THIS DIFFERENCE IN IQS...
I DON'T KNOW WHY, BUT I GET THE FEELING SOMEONE JUST SAID SOMETHING RUDE ABOUT ME.
...I DON'T THINK THE PROBLEM IS THE QUESTION ITSELF...

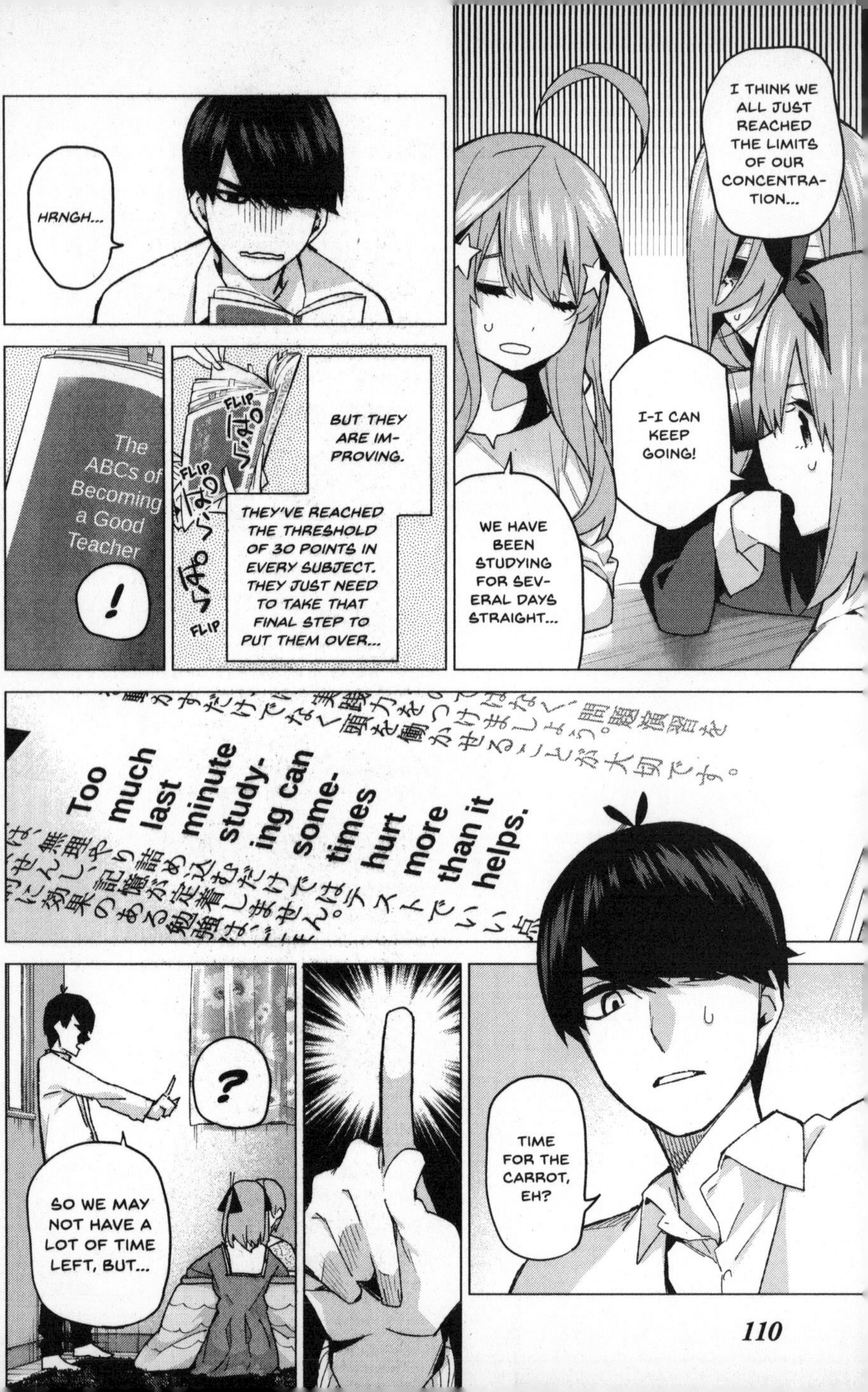

I THINK WE ALL JUST REACHED THE LIMITS OF OUR CONCENTRATION...
I-I CAN KEEP GOING!
WE HAVE BEEN STUDYING FOR SEVERAL DAYS STRAIGHT...
HRNGH...
BUT THEY ARE IMPROVING.
THEY'VE REACHED THE THRESHOLD OF 30 POINTS IN EVERY SUBJECT. THEY JUST NEED TO TAKE THAT FINAL STEP TO PUT THEM OVER...
FLIP
FLIP
FLIP
The ABCs of Becoming a Good Teacher
!
Too much last minute studying can sometimes hurt more than it helps.
TIME FOR THE CARROT, EH?
?
SO WE MAY NOT HAVE A LOT OF TIME LEFT, BUT...

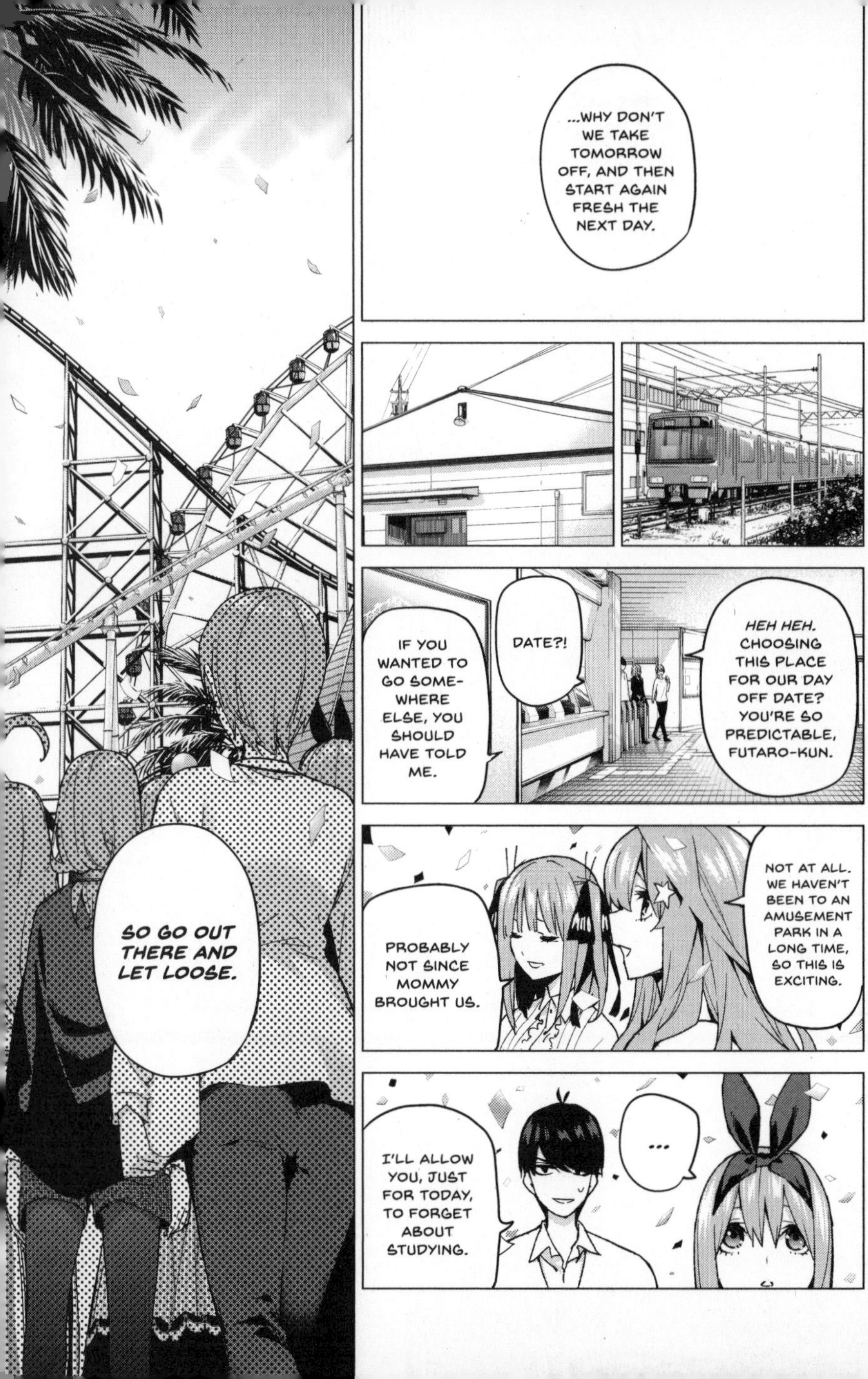
...WHY DON'T WE TAKE TOMORROW OFF, AND THEN START AGAIN FRESH THE NEXT DAY.
HEH HEH. CHOOSING THIS PLACE FOR OUR DAY OFF DATE? YOU'RE SO PREDICTABLE, FUTARO-KUN.
DATE?!
IF YOU WANTED TO GO SOME-WHERE ELSE, YOU SHOULD HAVE TOLD ME.
NOT AT ALL. WE HAVEN'T BEEN TO AN AMUSEMENT PARK IN A LONG TIME, SO THIS IS EXCITING.
PROBABLY NOT SINCE MOMMY BROUGHT US.
...
I'LL ALLOW YOU, JUST FOR TODAY, TO FORGET ABOUT STUDYING.
SO GO OUT THERE AND LET LOOSE.

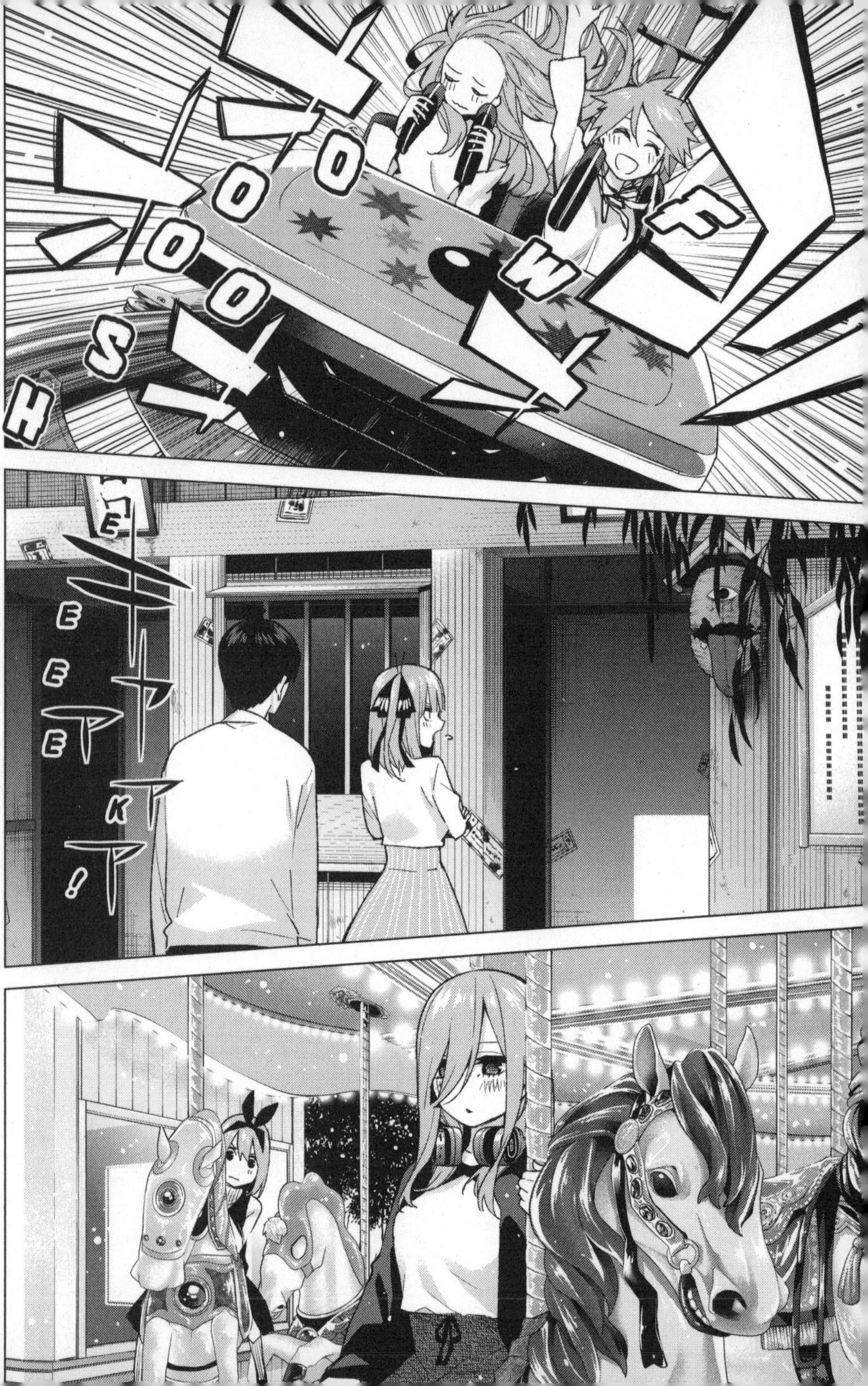
FWOOOOSH
EEEEK!

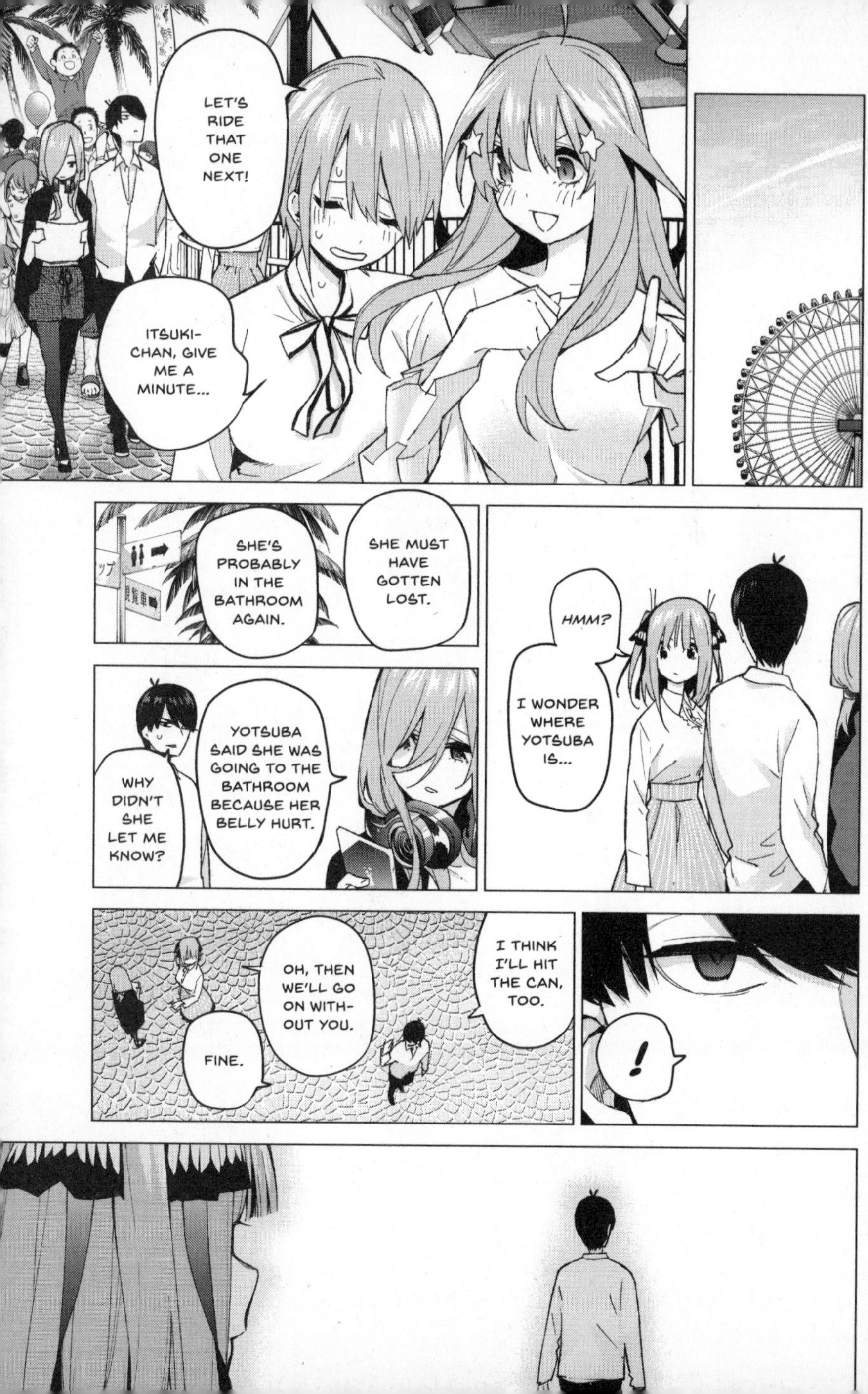
LET'S RIDE THAT ONE NEXT!
ITSUKI-CHAN, GIVE ME A MINUTE...
HMM?
I WONDER WHERE YOTSUBA IS...
SHE MUST HAVE GOTTEN LOST.
SHE'S PROBABLY IN THE BATHROOM AGAIN.
YOTSUBA SAID SHE WAS GOING TO THE BATHROOM BECAUSE HER BELLY HURT.
WHY DIDN'T SHE LET ME KNOW?
!
I THINK I'LL HIT THE CAN, TOO.
OH, THEN WE'LL GO ON WITH-OUT YOU.
FINE.

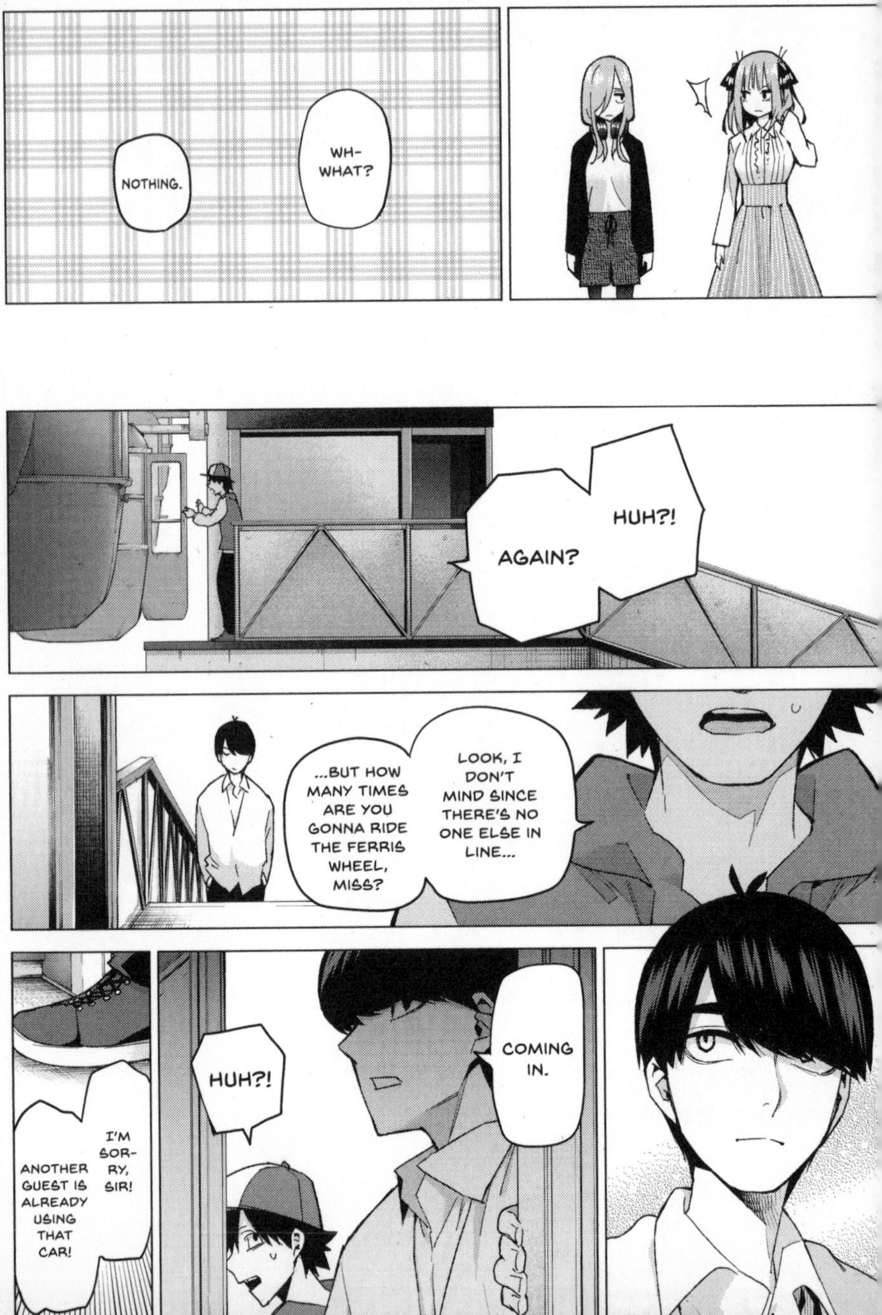
WH- WHAT?
NOTHING.
HUH?!
AGAIN?
LOOK, I DON'T MIND SINCE THERE'S NO ONE ELSE IN LINE...
...BUT HOW MANY TIMES ARE YOU GONNA RIDE THE FERRIS WHEEL, MISS?
COMING IN.
HUH?!
I'M SORRY, SIR!
ANOTHER GUEST IS ALREADY USING THAT CAR!

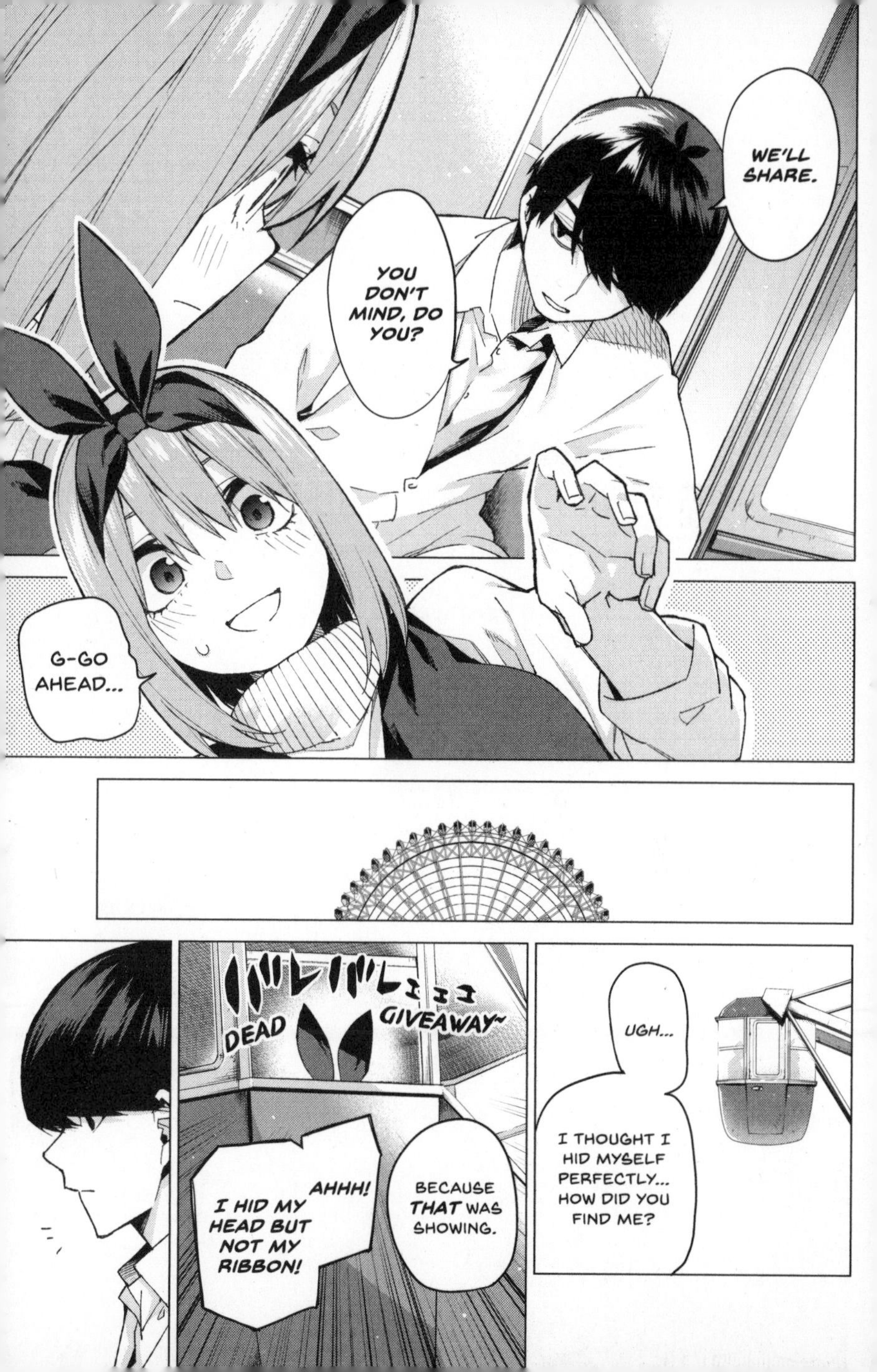
WE'LL SHARE.
YOU DON'T MIND, DO YOU?
G-GO AHEAD...
UGH...
I THOUGHT I HID MYSELF PERFECTLY... HOW DID YOU FIND ME?
DEAD GIVEAWAY~
BECAUSE *THAT* WAS SHOWING.
AHHH! I HID MY HEAD BUT NOT MY RIBBON!

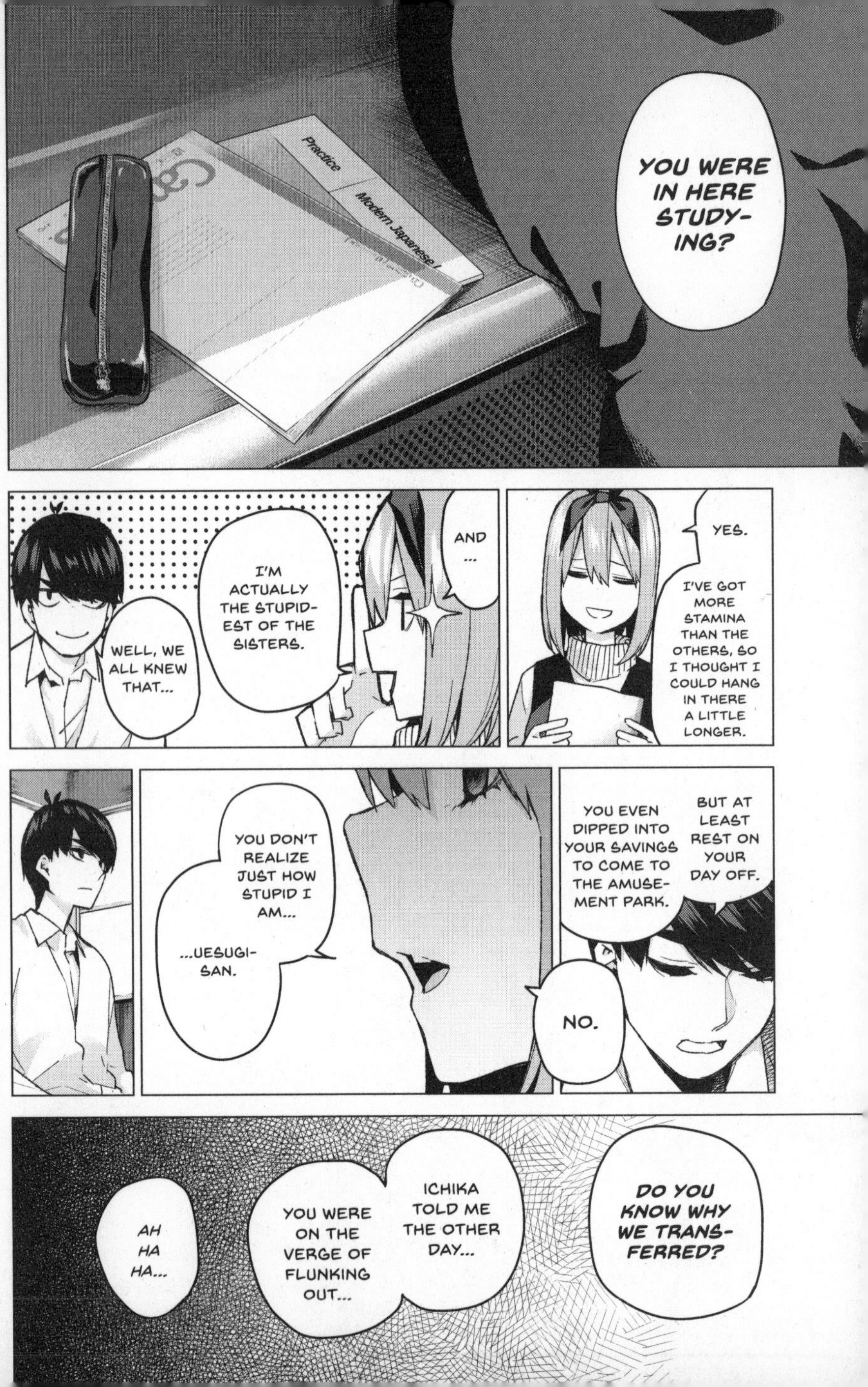
Practice
Modern Japanese I
YOU WERE IN HERE STUDYING?
YES.
I'VE GOT MORE STAMINA THAN THE OTHERS, SO I THOUGHT I COULD HANG IN THERE A LITTLE LONGER.
AND ...
I'M ACTUALLY THE STUPIDEST OF THE SISTERS.
WELL, WE ALL KNEW THAT...
BUT AT LEAST REST ON YOUR DAY OFF.
YOU EVEN DIPPED INTO YOUR SAVINGS TO COME TO THE AMUSEMENT PARK.
NO.
YOU DON'T REALIZE JUST HOW STUPID I AM...
...UESUGI-SAN.
DO YOU KNOW WHY WE TRANSFERRED?
ICHIKA TOLD ME THE OTHER DAY...
YOU WERE ON THE VERGE OF FLUNKING OUT...
AH HA HA...

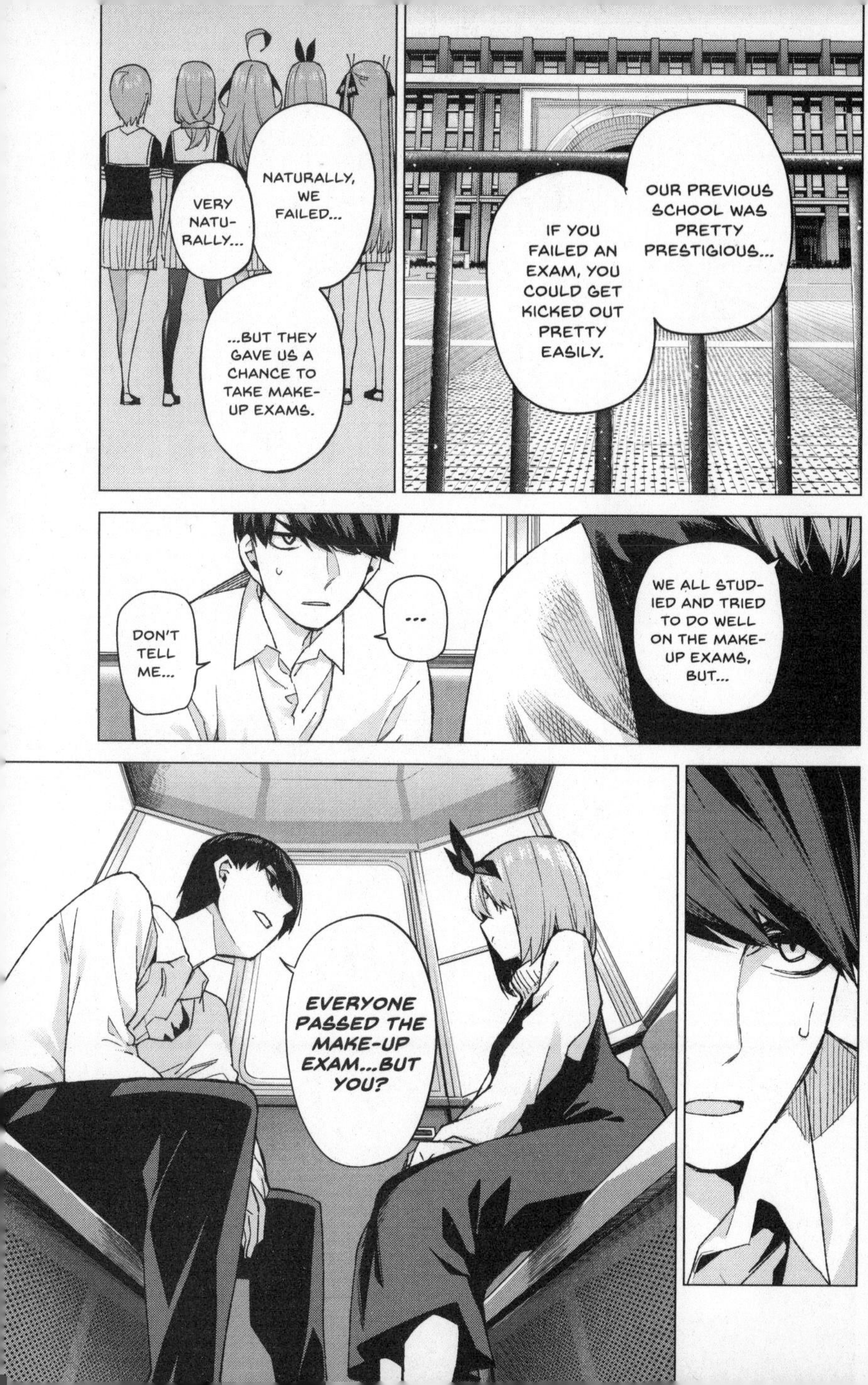
OUR PREVIOUS SCHOOL WAS PRETTY PRESTIGIOUS...
IF YOU FAILED AN EXAM, YOU COULD GET KICKED OUT PRETTY EASILY.
NATURALLY, WE FAILED...
VERY NATURALLY...
...BUT THEY GAVE US A CHANCE TO TAKE MAKE-UP EXAMS.
WE ALL STUDIED AND TRIED TO DO WELL ON THE MAKE-UP EXAMS, BUT...
...
DON'T TELL ME...
EVERYONE PASSED THE MAKE-UP EXAM...BUT YOU?

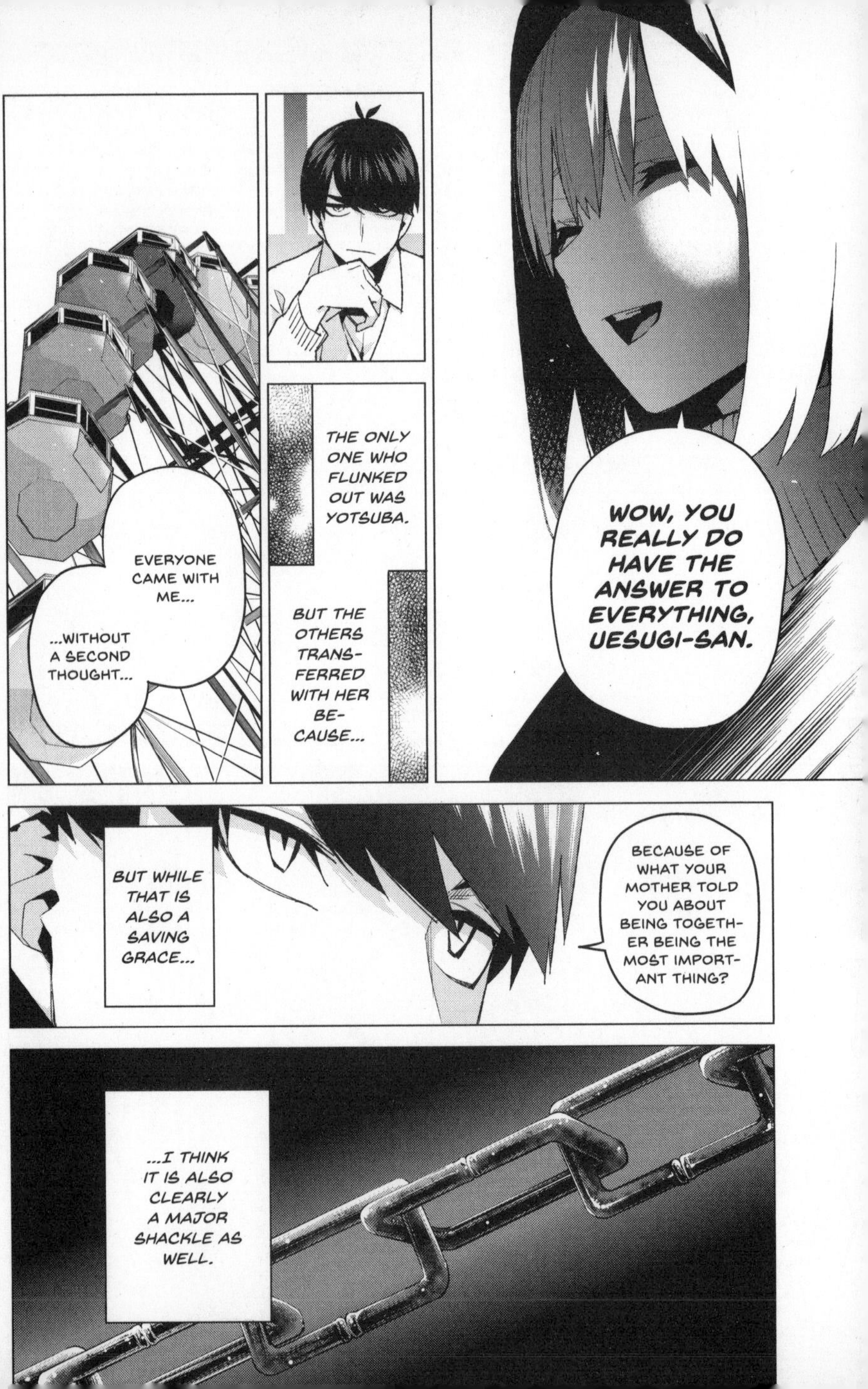
WOW, YOU REALLY DO HAVE THE ANSWER TO EVERYTHING, UESUGI-SAN.
THE ONLY ONE WHO FLUNKED OUT WAS YOTSUBA.
BUT THE OTHERS TRANSFERRED WITH HER BECAUSE...
EVERYONE CAME WITH ME...
...WITHOUT A SECOND THOUGHT...
BECAUSE OF WHAT YOUR MOTHER TOLD YOU ABOUT BEING TOGETHER BEING THE MOST IMPORTANT THING?
BUT WHILE THAT IS ALSO A SAVING GRACE...
...I THINK IT IS ALSO CLEARLY A MAJOR SHACKLE AS WELL.

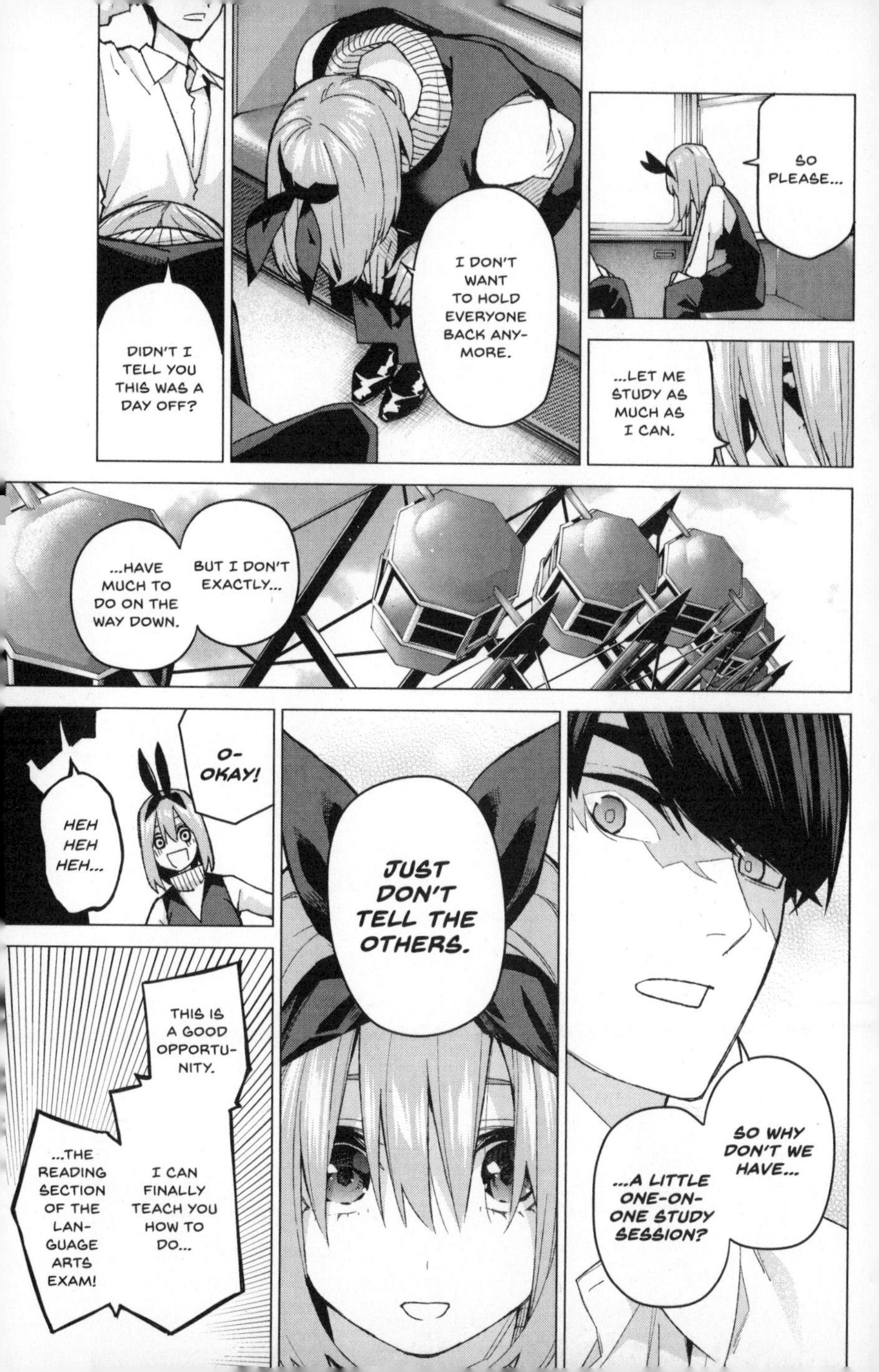
SO PLEASE...
...LET ME STUDY AS MUCH AS I CAN.
I DON'T WANT TO HOLD EVERYONE BACK ANY-MORE.
DIDN'T I TELL YOU THIS WAS A DAY OFF?
BUT I DON'T EXACTLY...
...HAVE MUCH TO DO ON THE WAY DOWN.
SO WHY DON'T WE HAVE...
...A LITTLE ONE-ON-ONE STUDY SESSION?
JUST DON'T TELL THE OTHERS.
O-OKAY!
HEH HEH HEH...
THIS IS A GOOD OPPORTU-NITY.
I CAN FINALLY TEACH YOU HOW TO DO...
...THE READING SECTION OF THE LAN-GUAGE ARTS EXAM!

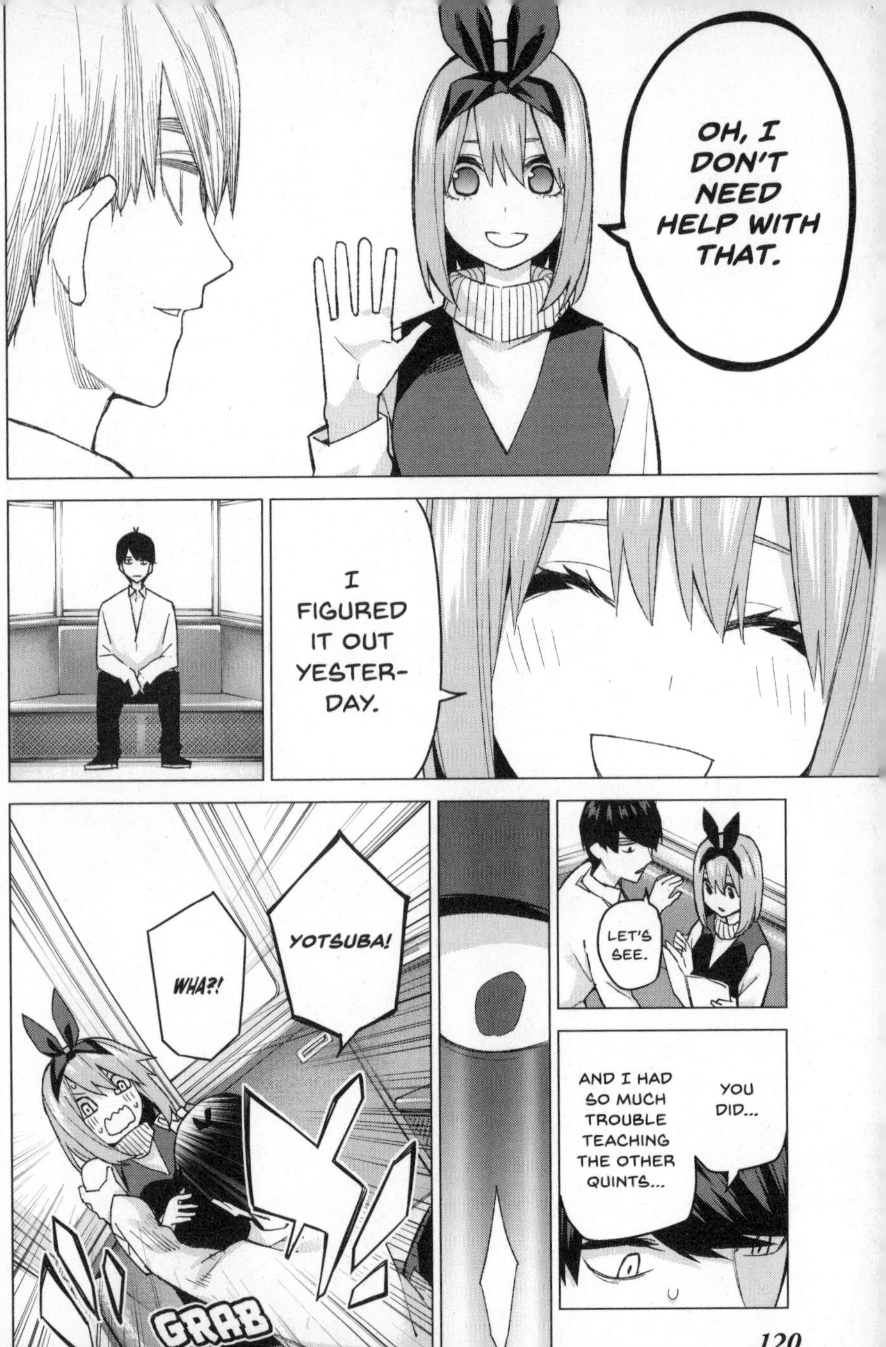
OH, I DON'T NEED HELP WITH THAT.
I FIGURED IT OUT YESTER-DAY.
LET'S SEE.
YOU DID...
AND I HAD SO MUCH TROUBLE TEACHING THE OTHER QUINTS...
YOTSUBA!
WHA?!
GRAB

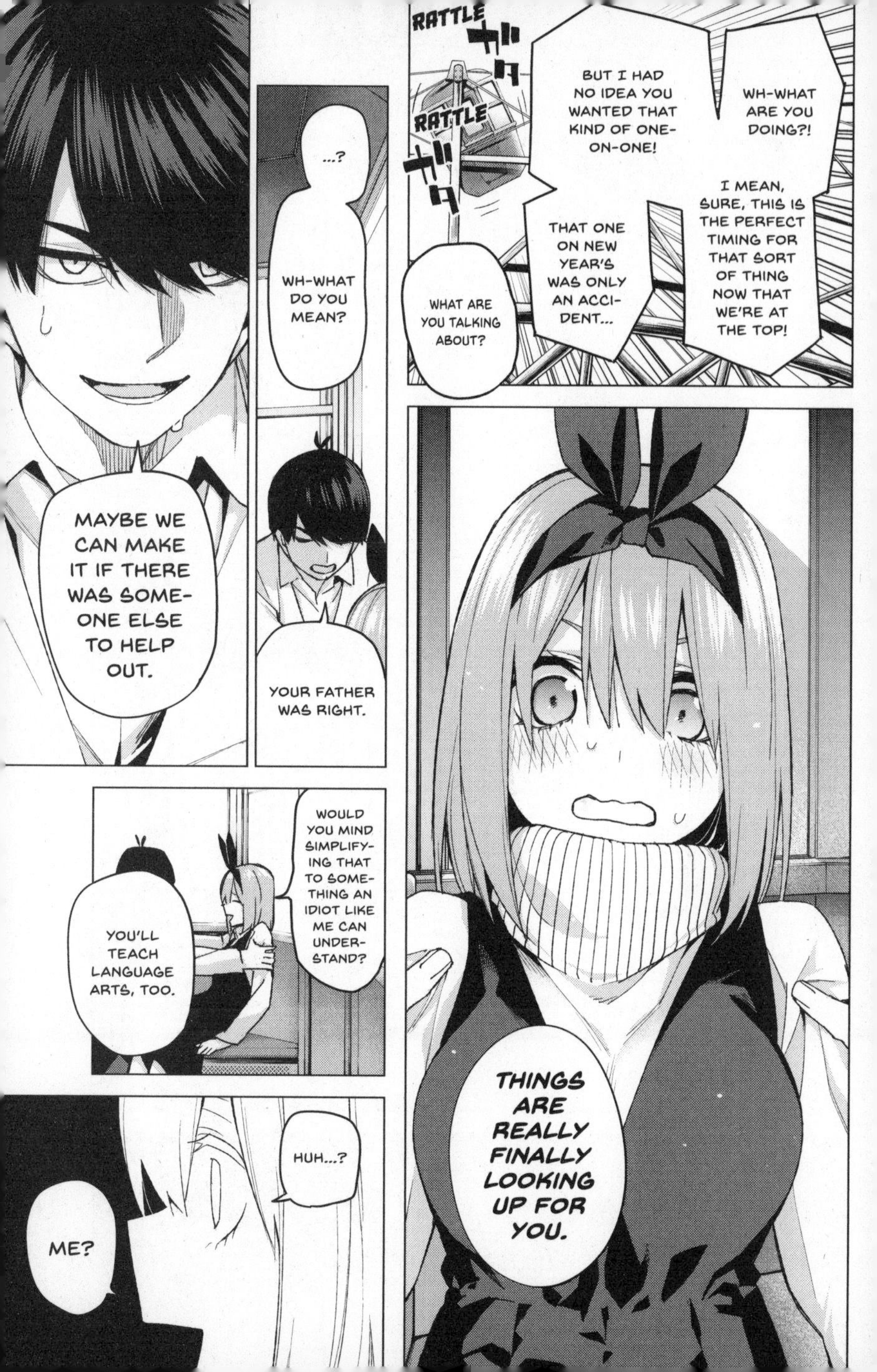
RATTLE
RATTLE
WH-WHAT ARE YOU DOING?!
I MEAN, SURE, THIS IS THE PERFECT TIMING FOR THAT SORT OF THING NOW THAT WE'RE AT THE TOP!
BUT I HAD NO IDEA YOU WANTED THAT KIND OF ONE-ON-ONE!
THAT ONE ON NEW YEAR'S WAS ONLY AN ACCIDENT...
WHAT ARE YOU TALKING ABOUT?
THINGS ARE REALLY FINALLY LOOKING UP FOR YOU.
...?
WH-WHAT DO YOU MEAN?
YOUR FATHER WAS RIGHT.
MAYBE WE CAN MAKE IT IF THERE WAS SOMEONE ELSE TO HELP OUT.
WOULD YOU MIND SIMPLIFYING THAT TO SOMETHING AN IDIOT LIKE ME CAN UNDERSTAND?
YOU'LL TEACH LANGUAGE ARTS, TOO.
HUH...?
ME?

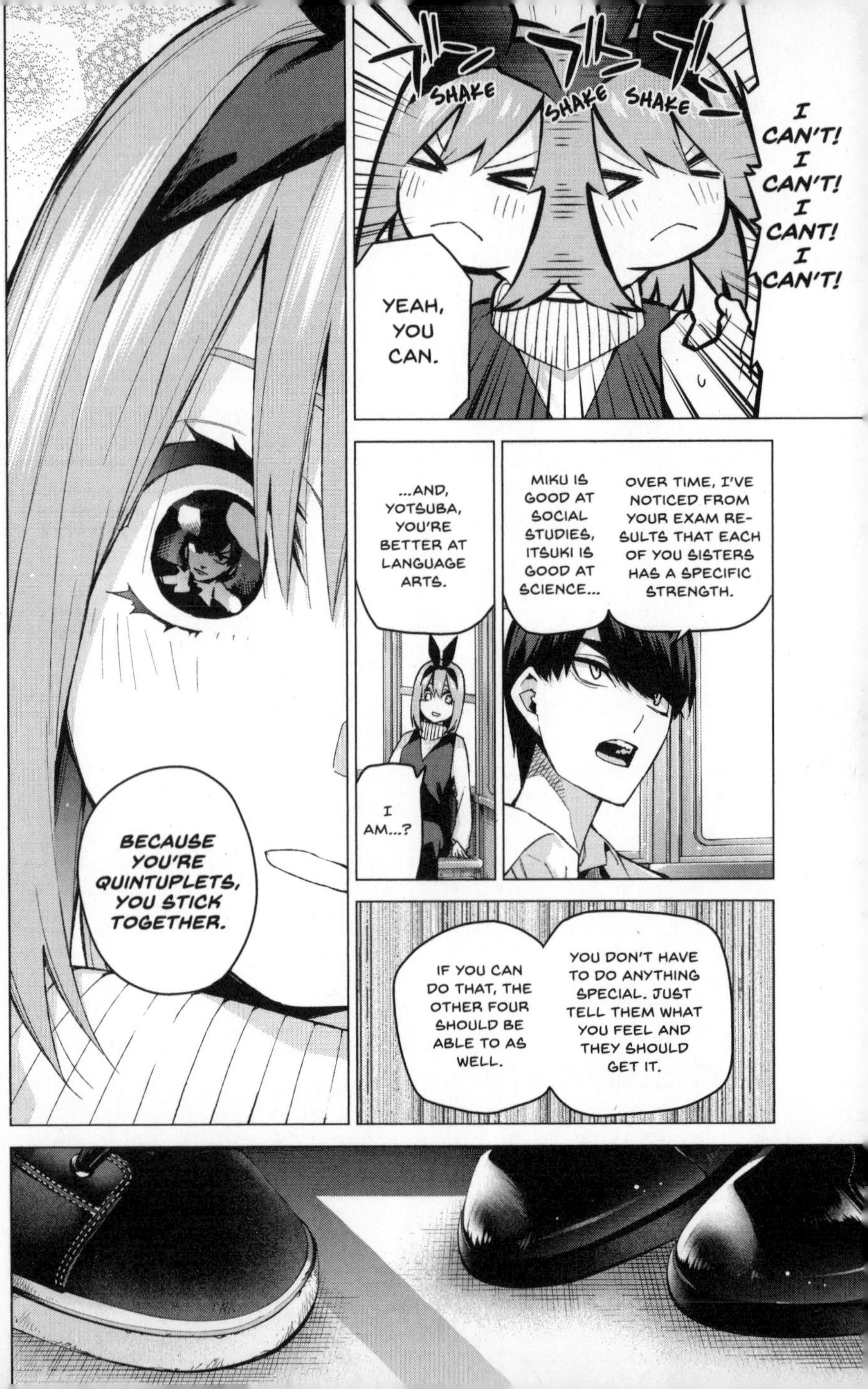
SHAKE
SHAKE
SHAKE
I CAN'T! I CAN'T! I CANT! I CAN'T!
YEAH, YOU CAN.
OVER TIME, I'VE NOTICED FROM YOUR EXAM RE-SULTS THAT EACH OF YOU SISTERS HAS A SPECIFIC STRENGTH.
MIKU IS GOOD AT SOCIAL STUDIES, ITSUKI IS GOOD AT SCIENCE...
...AND, YOTSUBA, YOU'RE BETTER AT LANGUAGE ARTS.
I AM...?
YOU DON'T HAVE TO DO ANYTHING SPECIAL. JUST TELL THEM WHAT YOU FEEL AND THEY SHOULD GET IT.
IF YOU CAN DO THAT, THE OTHER FOUR SHOULD BE ABLE TO AS WELL.
BECAUSE YOU'RE QUINTUPLETS, YOU STICK TOGETHER.

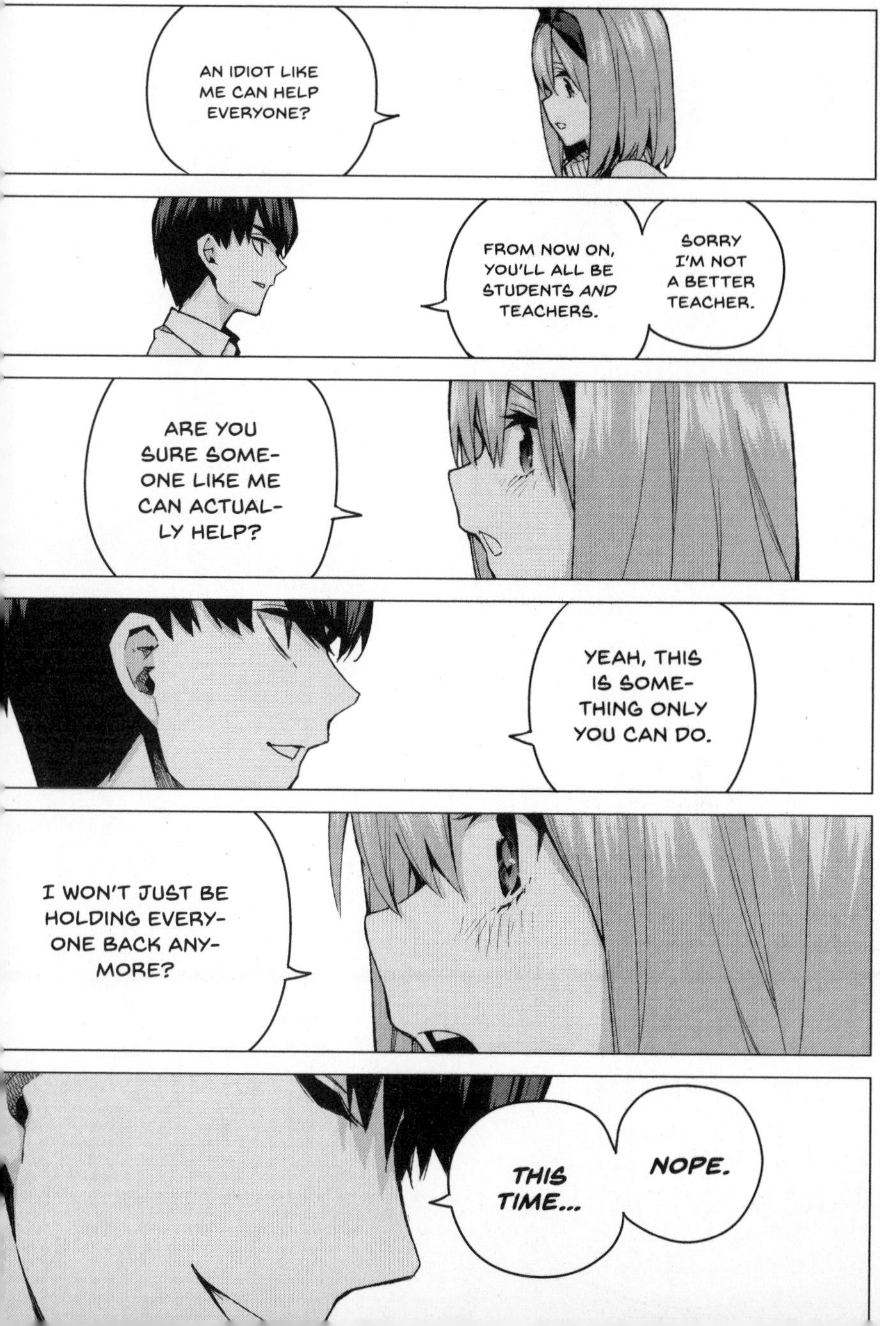

AN IDIOT LIKE ME CAN HELP EVERYONE?
SORRY I'M NOT A BETTER TEACHER.
FROM NOW ON, YOU'LL ALL BE STUDENTS *AND* TEACHERS.
ARE YOU SURE SOME-ONE LIKE ME CAN ACTUAL-LY HELP?
YEAH, THIS IS SOME-THING ONLY YOU CAN DO.
I WON'T JUST BE HOLDING EVERY-ONE BACK ANY-MORE?
NOPE.
THIS TIME...

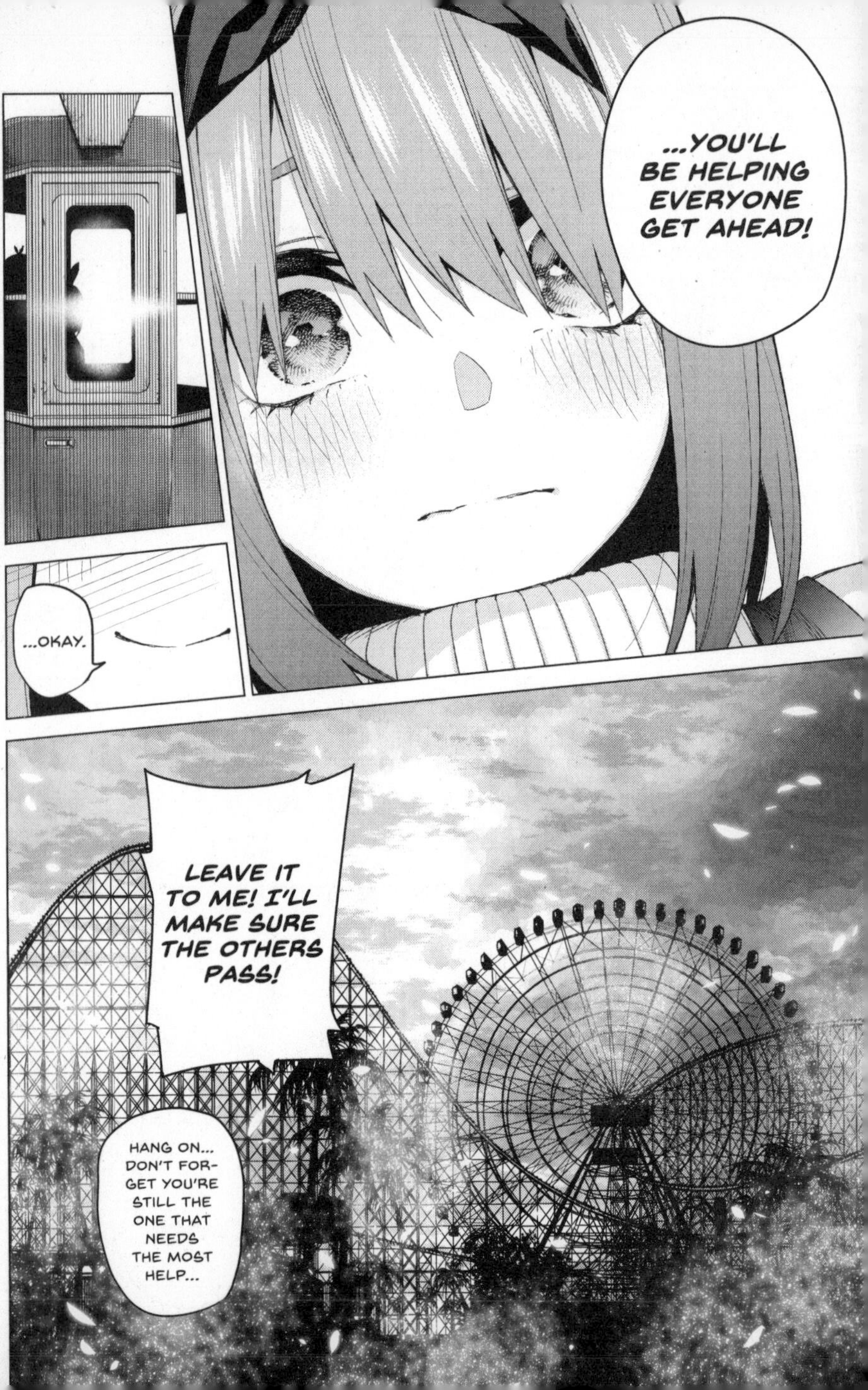
...YOU'LL BE HELPING EVERYONE GET AHEAD!
...OKAY.
LEAVE IT TO ME! I'LL MAKE SURE THE OTHERS PASS!
HANG ON... DON'T FOR-GET YOU'RE STILL THE ONE THAT NEEDS THE MOST HELP...

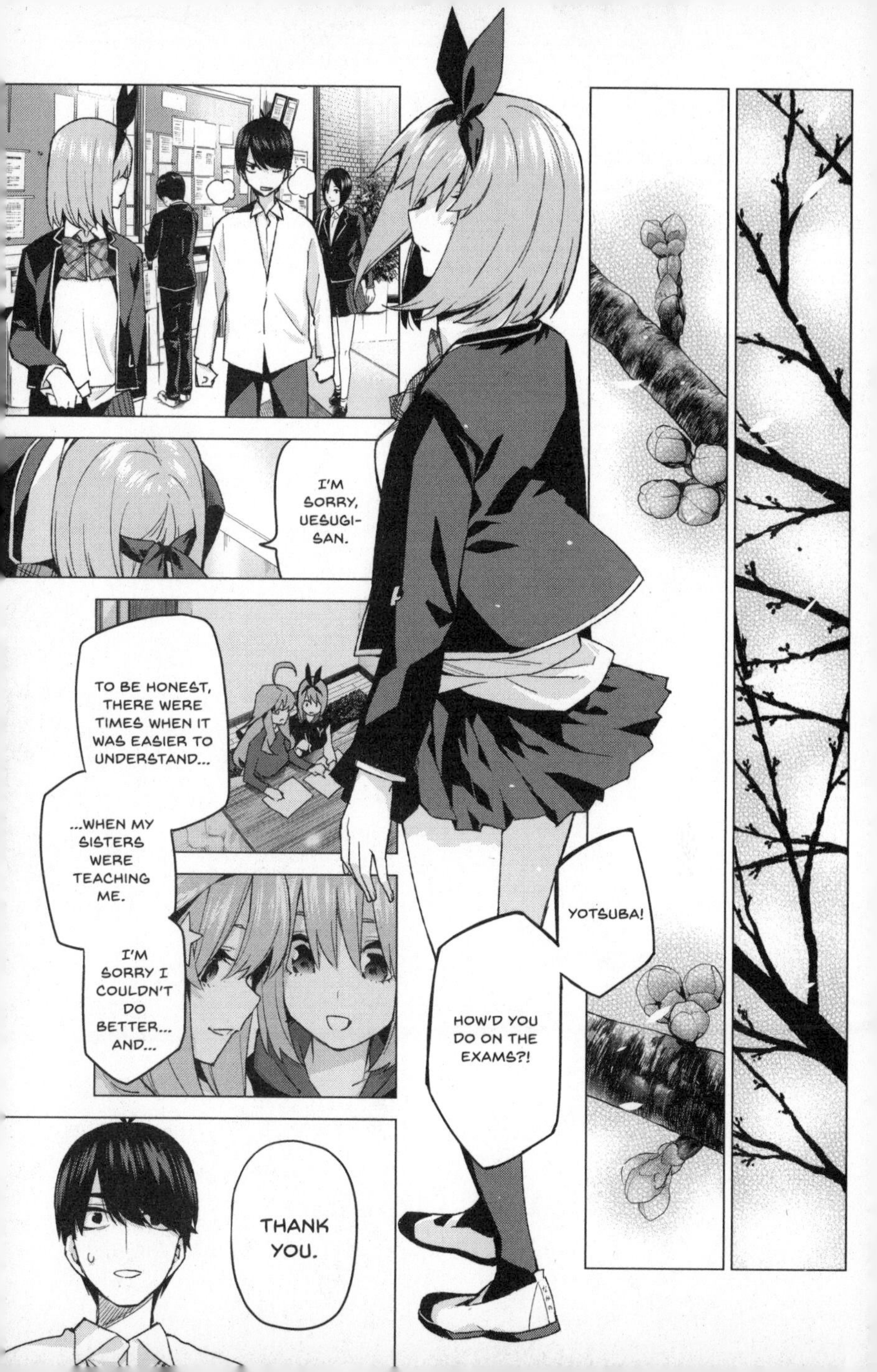
YOTSUBA!
HOW'D YOU DO ON THE EXAMS?!
I'M SORRY, UESUGI-SAN.
TO BE HONEST, THERE WERE TIMES WHEN IT WAS EASIER TO UNDERSTAND...
...WHEN MY SISTERS WERE TEACHING ME.
I'M SORRY I COULDN'T DO BETTER... AND...
THANK YOU.

Lan- guage Arts	Math	Science	Social Studies	English	Total
51	33	32	36	32	184

FOR THE FIRST TIME...I FEEL LIKE MY EFFORTS WERE RE- WARDED.

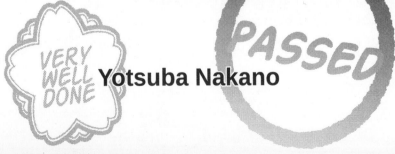

VERY WELL DONE

Yotsuba Nakano

PASSED

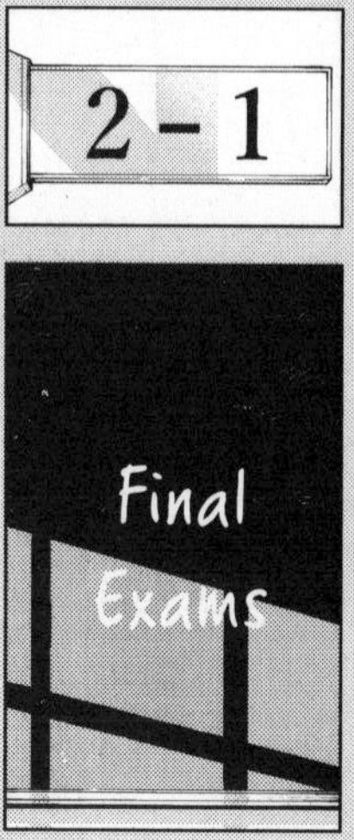
2-1
Final Exams

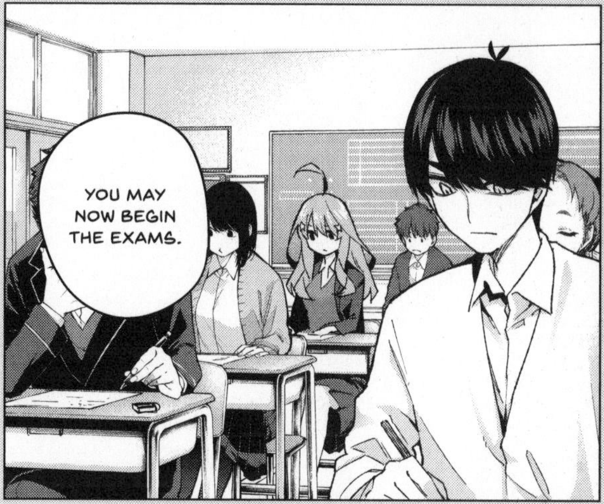
YOU MAY NOW BEGIN THE EXAMS.

CHAPTER 57
IF THE LAST EXAM WAS ITSUKI'S

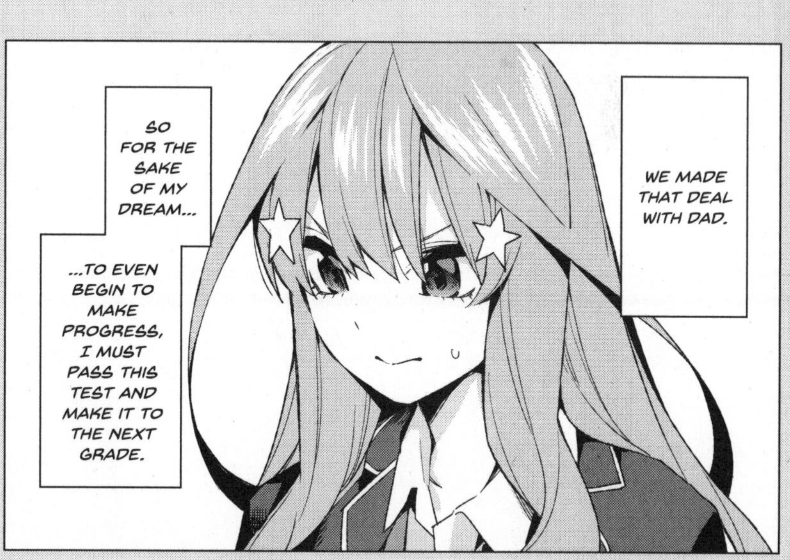
WE MADE THAT DEAL WITH DAD.
SO FOR THE SAKE OF MY DREAM...
...TO EVEN BEGIN TO MAKE PROGRESS, I MUST PASS THIS TEST AND MAKE IT TO THE NEXT GRADE.

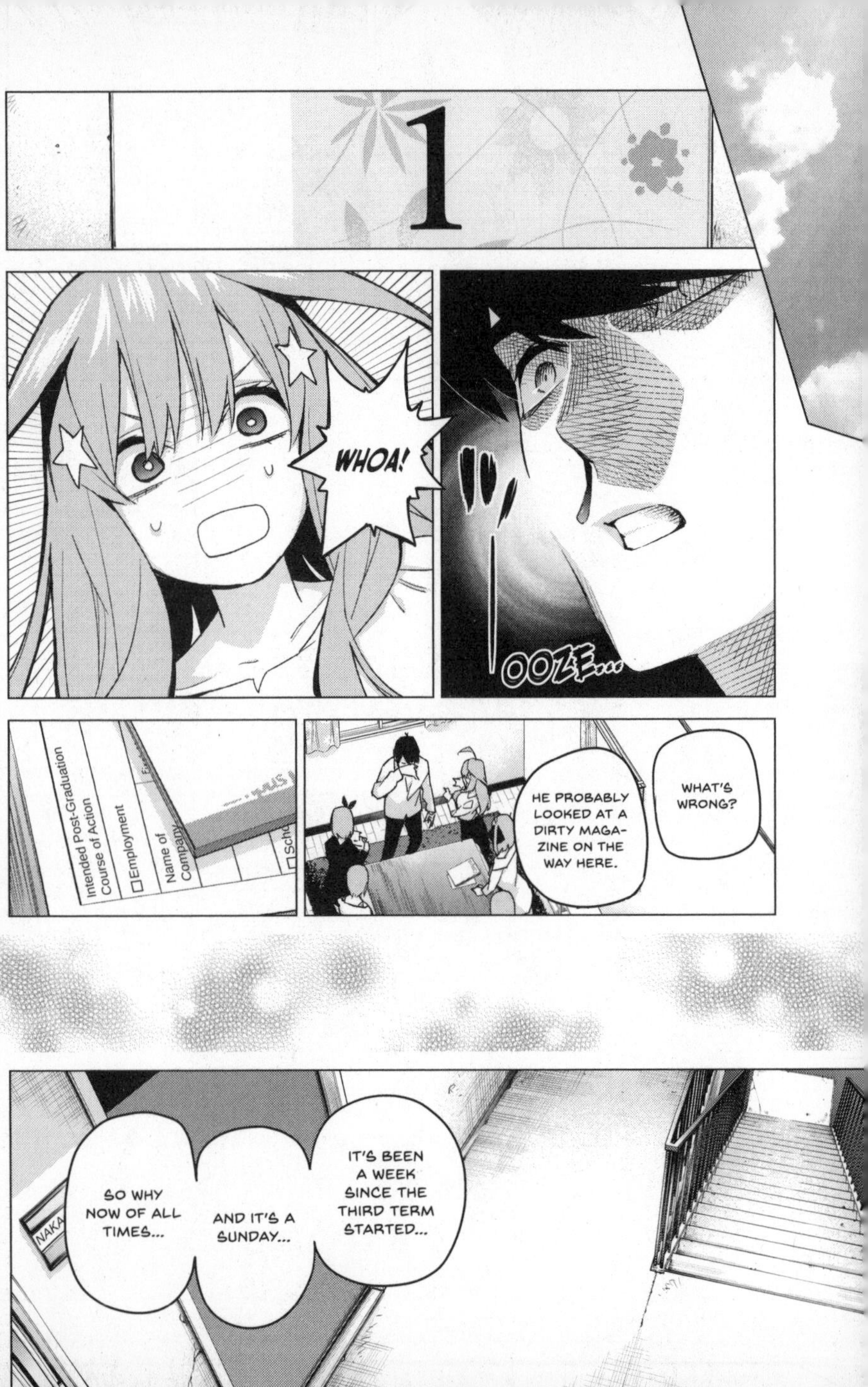
1
OOZE...
WHOA!
WHAT'S WRONG?
HE PROBABLY LOOKED AT A DIRTY MAGA-ZINE ON THE WAY HERE.
Intended Post-Graduation Course of Action
Employment
Name of Company
IT'S BEEN A WEEK SINCE THE THIRD TERM STARTED...
AND IT'S A SUNDAY...
SO WHY NOW OF ALL TIMES...

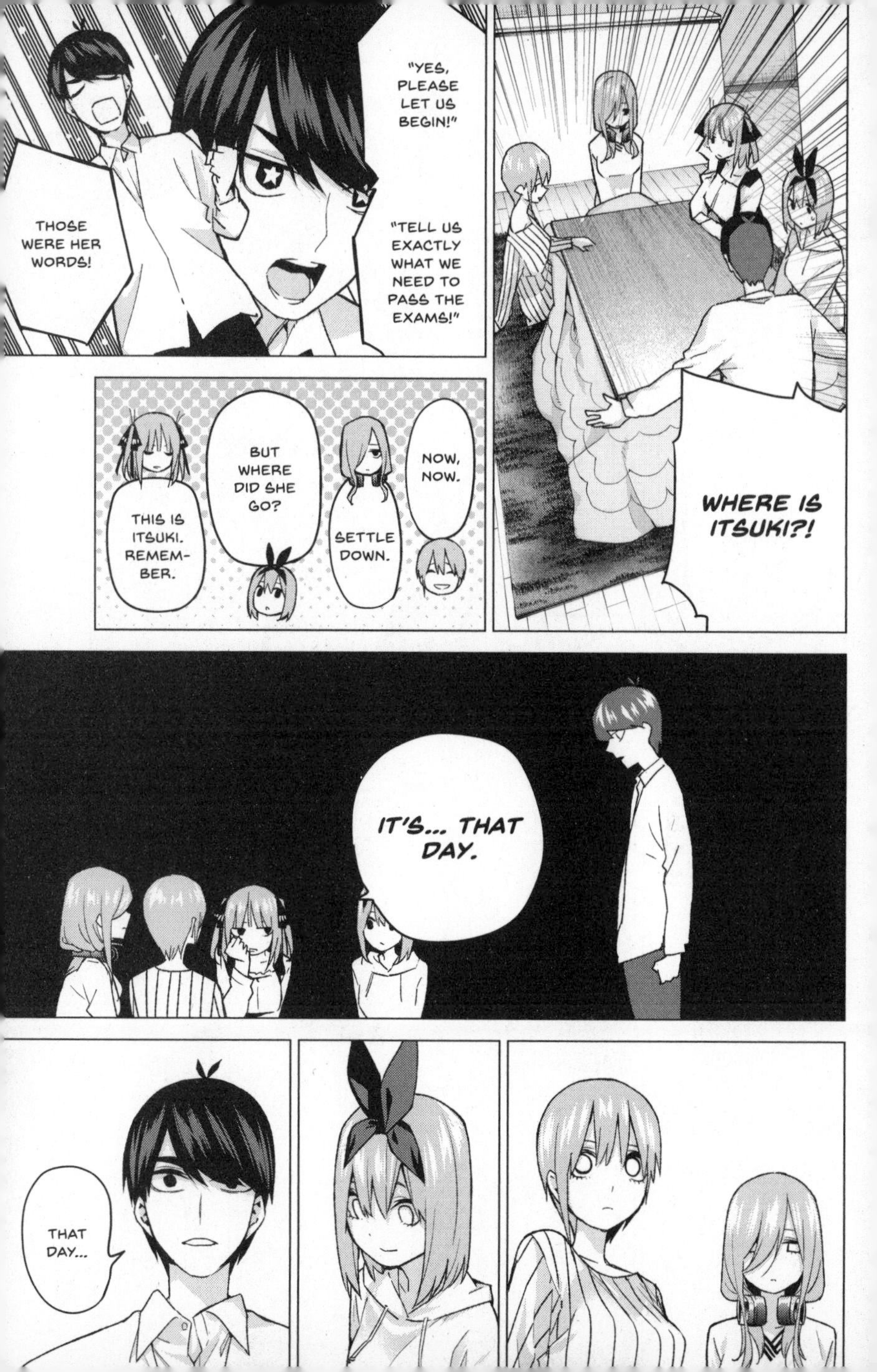

WHERE IS ITSUKI?!
"YES, PLEASE LET US BEGIN!"
"TELL US EXACTLY WHAT WE NEED TO PASS THE EXAMS!"
THOSE WERE HER WORDS!
NOW, NOW.
SETTLE DOWN.
BUT WHERE DID SHE GO?
THIS IS ITSUKI. REMEMBER.
IT'S... THAT DAY.
THAT DAY...

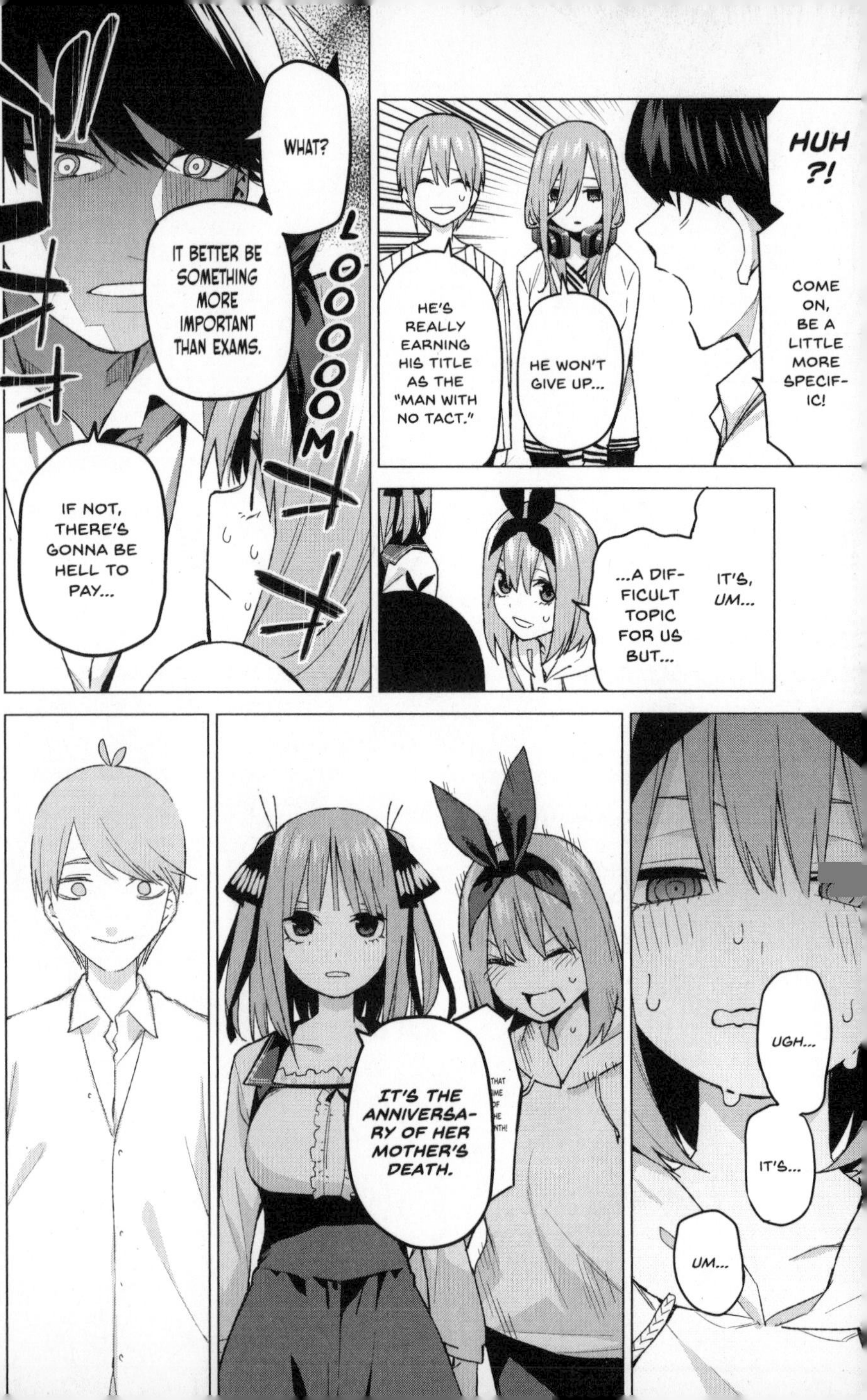
HUH ?!
COME ON, BE A LITTLE MORE SPECIF-IC!
HE WON'T GIVE UP...
HE'S REALLY EARNING HIS TITLE AS THE "MAN WITH NO TACT."
IT'S, UM...
...A DIF-FICULT TOPIC FOR US BUT...
WHAT?
IT BETTER BE SOMETHING MORE IMPORTANT THAN EXAMS.
LOOOOOOOM
IF NOT, THERE'S GONNA BE HELL TO PAY...
UGH...
IT'S...
UM...
IT'S THE ANNIVERSA-RY OF HER MOTHER'S DEATH.

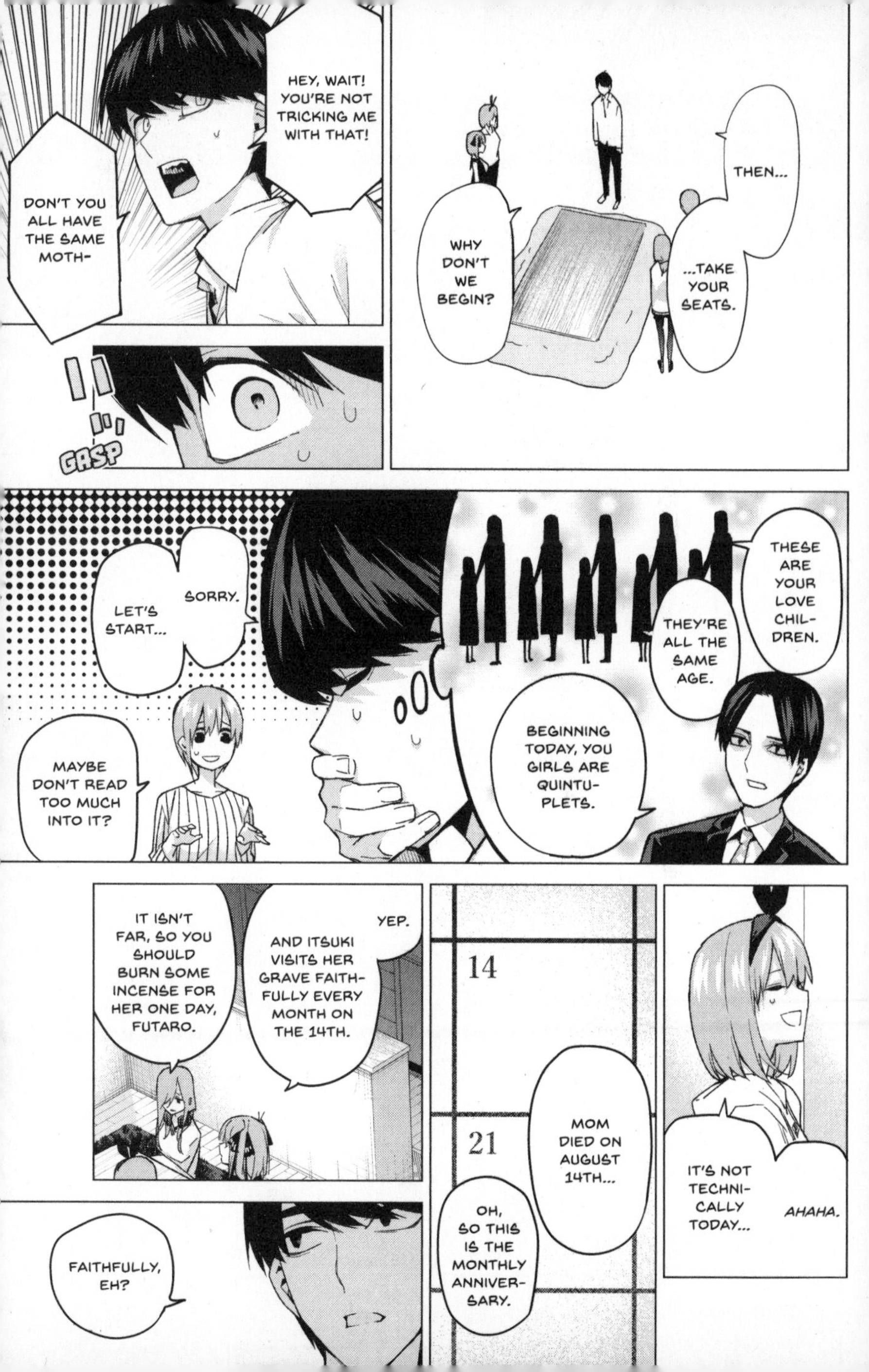
THEN...
...TAKE YOUR SEATS.
WHY DON'T WE BEGIN?
HEY, WAIT! YOU'RE NOT TRICKING ME WITH THAT!
DON'T YOU ALL HAVE THE SAME MOTH-
GASP
THESE ARE YOUR LOVE CHILDREN.
THEY'RE ALL THE SAME AGE.
BEGINNING TODAY, YOU GIRLS ARE QUINTUPLETS.
SORRY.
LET'S START...
MAYBE DON'T READ TOO MUCH INTO IT?
IT'S NOT TECHNICALLY TODAY...
AHAHA.
14
21
MOM DIED ON AUGUST 14TH...
OH, SO THIS IS THE MONTHLY ANNIVERSARY.
YEP.
AND ITSUKI VISITS HER GRAVE FAITHFULLY EVERY MONTH ON THE 14TH.
IT ISN'T FAR, SO YOU SHOULD BURN SOME INCENSE FOR HER ONE DAY, FUTARO.
FAITHFULLY, EH?

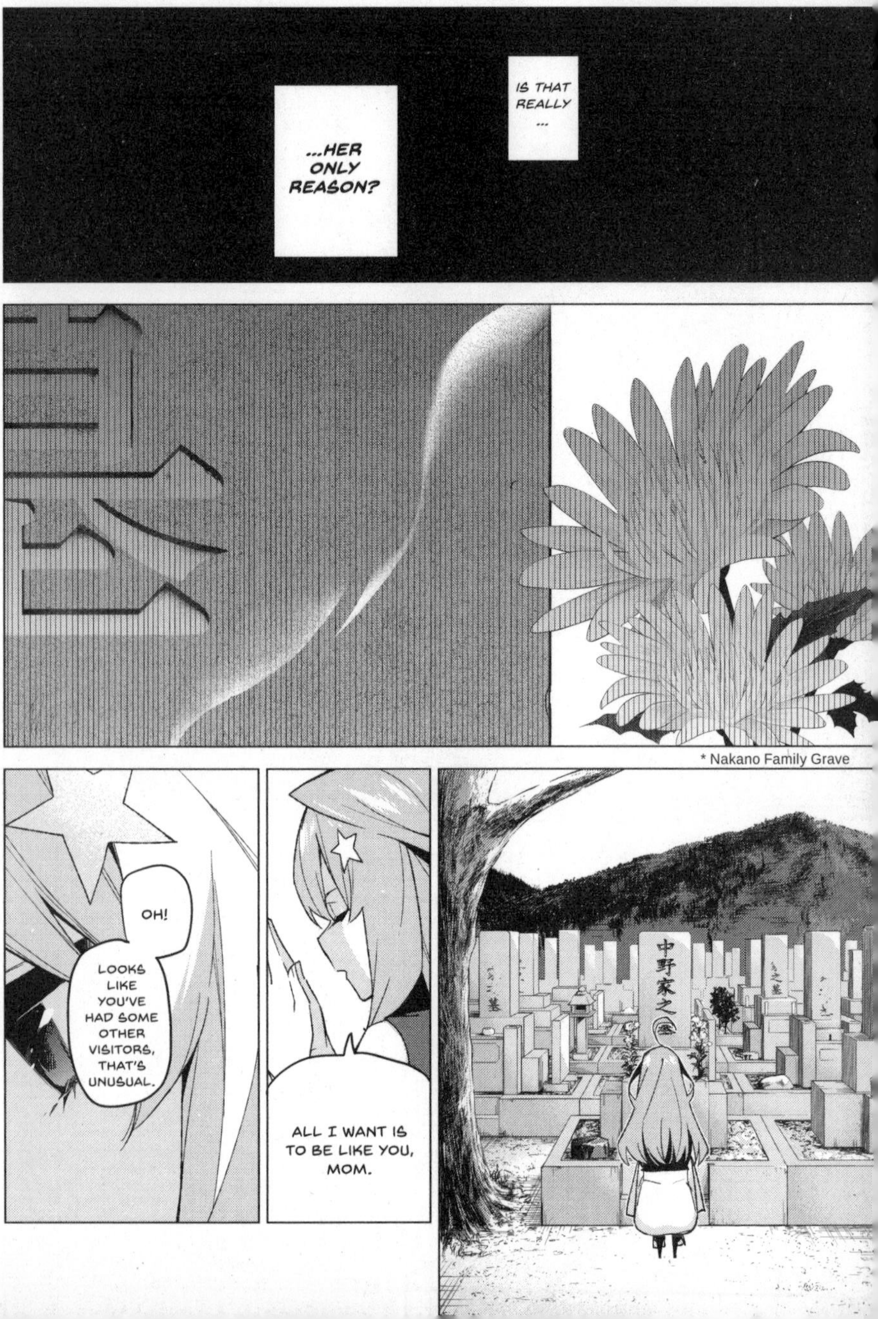
IS THAT REALLY ...
...HER ONLY REASON?
* Nakano Family Grave
ALL I WANT IS TO BE LIKE YOU, MOM.
OH!
LOOKS LIKE YOU'VE HAD SOME OTHER VISITORS, THAT'S UNUSUAL.

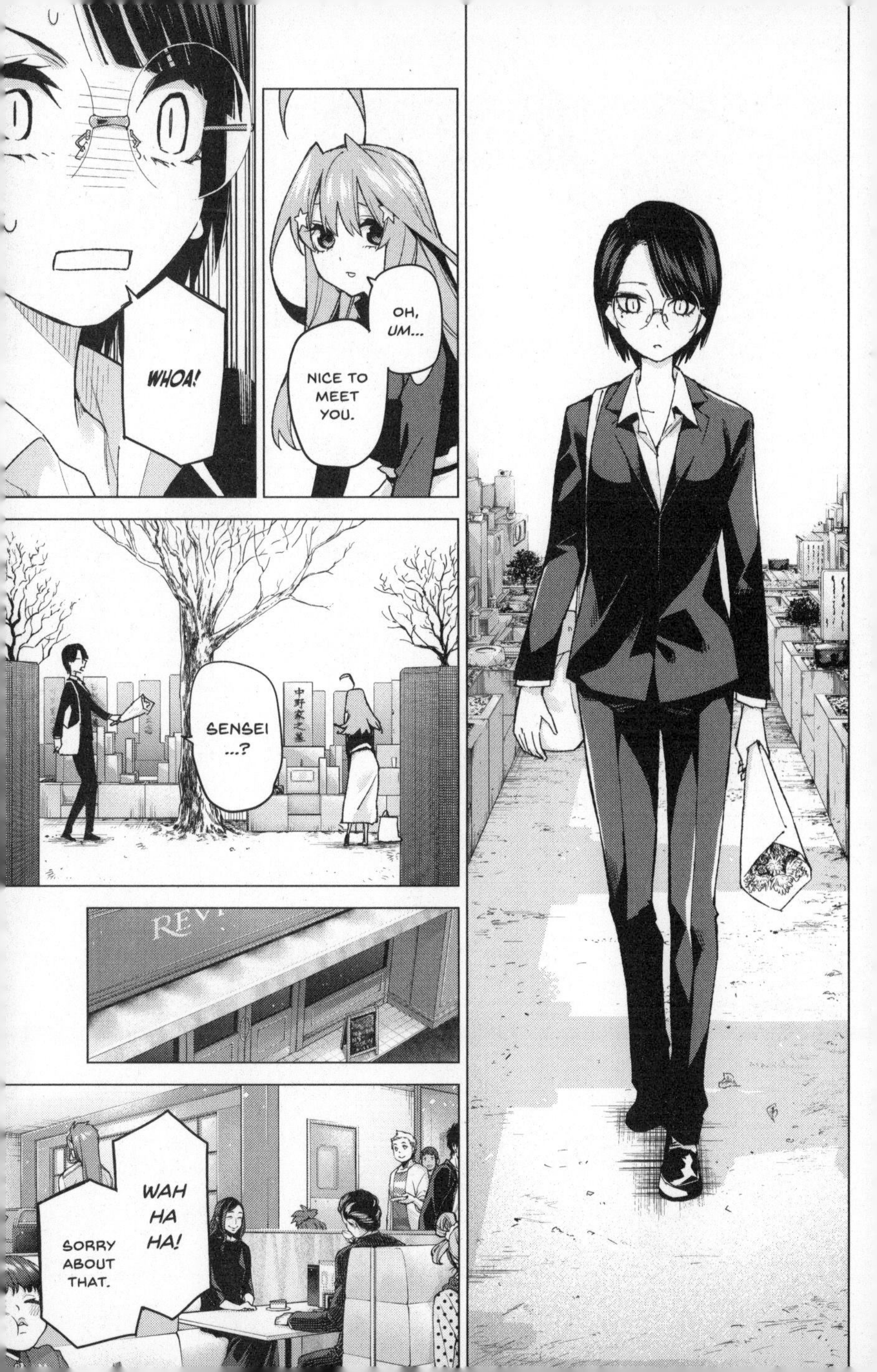
OH, UM...
NICE TO MEET YOU.
WHOA!
中野家之墓
SENSEI ...?
WAH HA HA!
SORRY ABOUT THAT.

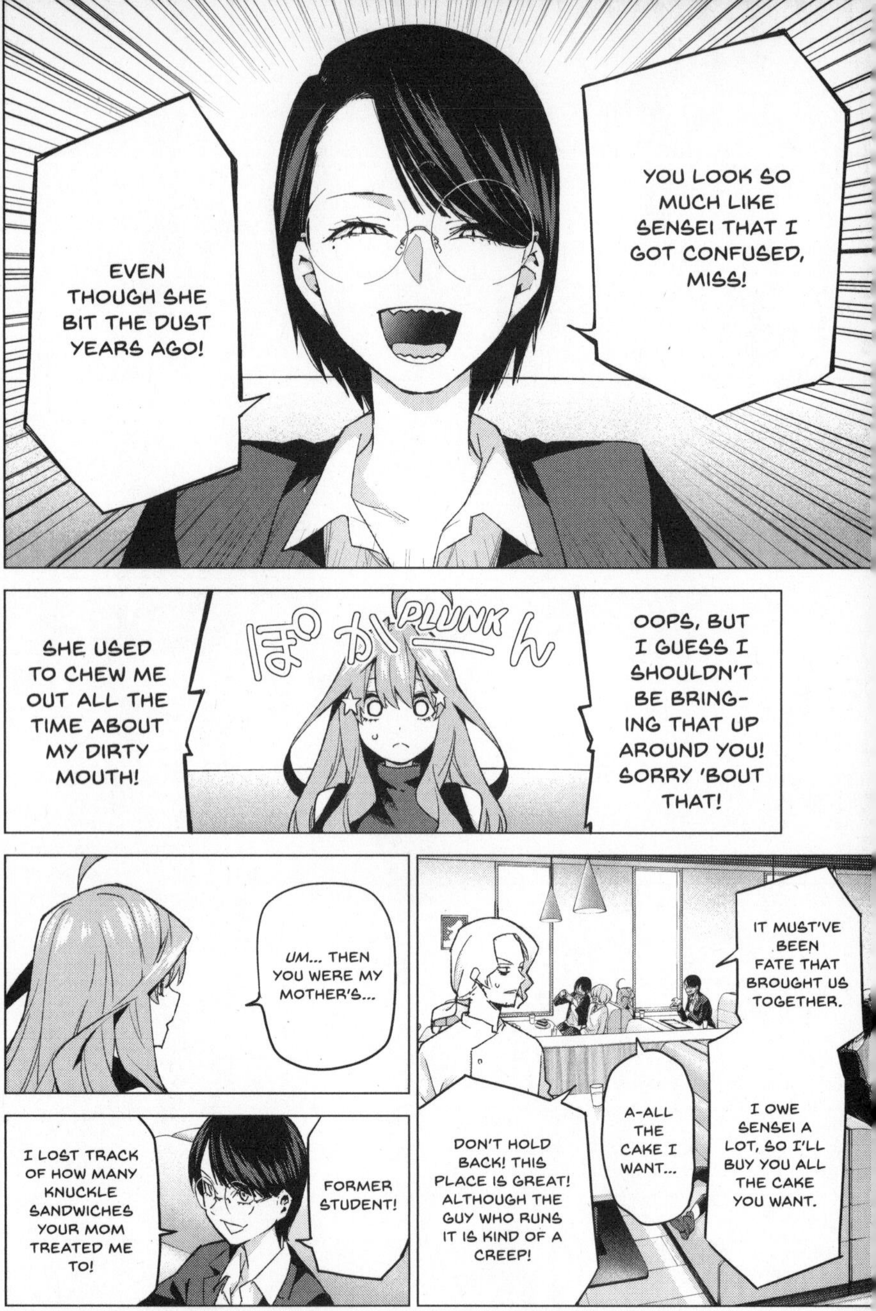
YOU LOOK SO MUCH LIKE SENSEI THAT I GOT CONFUSED, MISS!
EVEN THOUGH SHE BIT THE DUST YEARS AGO!
OOPS, BUT I GUESS I SHOULDN'T BE BRINGING THAT UP AROUND YOU! SORRY 'BOUT THAT!
ぽかーん
PLUNK
SHE USED TO CHEW ME OUT ALL THE TIME ABOUT MY DIRTY MOUTH!
IT MUST'VE BEEN FATE THAT BROUGHT US TOGETHER.
I OWE SENSEI A LOT, SO I'LL BUY YOU ALL THE CAKE YOU WANT.
A-ALL THE CAKE I WANT...
DON'T HOLD BACK! THIS PLACE IS GREAT! ALTHOUGH THE GUY WHO RUNS IT IS KIND OF A CREEP!
UM... THEN YOU WERE MY MOTHER'S...
FORMER STUDENT!
I LOST TRACK OF HOW MANY KNUCKLE SANDWICHES YOUR MOM TREATED ME TO!

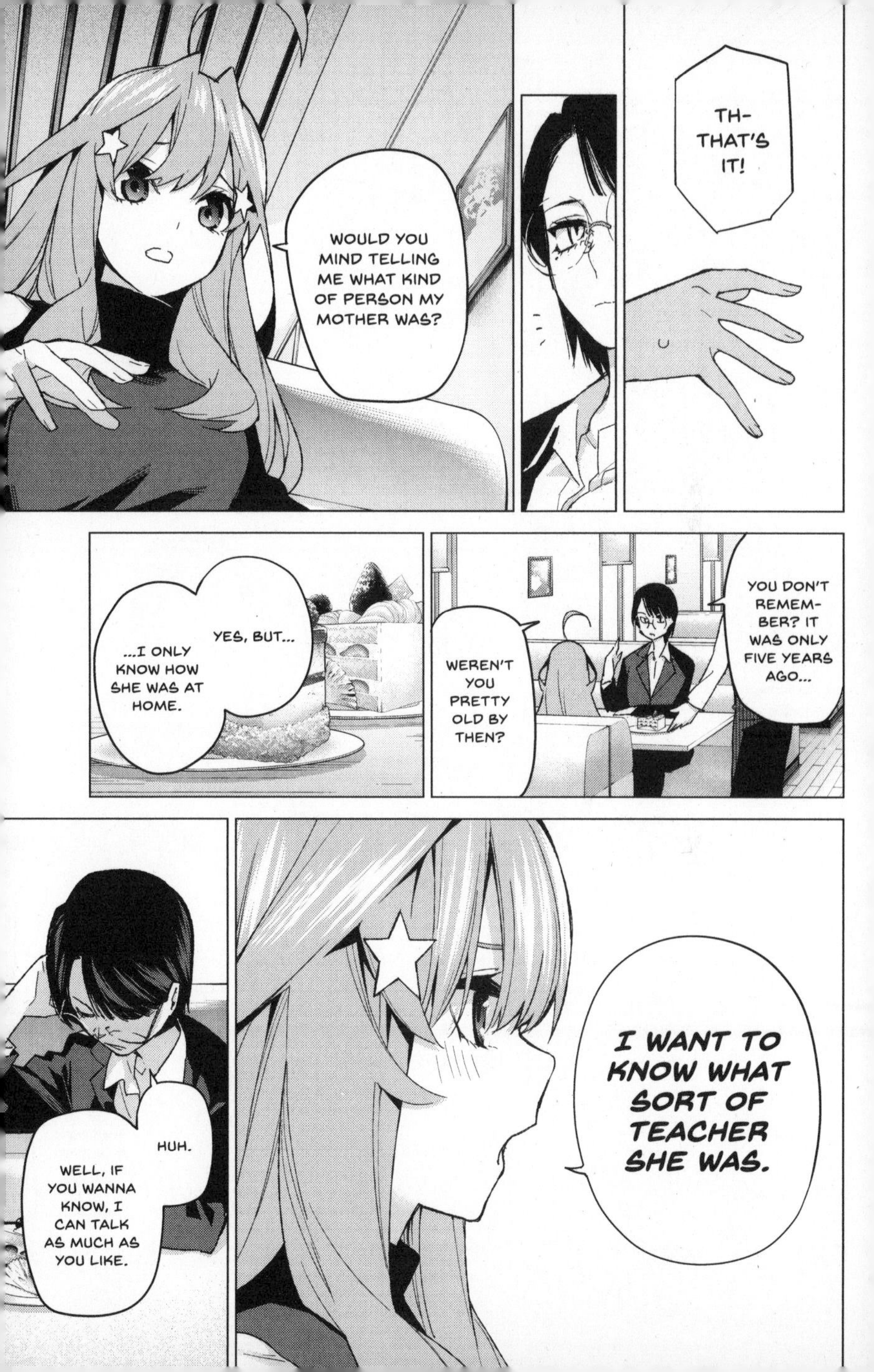
TH- THAT'S IT!
WOULD YOU MIND TELLING ME WHAT KIND OF PERSON MY MOTHER WAS?
YOU DON'T REMEM- BER? IT WAS ONLY FIVE YEARS AGO...
WEREN'T YOU PRETTY OLD BY THEN?
YES, BUT...
...I ONLY KNOW HOW SHE WAS AT HOME.
I WANT TO KNOW WHAT SORT OF TEACHER SHE WAS.
HUH.
WELL, IF YOU WANNA KNOW, I CAN TALK AS MUCH AS YOU LIKE.

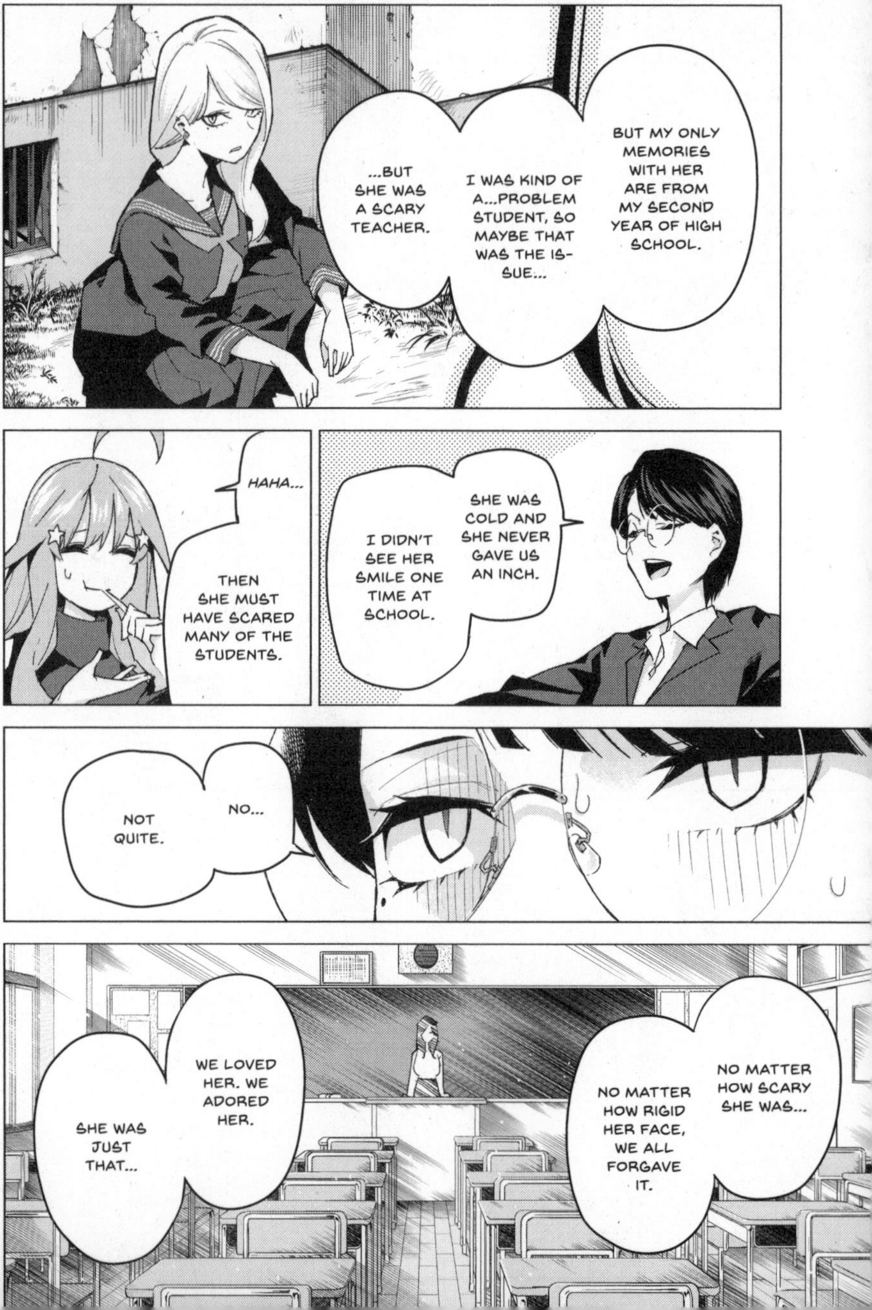
BUT MY ONLY MEMORIES WITH HER ARE FROM MY SECOND YEAR OF HIGH SCHOOL.
I WAS KIND OF A...PROBLEM STUDENT, SO MAYBE THAT WAS THE IS-SUE...
...BUT SHE WAS A SCARY TEACHER.
SHE WAS COLD AND SHE NEVER GAVE US AN INCH.
I DIDN'T SEE HER SMILE ONE TIME AT SCHOOL.
HAHA...
THEN SHE MUST HAVE SCARED MANY OF THE STUDENTS.
NO...
NOT QUITE.
NO MATTER HOW SCARY SHE WAS...
NO MATTER HOW RIGID HER FACE, WE ALL FORGAVE IT.
WE LOVED HER. WE ADORED HER.
SHE WAS JUST THAT...

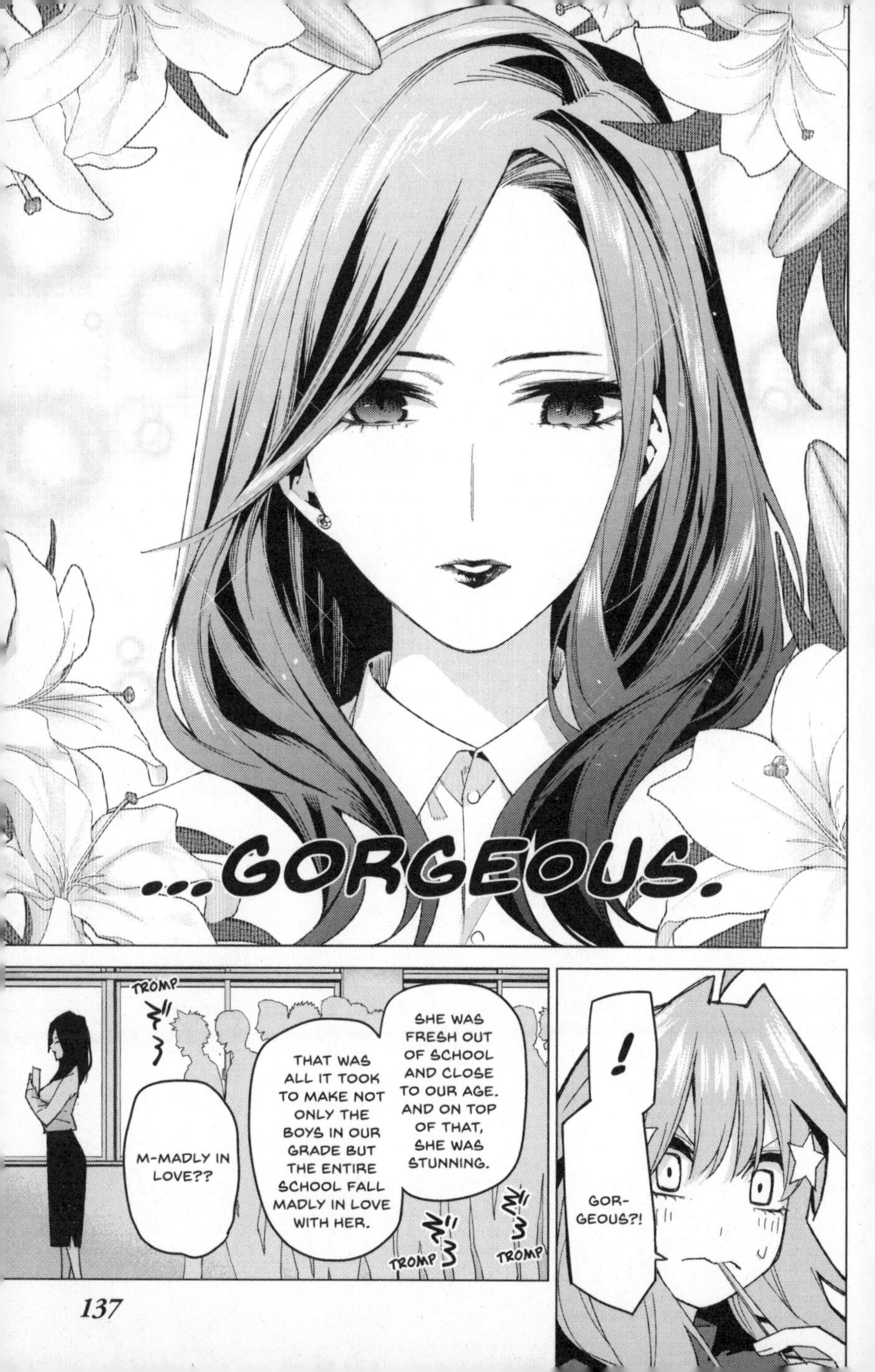
...GORGEOUS.
!
GOR-GEOUS?!
TROMP
SHE WAS FRESH OUT OF SCHOOL AND CLOSE TO OUR AGE. AND ON TOP OF THAT, SHE WAS STUNNING.
THAT WAS ALL IT TOOK TO MAKE NOT ONLY THE BOYS IN OUR GRADE BUT THE ENTIRE SCHOOL FALL MADLY IN LOVE WITH HER.
M-MADLY IN LOVE??
TROMP
TROMP

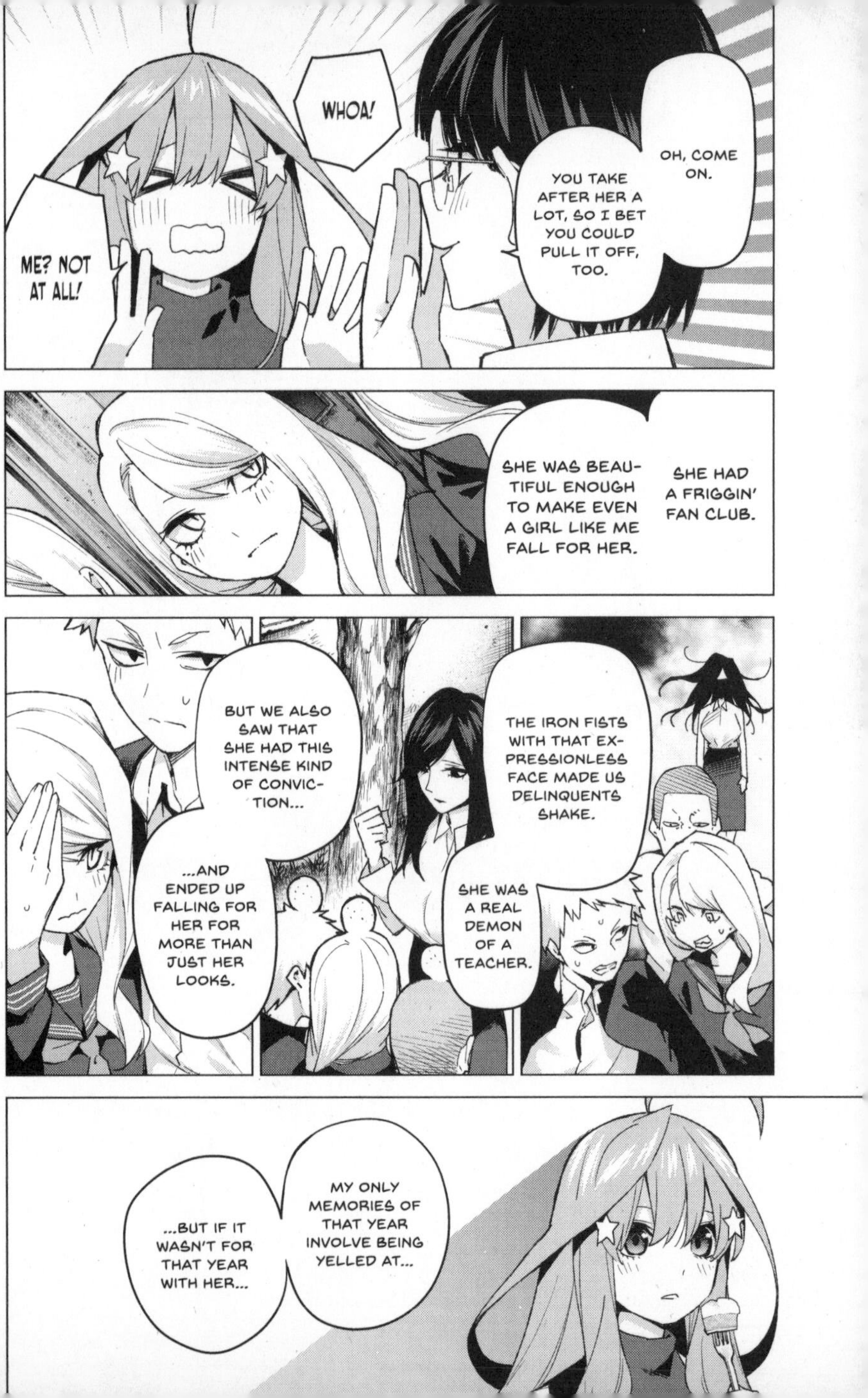
OH, COME ON.
YOU TAKE AFTER HER A LOT, SO I BET YOU COULD PULL IT OFF, TOO.
WHOA!
ME? NOT AT ALL!
SHE HAD A FRIGGIN' FAN CLUB.
SHE WAS BEAUTIFUL ENOUGH TO MAKE EVEN A GIRL LIKE ME FALL FOR HER.
THE IRON FISTS WITH THAT EXPRESSIONLESS FACE MADE US DELINQUENTS SHAKE.
SHE WAS A REAL DEMON OF A TEACHER.
BUT WE ALSO SAW THAT SHE HAD THIS INTENSE KIND OF CONVICTION...
...AND ENDED UP FALLING FOR HER FOR MORE THAN JUST HER LOOKS.
MY ONLY MEMORIES OF THAT YEAR INVOLVE BEING YELLED AT...
...BUT IF IT WASN'T FOR THAT YEAR WITH HER...

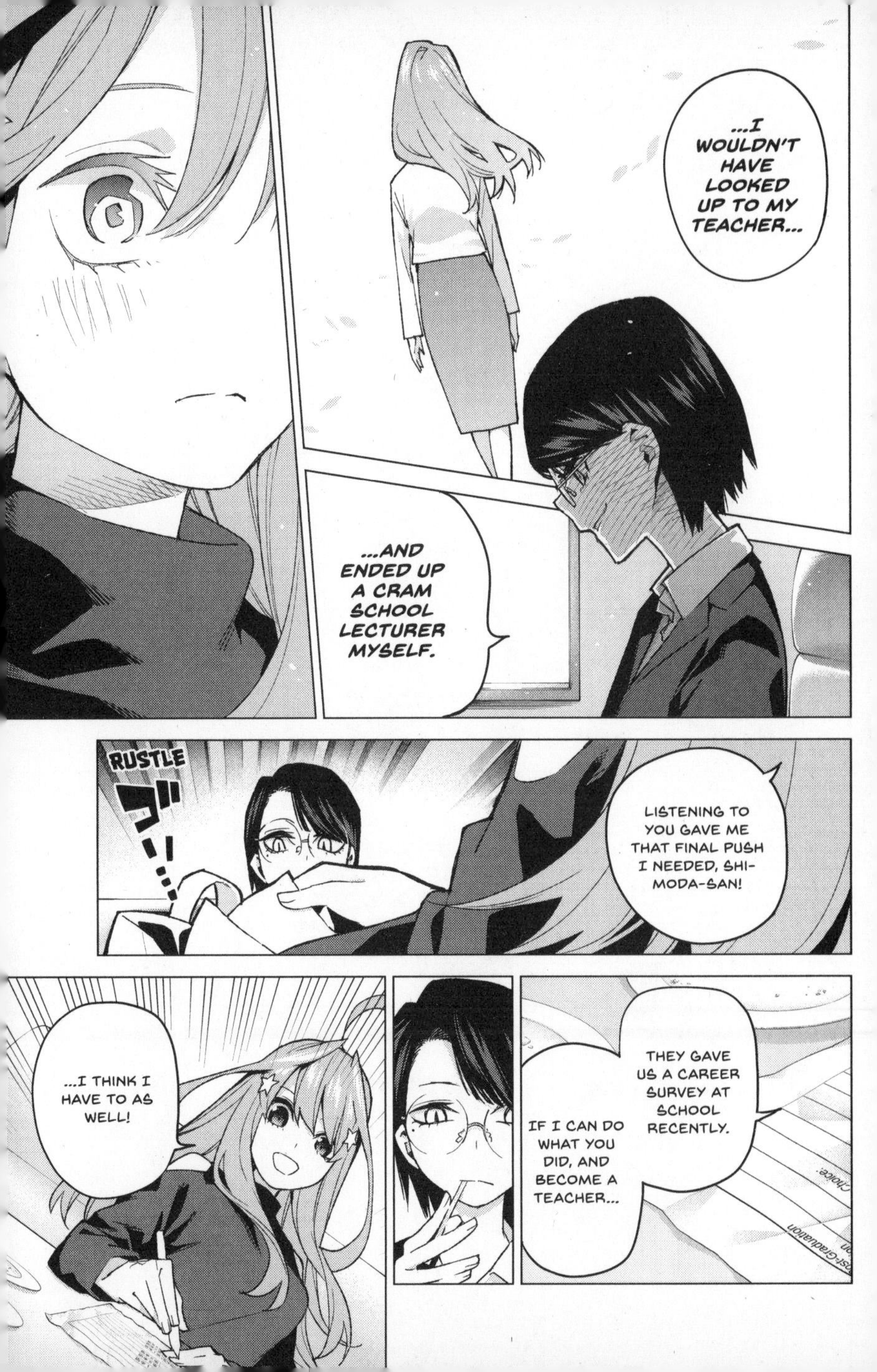
...I WOULDN'T HAVE LOOKED UP TO MY TEACHER...
...AND ENDED UP A CRAM SCHOOL LECTURER MYSELF.
LISTENING TO YOU GAVE ME THAT FINAL PUSH I NEEDED, SHI-MODA-SAN!
RUSTLE
THEY GAVE US A CAREER SURVEY AT SCHOOL RECENTLY.
IF I CAN DO WHAT YOU DID, AND BECOME A TEACHER...
...I THINK I HAVE TO AS WELL!

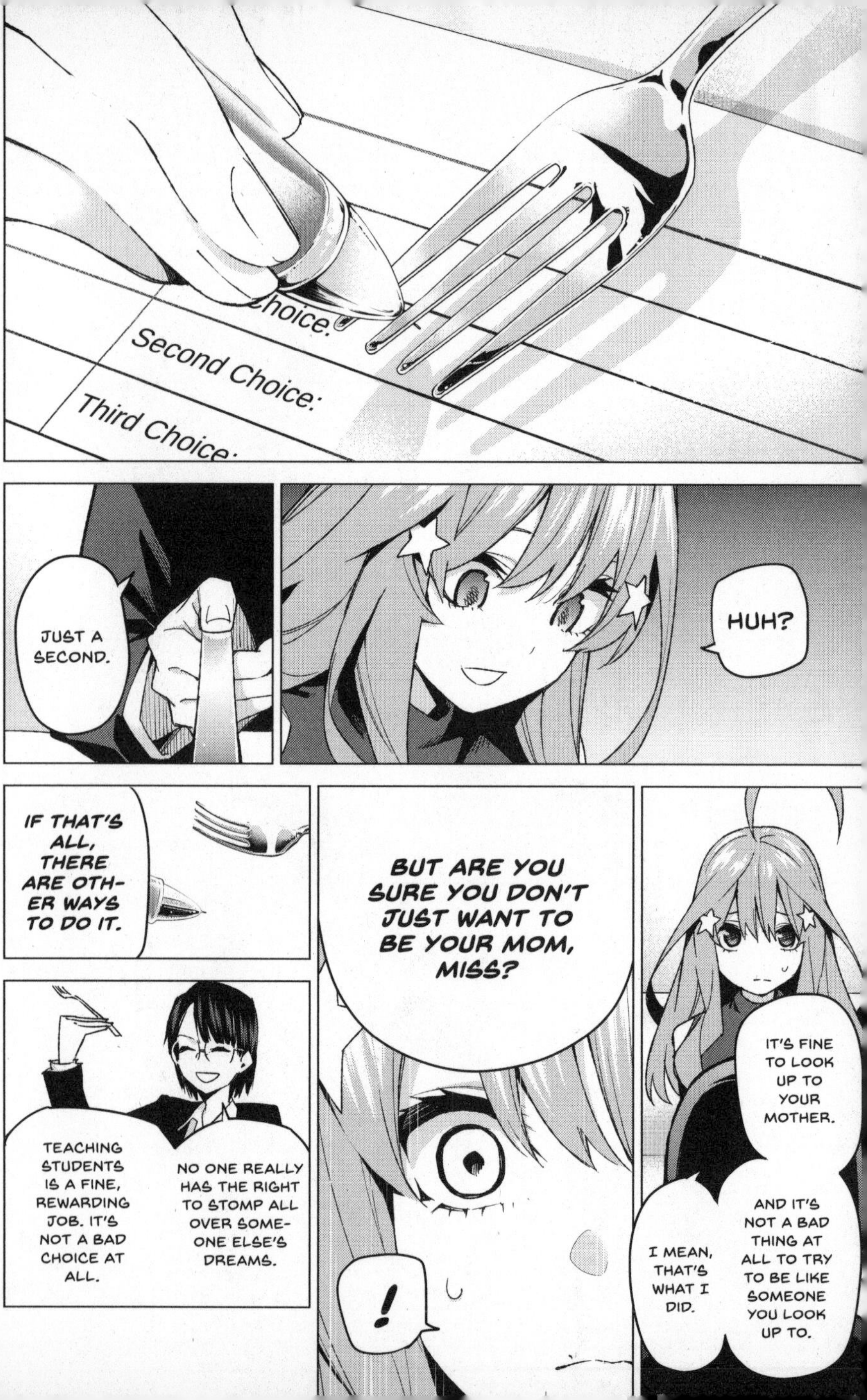

Second Choice:
Third Choice
JUST A SECOND.
HUH?
IF THAT'S ALL, THERE ARE OTH-ER WAYS TO DO IT.
TEACHING STUDENTS IS A FINE, REWARDING JOB. IT'S NOT A BAD CHOICE AT ALL.
NO ONE REALLY HAS THE RIGHT TO STOMP ALL OVER SOME-ONE ELSE'S DREAMS.
IT'S FINE TO LOOK UP TO YOUR MOTHER.
AND IT'S NOT A BAD THING AT ALL TO TRY TO BE LIKE SOMEONE YOU LOOK UP TO.
I MEAN, THAT'S WHAT I DID.
BUT ARE YOU SURE YOU DON'T JUST WANT TO BE YOUR MOM, MISS?
!

BUT ONLY IF THERE'S A REASON YOU WANT TO BE A TEACHER.

2

LET'S EXCHANGE CONTACT INFORMATION.

SHE ATE A LOT...

I...

OOPS! HERE I AM LECTURING YOU ON MY OFF HOURS. I'VE GOTTA FIX THAT HABIT.

NEXT TIME YOU FEEL LIKE HEARING ABOUT YOUR MOM...

...LET'S MEET UP AGAIN.

Wed	Thur
31	1
7	8
14	15

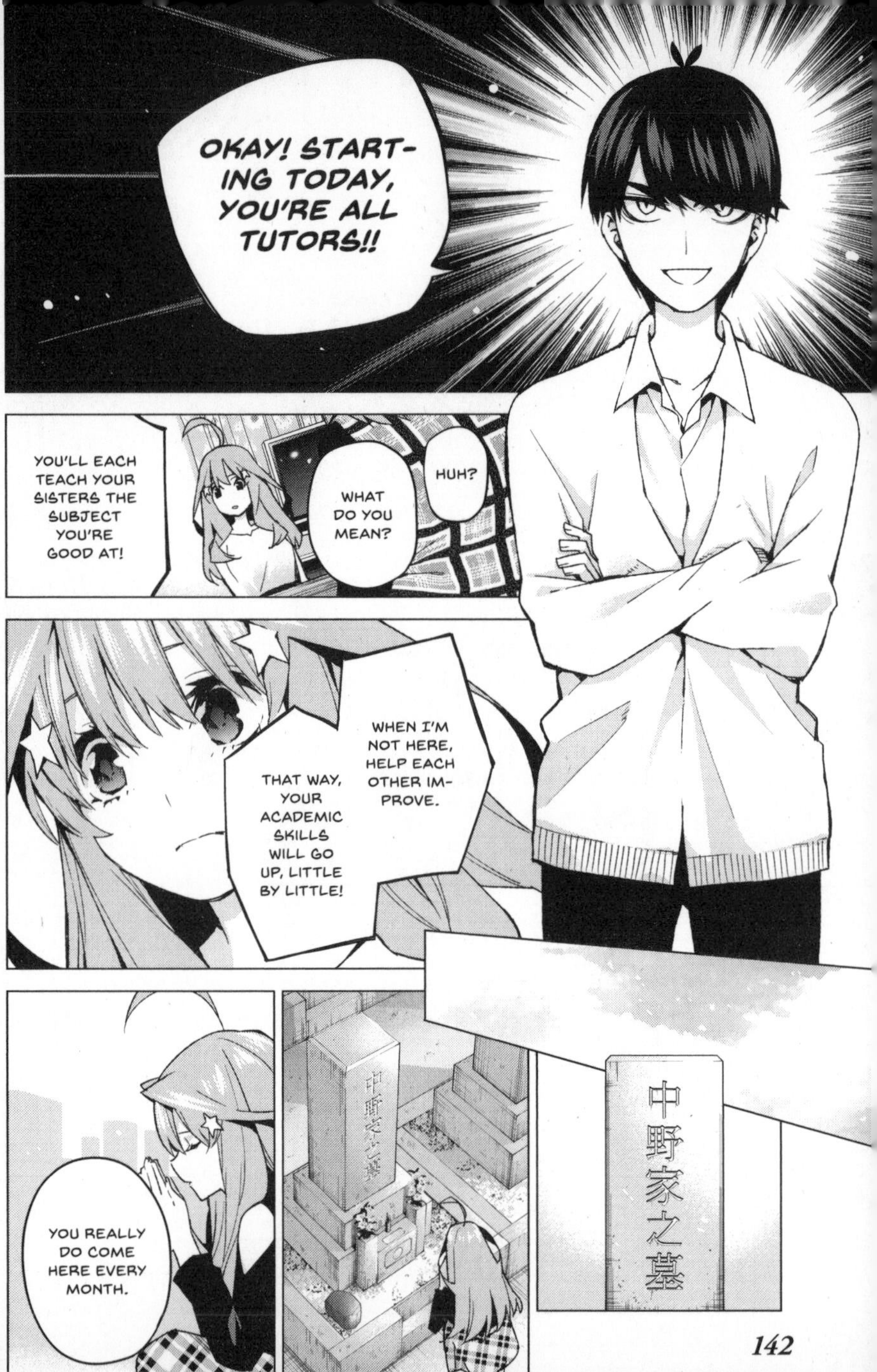
OKAY! START-ING TODAY, YOU'RE ALL TUTORS!!
HUH?
WHAT DO YOU MEAN?
YOU'LL EACH TEACH YOUR SISTERS THE SUBJECT YOU'RE GOOD AT!
WHEN I'M NOT HERE, HELP EACH OTHER IM-PROVE.
THAT WAY, YOUR ACADEMIC SKILLS WILL GO UP, LITTLE BY LITTLE!
中野家之墓
YOU REALLY DO COME HERE EVERY MONTH.

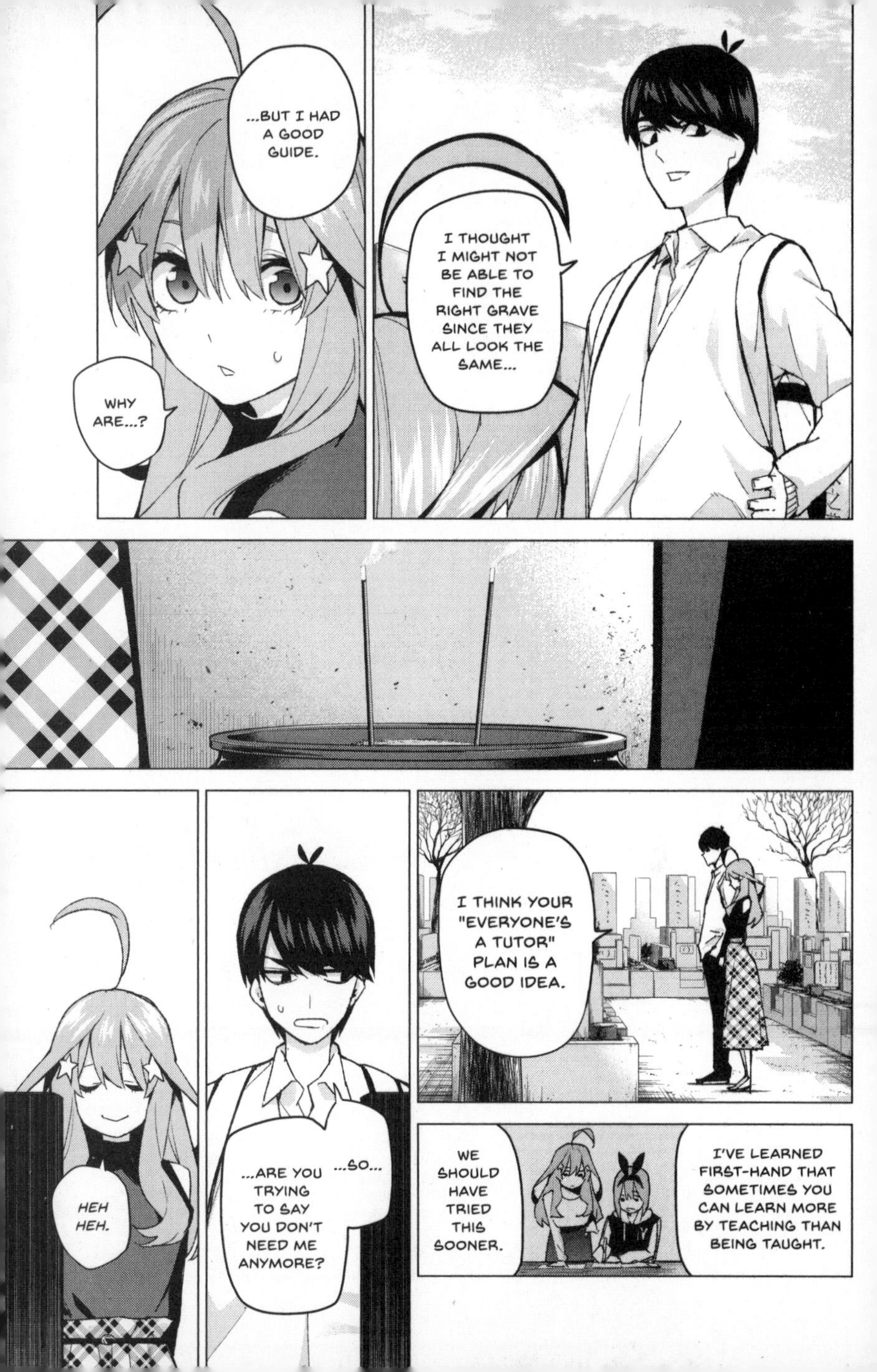
I THOUGHT I MIGHT NOT BE ABLE TO FIND THE RIGHT GRAVE SINCE THEY ALL LOOK THE SAME...
...BUT I HAD A GOOD GUIDE.
WHY ARE...?
I THINK YOUR "EVERYONE'S A TUTOR" PLAN IS A GOOD IDEA.
I'VE LEARNED FIRST-HAND THAT SOMETIMES YOU CAN LEARN MORE BY TEACHING THAN BEING TAUGHT.
WE SHOULD HAVE TRIED THIS SOONER.
...SO...
...ARE YOU TRYING TO SAY YOU DON'T NEED ME ANYMORE?
HEH HEH.

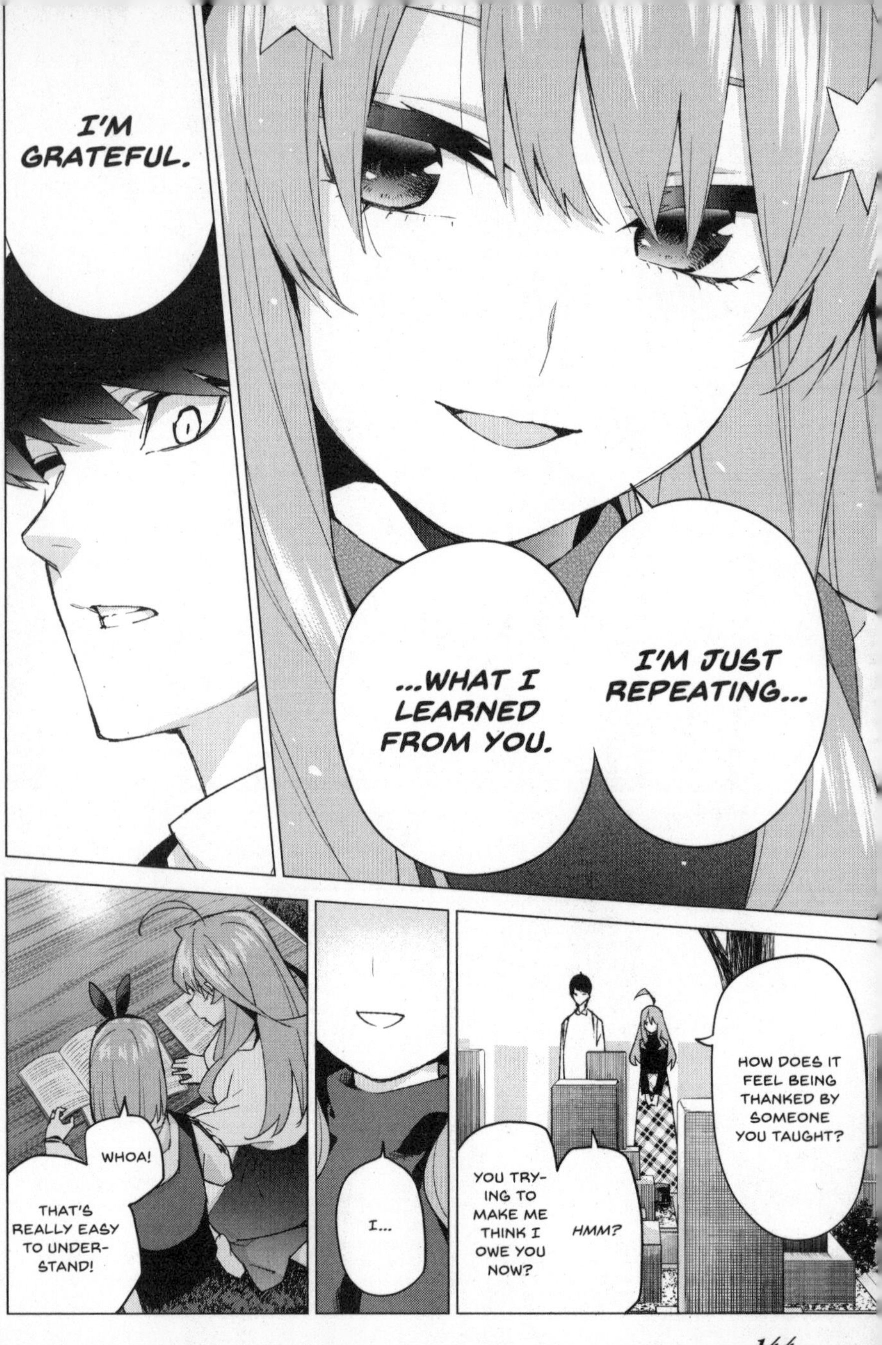
I'M JUST REPEATING...
...WHAT I LEARNED FROM YOU.
I'M GRATEFUL.
HOW DOES IT FEEL BEING THANKED BY SOMEONE YOU TAUGHT?
HMM?
YOU TRYING TO MAKE ME THINK I OWE YOU NOW?
I...
WHOA!
THAT'S REALLY EASY TO UNDERSTAND!

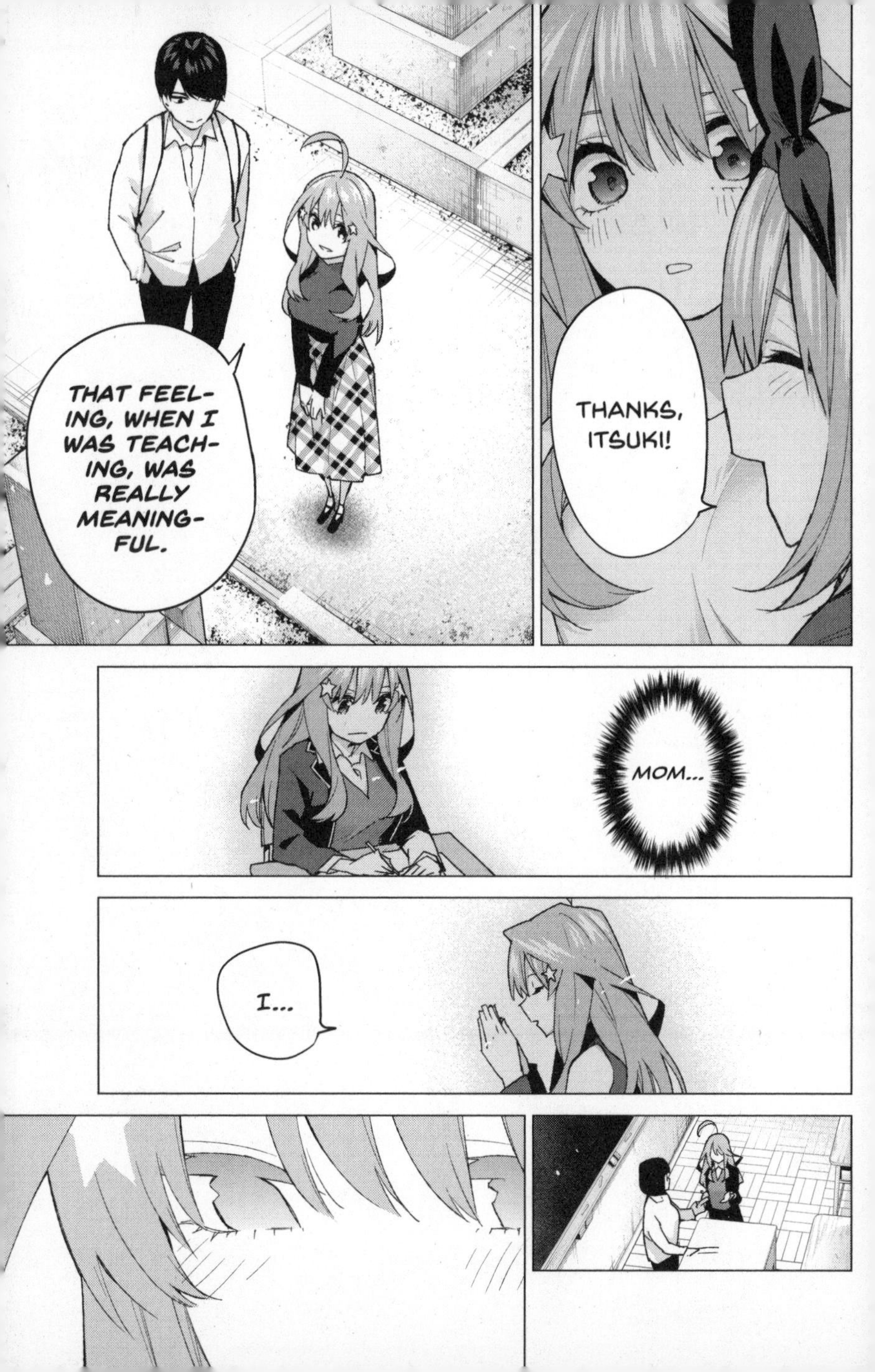
THANKS, ITSUKI!
THAT FEELING, WHEN I WAS TEACHING, WAS REALLY MEANINGFUL.
MOM...
I...

Language Arts	Math	Science	Social Studies	English	Total
47	35	70	32	40	224

...I AM GOING TO BE A TEACHER.

VERY WELL DONE

Itsuki Nakano

PASSED

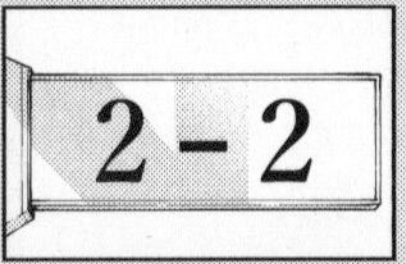
2-2

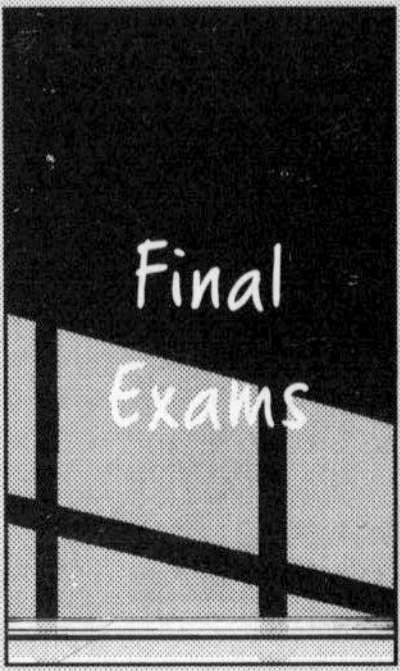
Final Exams

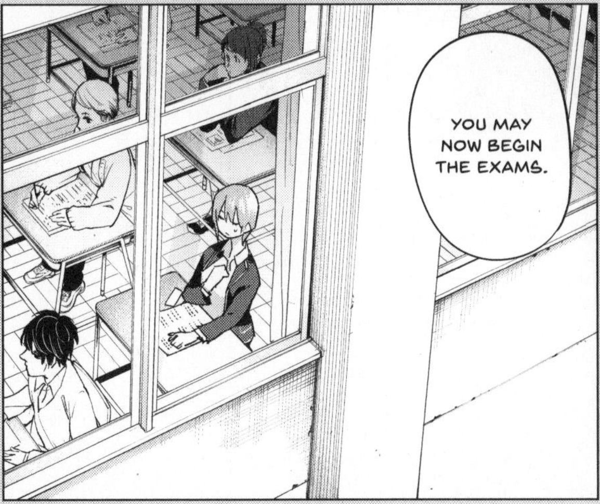
YOU MAY NOW BEGIN THE EXAMS.

CHAPTER 58
IF THE LAST EXAM WAS ICHIKA'S

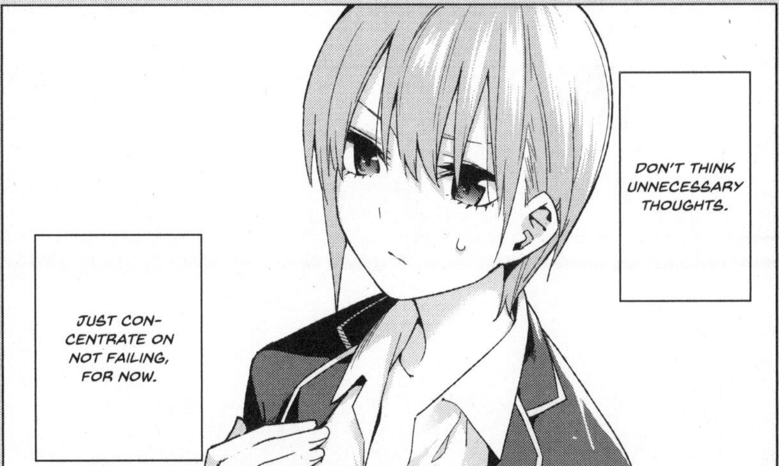
DON'T THINK UNNECESSARY THOUGHTS.
JUST CON-CENTRATE ON NOT FAILING, FOR NOW.

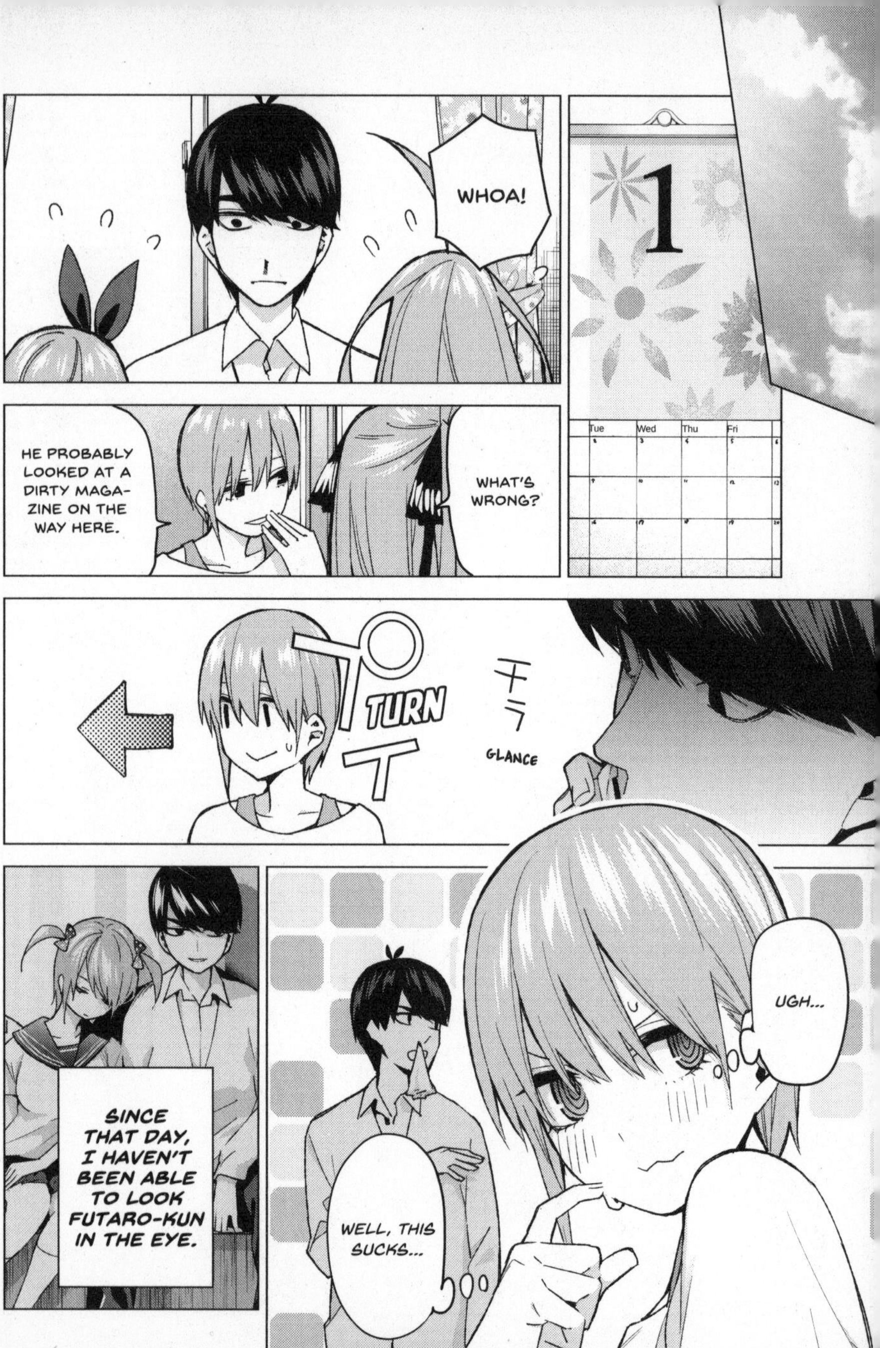
1
Tue
Wed
Thu
Fri
WHOA!
WHAT'S WRONG?
HE PROBABLY LOOKED AT A DIRTY MAGAZINE ON THE WAY HERE.
チラ
GLANCE
TURN
UGH...
WELL, THIS SUCKS...
SINCE THAT DAY, I HAVEN'T BEEN ABLE TO LOOK FUTARO-KUN IN THE EYE.

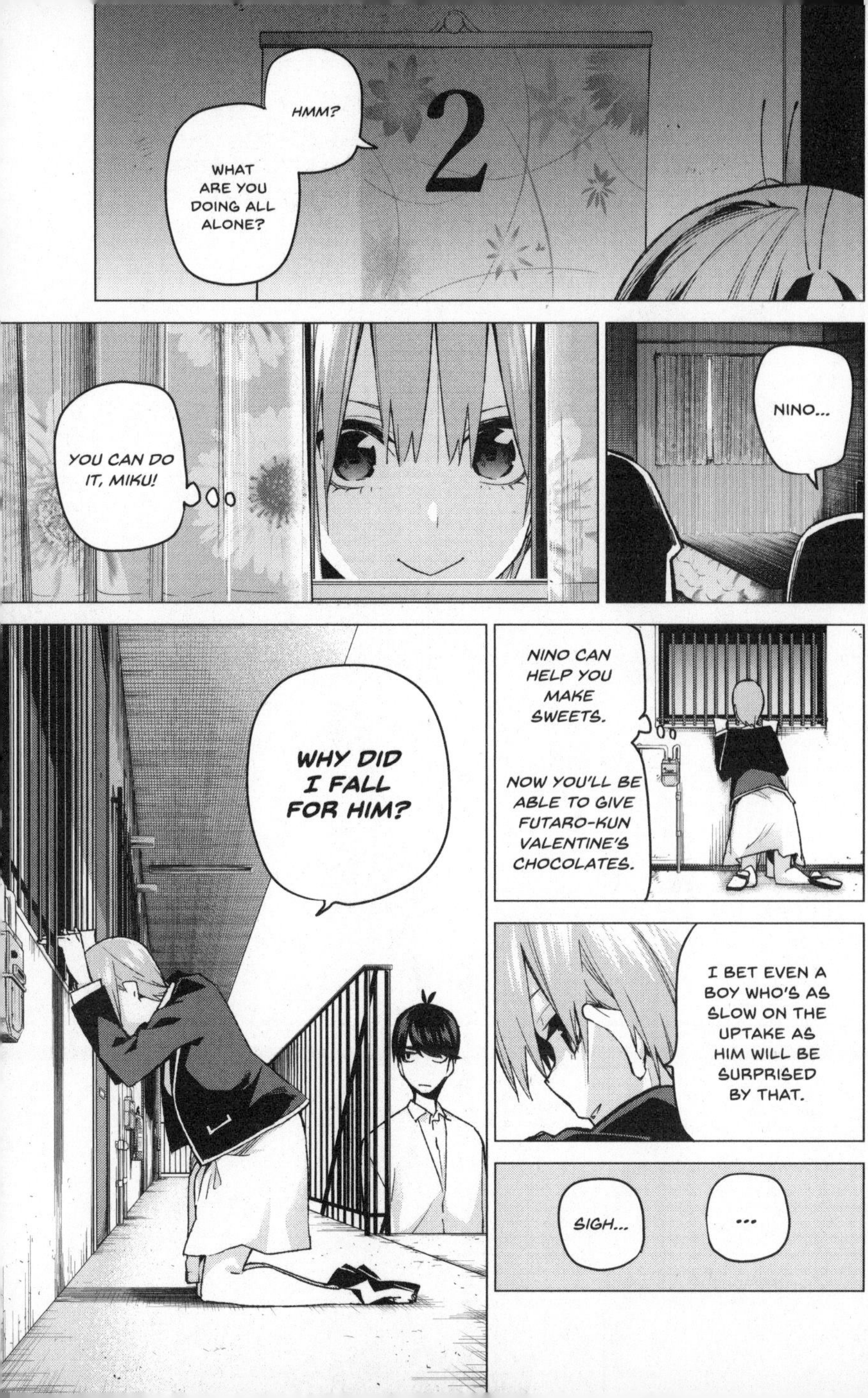
2
HMM?
WHAT ARE YOU DOING ALL ALONE?
NINO...
YOU CAN DO IT, MIKU!
NINO CAN HELP YOU MAKE SWEETS.
NOW YOU'LL BE ABLE TO GIVE FUTARO-KUN VALENTINE'S CHOCOLATES.
I BET EVEN A BOY WHO'S AS SLOW ON THE UPTAKE AS HIM WILL BE SURPRISED BY THAT.
...
SIGH...
WHY DID I FALL FOR HIM?

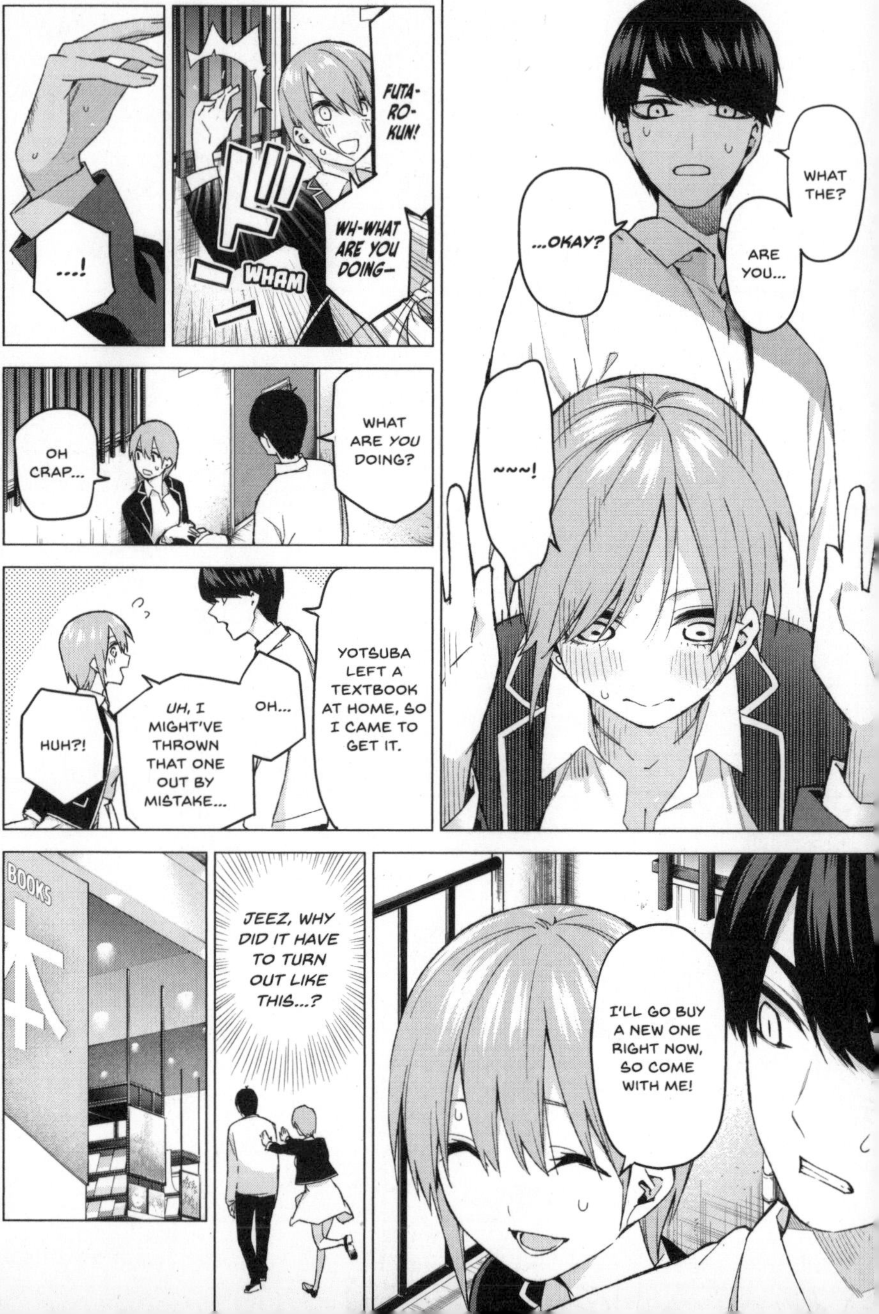
WHAT THE?
ARE YOU...
...OKAY?
~~~!
FUTA-RO-KUN!
WH-WHAT ARE YOU DOING—
WHAM
...!
WHAT ARE YOU DOING?
OH CRAP...
YOTSUBA LEFT A TEXTBOOK AT HOME, SO I CAME TO GET IT.
OH...
UH, I MIGHT'VE THROWN THAT ONE OUT BY MISTAKE...
HUH?!
I'LL GO BUY A NEW ONE RIGHT NOW, SO COME WITH ME!
JEEZ, WHY DID IT HAVE TO TURN OUT LIKE THIS...?
BOOKS
本
~~~

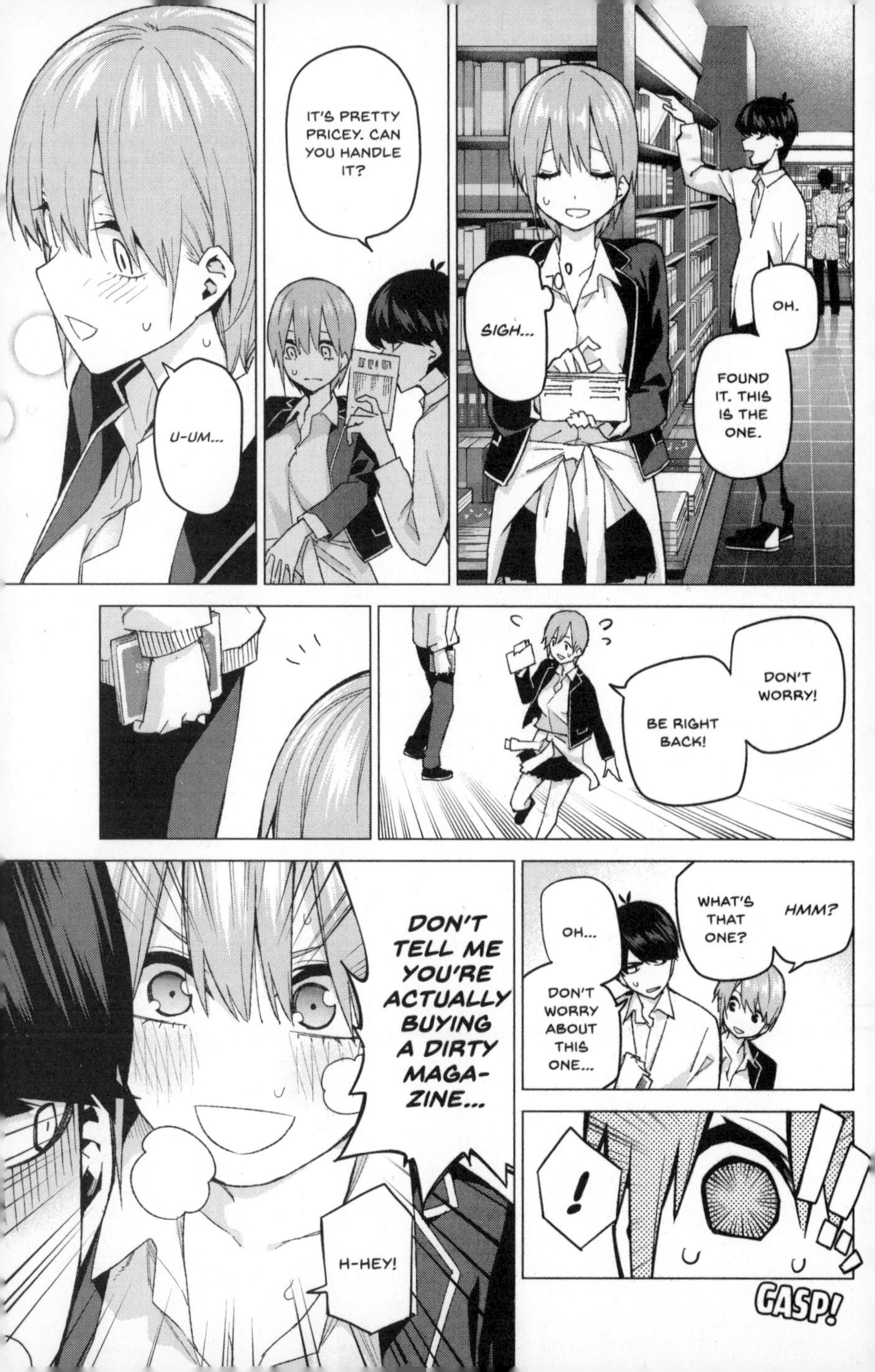
OH.
FOUND IT. THIS IS THE ONE.
SIGH...
IT'S PRETTY PRICEY. CAN YOU HANDLE IT?
U-UM...
DON'T WORRY!
BE RIGHT BACK!
HMM?
WHAT'S THAT ONE?
OH...
DON'T WORRY ABOUT THIS ONE...
!
!!
GASP!
DON'T TELL ME YOU'RE ACTUALLY BUYING A DIRTY MAGA-ZINE...
H-HEY!

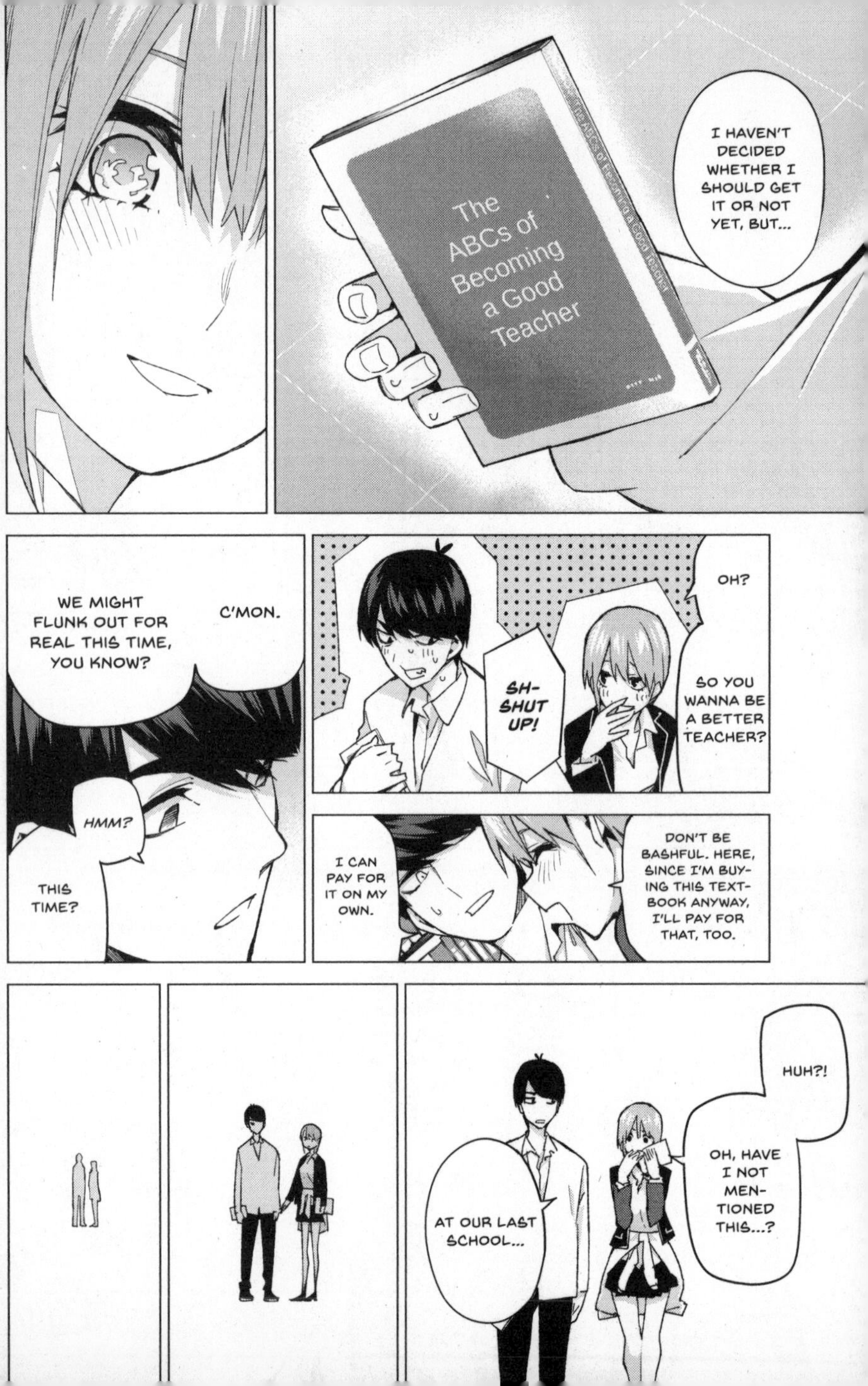
The ABCs of Becoming a Good Teacher
I HAVEN'T DECIDED WHETHER I SHOULD GET IT OR NOT YET, BUT...
OH?
SO YOU WANNA BE A BETTER TEACHER?
SH-SHUT UP!
DON'T BE BASHFUL. HERE, SINCE I'M BUYING THIS TEXTBOOK ANYWAY, I'LL PAY FOR THAT, TOO.
I CAN PAY FOR IT ON MY OWN.
C'MON.
WE MIGHT FLUNK OUT FOR REAL THIS TIME, YOU KNOW?
HMM?
THIS TIME?
HUH?!
OH, HAVE I NOT MENTIONED THIS...?
AT OUR LAST SCHOOL...

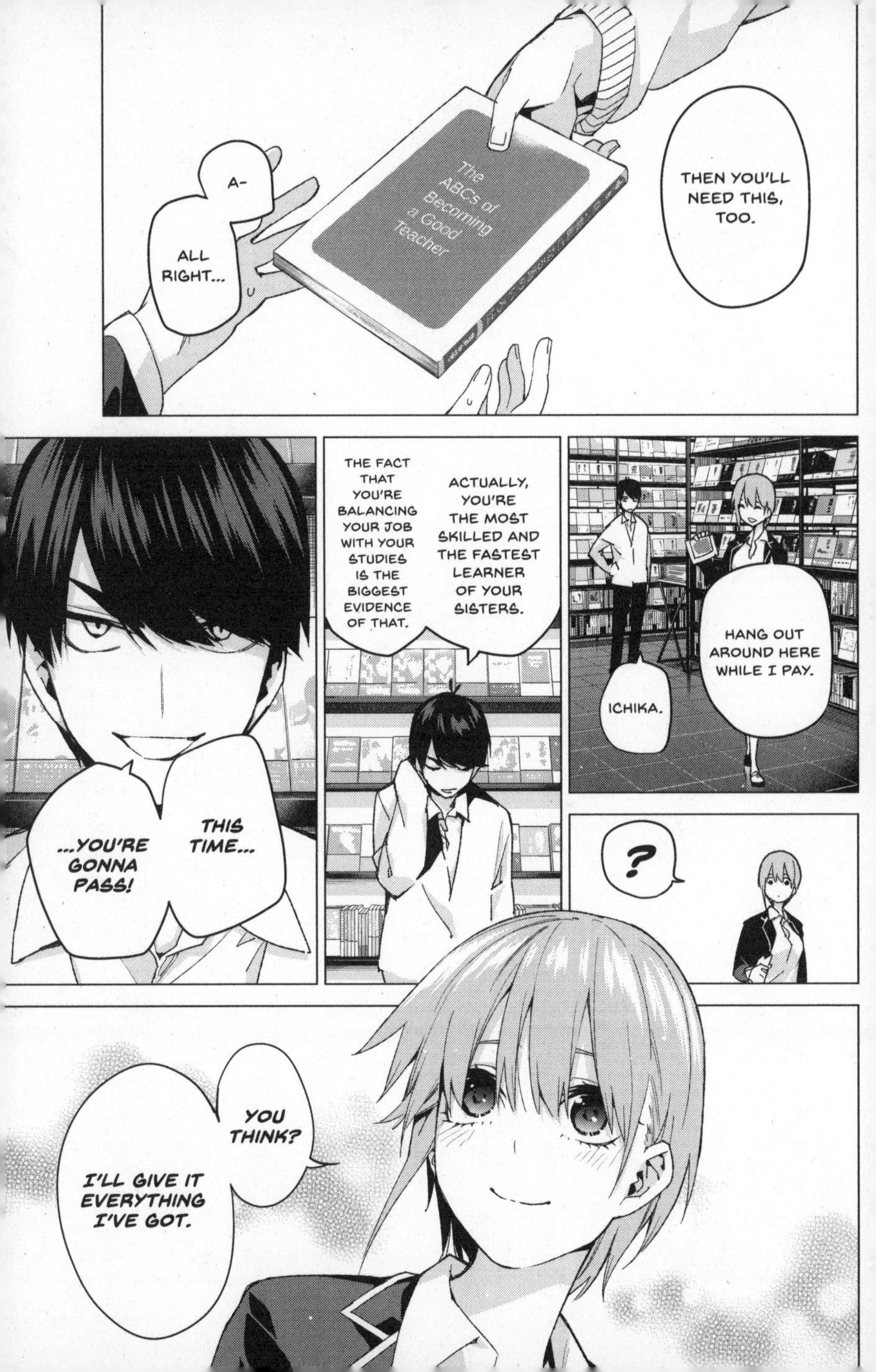
THEN YOU'LL NEED THIS, TOO.
The ABCs of Becoming a Good Teacher
A-
ALL RIGHT...
HANG OUT AROUND HERE WHILE I PAY.
ICHIKA.
?
ACTUALLY, YOU'RE THE MOST SKILLED AND THE FASTEST LEARNER OF YOUR SISTERS.
THE FACT THAT YOU'RE BALANCING YOUR JOB WITH YOUR STUDIES IS THE BIGGEST EVIDENCE OF THAT.
THIS TIME...
...YOU'RE GONNA PASS!
YOU THINK?
I'LL GIVE IT EVERYTHING I'VE GOT.

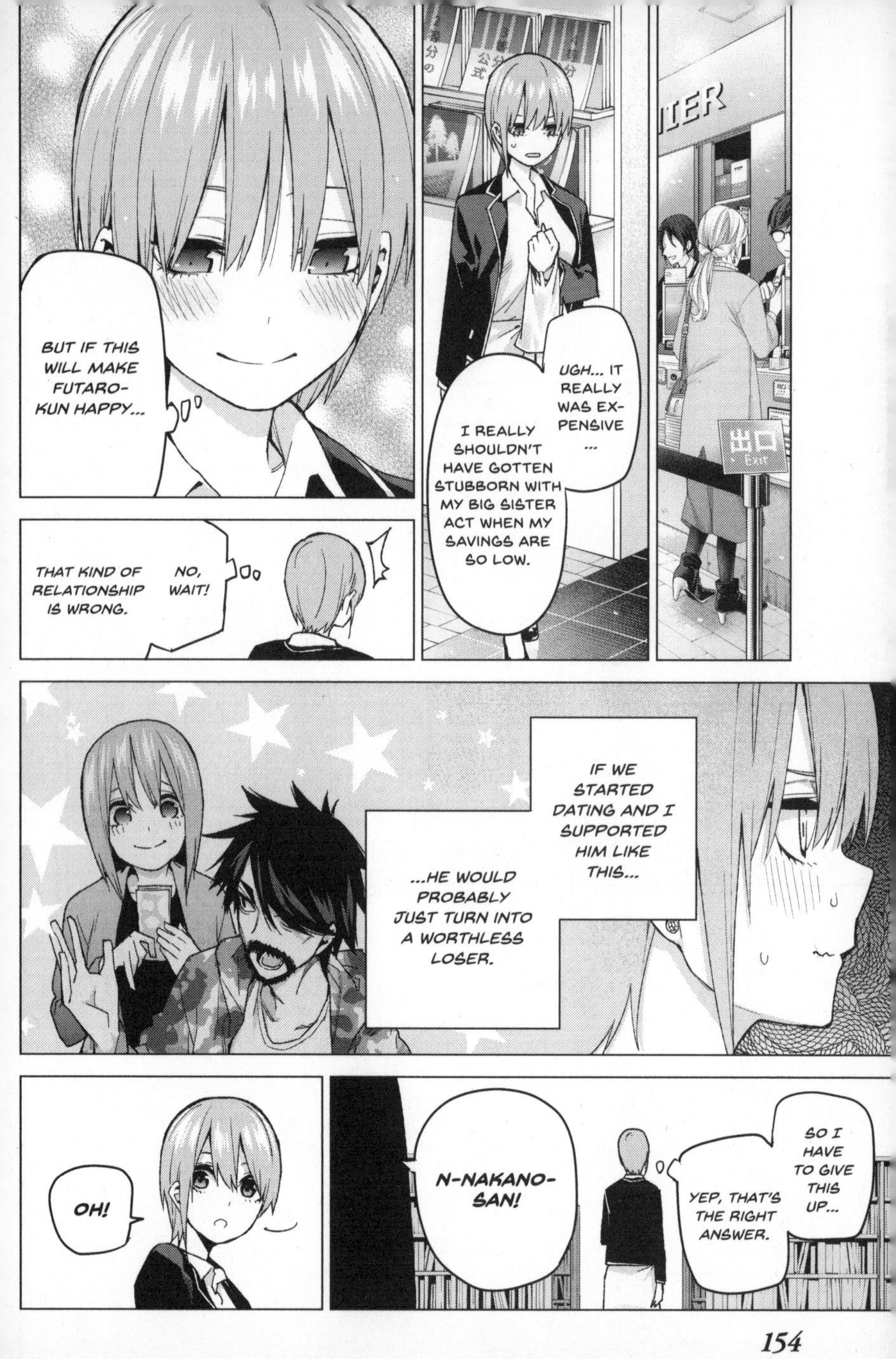
出口
Exit
UGH... IT REALLY WAS EX-PENSIVE...
I REALLY SHOULDN'T HAVE GOTTEN STUBBORN WITH MY BIG SISTER ACT WHEN MY SAVINGS ARE SO LOW.
BUT IF THIS WILL MAKE FUTARO-KUN HAPPY...
NO, WAIT!
THAT KIND OF RELATIONSHIP IS WRONG.
IF WE STARTED DATING AND I SUPPORTED HIM LIKE THIS...
...HE WOULD PROBABLY JUST TURN INTO A WORTHLESS LOSER.
SO I HAVE TO GIVE THIS UP...
YEP, THAT'S THE RIGHT ANSWER.
N-NAKANO-SAN!
OH!

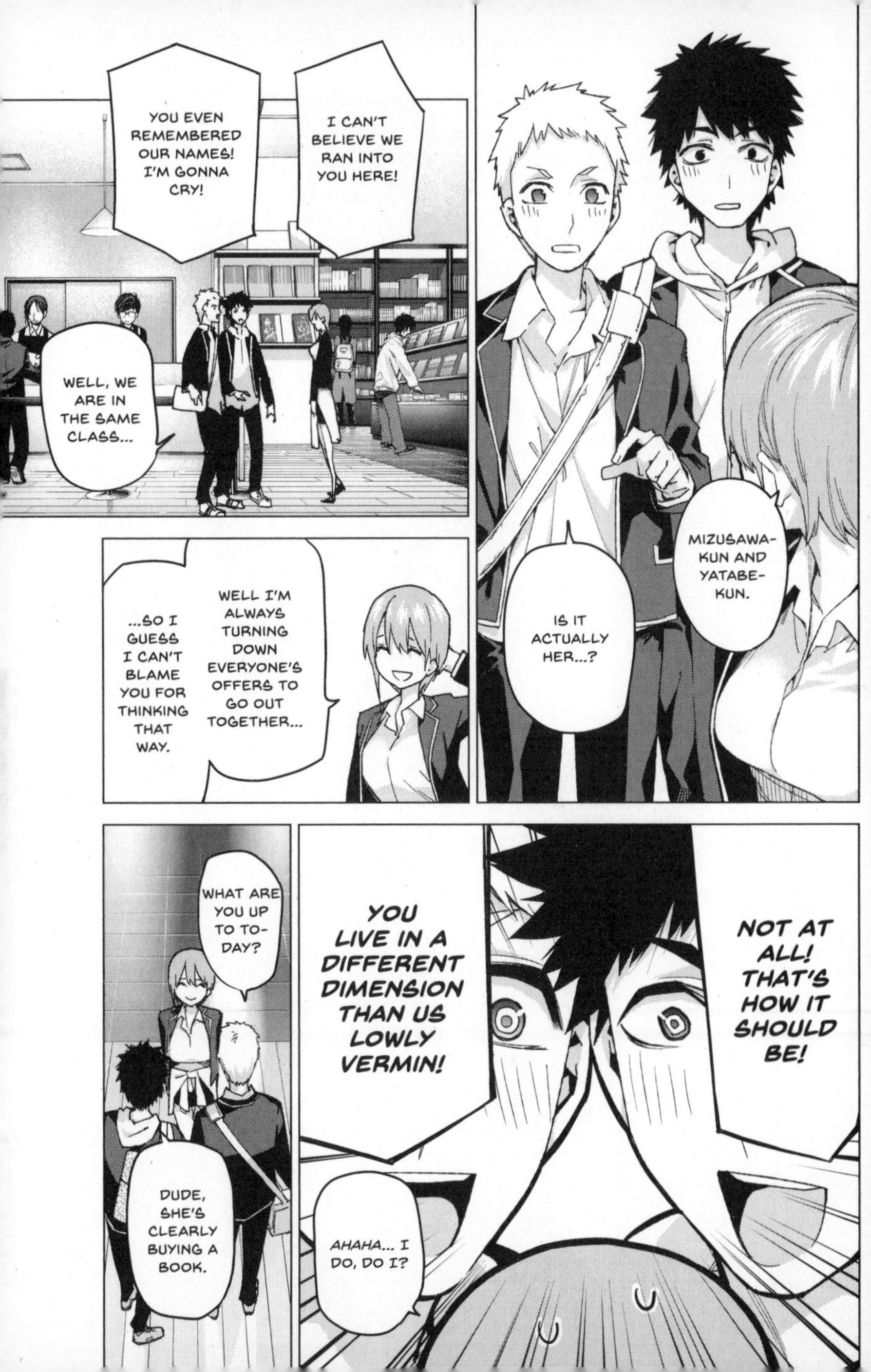
MIZUSAWA-KUN AND YATABE-KUN.
IS IT ACTUALLY HER...?
I CAN'T BELIEVE WE RAN INTO YOU HERE!
YOU EVEN REMEMBERED OUR NAMES! I'M GONNA CRY!
WELL, WE ARE IN THE SAME CLASS...
WELL I'M ALWAYS TURNING DOWN EVERYONE'S OFFERS TO GO OUT TOGETHER...
...SO I GUESS I CAN'T BLAME YOU FOR THINKING THAT WAY.
NOT AT ALL! THAT'S HOW IT SHOULD BE!
YOU LIVE IN A DIFFERENT DIMENSION THAN US LOWLY VERMIN!
AHAHA... I DO, DO I?
WHAT ARE YOU UP TO TO-DAY?
DUDE, SHE'S CLEARLY BUYING A BOOK.

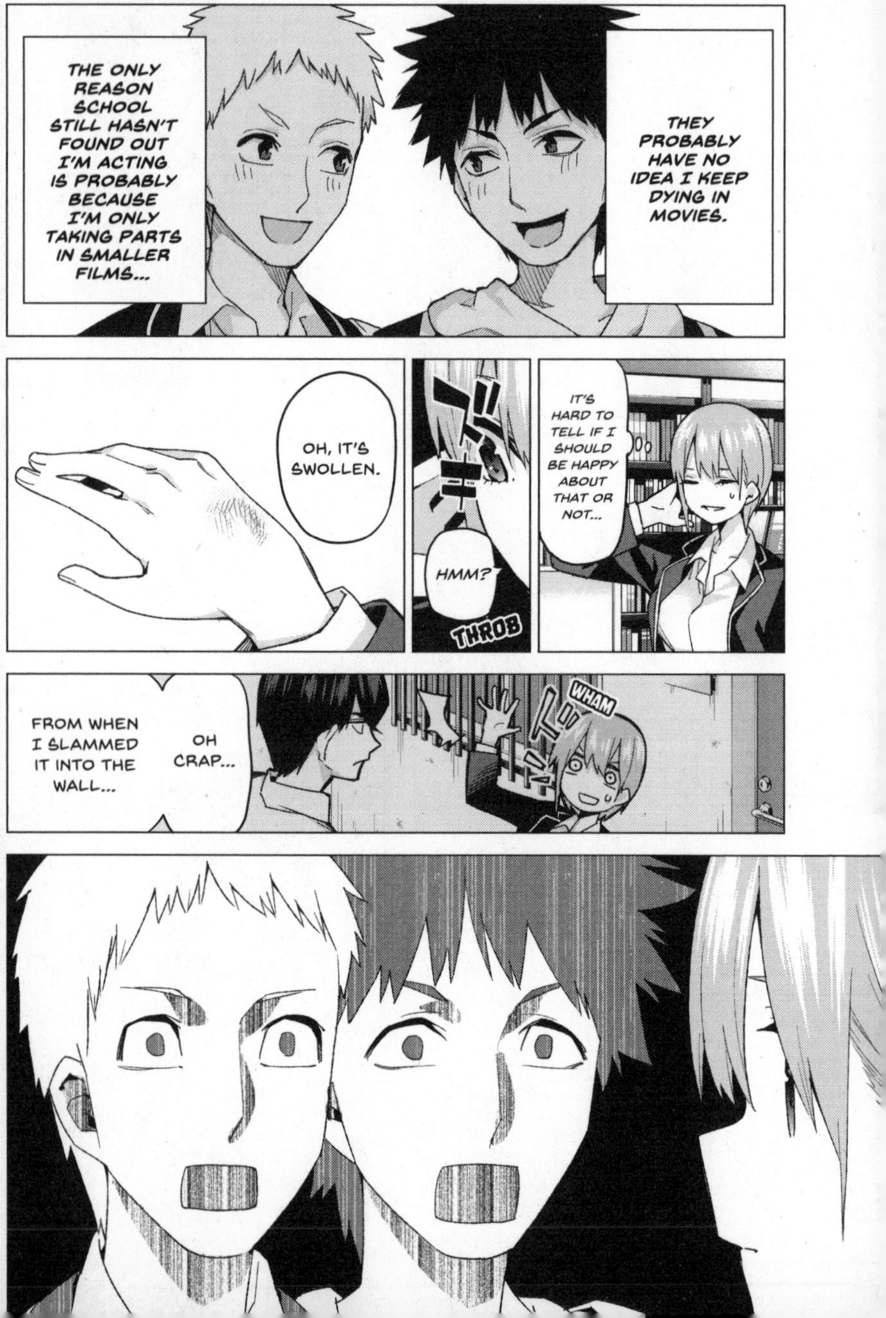
THEY PROBABLY HAVE NO IDEA I KEEP DYING IN MOVIES.
THE ONLY REASON SCHOOL STILL HASN'T FOUND OUT I'M ACTING IS PROBABLY BECAUSE I'M ONLY TAKING PARTS IN SMALLER FILMS...
IT'S HARD TO TELL IF I SHOULD BE HAPPY ABOUT THAT OR NOT...
HMM?
THROB
OH, IT'S SWOLLEN.
WHAM
OH CRAP...
FROM WHEN I SLAMMED IT INTO THE WALL...

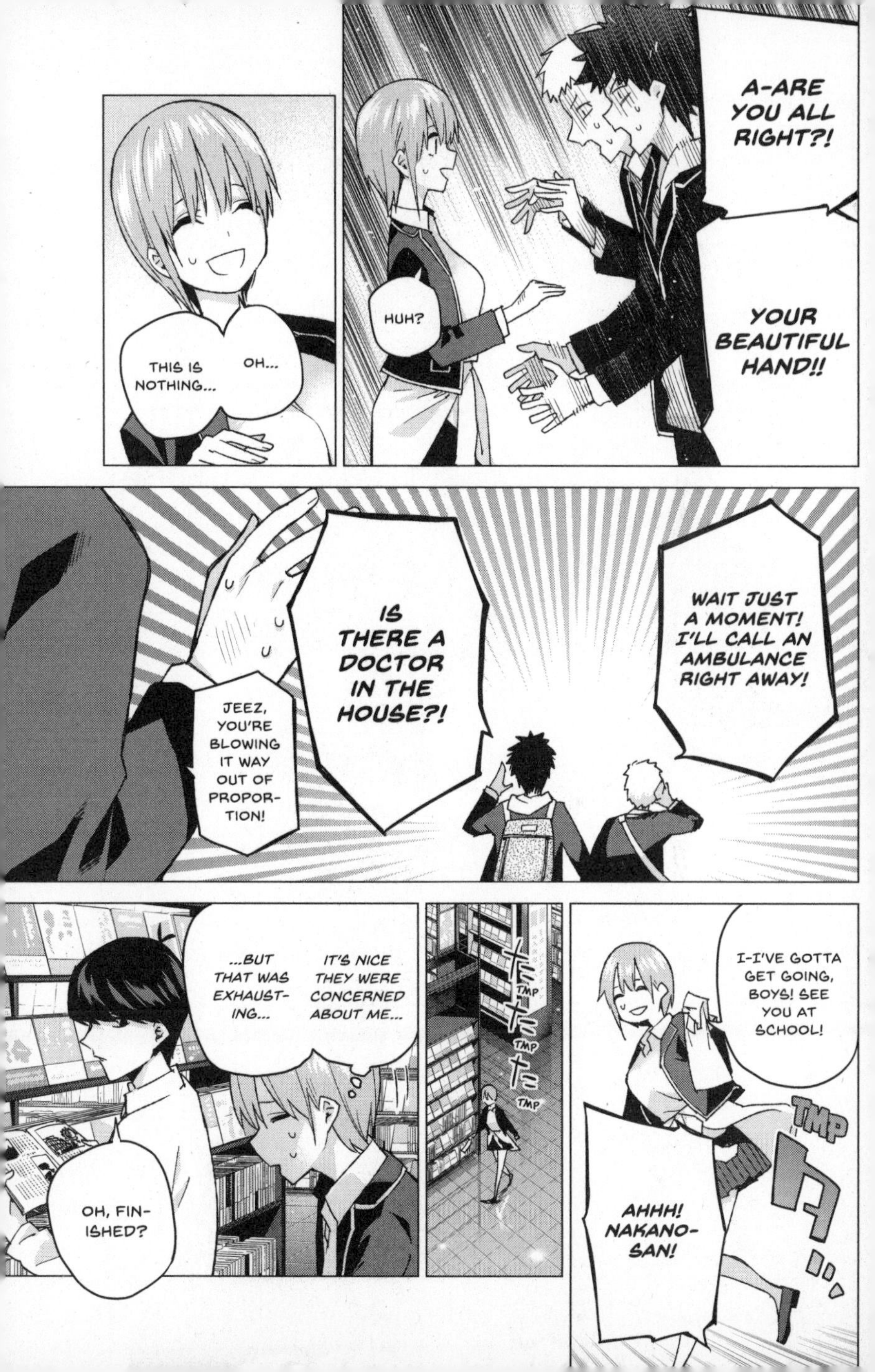
A-ARE YOU ALL RIGHT?!
YOUR BEAUTIFUL HAND!!
HUH?
OH...
THIS IS NOTHING...
WAIT JUST A MOMENT! I'LL CALL AN AMBULANCE RIGHT AWAY!
IS THERE A DOCTOR IN THE HOUSE?!
JEEZ, YOU'RE BLOWING IT WAY OUT OF PROPOR-TION!
I-I'VE GOTTA GET GOING, BOYS! SEE YOU AT SCHOOL!
TMP
AHHH! NAKANO-SAN!
TMP
TMP
TMP
IT'S NICE THEY WERE CONCERNED ABOUT ME...
...BUT THAT WAS EXHAUST-ING...
OH, FIN-ISHED?

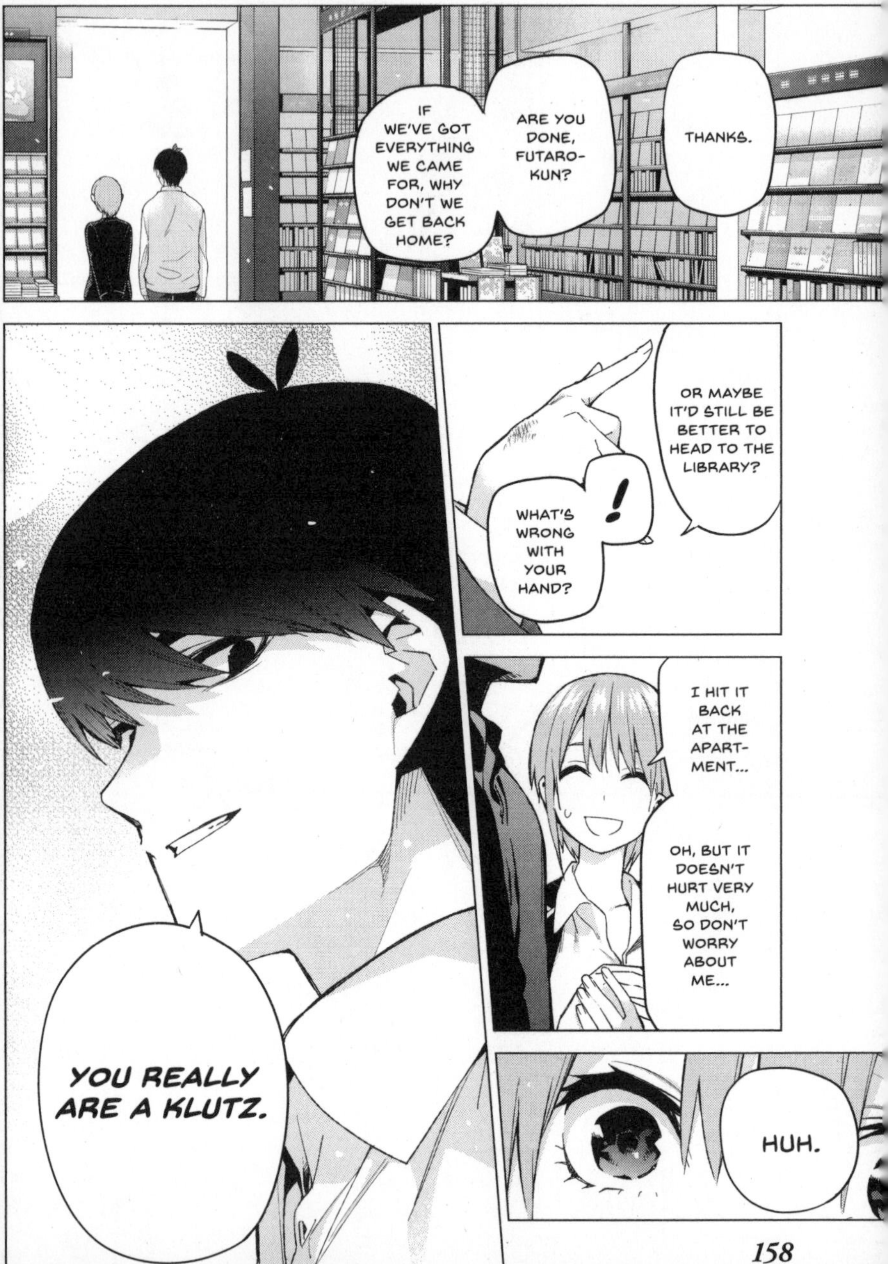
THANKS.
ARE YOU DONE, FUTARO-KUN?
IF WE'VE GOT EVERYTHING WE CAME FOR, WHY DON'T WE GET BACK HOME?
OR MAYBE IT'D STILL BE BETTER TO HEAD TO THE LIBRARY?
!
WHAT'S WRONG WITH YOUR HAND?
I HIT IT BACK AT THE APARTMENT...
OH, BUT IT DOESN'T HURT VERY MUCH, SO DON'T WORRY ABOUT ME...
HUH.
YOU REALLY ARE A KLUTZ.

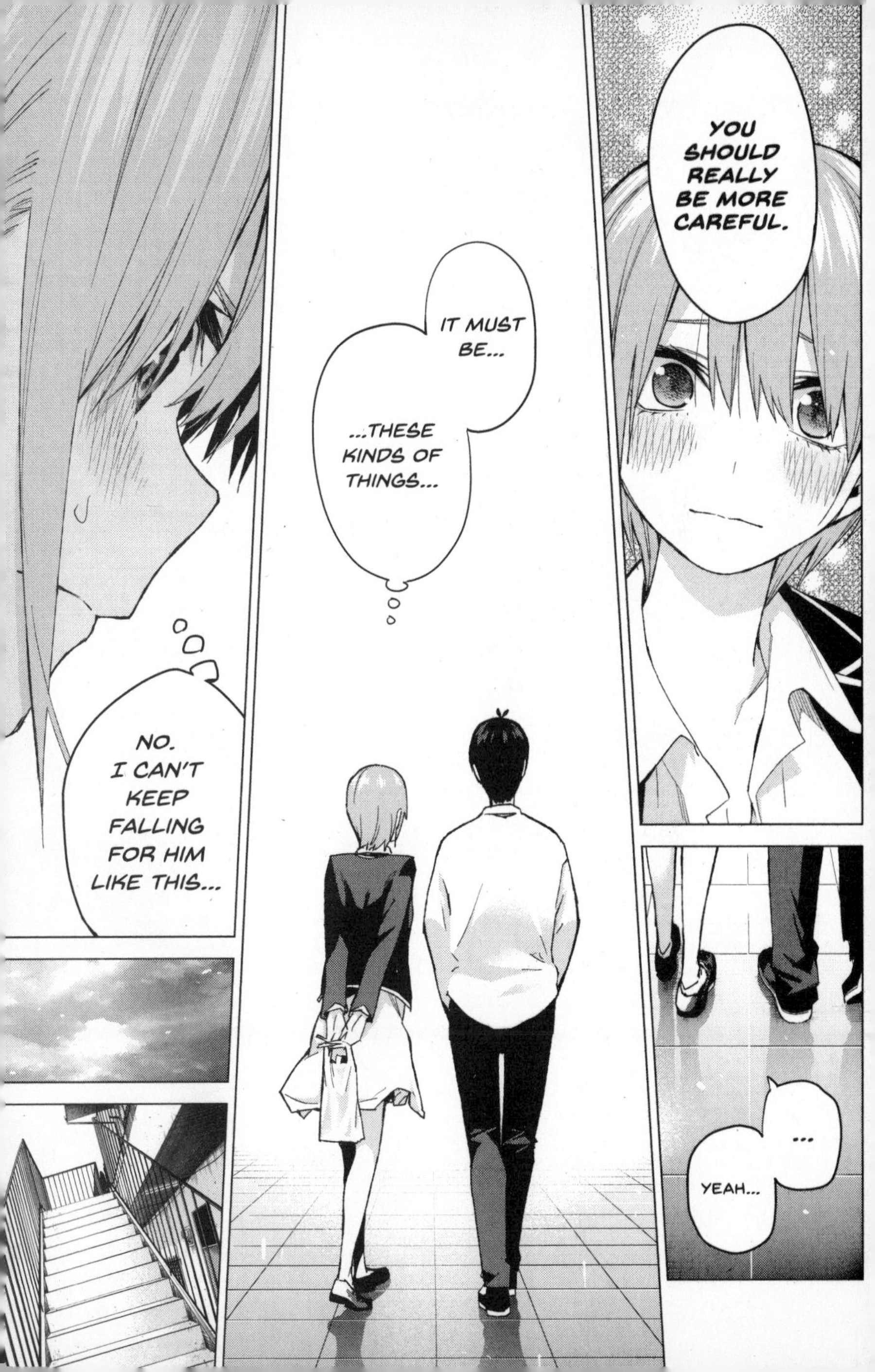

YOU SHOULD REALLY BE MORE CAREFUL.
...
YEAH...
IT MUST BE...
...THESE KINDS OF THINGS...
NO. I CAN'T KEEP FALLING FOR HIM LIKE THIS...

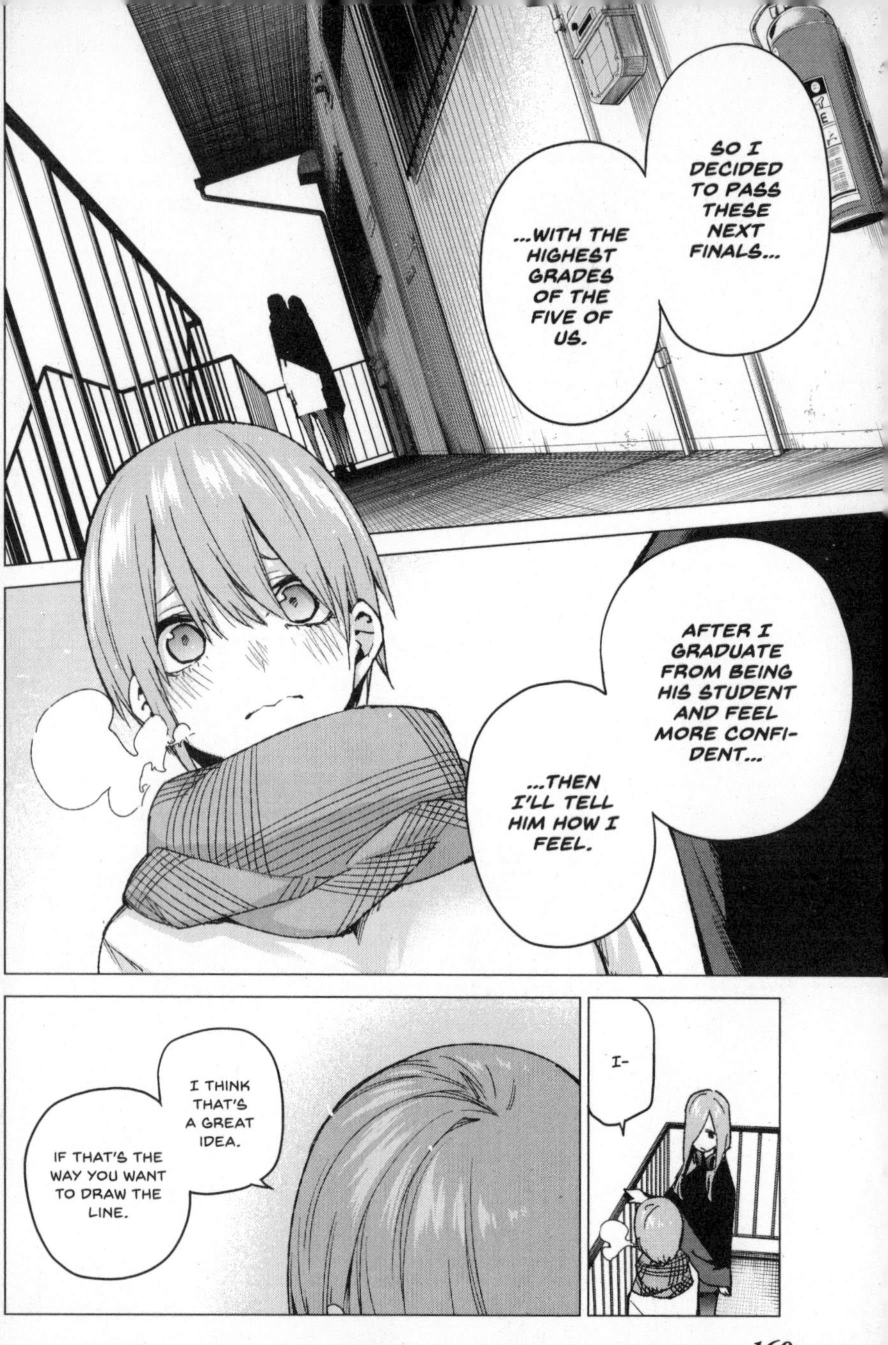
SO I DECIDED TO PASS THESE NEXT FINALS...
...WITH THE HIGHEST GRADES OF THE FIVE OF US.
AFTER I GRADUATE FROM BEING HIS STUDENT AND FEEL MORE CONFI-DENT...
...THEN I'LL TELL HIM HOW I FEEL.
I-
I THINK THAT'S A GREAT IDEA.
IF THAT'S THE WAY YOU WANT TO DRAW THE LINE.

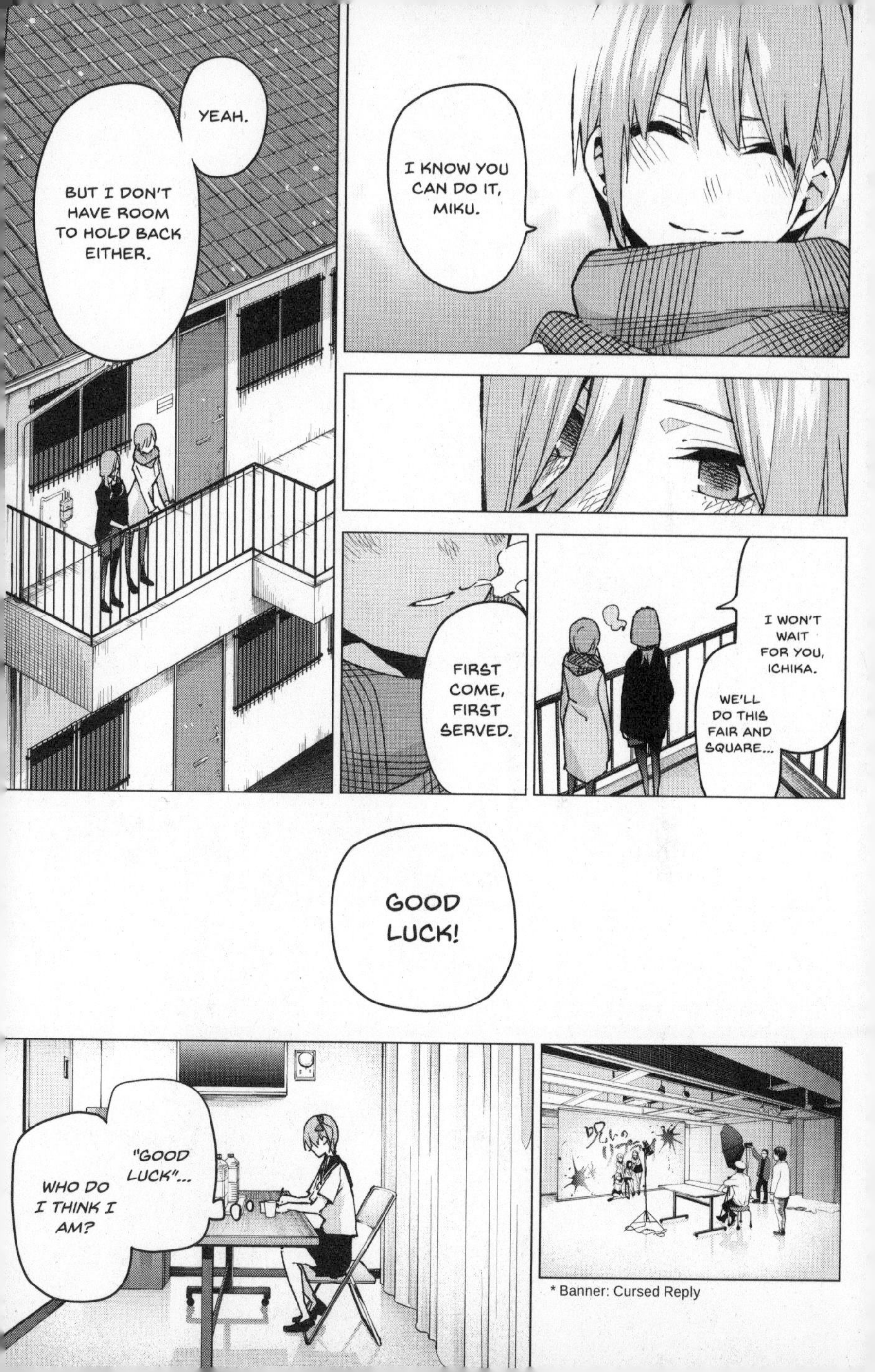
I KNOW YOU CAN DO IT, MIKU.
I WON'T WAIT FOR YOU, ICHIKA.
WE'LL DO THIS FAIR AND SQUARE...
FIRST COME, FIRST SERVED.
YEAH.
BUT I DON'T HAVE ROOM TO HOLD BACK EITHER.
GOOD LUCK!
"GOOD LUCK"...
WHO DO I THINK I AM?

* Banner: Cursed Reply

MIKU KEEPS CHANGING...
JUST MAKE SURE YOU DON'T HAVE ANY RE-GRETS!
NAKANO-SAN, STANDBY!
OKAY!
WHY DON'T YOU TAKE A LITTLE BREAK, ICHIKA-CHAN?
AHAHA, BUT I'M A STUDENT.
BECAUSE THINGS WON'T KEEP GOING LIKE THIS FOREVER.
I'M THE ONE WHO SAID IT, BUT I...
UGH... I'D BET-TER GO TO SLEEP FOR THE NIGHT ...
...AND PICK UP AGAIN TO-MORROW...
THINGS WON'T KEEP GOING LIKE THIS...
WH
O
AP
JUST A LITTLE LONGER!

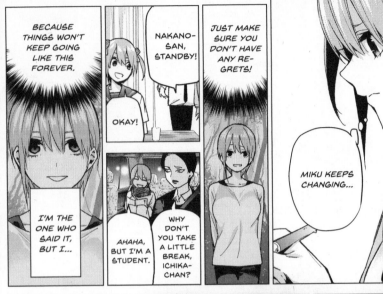

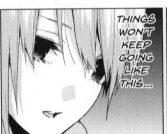

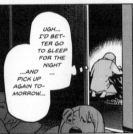

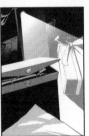

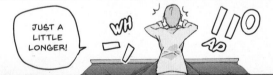

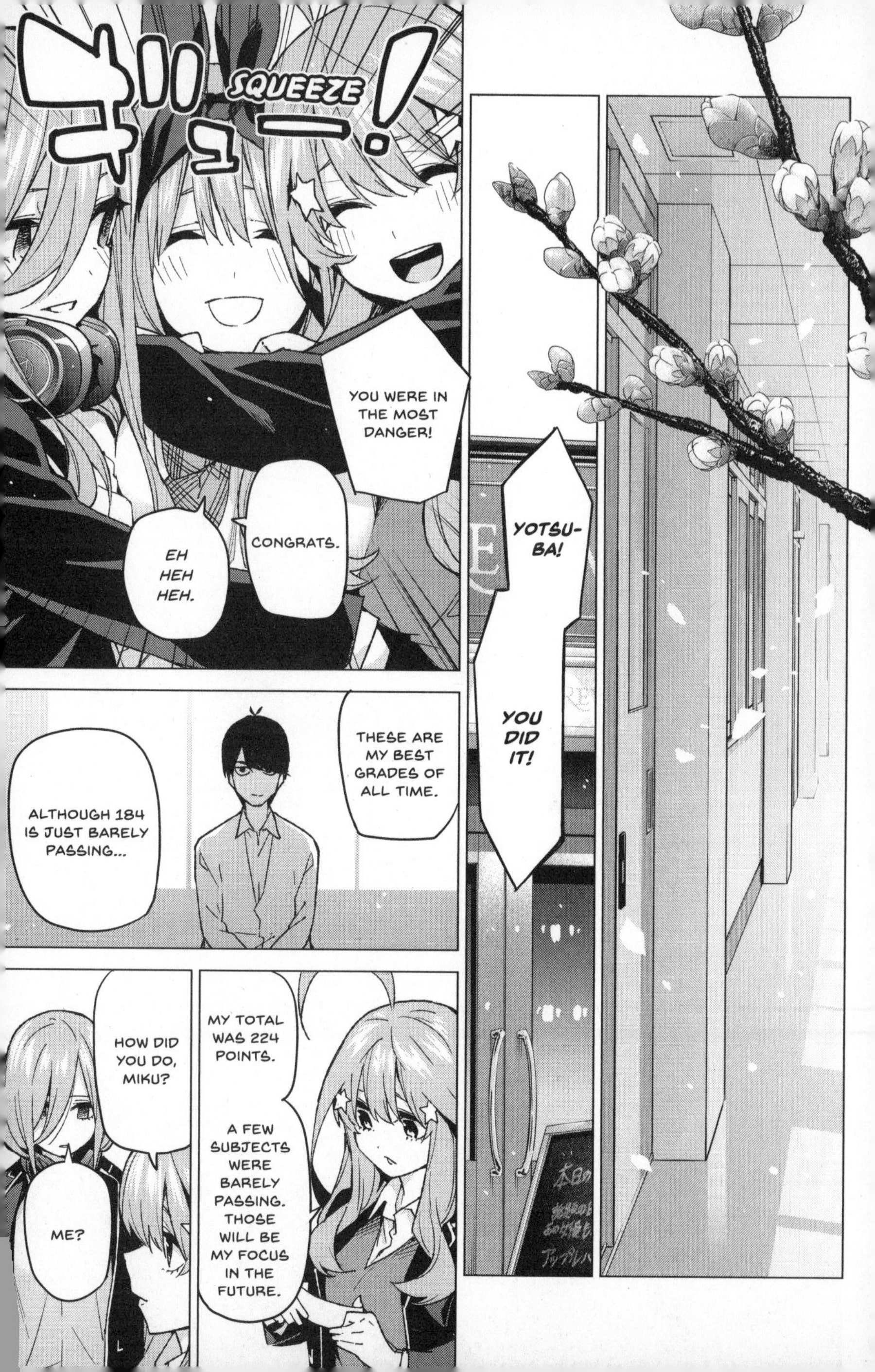
YOTSUBA!
YOU DID IT!
SQUEEZE
YOU WERE IN THE MOST DANGER!
CONGRATS.
EH HEH HEH.
THESE ARE MY BEST GRADES OF ALL TIME.
ALTHOUGH 184 IS JUST BARELY PASSING...
MY TOTAL WAS 224 POINTS.
A FEW SUBJECTS WERE BARELY PASSING. THOSE WILL BE MY FOCUS IN THE FUTURE.
HOW DID YOU DO, MIKU?
ME?

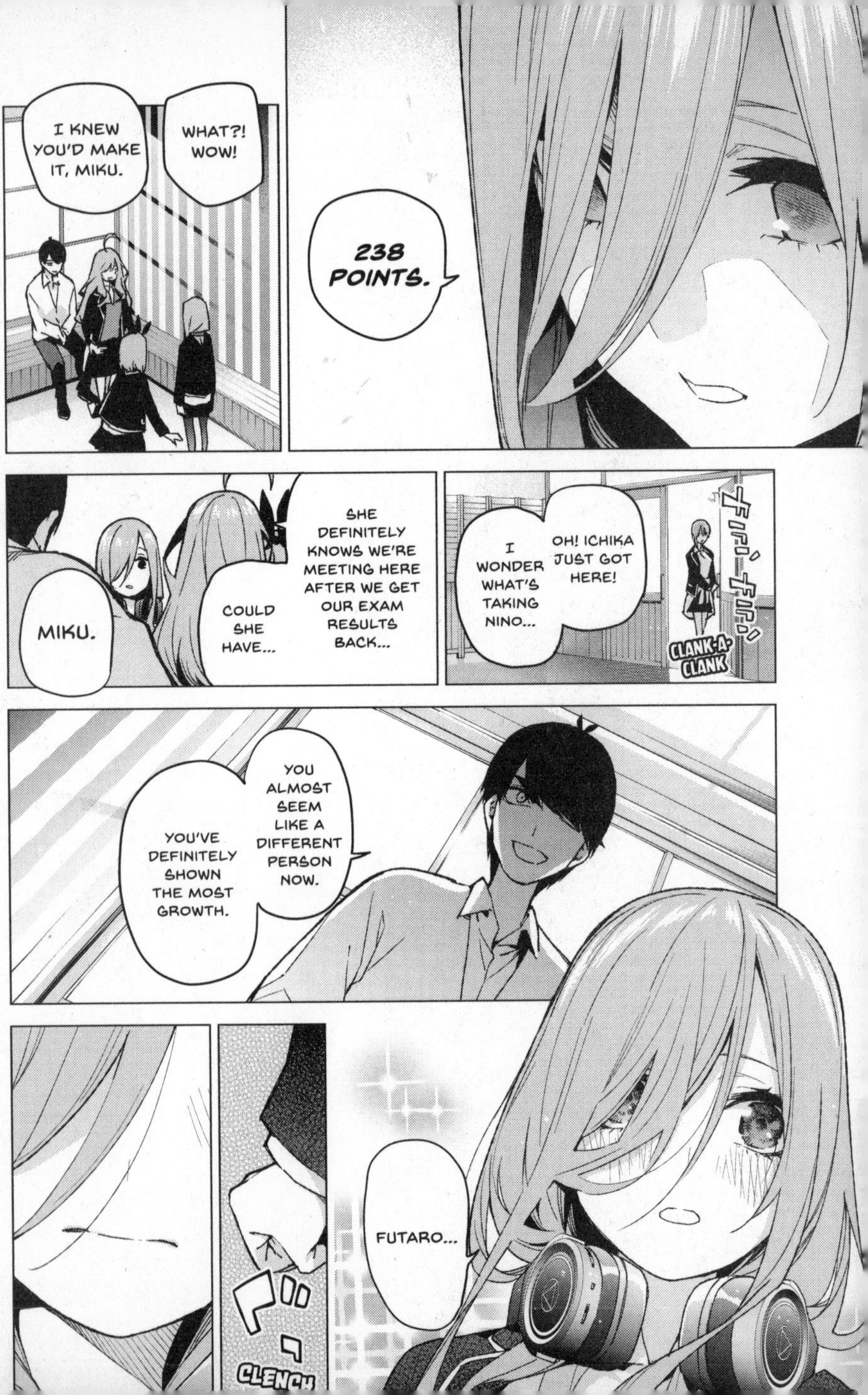
238 POINTS.
WHAT?! WOW!
I KNEW YOU'D MAKE IT, MIKU.
OH! ICHIKA JUST GOT HERE!
I WONDER WHAT'S TAKING NINO...
CLANK-A-CLANK
SHE DEFINITELY KNOWS WE'RE MEETING HERE AFTER WE GET OUR EXAM RESULTS BACK...
COULD SHE HAVE...
MIKU.
YOU ALMOST SEEM LIKE A DIFFERENT PERSON NOW.
YOU'VE DEFINITELY SHOWN THE MOST GROWTH.
FUTARO...
CLENCH

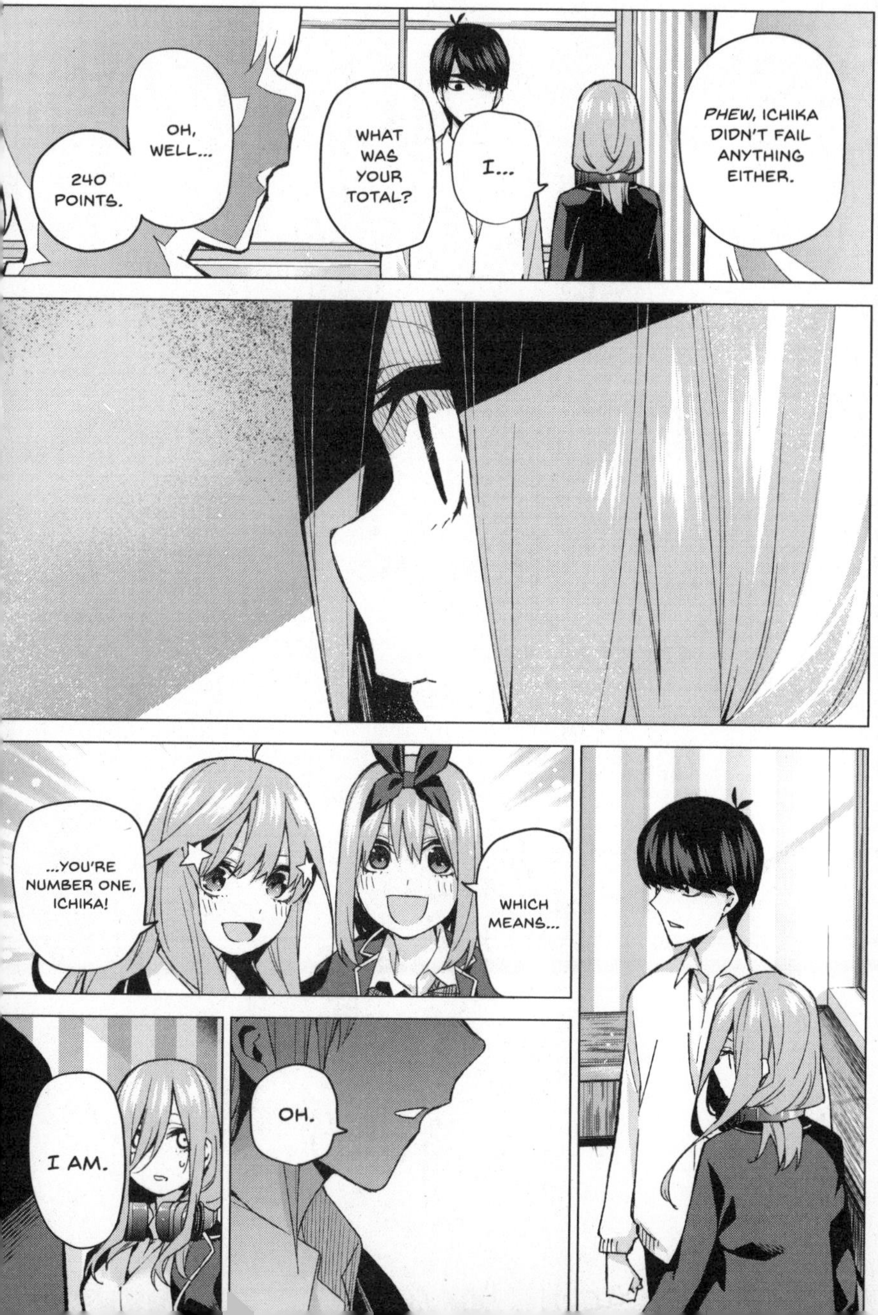
PHEW, ICHIKA DIDN'T FAIL ANYTHING EITHER.
I...
WHAT WAS YOUR TOTAL?
OH, WELL...
240 POINTS.
WHICH MEANS...
...YOU'RE NUMBER ONE, ICHIKA!
OH.
I AM.

Lan- guage Arts	Math	Science	Social Studies	English	Total
38	63	52	40	47	240

NAILED IT.

VERY WELL DONE

Ichika Nakano

PASSED

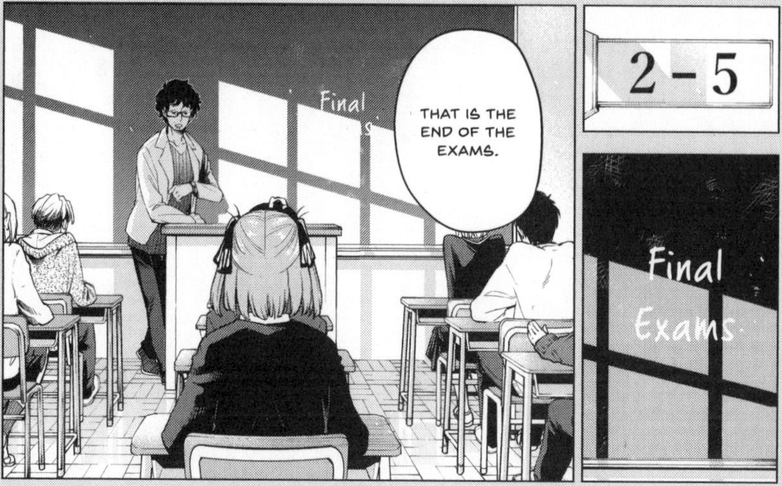
2 – 5
Final Exams
Final
THAT IS THE END OF THE EXAMS.

CHAPTER 59
IF THE LAST EXAM WAS NINO'S

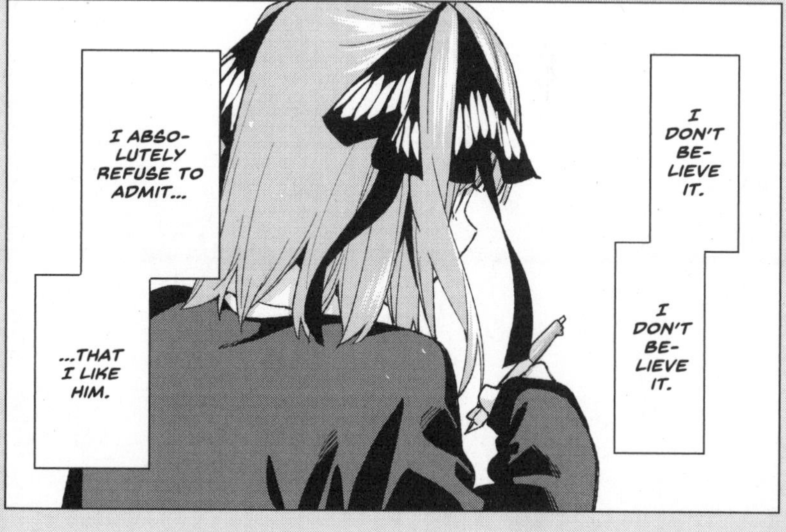
I DON'T BE-LIEVE IT.
I ABSO-LUTELY REFUSE TO ADMIT...
I DON'T BE-LIEVE IT.
...THAT I LIKE HIM.

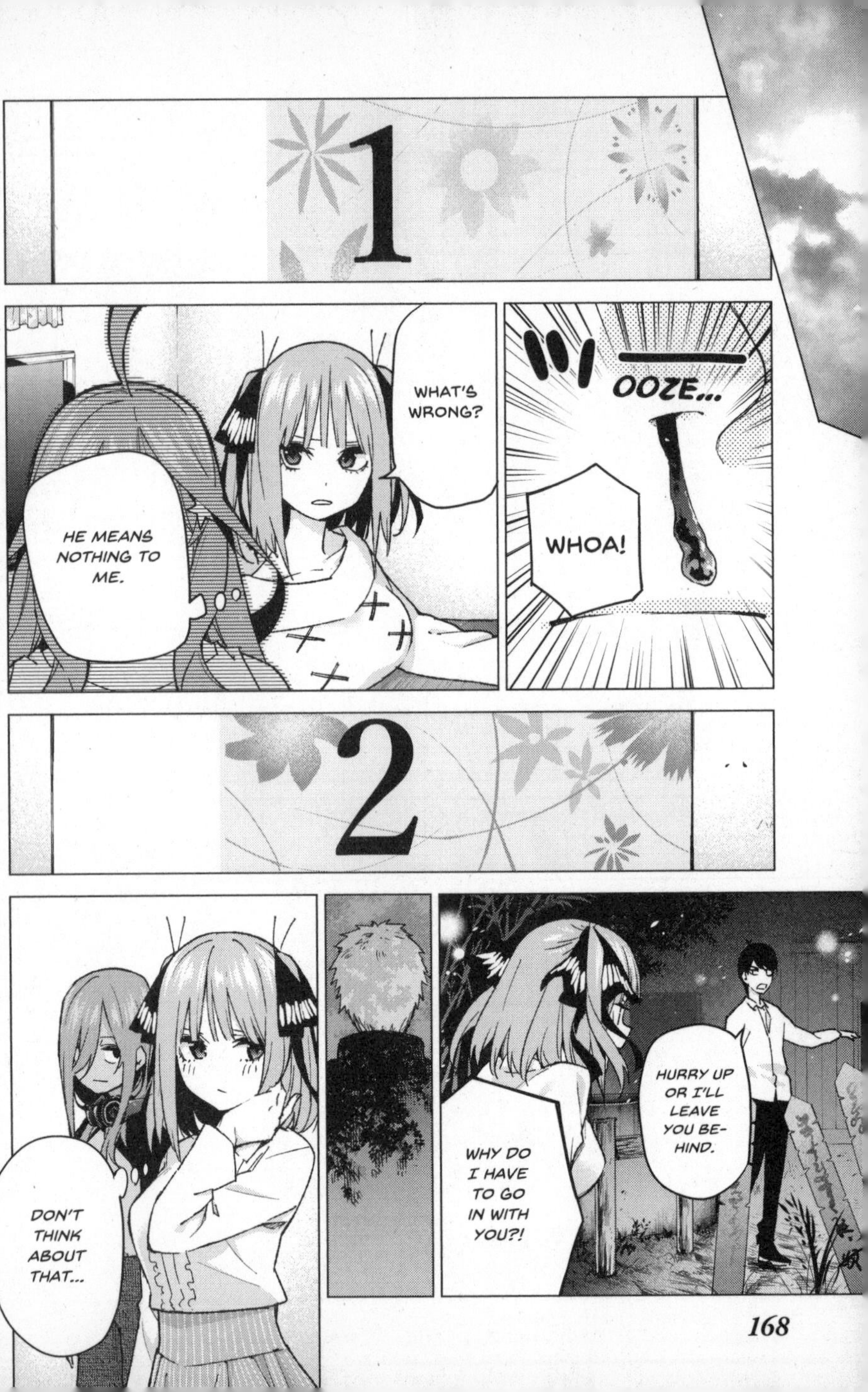
1
OOZE...
WHOA!
WHAT'S WRONG?
HE MEANS NOTHING TO ME.
2
...
HURRY UP OR I'LL LEAVE YOU BE-HIND.
WHY DO I HAVE TO GO IN WITH YOU?!
DON'T THINK ABOUT THAT...

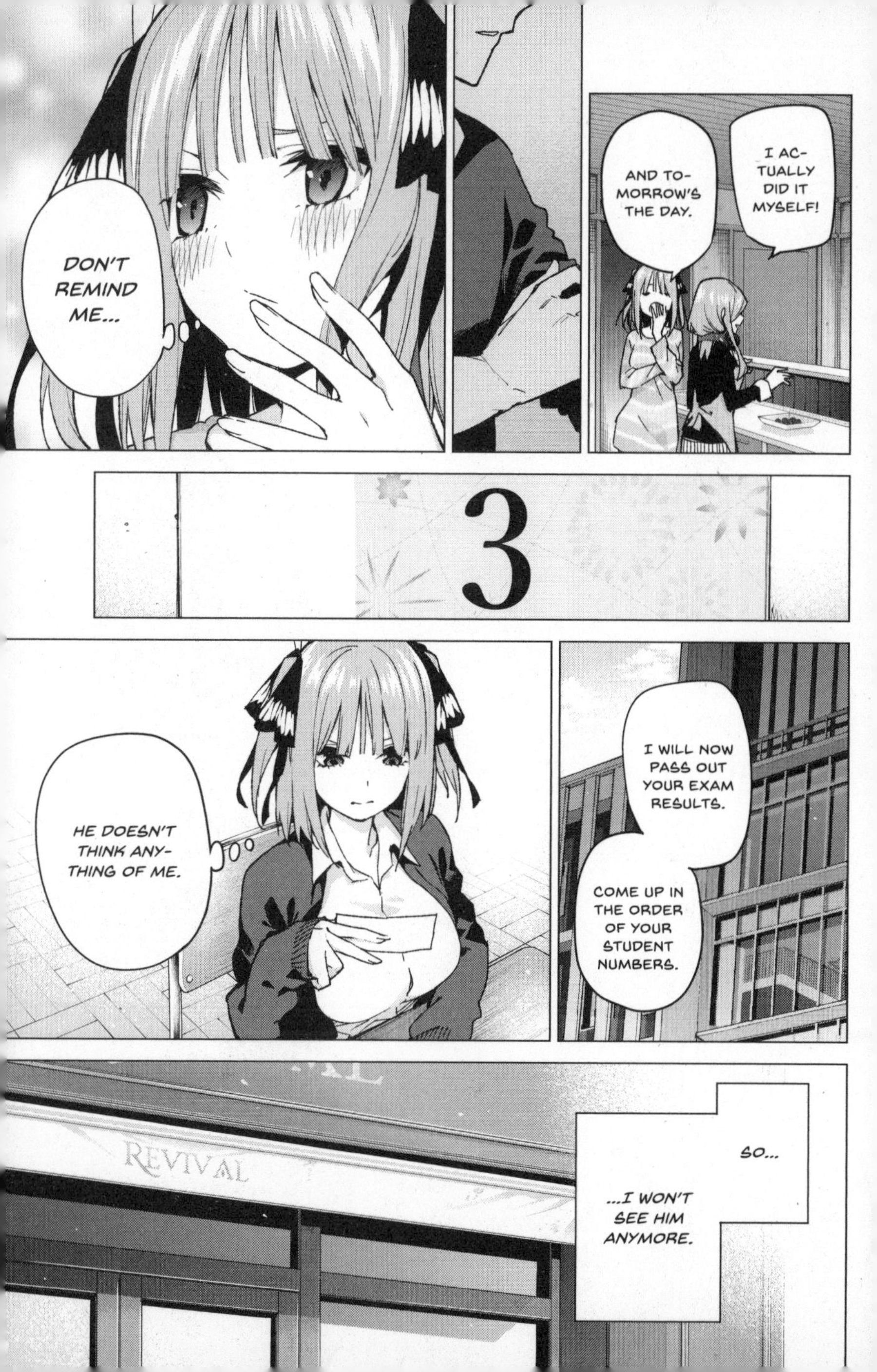
I ACTUALLY DID IT MYSELF!
AND TOMORROW'S THE DAY.
DON'T REMIND ME...
3
I WILL NOW PASS OUT YOUR EXAM RESULTS.
COME UP IN THE ORDER OF YOUR STUDENT NUMBERS.
HE DOESN'T THINK ANYTHING OF ME.
SO...
...I WON'T SEE HIM ANYMORE.
REVIVAL

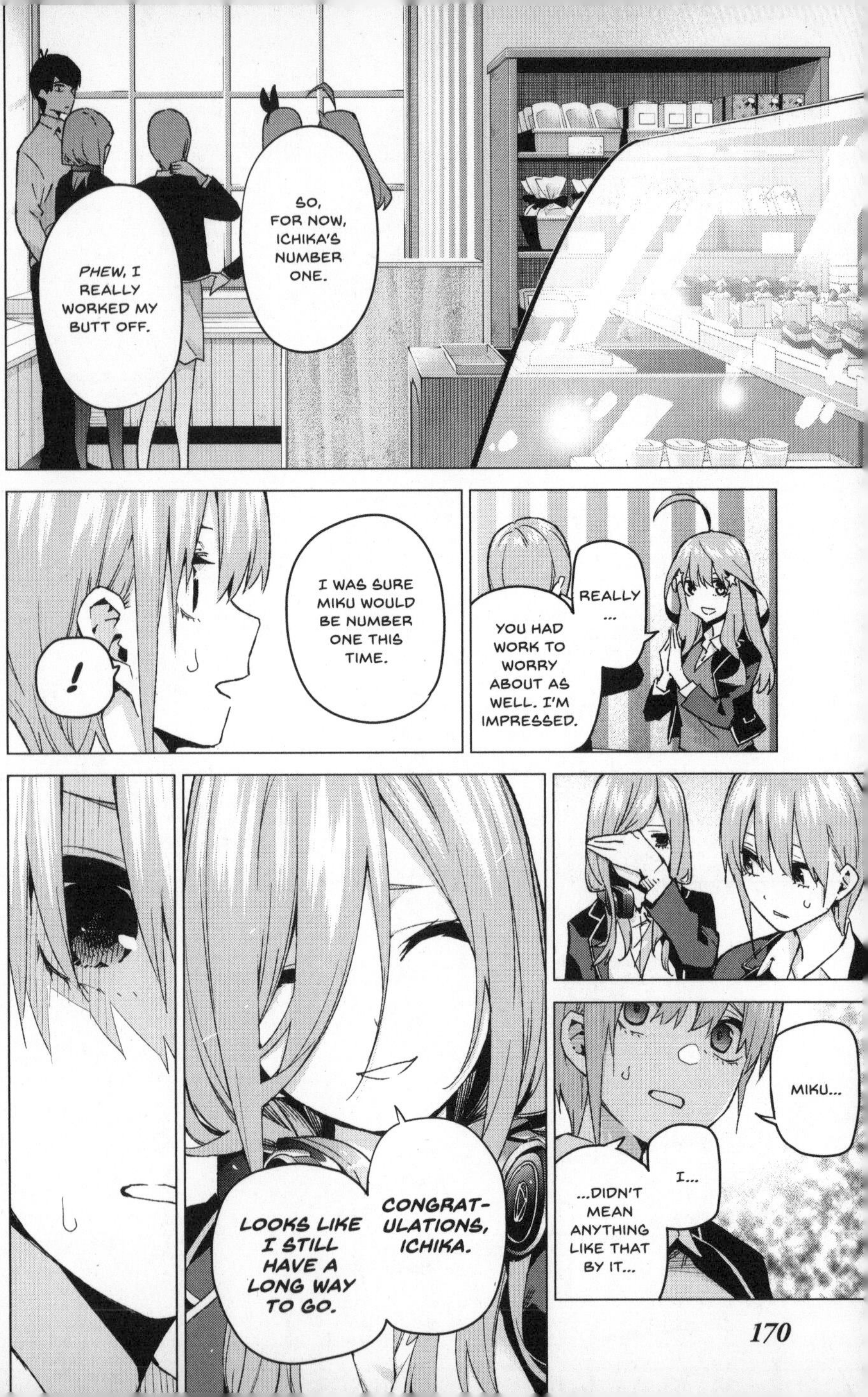
SO, FOR NOW, ICHIKA'S NUMBER ONE.
PHEW, I REALLY WORKED MY BUTT OFF.
REALLY...
YOU HAD WORK TO WORRY ABOUT AS WELL. I'M IMPRESSED.
I WAS SURE MIKU WOULD BE NUMBER ONE THIS TIME.
!
MIKU...
I...
...DIDN'T MEAN ANYTHING LIKE THAT BY IT...
CONGRAT-ULATIONS, ICHIKA.
LOOKS LIKE I STILL HAVE A LONG WAY TO GO.

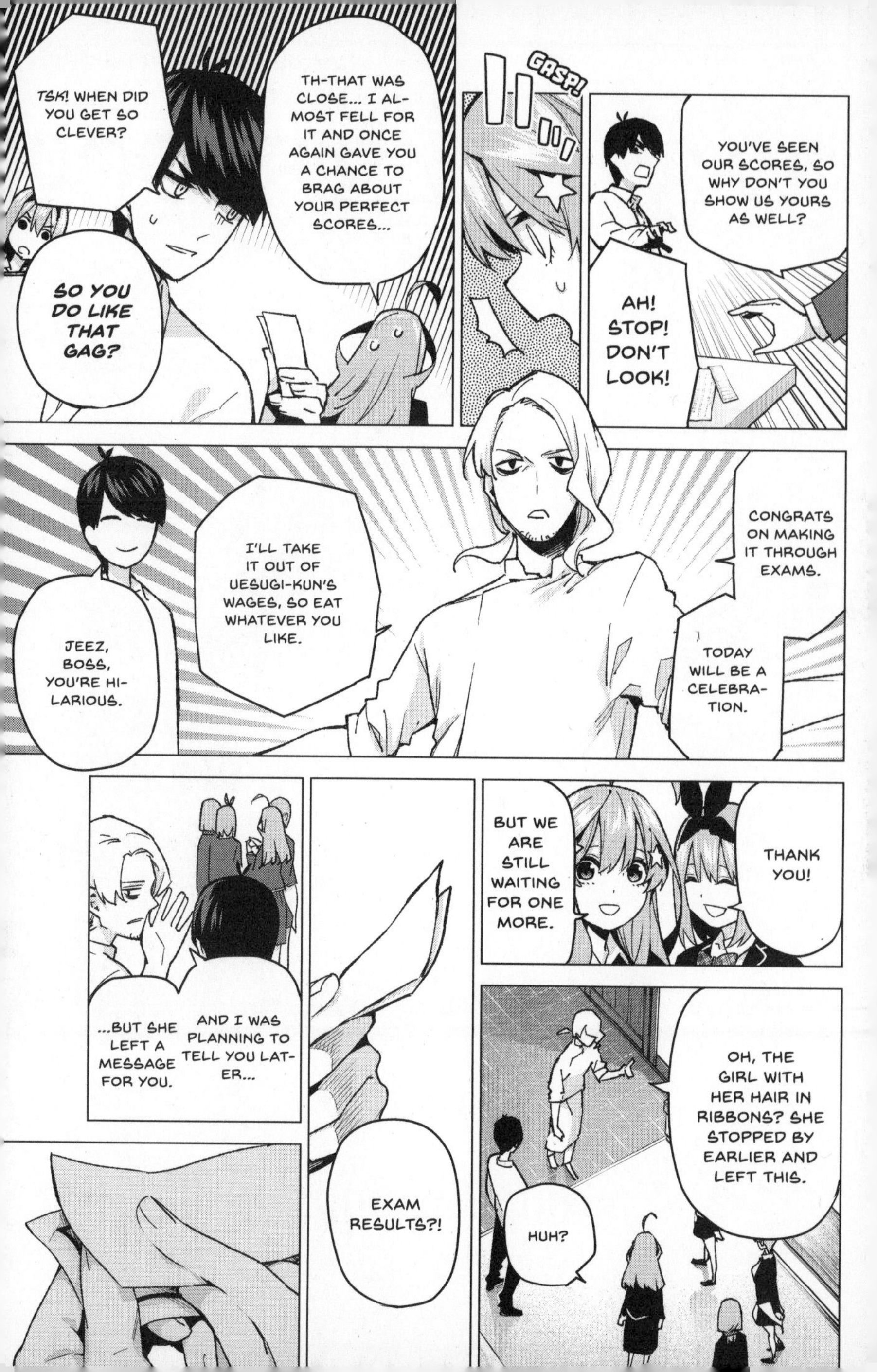
YOU'VE SEEN OUR SCORES, SO WHY DON'T YOU SHOW US YOURS AS WELL?
AH! STOP! DON'T LOOK!
GASP!
TH-THAT WAS CLOSE... I AL-MOST FELL FOR IT AND ONCE AGAIN GAVE YOU A CHANCE TO BRAG ABOUT YOUR PERFECT SCORES...
TSK! WHEN DID YOU GET SO CLEVER?
SO YOU DO LIKE THAT GAG?
CONGRATS ON MAKING IT THROUGH EXAMS.
TODAY WILL BE A CELEBRA-TION.
I'LL TAKE IT OUT OF UESUGI-KUN'S WAGES, SO EAT WHATEVER YOU LIKE.
JEEZ, BOSS, YOU'RE HI-LARIOUS.
THANK YOU!
BUT WE ARE STILL WAITING FOR ONE MORE.
OH, THE GIRL WITH HER HAIR IN RIBBONS? SHE STOPPED BY EARLIER AND LEFT THIS.
HUH?
EXAM RESULTS?!
AND I WAS PLANNING TO TELL YOU LAT-ER...
...BUT SHE LEFT A MESSAGE FOR YOU.

Language Arts	Math	Science	Social Studies	English	Total
32	33	40	48	56	209

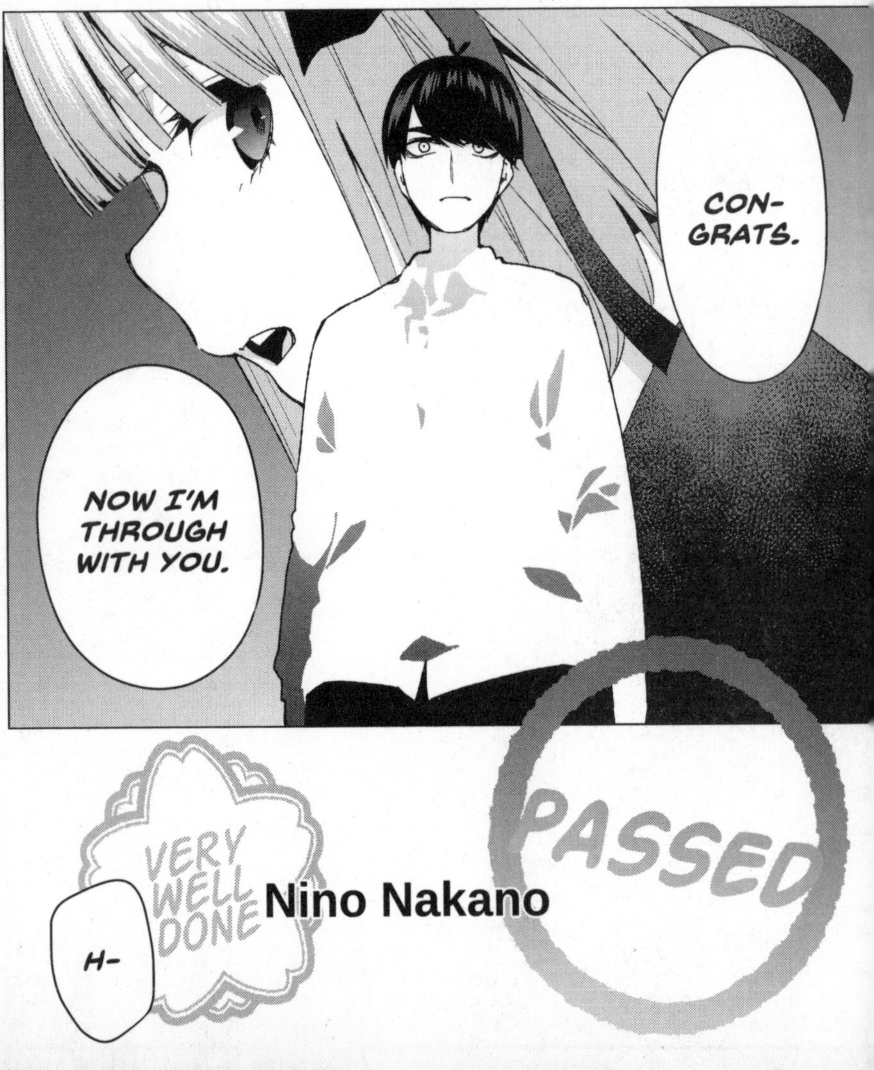
CON-GRATS.
NOW I'M THROUGH WITH YOU.
PASSED
Nino Nakano
VERY WELL DONE
H-

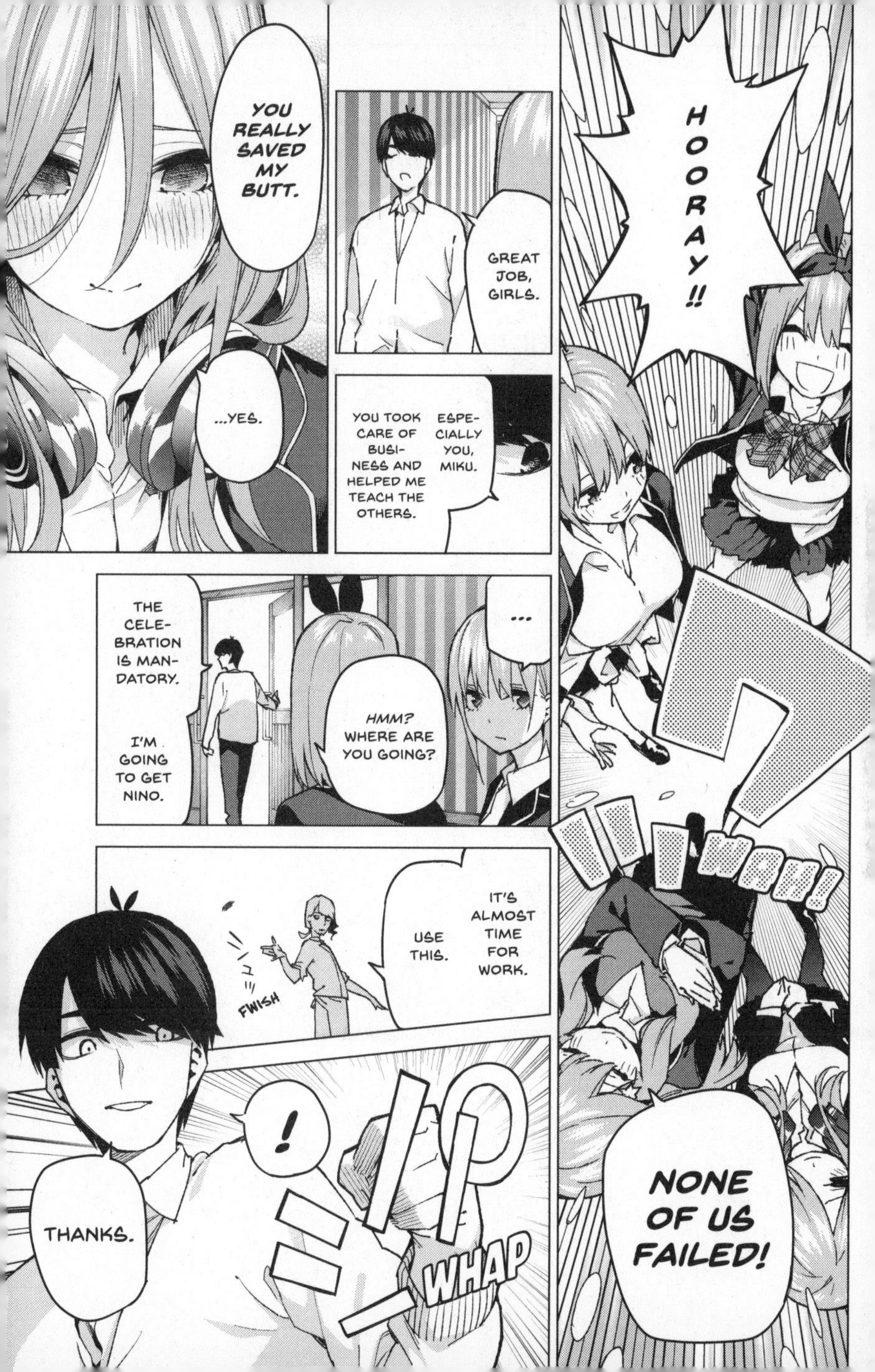
HOORAY!!
WAH!
NONE OF US FAILED!
GREAT JOB, GIRLS.
ESPECIALLY YOU, MIKU.
YOU TOOK CARE OF BUSINESS AND HELPED ME TEACH THE OTHERS.
YOU REALLY SAVED MY BUTT.
...YES.
...
HMM? WHERE ARE YOU GOING?
THE CELEBRATION IS MANDATORY.
I'M GOING TO GET NINO.
IT'S ALMOST TIME FOR WORK.
USE THIS.
FWISH
!
WHAP
THANKS.

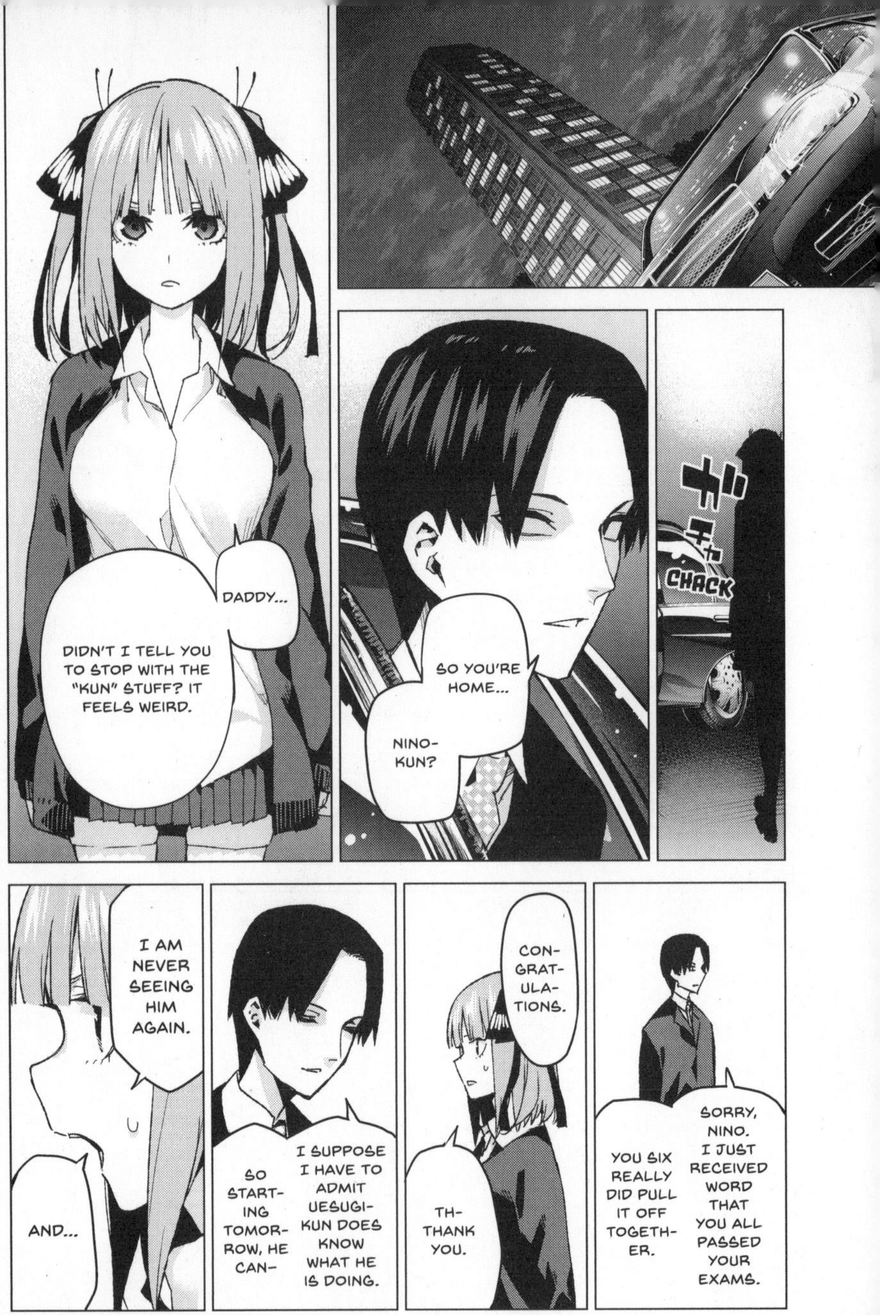
ガチャ
CHACK
SO YOU'RE HOME...
NINO-KUN?
DADDY...
DIDN'T I TELL YOU TO STOP WITH THE "KUN" STUFF? IT FEELS WEIRD.
SORRY, NINO. I JUST RECEIVED WORD THAT YOU ALL PASSED YOUR EXAMS.
YOU SIX REALLY DID PULL IT OFF TOGETHER.
CONGRATULATIONS.
TH-THANK YOU.
I SUPPOSE I HAVE TO ADMIT UESUGI-KUN DOES KNOW WHAT HE IS DOING.
SO STARTING TOMORROW, HE CAN-
I AM NEVER SEEING HIM AGAIN.
AND...

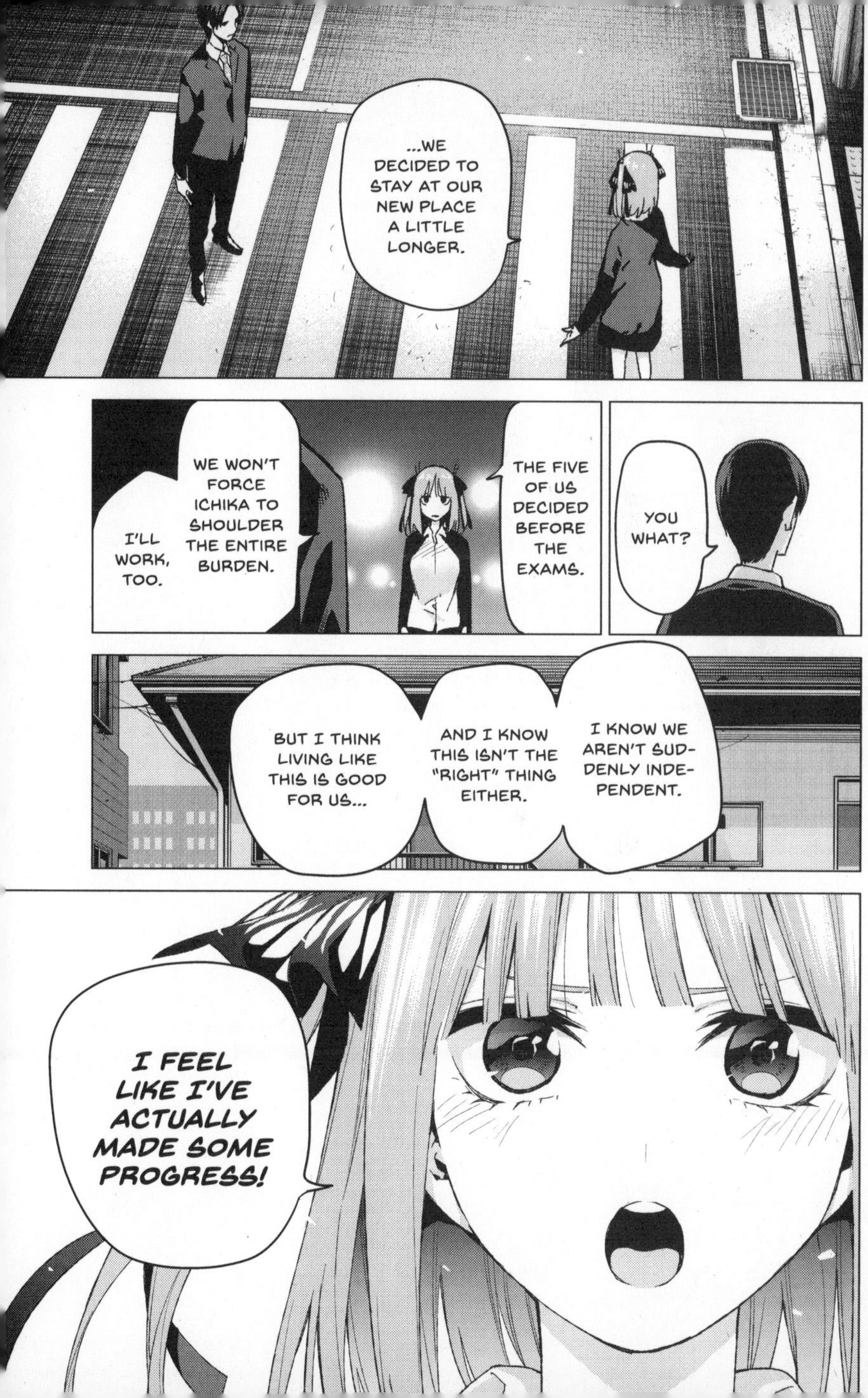
...WE DECIDED TO STAY AT OUR NEW PLACE A LITTLE LONGER.
YOU WHAT?
THE FIVE OF US DECIDED BEFORE THE EXAMS.
WE WON'T FORCE ICHIKA TO SHOULDER THE ENTIRE BURDEN.
I'LL WORK, TOO.
I KNOW WE AREN'T SUDDENLY INDEPENDENT.
AND I KNOW THIS ISN'T THE "RIGHT" THING EITHER.
BUT I THINK LIVING LIKE THIS IS GOOD FOR US...
I FEEL LIKE I'VE ACTUALLY MADE SOME PROGRESS!

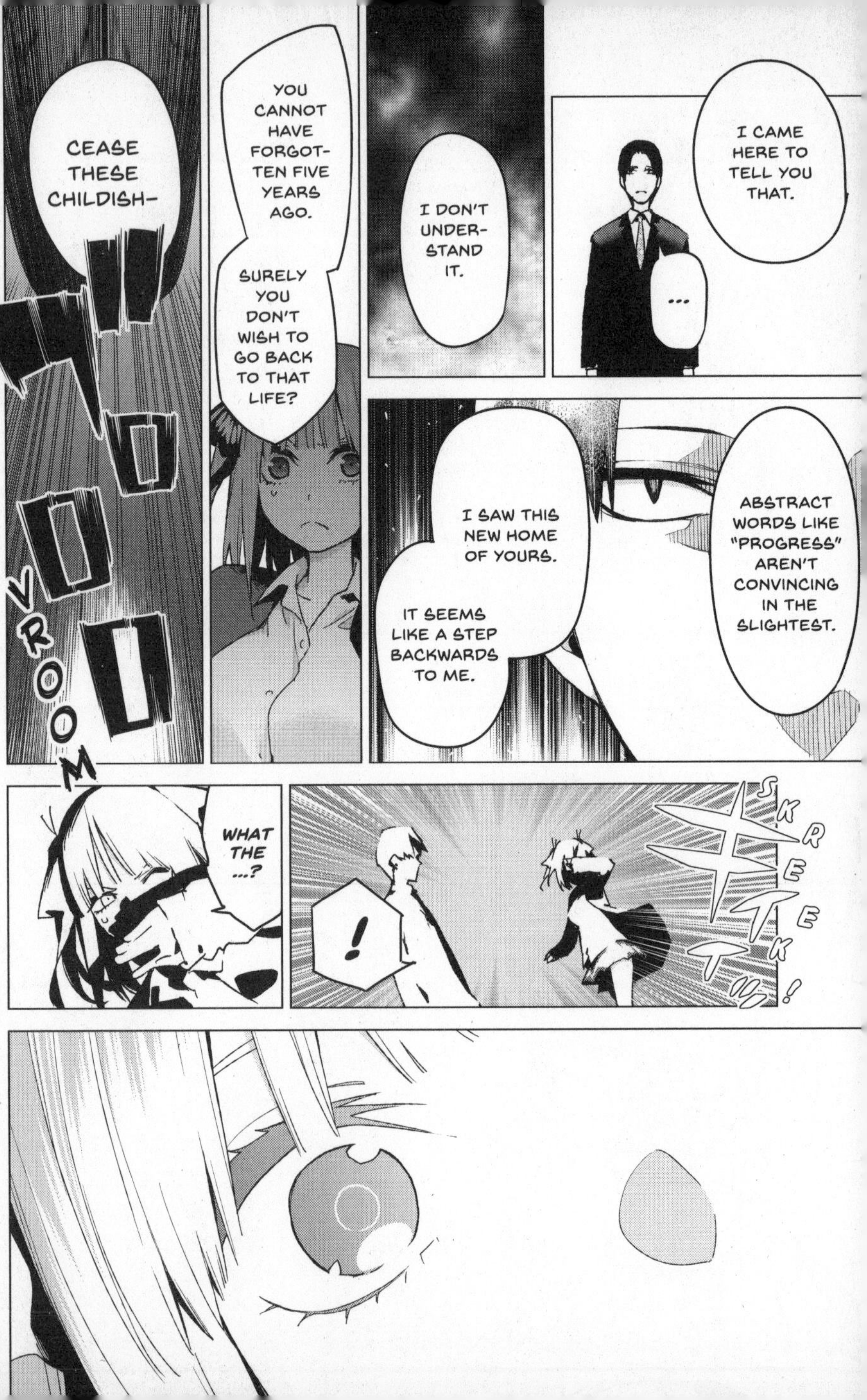
I CAME HERE TO TELL YOU THAT.
...
I DON'T UNDERSTAND IT.
ABSTRACT WORDS LIKE "PROGRESS" AREN'T CONVINCING IN THE SLIGHTEST.
I SAW THIS NEW HOME OF YOURS.
IT SEEMS LIKE A STEP BACKWARDS TO ME.
YOU CANNOT HAVE FORGOTTEN FIVE YEARS AGO.
SURELY YOU DON'T WISH TO GO BACK TO THAT LIFE?
CEASE THESE CHILDISH-
VROOM
SKREETCK!!
!
WHAT THE ...?

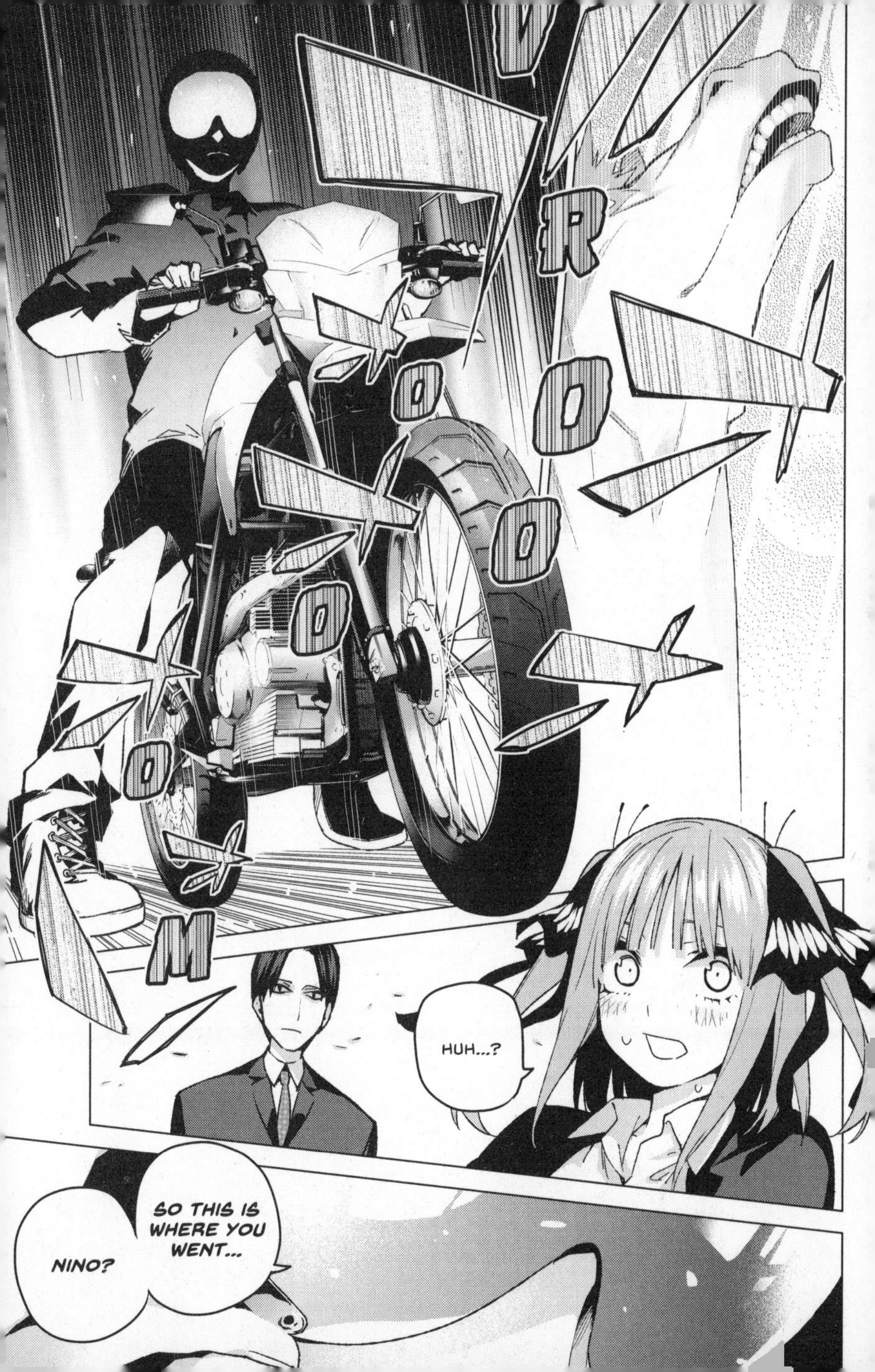
VROOOOOM
HUH...?
SO THIS IS WHERE YOU WENT...
NINO?

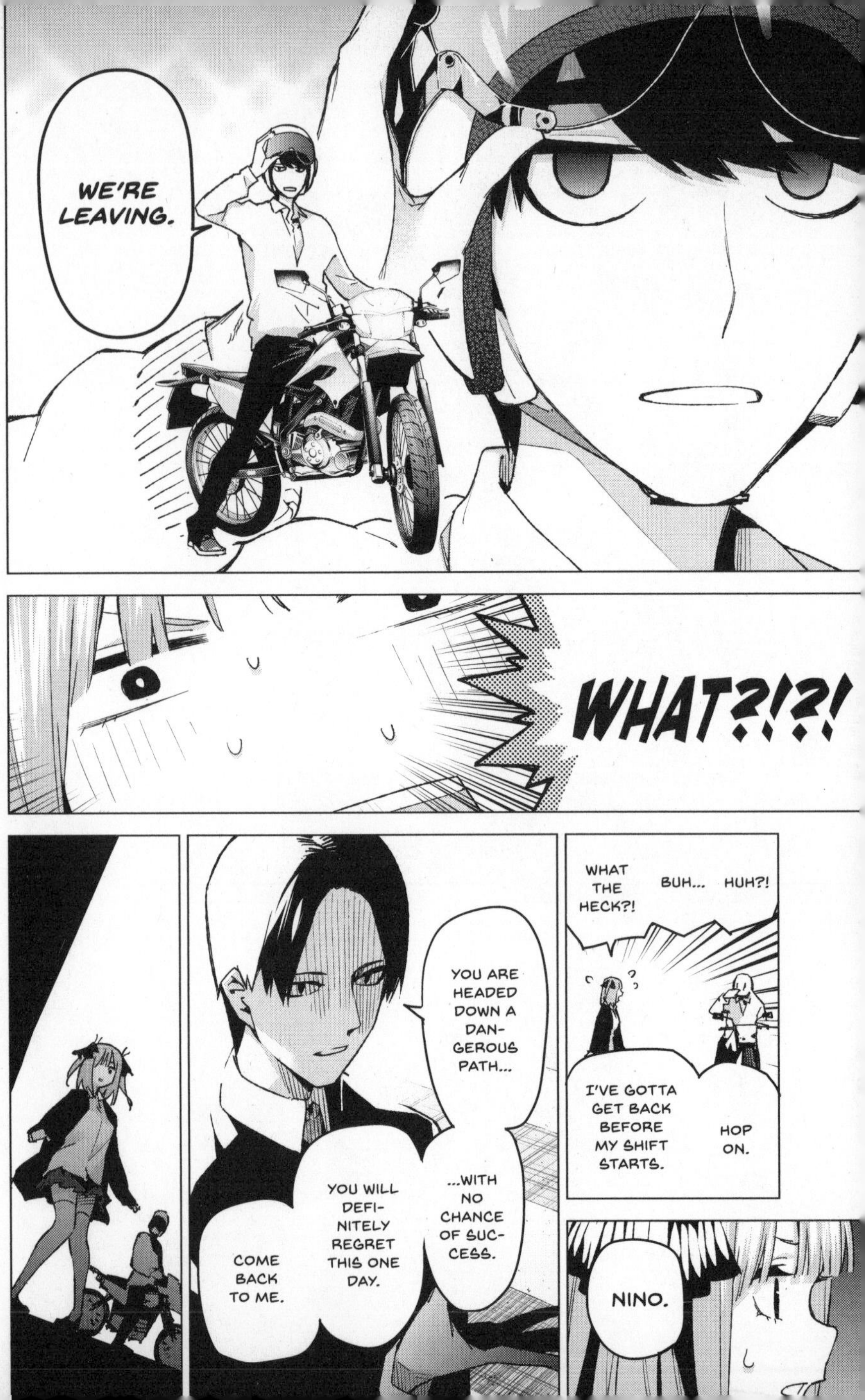
WE'RE LEAVING.
WHAT?!?!
HUH?!
BUH...
WHAT THE HECK?!
HOP ON.
I'VE GOTTA GET BACK BEFORE MY SHIFT STARTS.
NINO.
YOU ARE HEADED DOWN A DANGEROUS PATH...
...WITH NO CHANCE OF SUCCESS.
YOU WILL DEFINITELY REGRET THIS ONE DAY.
COME BACK TO ME.

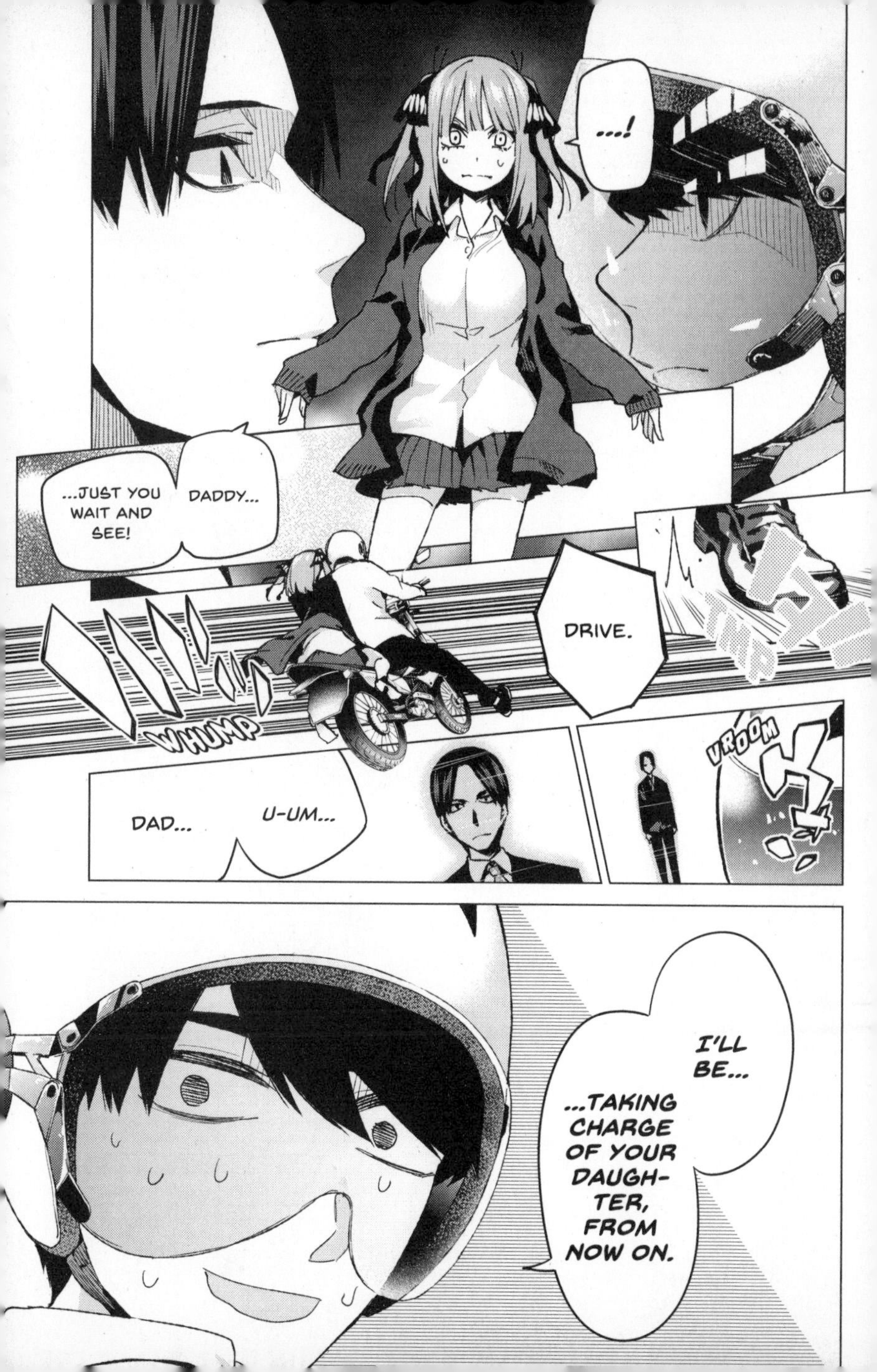
...!
DADDY...
...JUST YOU WAIT AND SEE!
DRIVE.
WHUMP
VROOM
U-UM...
DAD...
I'LL BE...
...TAKING CHARGE OF YOUR DAUGHTER, FROM NOW ON.

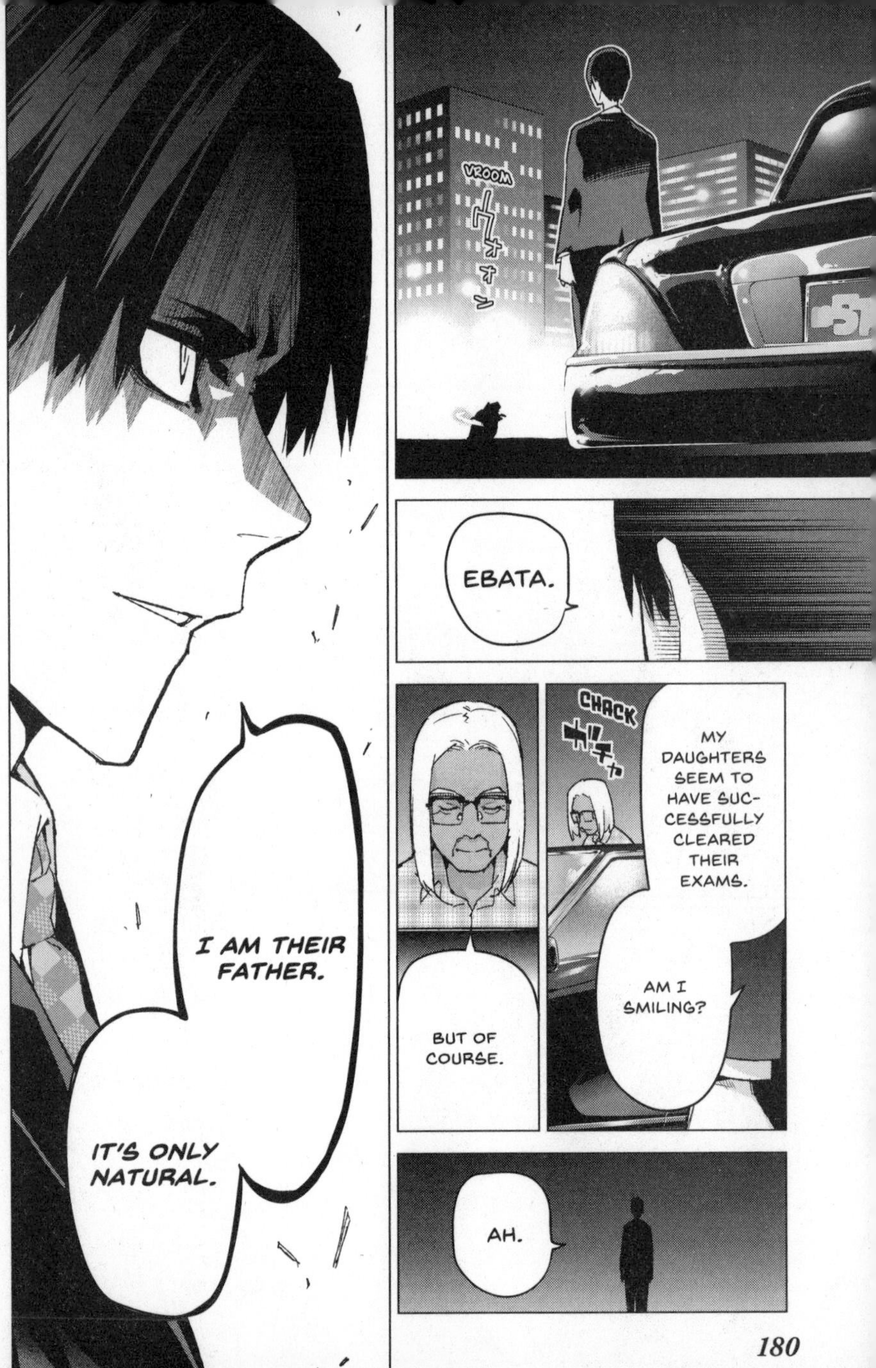
VROOM
EBATA.
CHACK
MY DAUGHTERS SEEM TO HAVE SUC-CESSFULLY CLEARED THEIR EXAMS.
AM I SMILING?
BUT OF COURSE.
AH.
I AM THEIR FATHER.
IT'S ONLY NATURAL.

* Helmets are required by law.

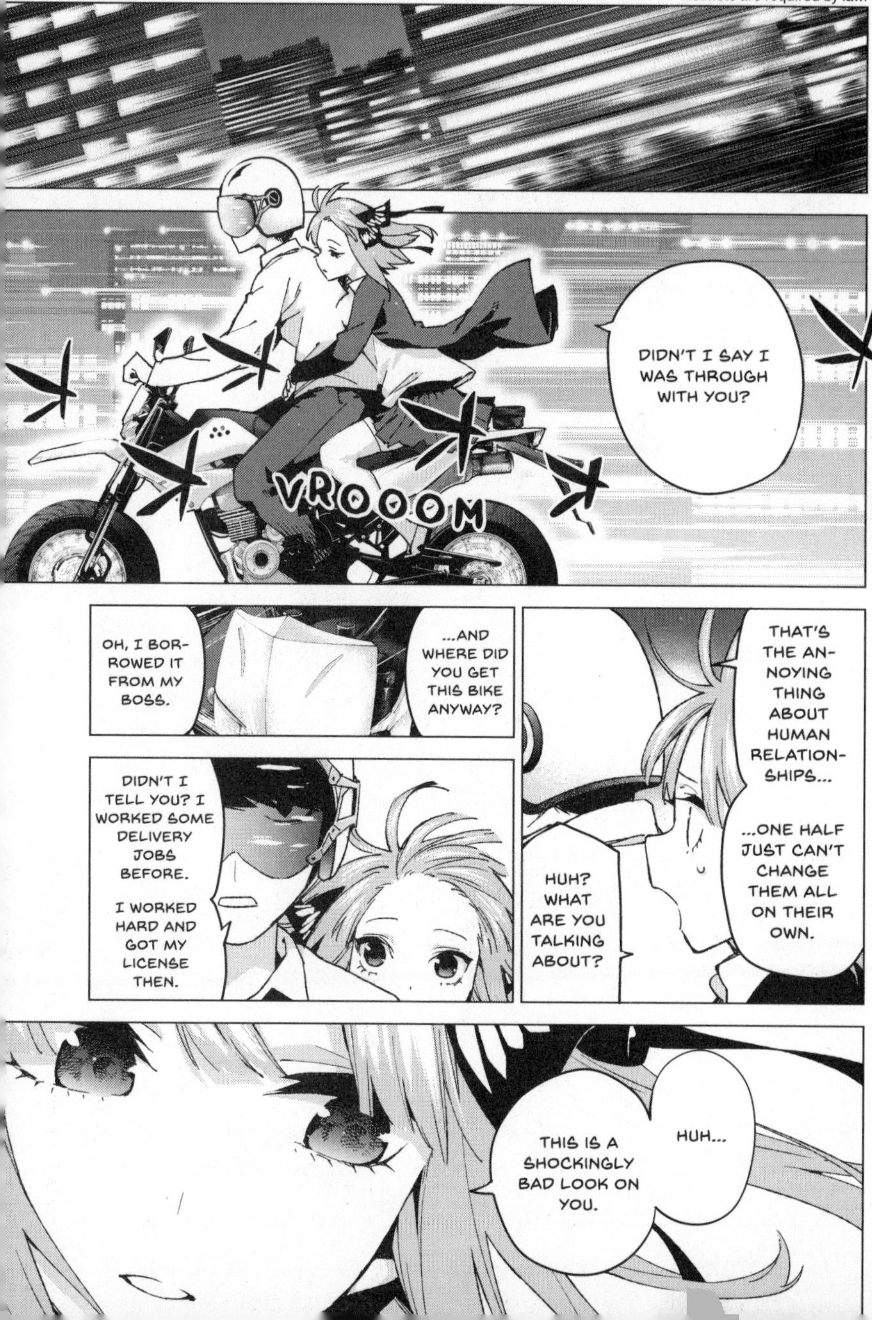
DIDN'T I SAY I WAS THROUGH WITH YOU?
VROOOM
THAT'S THE ANNOYING THING ABOUT HUMAN RELATIONSHIPS...
...ONE HALF JUST CAN'T CHANGE THEM ALL ON THEIR OWN.
HUH? WHAT ARE YOU TALKING ABOUT?
...AND WHERE DID YOU GET THIS BIKE ANYWAY?
OH, I BORROWED IT FROM MY BOSS.
DIDN'T I TELL YOU? I WORKED SOME DELIVERY JOBS BEFORE.
I WORKED HARD AND GOT MY LICENSE THEN.
HUH...
THIS IS A SHOCKINGLY BAD LOOK ON YOU.

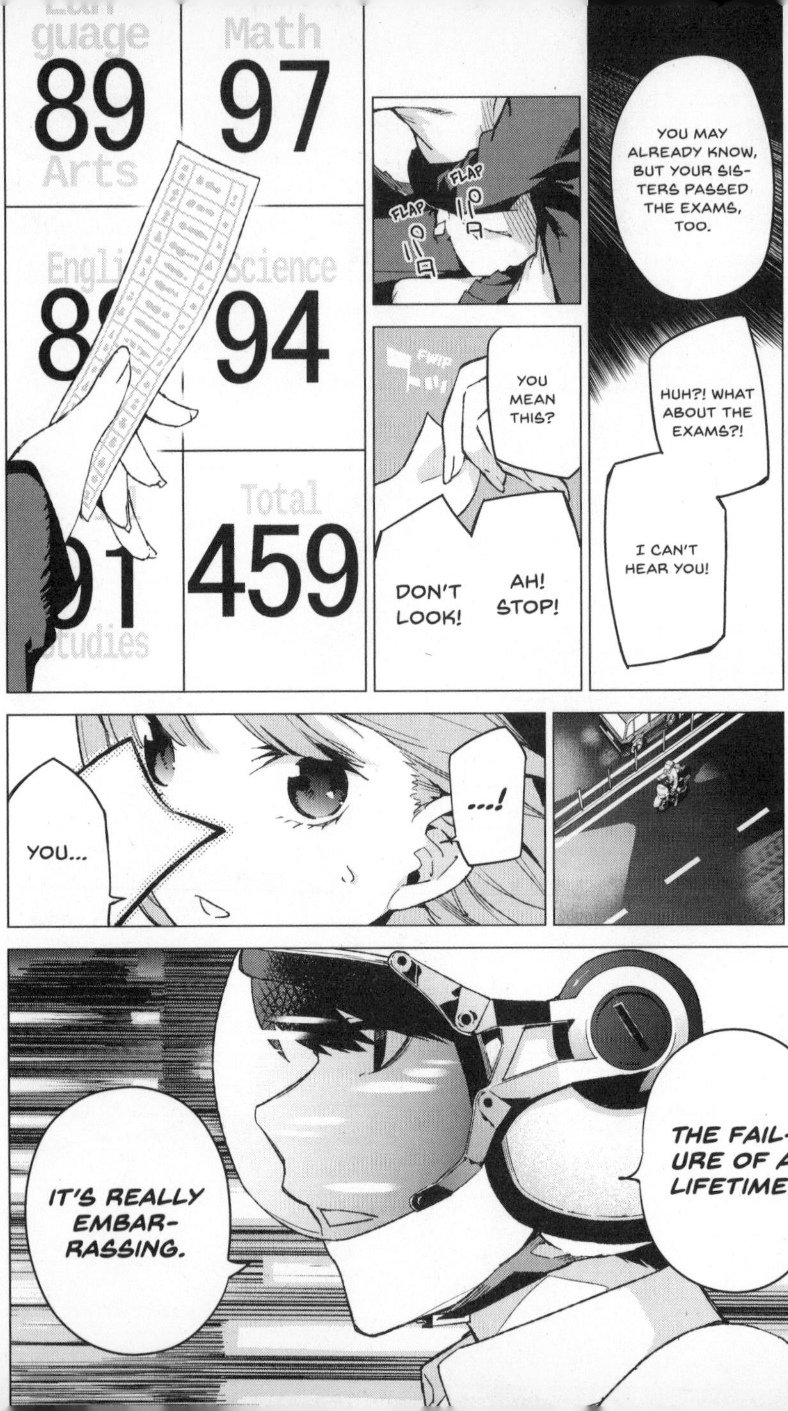
YOU MAY ALREADY KNOW, BUT YOUR SIS-TERS PASSED THE EXAMS, TOO.
HUH?! WHAT ABOUT THE EXAMS?!
I CAN'T HEAR YOU!
FLAP
FLAP
FWIP
YOU MEAN THIS?
AH! STOP!
DON'T LOOK!
guage
89
Arts
Math
97
Science
94
Studies
Total
459
...!
YOU...
THE FAIL-URE OF A LIFETIME.
IT'S REALLY EMBAR-RASSING.

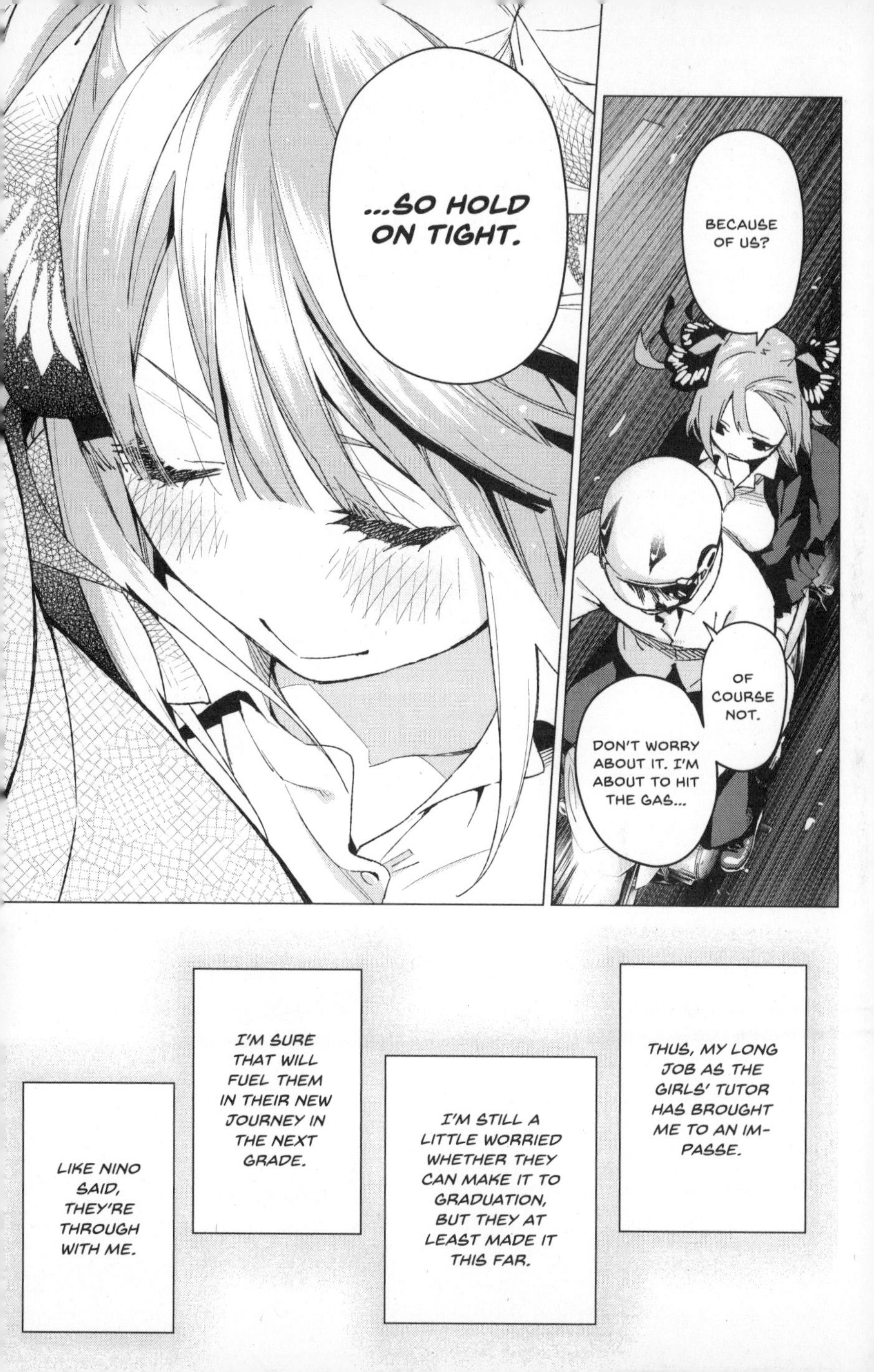
BECAUSE OF US?
OF COURSE NOT.
DON'T WORRY ABOUT IT. I'M ABOUT TO HIT THE GAS...
...SO HOLD ON TIGHT.
THUS, MY LONG JOB AS THE GIRLS' TUTOR HAS BROUGHT ME TO AN IM-PASSE.
I'M STILL A LITTLE WORRIED WHETHER THEY CAN MAKE IT TO GRADUATION, BUT THEY AT LEAST MADE IT THIS FAR.
I'M SURE THAT WILL FUEL THEM IN THEIR NEW JOURNEY IN THE NEXT GRADE.
LIKE NINO SAID, THEY'RE THROUGH WITH ME.

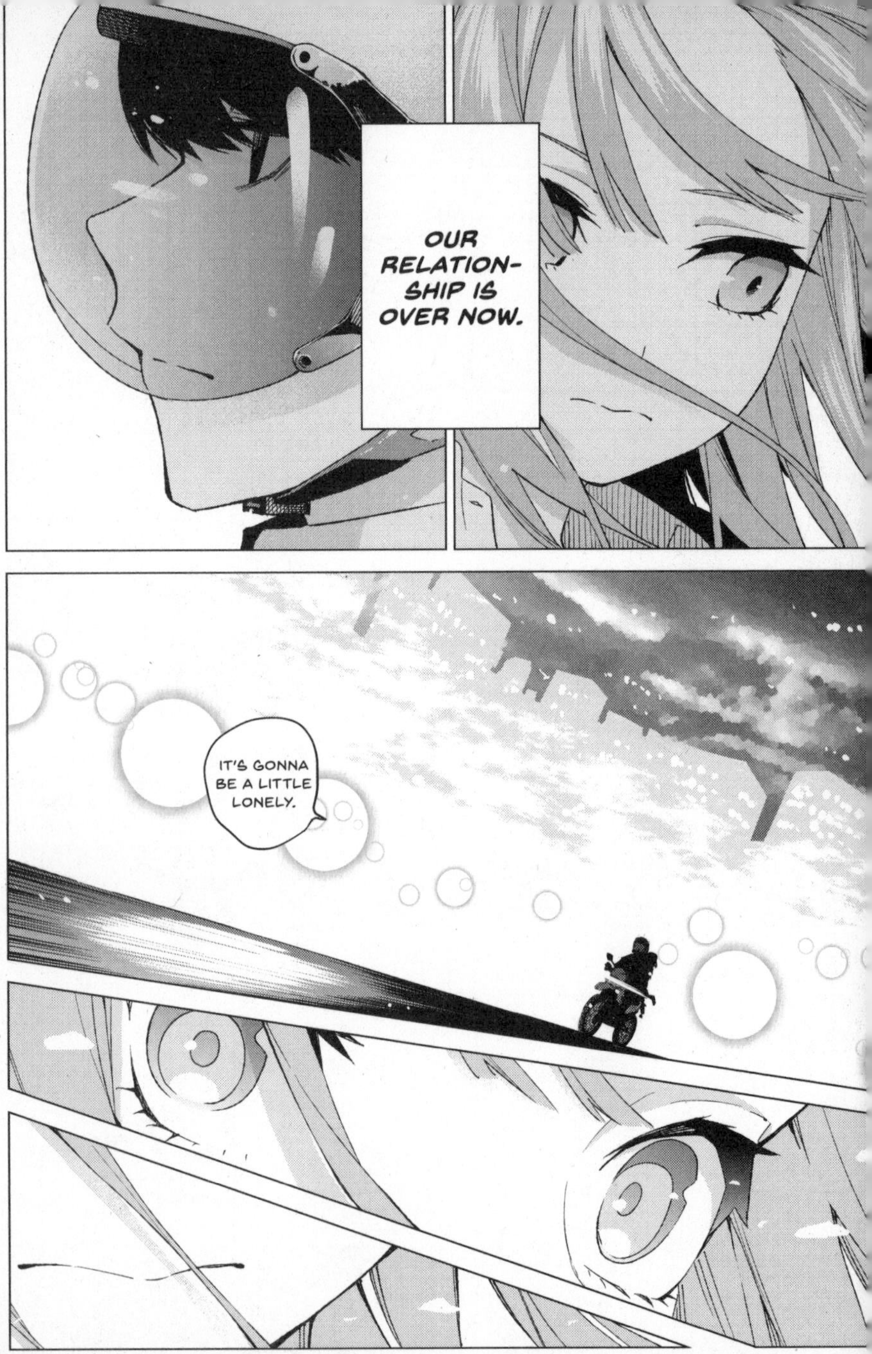
OUR RELATION-SHIP IS OVER NOW.
IT'S GONNA BE A LITTLE LONELY.

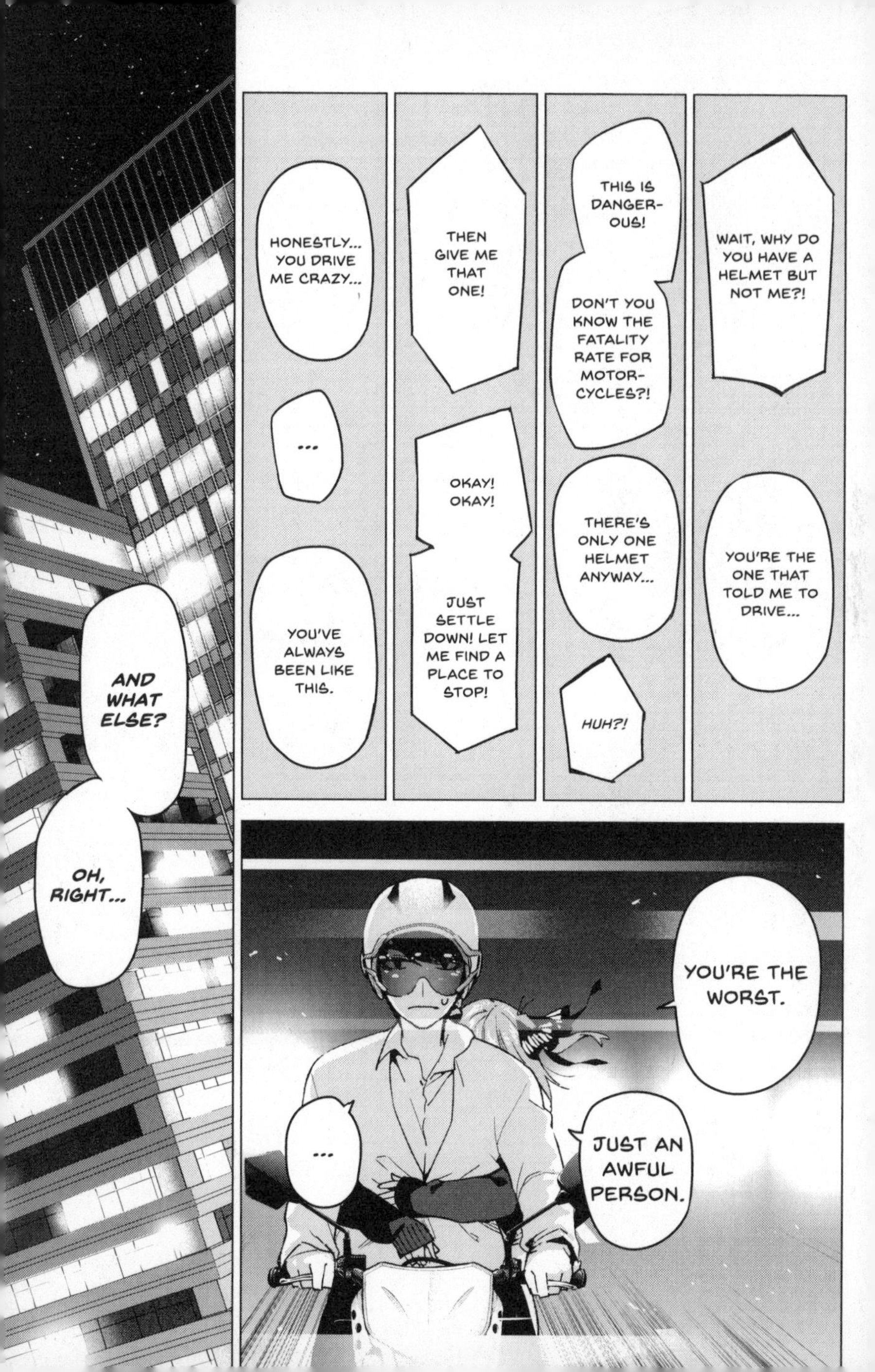
WAIT, WHY DO YOU HAVE A HELMET BUT NOT ME?!
YOU'RE THE ONE THAT TOLD ME TO DRIVE...
THIS IS DANGEROUS!
DON'T YOU KNOW THE FATALITY RATE FOR MOTORCYCLES?!
THERE'S ONLY ONE HELMET ANYWAY...
HUH?!
THEN GIVE ME THAT ONE!
OKAY! OKAY!
JUST SETTLE DOWN! LET ME FIND A PLACE TO STOP!
HONESTLY... YOU DRIVE ME CRAZY...
...
YOU'VE ALWAYS BEEN LIKE THIS.
YOU'RE THE WORST.
JUST AN AWFUL PERSON.
...
AND WHAT ELSE?
OH, RIGHT...

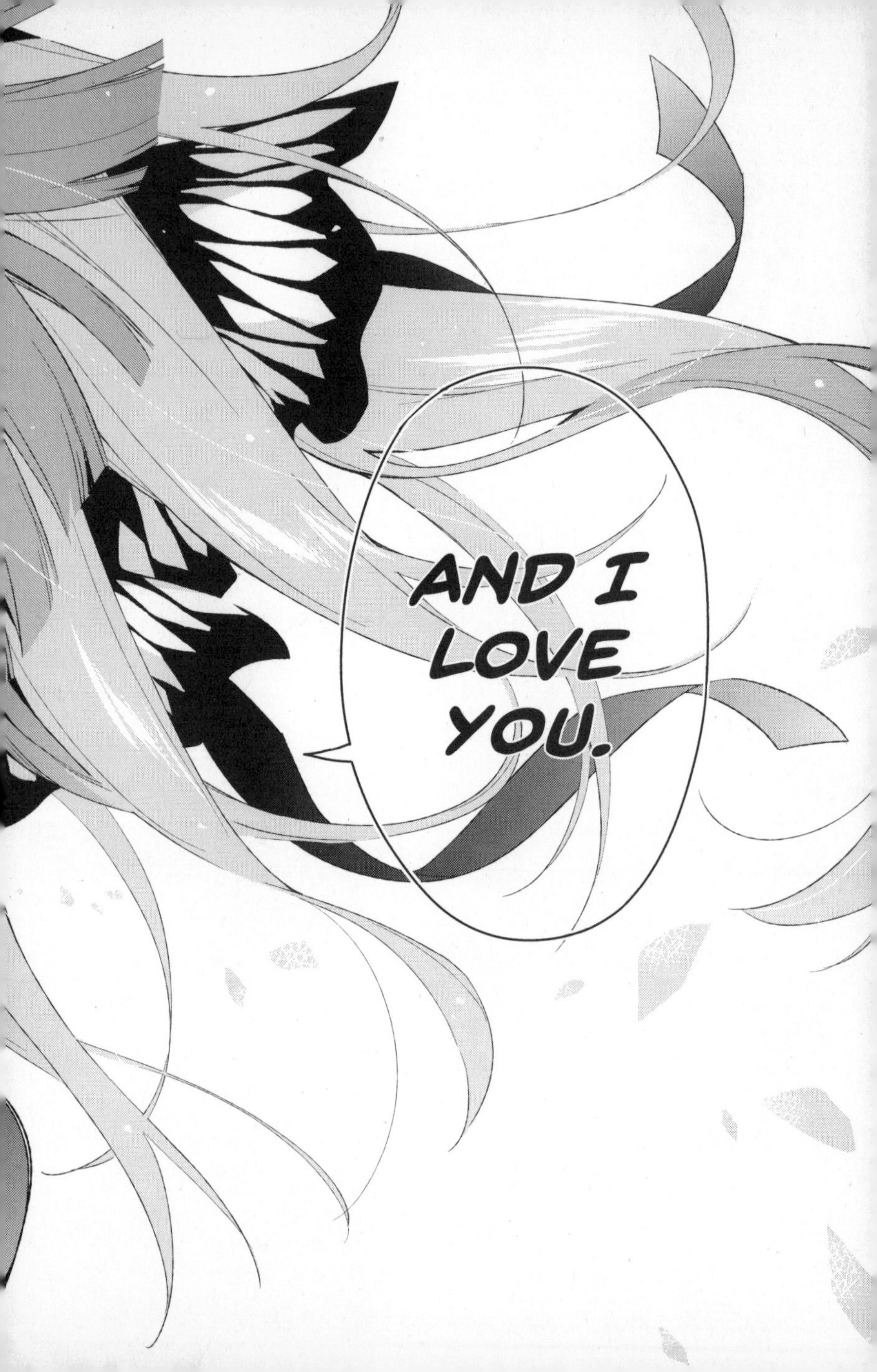
AND I LOVE YOU.

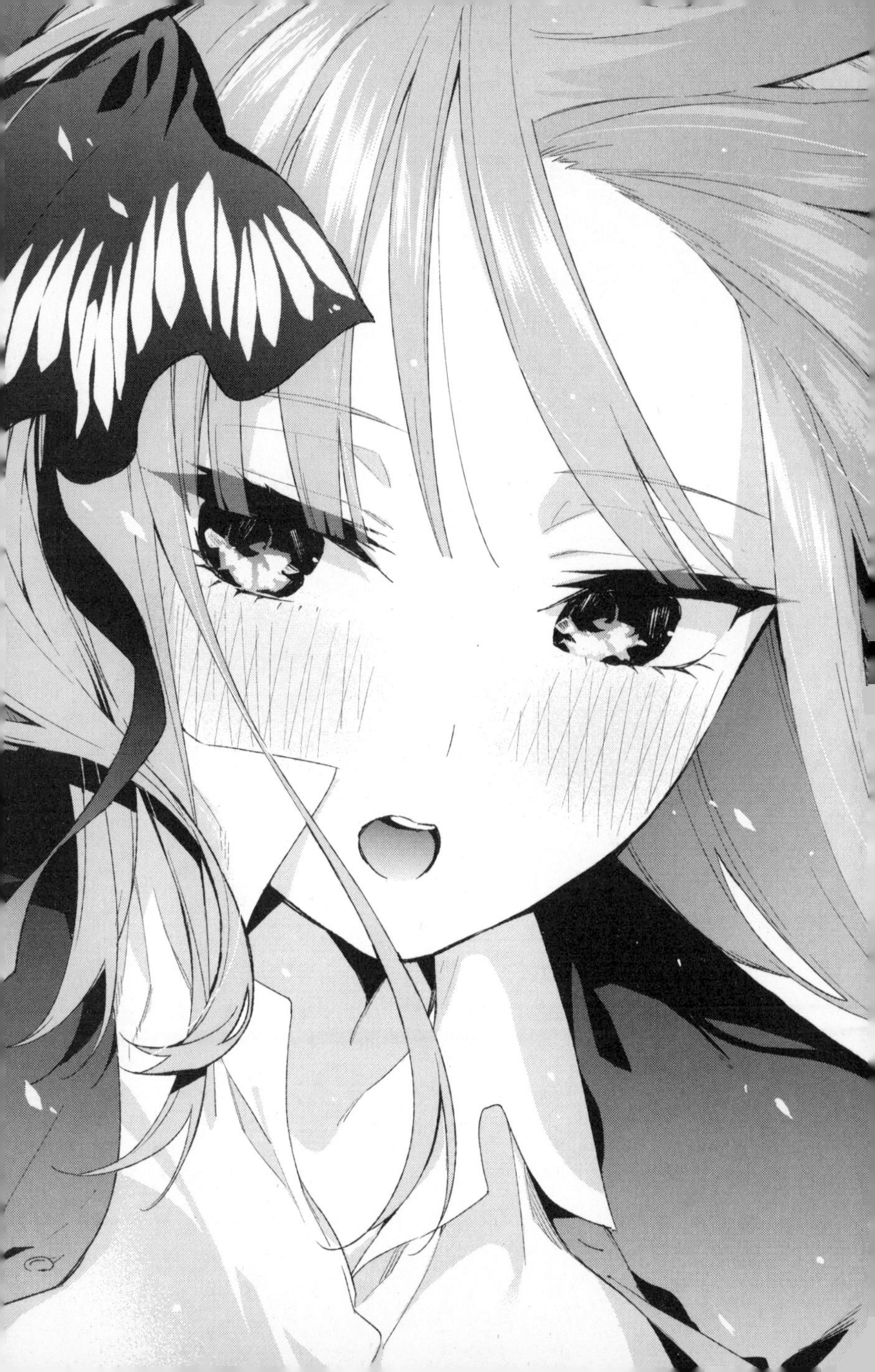

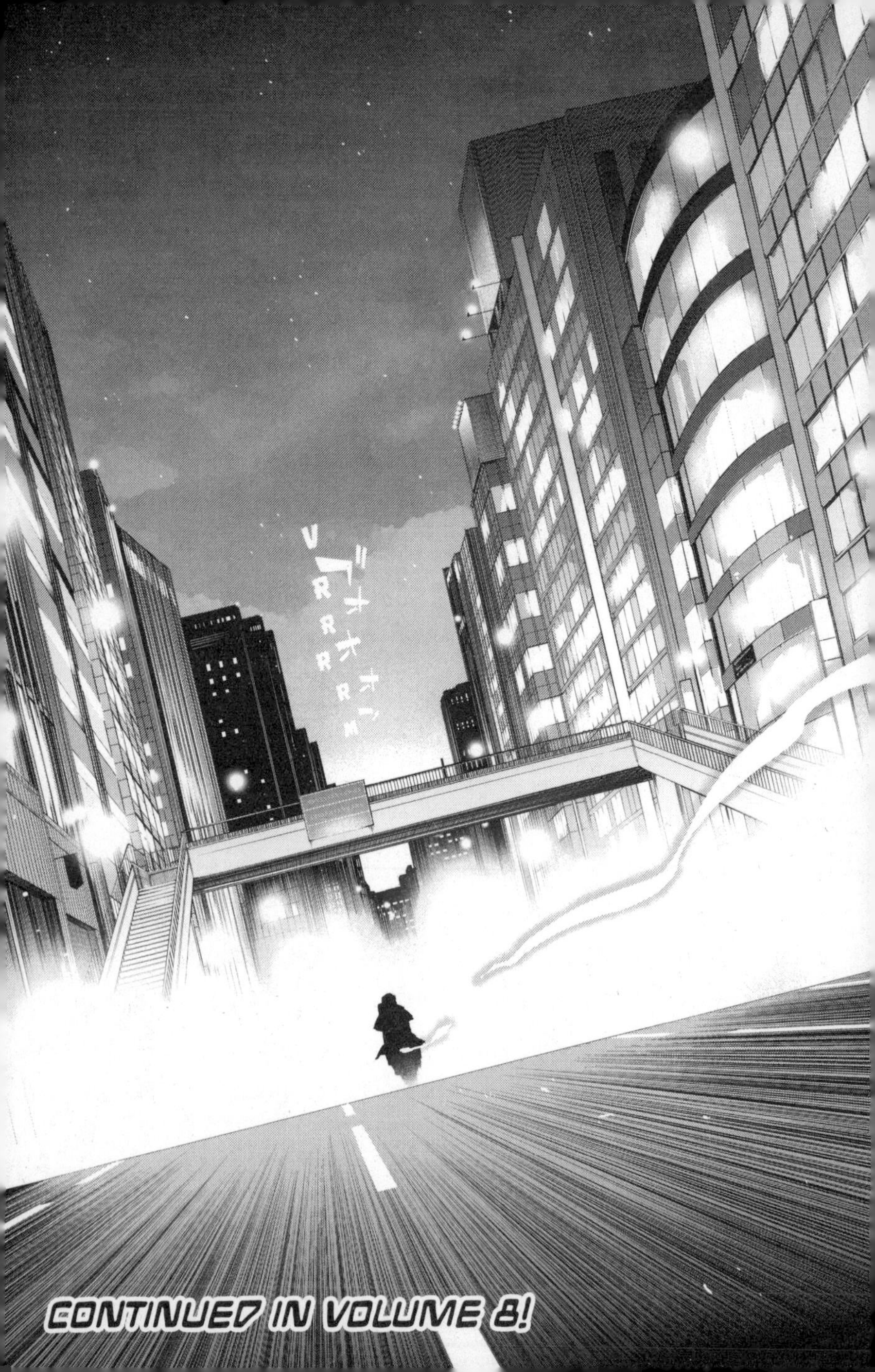
ブオオオーッ
VRRRRM
CONTINUED IN VOLUME 8!

THE QUINTUPLETS SHARE A BUNNY

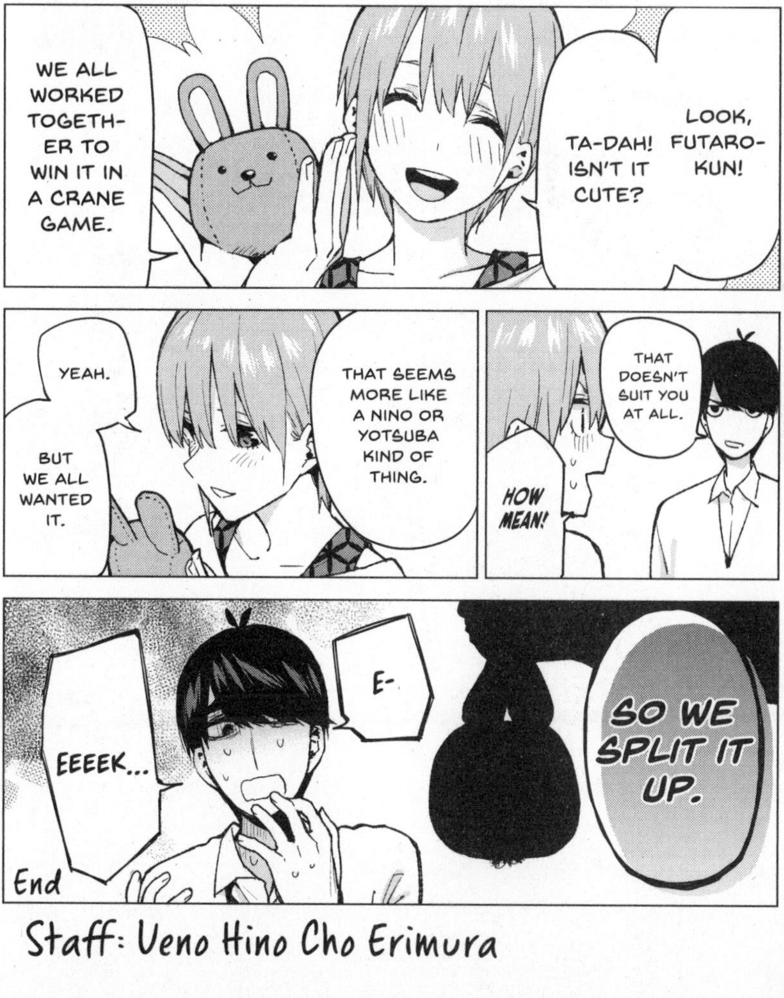
LOOK, FUTARO-KUN!
TA-DAH! ISN'T IT CUTE?
WE ALL WORKED TOGETH-ER TO WIN IT IN A CRANE GAME.
THAT DOESN'T SUIT YOU AT ALL.
HOW MEAN!
THAT SEEMS MORE LIKE A NINO OR YOTSUBA KIND OF THING.
YEAH.
BUT WE ALL WANTED IT.
SO WE SPLIT IT UP.
E-
EEEEK...
End

Staff: Ueno Hino Cho Erimura

Princess Jellyfish

Akiko Higashimura

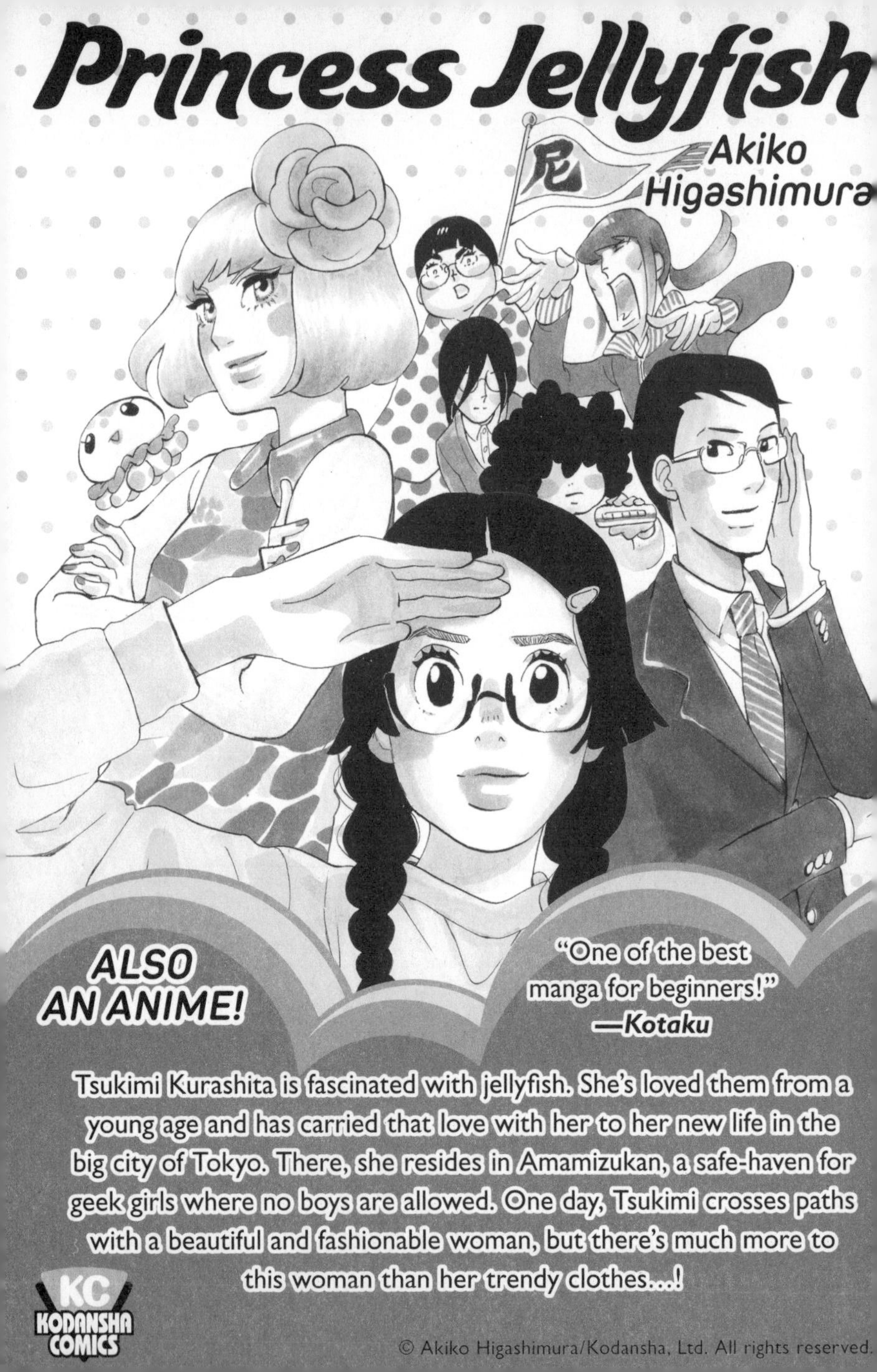

ALSO AN ANIME!

"One of the best manga for beginners!"
—Kotaku

Tsukimi Kurashita is fascinated with jellyfish. She's loved them from a young age and has carried that love with her to her new life in the big city of Tokyo. There, she resides in Amamizukan, a safe-haven for geek girls where no boys are allowed. One day, Tsukimi crosses paths with a beautiful and fashionable woman, but there's much more to this woman than her trendy clothes...!

KC KODANSHA COMICS

‹ KAMOME ›
SHIRAHAMA

Witch Hat Atelier

A magical manga adventure for fans of Disney and Studio Ghibli!

Witch Hat Atelier © Kamome Shirahama/Kodansha Ltd

The magical adventure that took Japan by storm is finally here, from acclaimed DC and Marvel cover artist Kamome Shirahama!

In a world where everyone takes wonders like magic spells and dragons for granted, Coco is a girl with a simple dream: She wants to be a witch. But everybody knows magicians are born, not made, and Coco was not born with a gift for magic. Resigned to her un-magical life, Coco is about to give up on her dream to become a witch...until the day she meets Qifrey, a mysterious, traveling magician. After secretly seeing Qifrey perform magic in a way she's never seen before, Coco soon learns what everybody "knows" might not be the truth, and discovers that her magical dream may not be as far away as it may seem...

EDENSZERO
エデンズゼロ

HIRO MASHIMA IS BACK! JOIN THE CREATOR OF *FAIRY TAIL* AS HE TAKES TO THE STARS FOR ANOTHER THRILLING SAGA!

EDENS ZERO © Hiro Mashima/Kodansha, Ltd.

A high-flying space adventure! All the steadfast friendship and wild fighting you've been waiting for...IN SPACE!

At Granbell Kingdom, an abandoned amusement park, Shiki has lived his entire life among machines. But one day, Rebecca and her cat companion Happy appear at the park's front gates. Little do these newcomers know that this is the first human contact Granbell has had in a hundred years! As Shiki stumbles his way into making new friends, his former neighbors stir at an opportunity for a robo-rebellion... And when his old homeland becomes too dangerous, Shiki must join Rebecca and Happy on their spaceship and escape into the boundless cosmos.

KC KODANSHA COMICS

CUTE ANIMALS AND LIFE LESSONS, PERFECT FOR ASPIRING PET VETS OF ALL AGES!

YUZU THE PET VET

KODANSHA COMICS

1

BY **MINGO ITO**

In collaboration with
NIPPON COLUMBIA CO., LTD.

Yuzu the Pet Vet © Mingo Ito / NIPPON COLUMBIA CO. LTD / Kodansha Ltd.

For an 11-year-old, Yuzu has a lot on her plate. When her mom gets sick and has to be hospitalized, Yuzu goes to live with her uncle who runs the local veterinary clinic. Yuzu's always been scared of animals, but she tries to help out. Through all the tough moments in her life, Yuzu realizes that she can help make things all right with a little help from her animal pals, peers, and kind grown-ups.

Every new patient is a furry friend in the making!

The adorable new odd-couple cat comedy manga from the creator of the beloved *Chi's Sweet Home*, in full color!

Sue & Tai-chan

Konami Kanata

Sue is an aging housecat who's looking forward to living out her life in peace... but her plans change when the mischievous black tomcat Tai-chan enters the picture! Hey! Sue never signed up to be a catsitter! *Sue & Tai-chan* is the latest from the reigning meow-narch of cute kitty comics, Konami Kanata.

THE SWEET SCENT OF LOVE IS IN THE AIR! FOR FANS OF OFFBEAT ROMANCES LIKE *WOTAKOI*

VOL. 1

Sweat and Soap © Kintetsu Yamada / Kodansha Ltd.

In an office romance, there's a fine line between sexy and awkward... and that line is where Asako — a woman who sweats copiously — meets Koutarou — a perfume developer who can't get enough of Asako's, er, scent. Don't miss a romcom manga like no other!

KC KODANSHA COMICS

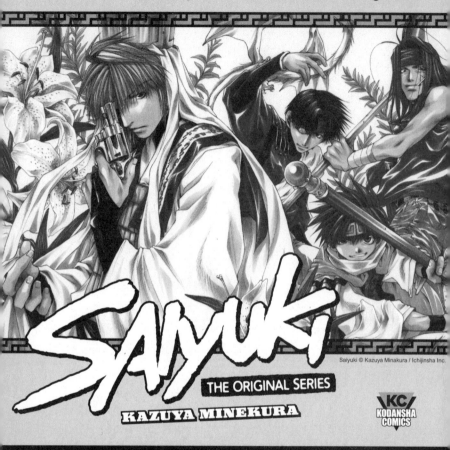

Futaro Uesugi is a second-year in high school, scraping to get by and pay off his family's debt. The only thing he can do is study, so when Futaro receives a part-time job offer to tutor the five daughters of a wealthy businessman, he can't pass it up. Little does he know, these five beautiful sisters are quintuplets, but the only thing they have in common...is that they're all terrible at studying!

THE QUINTESSENTIAL QUINTUPLETS

negi haruba

KC KODANSHA COMICS

A SMART, NEW ROMANTIC COMEDY FOR FANS OF *SHORTCAKE CAKE* AND *TERRACE HOUSE!*

A romance manga starring high school girl Meeko, who learns to live on her own in a boarding house whose living room is home to the odd (but handsome) Matsunaga-san. She begins to adjust to her new life away from her parents, but Meeko soon learns that no matter how far away from home she is, she's still a young girl at heart — especially when she finds herself falling for Matsunaga-san.

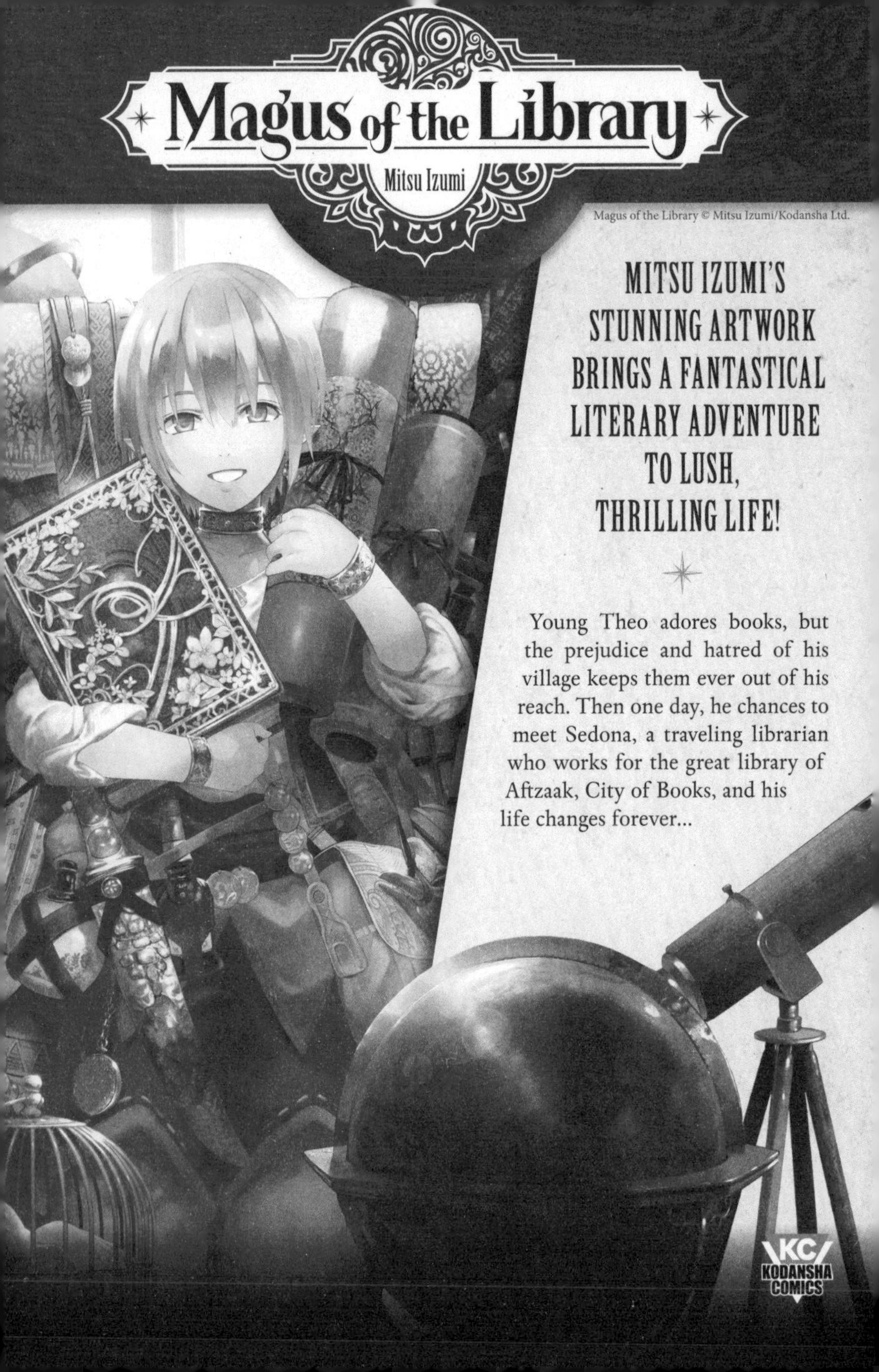

Magus of the Library

Mitsu Izumi

MITSU IZUMI'S STUNNING ARTWORK BRINGS A FANTASTICAL LITERARY ADVENTURE TO LUSH, THRILLING LIFE!

Young Theo adores books, but the prejudice and hatred of his village keeps them ever out of his reach. Then one day, he chances to meet Sedona, a traveling librarian who works for the great library of Aftzaak, City of Books, and his life changes forever...

PERFECT WORLD

Rie Aruga

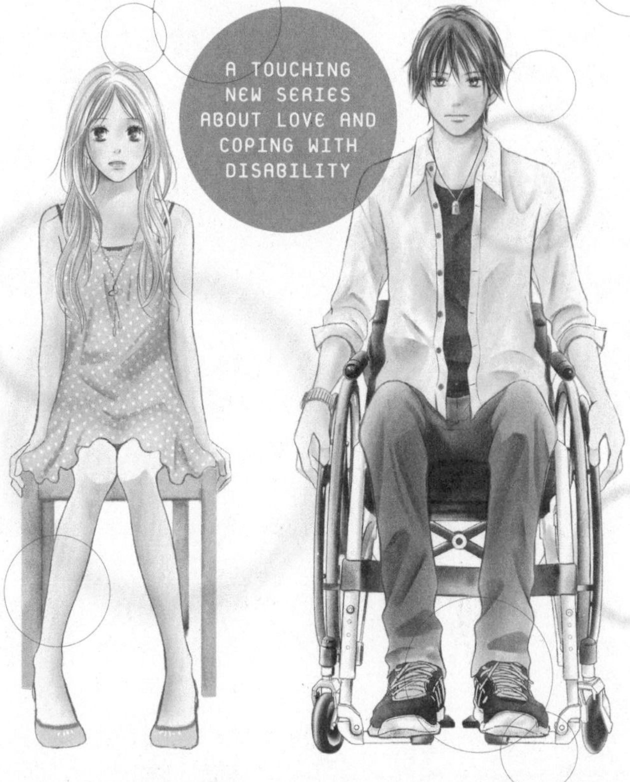
A TOUCHING NEW SERIES ABOUT LOVE AND COPING WITH DISABILITY

An office party reunites Tsugumi with her high school crush Itsuki. He's realized his dream of becoming an architect, but along the way, he experienced a spinal injury that put him in a wheelchair. Now Tsugumi's rekindled feelings will butt up against prejudices she never considered — and Itsuki will have to decide if he's ready to let someone into his heart...

"Depicts with great delicacy and courage the difficulties some with disabilities experience getting involved in romantic relationships... Rie Aruga refuses to romanticize, pushing her heroine to face the reality of disability. She invites her readers to the same tasks of empathy, knowledge and recognition."
—Slate.fr

"An important entry [in manga romance]... The emotional core of both plot and characters indicates thoughtfulness... [Aruga's] research is readily apparent in the text and artwork, making this feel like a real story."
—Anime News Network

KC KODANSHA COMICS

SKATING THRILLS AND ICY CHILLS WITH THIS NEW TINGLY ROMANCE SERIES!

A rom-com on ice, perfect for fans of *Princess Jellyfish* and *Wotakoi*. Kokoro is the talk of the figure-skating world, winning trophies and hearts. But little do they know... he's actually a huge nerd! From the beloved creator of *You're My Pet* (*Tramps Like Us*).

Chitose is a serious young woman, working for the health magazine *SASSO*. Or at least, she would be, if she wasn't constantly getting distracted by her childhood friend, international figure skating star Kokoro Kijinami! In the public eye and on the ice, Kokoro is a gallant, flawless knight, but behind his glittery costumes and breathtaking spins lies a secret: He's actually a hopelessly romantic otaku, who can only land his quad jumps when Chitose is on hand to recite a spell from his favorite magical girl anime!

KC
KODANSHA
COMICS

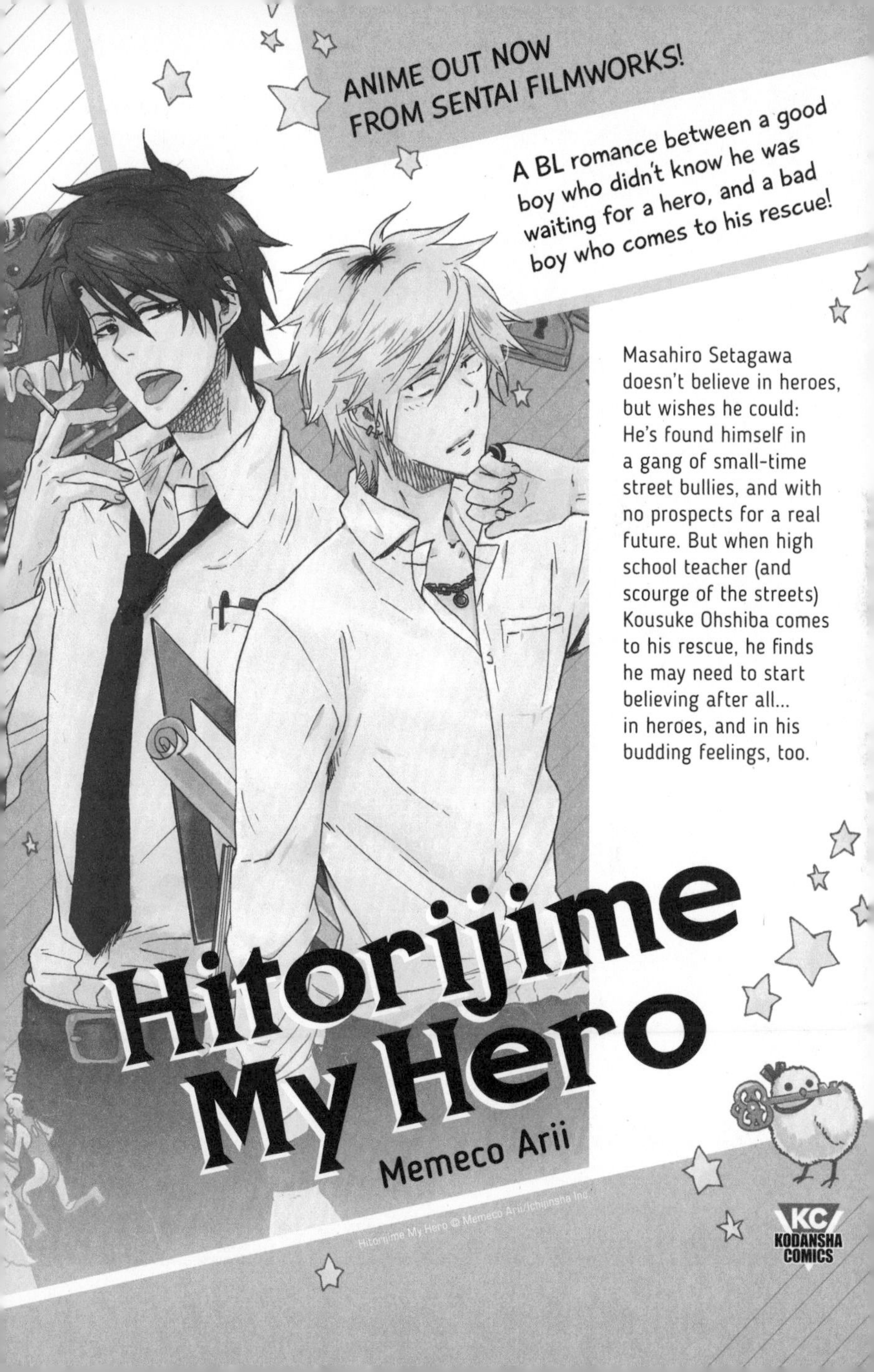
ANIME OUT NOW FROM SENTAI FILMWORKS!
A BL romance between a good boy who didn't know he was waiting for a hero, and a bad boy who comes to his rescue!
Masahiro Setagawa doesn't believe in heroes, but wishes he could: He's found himself in a gang of small-time street bullies, and with no prospects for a real future. But when high school teacher (and scourge of the streets) Kousuke Ohshiba comes to his rescue, he finds he may need to start believing after all... in heroes, and in his budding feelings, too.
Hitorijime My Hero
Memeco Arii
Hitorijime My Hero © Memeco Arii/Ichijinsha Inc.
KC KODANSHA COMICS

A dark and sexy body-horror action manga perfect for fans of *Prison School* and *High School of the Dead*!

Shuichi Kagaya is a smart kid, and most smart kids his age would be thinking about college. Shuichi is also a monster, and he's smart enough to know that monsters don't go to college. But after he uses his monstrous form to save his classmate Claire Aoki, it doesn't matter what his plans for the future were, because he's not the one making the decisions anymore. Now that the seductive, sadistic Claire knows Shuichi's secret, she's got her own ideas about what a monster is good for—because he's not the first monster she's met...

KC
KODANSHA COMICS

GLEIPNIR

Gleipnir © Sun Takeda/Kodansha Ltd.

"You and me together...we would be unstoppable."

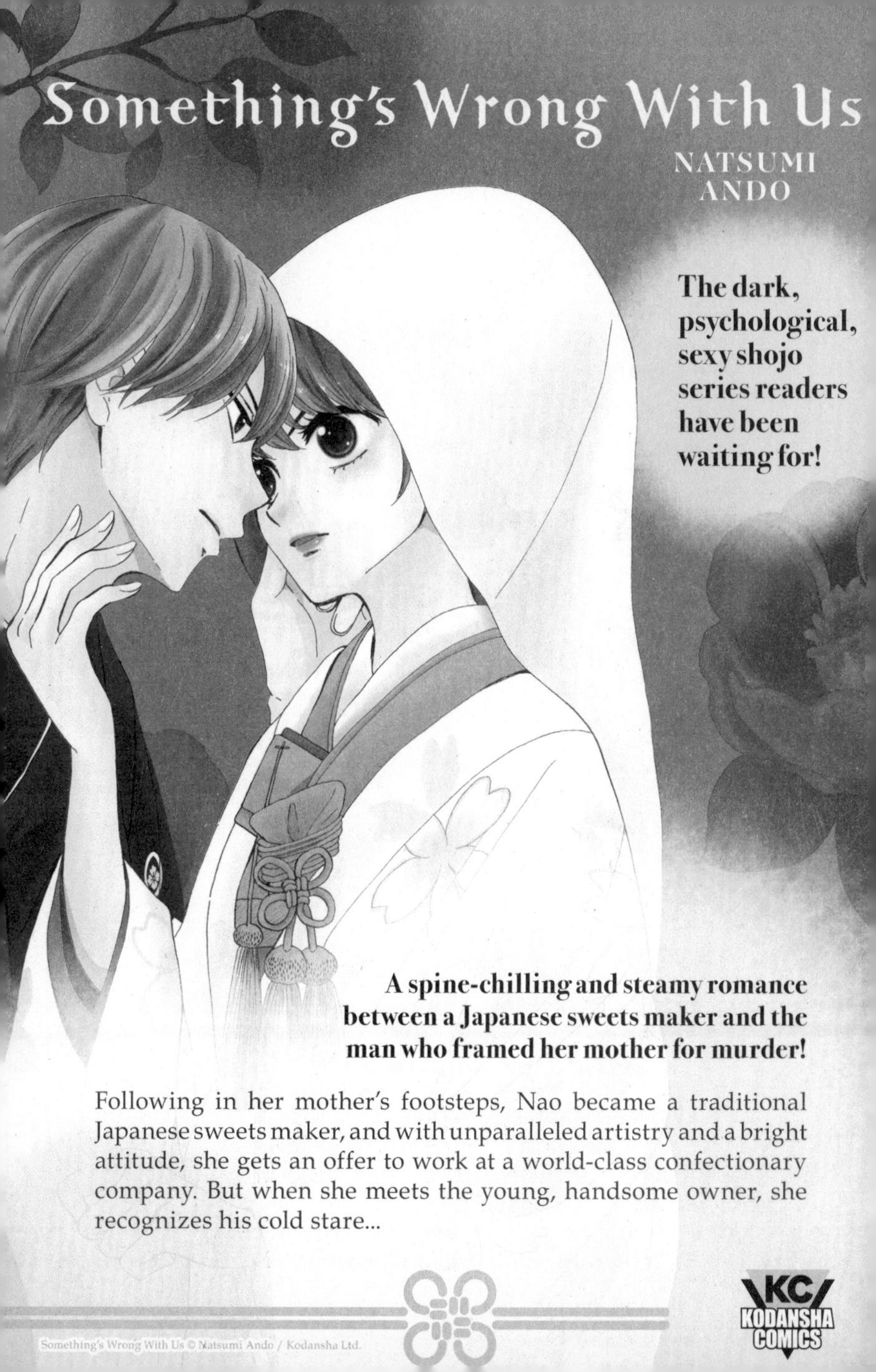
Something's Wrong With Us
NATSUMI ANDO
The dark, psychological, sexy shojo series readers have been waiting for!
A spine-chilling and steamy romance between a Japanese sweets maker and the man who framed her mother for murder!
Following in her mother's footsteps, Nao became a traditional Japanese sweets maker, and with unparalleled artistry and a bright attitude, she gets an offer to work at a world-class confectionary company. But when she meets the young, handsome owner, she recognizes his cold stare...
KC KODANSHA COMICS
Something's Wrong With Us © Natsumi Ando / Kodansha Ltd.

Young characters and steampunk setting, like *Howl's Moving Castle* and *Battle Angel Alita*

Beyond the Clouds © 2018 Nicke / Ki-oon

A boy with a talent for machines and a mysterious girl whose wings he's fixed will take you beyond the clouds! In the tradition of the high-flying, resonant adventure stories of Studio Ghibli comes a gorgeous tale about the longing of young hearts for adventure and friendship!

A Kodansha Comics Trade Paperback Original
The Quintessential Quintuplets 7 copyright © 2018 Negi Haruba
English translation copyright © 2020 Negi Haruba

All rights reserved.

Published in the United States by Kodansha Comics, an imprint of Kodansha USA Publishing, LLC, New York.

Publication rights for this English edition arranged through Kodansha Ltd., Tokyo.

First published in Japan in 2018 by Kodansha Ltd., Tokyo as *Gotoubun no hanayome*, volume 7.

ISBN 978-1-63236-899-7

Cover Design: Saya Takagi (RedRooster)

Printed in Italy by Grafica Veneta S.p.A.

www.kodanshacomics.com

9 8 7 6 5 4
Translation: Steven LeCroy
Lettering: Jan Lan Ivan Concepcion
Editing: Nathaniel Gallant, Thalia Sutton
Additional Layout: Belynda Ungurath
Editorial Assistance: YKS Services LLC/SKY Japan, INC.
Kodansha Comics edition cover design by Phil Balsman

Publisher: Kiichiro Sugawara
Managing editor: Maya Rosewood
Vice president of marketing & publicity: Naho Yamada

Director of publishing services: Ben Applegate
Associate director of operations: Stephen Pakula
Publishing services managing editor: Noelle Webster
Assistant production manager: Emi Lotto